THE OFFICIAL WORLD

THE
OFFICIAL
WORLD

MARK SELTZER

DUKE UNIVERSITY PRESS
DURHAM AND LONDON   2016

© 2016 Duke University Press

Printed in the United States of America on acid-free paper ∞
Designed by Heather Hensley
Typeset in Minion Pro by Westchester Publishing Services

Library of Congress Cataloging-in-Publication Data
Seltzer, Mark, [date] author.
The official world / Mark Seltzer.
pages cm
Includes bibliographical references and index.
ISBN 978-0-8223-6086-5 (hardcover : alk. paper)
ISBN 978-0-8223-6100-8 (pbk. : alk. paper)
ISBN 978-0-8223-7445-9 (e-book)
1. Suspense fiction—History and criticism. 2. Crime in popular culture.
3. Crime in mass media. 4. Literature and society. I. Title.
PN3448.S86S45 2016
809.3'872—dc23 2015031594

Cover art: Naoko Tanaka, *Absolute Helligkeit*, 2012. Still image of the
performance. Courtesy of the artist.

CONTENTS

I • THE DAILY PLANET

ONE

INTRODUCTION TO
THE OFFICIAL WORLD

"Superman is, after all, an alien life form," the horror genre writer Clive Barker notes in his introduction to Neil Gaiman's graphic novel *The Doll's House*: "He's simply the acceptable face of invading realities." He may have noted too that the acceptable face that an invading alien life form takes—in a type of world that consists of both itself and an unremitting commentary on itself—is that of a mild-mannered reporter on the *Daily Planet*.[1]

In the pages that follow I mean to set out the pedagogical principles of such a self-reporting world, and the type of society it stages: a self-inciting, self-legislating, and self-depictive form of life that I redescribe as "the official world."

The globe and the reporter. The syncing of the two makes for what the historian of the Renaissance Jacob Burkhardt describes as the modern age's two great concurrent discoveries: "the discovery of the world and man."[2] And that makes for a two-sided discovery, alter and ego: the opening to the great outside, the great outdoors, and to the interior, a new continent of self-reflection—and so its self-reporting.

We might take the broad view on this, one coextensive with the long modernity: the advent of the world as worldview, and so a world recast by the presence of alternatives.[3] As Niklas Luhmann puts it, "It would be difficult to deny that in our present historical circumstances we are very concerned about not simply what modern society is but how it observes and describes itself and its environment."[4] Such an observation has by now achieved the undeniability of self-evidence. It is, as George Spencer-Brown puts it, "the form in which our way of talking about our ordinary living experience can

Figure 1.1. The Self-Reporting World in Person.

be seen to be cradled."[5] But what exactly then is it evidence of? What is the character of a modern society that consists of both itself and its continuous autodescription? Bound to its self-description, the "cradle rocks over an abyss"—self-suspended from moment to moment.[6] These forms of suspendedness and their zoned spaces—at once gamelike, violent, yet extremely formal—are elements of an official world.

What I want to set out here are some relatively recent examples of the form of a social-systemic organization that metastasized across the five-hundred-year range of what has alternatively been called the age of discovery, the age of globalization, and the bourgeois half-millennium: an age coming to realization, or to term, in the epoch of social systems and its anthropotechnics—or art with humans.[7] The term "anthropotechnics" has been used for some time to describe human-technical assemblages, particularly in accounts of robotics and automatonic actions. The larger use concerns practices and forms of life (we can think here of Wittgenstein's language games or Foucault's power-discourse games) that enter into what the American suspense writer Patricia Highsmith calls "games for the living." This art with humans, these repeated practices and ego-technics, these informalized games mark out the grids, outlines, and practice zones of the official world: its form games.

There is an extended arc to the anthropotechnic turn, and to the putting into place of the improbable prospect of an autotropic planet: its imperatives and its repeating exercises; its precincts, circuits, and observation zones; its ways of relating the immanence of the system to its environment; and so of soliciting, and processing, what I will describe as news from the outside. The crux of the matter is that the theoretical object, the globe, includes but goes beyond the aesthetic geometry of round things. It includes—as Peter Sloterdijk has traced in rich detail—its shape, its history, and its turning: the provisions of a world of compulsive, repeatable, and reversible movements; interiors and projections; ventures and returns, or revenues.

We are familiar too by now with the passage from the age of globalization to the global age. To the present that runs, as the sports idiom has it, in the added or "injury time" of the modern epoch: the repeated repeating of a social world-system.

This is the crystallization of a synchronous world, and its depictive media. It is now alternatively depicted, for example, as the "pristine culture of capitalism" or as the "Anthropocene." These may be seen as alternating descriptions of a real subsumption, either a synchronized or a trumped world, and hence a periodization in the idiom of the capitalist sublime. That begins to indicate the reincarnative character of a self-organized world and its serial forms of life and death and life.

These are depictions of a self-turned earth. Here is the novelist Cormac McCarthy on it: "Across the pieced land they watched a man turning the earth with an ox yoked by its horns to a singlehanded plow. The plow was of a type that was old in Egypt and was little more than a treeroot. They mounted up and rode on."[8] An extraordinary condensation of history, history as natural history, marks these contracted lines—and the species that singlehandedly if violently yokes them together, and, collaterally, watches that. This is a small diorama of the Anthropocene, one serving to indicate then that this term, the Anthropocene, less tells a new story than correlates an old one to the observation and depiction that enter into it. That correlationism has now arrived as its own theme—in this case, as the prerequisite of the form of the novel itself.[9]

The correlation of world and worldview has now, across a range of fields—disciplines apparently are still seen as pieced plots of earth—come into view and so into question. It shows a reality and watches it being made: a picture of motion, it (like a motion picture) realizes what it stages and shows that.[10] Such a coming into view appears as a turn taken in the history of a self-turned and self-observed planet—a series of turns I will be calling "the turn

turn."[11] In McCarthy's fiction of such a "crossing," this is an overturned and so uprooted world: one on the move and made for people with plans, and upwardly mobile, on the move up and on. There is encrypted here the great shift from vertical to upward mobility as the practice of modernity. It is as if one can daily turn the earth beneath one's own feet.[12]

This epoch is what I have worked to describe, over the last several years, as the official world. The range-finding episodes set out in these pages are commentaries on some of the demarcation zones and practices, ascetics and aesthetics, of the official world. The intent is that this concept may then step-by-step accrue some indication of what Alexander Kluge has described as "the precision of rough ideas."[13]

The Premises of the Official World

The argument of this book can be stated simply: a modern world comes to itself by staging its own conditions. A modern world is a self-conditioning and self-reporting one. If, prior to the nineteenth century, society could not describe itself, now it cannot stop describing itself—in an attempt to keep up with what it is at every moment bringing about.[14]

Or, as the great science-fiction writer Stanislaw Lem neatly put it: "In the Eolithic age there were no seminars on whether to invent the Paleolithic."[15] A modern society—which is to say, a continuously self-monitoring, auto-updating, and modernizing one—is what Emile Durkheim (inaugurating modern sociology, and so indicating a society on the way to self-description) described as an "almost sui generis" society. The autotropic character of that world makes up what Durkheim also would call a social fact.

It is necessary to set out these common, and, for the most part, well-known observations, since the conditions I mean to describe in these chapters—conditions at once familiar and surreal—depend on the background reality they, from moment to moment, hold in animated suspense. That reality is a complex infrastructure stabilized by its own tensions—like one of its iconic architectural forms, the suspension bridge.

There are three general premises to this argument.

First, if a modern world comes to itself by staging its own conditions, it must consist both of itself and its self-description, denotation, or registration. A modern society, to the extent that it is modern, takes note of itself as it goes along. It posits what Roland Barthes calls the now "most ordinary exercise of our language, which is commentary."[16] In doing so, it curates a world.

Second, if a modern world is a self-reporting one, a modern society must be bound to what Max Weber, early on, described as the self-documenting qualities and self-descriptive techniques that are the defining attributes of the second modernization. The modern world is an official world not merely in its administrative a priori, and not merely in the spreading of self-administration across the zones that make up the near-continuum of the modern social field. The administrative a priori consists in the bending of the will to know the real to the will to produce the real. The official world not merely denotes itself as it goes. Its operations, beyond that, mean that taking note of the fact is a fact-producing act.[17] If it stops commenting on itself, it dies.

Third, the model for this self-staging world is then the modern work of art. We know that the modern work of art interrogates itself with an unremitting and unsparing intensity as to its own nature and singularity. We know too that this leads thinking in a circle, by leading art back to the expression of its own conditions. The work of art thus epitomizes an autonomous, reflexive, and so self-epitomizing world.[18]

But reflexivity today is cheap. I am tempted to say, "It's free." Hence to the extent that it does so, the work of art is then both exceptional and exemplary in what we can call the epoch of social systems. It is exceptional in its autonomous relation to, as they say, the "outside" world. It is exemplary in that it provides the very model of the autonomization of that world, its stand-alone, internalized, and demarcated character.[19] In this way, the artwork not merely makes the world appear in the world, but too unceasingly marks that it does so.[20] It openly displays its own principle of production. The modern social system and its demarcation zones—like the modern work of art—perform their own unity (see part II).[21]

The artwork stages what it does, and, in doing so, enacts what it shows. Staging and acting (as in motion pictures) oscillate, each in turn interrupting and taking the place of the other. This resembles a magic trick, a self-exposed one: "There is no reality if one cannot ask about there being one."[22] The self-exposition is part of the routine, undoing in effect the privilege routinely accorded to reflexivity. Yet the routinization of disenchantment has (with apologies to Weber) its own charisma. The self-exposed trick requires, for its analysis, less an archaeology of knowledge than, as it were, an archaeology of knowingness. It is necessary then to look at the aesthetic and social function of these routines. To look not least, for example, at the social function of one of the practical working models of what the microsociologist Erving Goffman calls "our indoor social life": the practical joke (see part IV).

This self-staging opens to view the paradoxical status of the sui generis artwork in the company of contemporary social systems: modeling each other, they produce a reality in suspense. But—and crucially—this means that the systemic, reciprocal, and repercussive character of action in the official world then poses a basic difficulty of interpretation and perception, and so of aesthetics (as a science of the a prioris of perception).

That difficulty may be framed in these terms. The reflexive character of the demarcation zones that make up the official world has a singular, and peculiar, independence from, or even indifference to, aesthetic and philosophical expressions of the theory of reflection. Reflexivity without interiority, and operating on its own. That adapts, in effect, the most basic and rudimentary lesson of cybernetics—that reflexivity is a property of matter, not a privilege of human cognition—and applies it to itself.[23]

That generalization of reflection is only part of the difficulty. A reflexivity without interiority means this: an externalized reflexivity that posits a coming together, or assembly, of individuals outside themselves. The American novelist Theodore Dreiser traced it early on, in his first novel, *Sister Carrie* (1900). This estranged or extraverted reflection consists in "little audible links, chaining together great inaudible feelings or purposes": like the links of a chain letter or the phatic (channel-checking) function of an incessant twittering.

It is necessary to reconsider the significance of this compulsive exteriority of purposes and feelings. The most ordinary exercise of continuous commentary is visible not least in academico-professional circles: the semi-auditory clattering of thousands of keyboards set in motion, across the academic archipelago of lectures and seminars, by a contagious, self-promotional stenographic fervor. Twitters sent up like the little paper ribbons of writing tied to the latticework outside Shinto shrines, and some Zen temples, in Japan—appeals sent up to the great outside.[24] (It may be possible to see the rotational system of the academic conference—the extreme narrowness of professional citation circles, its self-repeating imperatives, its papers and name-tags—as the professional rezoning of a reincarnative form of life, via practices of compulsory, or compulsive, self-boosterism.)

A renewed ascetics of self-boosterism has emerged, one designed for the upwardly, if not exactly the vertically, mobile. Its ego-technic devices—rechristened social media—realign ascetic practices of the self to a self-promotional zeal. This pristine form of professionalism has affinities with the life-counseling industry that burgeoned in the mid-twentieth-century United States. It has affinities (it will be seen) with movements like Scientology and its streamlined corporatist spin-offs (with a wide following among corporate middle-managerial types open to, as one of these programs describes it, "Miracles Around Money"). The Weberian work ethic redesigned for self-designers is a fundamental attribute of the realized official world, an ongoing refashioning of ascetic practices of vertical mobility for calisthenics in upward mobility. (Yet the new asceticism—no pain, no gain, in repeated sets—retains a spiritual residue of devotionalism, in the form of an exteriorized and impersonal self-devotion. Or, as my solar cult fitness center Equinox puts it, "It's Not Fitness, It's Life." I will return to what "it" is.) Self-boosterism is a formal property of an autotropic and self-stimulative world. This type of world is one not merely in a continual state of suspense—the milieu of "men in space," to borrow the title of Tom McCarthy's first novel—but in stricto sensu self-suspended. (Superman, it may be recalled, did not at first fly; he leaped.)

These circuits are, among many others, versions of the stranger-intimacies of contemporary social systems, and the feelings and purposes incited and carried by their ego-technic media. This in turn enters into the collective autism that Sartre, describing the function of seriality in modern society, called the practico-inert.[25]

The presupposition of exteriority is crucial here. That is the case not merely because any immune system, from moment to moment—acting in a world of effects—is perpetually marking the distinction between what it is and what is external to it, and so perpetually attuned to news from the outside.[26] It might be said then that, stated simply, the official world does not have a boundary; it is a boundary. Or, put differently, a system needs a limit. The reflex question then, "What is 'outside' the official world?" is the question that it, from moment to moment to moment, puts to itself.

Its operations consist in renewing, recording, filing, retrieving, reenacting it. The intramuralized world knows, that is, that it has another side, an outside, and must reckon with this paradox at every moment. As in the extremely formal conditions in the playing out of a game, it is necessary to frame, demarcate, and report it—and in this sense see through it and reflect on it—in order to play the game, and to mark its distinction from the world that it, at the very same time, models.[27]

Here appears one of the great paradoxes in what the microsociologist Erving Goffman calls (in *The Presentation of Self in Everyday Life*) our "indoor social life" and its reenactive institutions. The paradox is this: that the strict internality of self-organizing systems allows for, or requires, the objective exteriorization of act and value. The second is the paradoxical function of the first. This is, in sum, the externalization of action, and the exteriorization of valuation, that marks the intramural or enclaved form of social-systemic operations. That externalization of act and value extends from its initial trial period, utilitarianism, around 1800. It is generalized through the formalization practices, and so application, of the principles of scientific or systemic management and the control revolution, around 1900. It disseminates across the social field, via second-order systems theory and practice, from the mid-twentieth century forward. The expansion and realization of its action zones is one marker of the transition from a modern age (which knows this) and a modern world (which enacts it, controlling its own climate). It includes, among its many presentation media, the social-semantic function of the novel and its popular genre forms—not least, it will be seen, the forms and practices of the suspense novel.

Suspendedness

My literary examples are drawn in larger part from the "suspense" mode and its autogenic, self-stressed, and suspended worlds. Suspense as world and as worldview: its serial reenactments, compulsive mobilities, and lethal but reincarnative drives. My interest, however, is less in the genre than in the reenactive practices it generically models and presupposes, and puts in perpetual, and turbulent, motion.

The form of the suspense novel becomes in our time a self-supporting argument for these autotropic processes, and for staging the protocols, practices, and spaces of the official world. Suspense fiction is the voice of this autogenic, self-stressed, and suspended state at its purest. It is a genre premised on a psychosemantics that we might call the mood of systems. That is, if we bear in mind—given the segmented differentiation of the disparate systems that make up a multiverse world—that (as Emerson expressed it) "our moods do not believe in each other."[28]

Self-stress, compulsive mobility, the ascetics of projective externalization, and the aesthetics of exploding persons and things: these are the modal forms of the daily planet today and indicators of the violence it induces and subjects itself to. This is why it becomes plausible to see the exigencies of an overdeveloped and overcommunicative, and so a doomed, planet to be treatable as mood disorders. Say, melancholia in Lars von Trier; or recreational psychopathy in J. G. Ballard's fiction; or fugue in Ballard's brilliant reenactor, Tom McCarthy; or necronautical fury in the catastrophic-modernization novels of the Japanese novelist Yukio Mishima; or, all of these, in the apprehensively violent and autistic Cold War novels of the American suspense writer Patricia Highsmith.

The suspense novel stages "precarious life"—the phrase is from Highsmith's first novel, *Strangers on a Train*. Suspense fiction, that is, erects stages for the countless secondary worlds, the reflexive action-and-reaction zones, that make up the official world. Its performative dimension is autotropic violence: self-induced, serial, and reenactive. This is a Cold War form of violence suspended in its premonition and induced in its preemption. Its demarcation zones everywhere operate under what Highsmith calls "the weight of officialism." Suspendedness is its primary aesthetic category. It is not for nothing that the great dream of Guy Haines, the architect turned killer in *Strangers*, is to build a white suspension bridge. It is, we are meant to see, a bridge to nowhere: a structure held in place and supported by its own tensions, and nothing else.

For this reason, Highsmith's pathographies of the official world will serve as something of a throughput, albeit an intermittent one, in these chapters. Highsmith's work is a border case, but so a border-delineating one: a way of drawing the chalk-white outlines of the reenactment zones that make up the operations of an official world.

The Human Pyramid

Suspendedness and its practices then. Consider this moment in Highsmith's best-known novel, *The Talented Mr. Ripley*. The novel's action pivots on the observation of a "game." That game involves the body-to-body building of a "human pyramid" and it is this scene that stimulates Tom's first killing (the first in a series, setting off a series of suspense novels).

> Tom watched with interest as a human pyramid was building, feet braced on bulging thighs, hands gripping forearms. He could hear their "Allez!" and their "Un-deux!" . . ."Look!" Tom said. "There goes the top!" He stood still to watch the smallest one, a boy of about seventeen, as he was boosted to the shoulders of the centre man in the three top men. He stood poised, his arms open, as if receiving applause. "Bravo!" Tom shouted.
>
> Tom looked at Dickie. Dickie was looking at a couple of men sitting near by on the beach.
>
> "Ten thousand saw I at a glance, nodding their heads in sprightly dance," Dickie said sourly to Tom.[29]

The human pyramid—as a game, a spectacle, and a form—is a living diagram, no doubt one both timeless and timely. It has here a precise meaning. It is—via a geometry of bodies akin to pornographic action—a paradigm of a modern social order or, more exactly, the perception of that order in sensuous terms.[30]

The pyramid involves, above all, a shift from person to position, and their exact correlation—again, a defining principle of the second modernity. Here one sees the arranged and stacked cubicles of individuals, sorted into the functions that make them up, interlocked to form the parts of a self-braced whole. This is the thrilled spectacle of persons as the effect of mechanic or formal assemblages, segmented, specialized, collated, each one in position in that its position defines what it is.

The administrative a priori is reenacted in game form. The office building—the skyscraper—evokes (as Rem Koolhaas observes, in *Delirious New York*) stacks of money.[31] It evokes too (as C. Wright Mills observes, in "White Collar") stacks of files: "Each office within the skyscraper is a segment of the enormous file."[32] The stacked pyramidic form here also, in the unfolding of this passage, eroticizes a failure of self-difference, in the aggregate, as a failure of sexual difference. (This makes for a series of substitutions—propped on the schoolboy quotation from Wordsworth's "Daffodils"—such that that numerous self-sameness ignites the charge of sex-sameness.) It is, in short, impossible to consider excitation in Highsmith, among others, apart from her modeling of a sociality premised on the performative principles of action in the systems epoch. And impossible to consider that systems epoch in turn apart from its achievement of self-conditioned and self-evaluated form and its self-observed observation.

A metastasized officialism. It may be, as Adorno put it, that the system is the belly-turned-mind. Yet one finds here something like the reverse side, the somatization of the system. It is a model, an exercise, a performance, and a worldview instrument. Its premise: autogenic stress as a form of life.

The suspense novel—the form of the human pyramid is the very model of suspense, the suspension of bodies in the name of some superior form—stages that suspense. It provides a narrative of ungovernable copying and the self-incited, physical thrill of risk taking and serial games of self-endangerment. It is not merely that Tom is everywhere "still pretending, uncontrollably."[33] The novel does the same. Ripley's games—in the border zones of bodily controllability and its panic/thrill—are then the formal conditions for novel reading and analogues of it: these forms of copying are copied into each other.

The analogues at work in moments such as these are technologies of auto-stimulation. Their internalized character makes it possible for the space of the game, the scene of the crime, and the form of the work of art to refer back to each other in circular fashion—and so to provide, as it were, the conditions for the continuous rotation of the elements of a self-induced world.

That presupposes the rotary system of modern, systematically-managed economic processes—and their transfer into aesthetic terms. (Consider the art world's turn to process and performance over production and objectivism.) Again and again, in suspense art, everything solid melts into air. But the stage for the autonomous presentation of weightlessness in the shape of expert performance is the logic both of the human pyramid and of "men in space": in the refined air of a self-conditioned world. (It is the logic of reincarnation stories that, for example, tie together, across great divides, recent films like *Gravity* and *The Master*, or recent novels, it will be seen, like Max Brooks's *World War Z* and McCarthy's *Remainder*.)

Here I ask you to attend to one further element in the spectacle of the human pyramid and the worldview it installs. "They must be professionals," the compulsively imitative and autogenically talented Tom Ripley observes of the acrobats. Yet this is a professionalism that, in its system-immanent terms, looks as hyperproductive, and as uselessly self-referential, as the formation of improbable geometric figures out of acrobatic bodies on a beach.[34]

We might see this form of professionalism as the realization or bitter end of the spirit of rationalization. Weber, we recall, in "Science as Profession [Vocation]" (*Wissenschaft als Beruf*) described the academic vocation in terms of a systemic blindness to all that is outside. He traced, in *The Protestant Ethic and the Spirit of Capitalism*, the more general and ultimate outcome of this unremitting and blindly internalized activity: its ultimate refinement to, purely and simply, and whatever its ends, "the irrational sense of having done one's job well."[35]

Or, as Robert Ludlum puts it in his suspense novel, *The Bourne Identity*, describing the secret agent and perpetually reborn killer Bourne's attempts at self-description and self-identification: "It was not professional, and if he had learned anything about himself during the past forty-eight hours it was that he *was* a professional. Of what he had no idea, but the status was not debatable."[36]

Disinhibition Training

At this point we might bear in mind that a discipline is also a practice, an immune system, an exercise, a personal training, an asceticism, a course of life that is not exactly a curriculum vitae. A form of life for people with plans, or at least planners. Here is another snapshot of what, via the suspense novel, this irrational discipline in having done one's job well looks like, in the planetary transition from the ascetics of vertical mobility (transcendence) to that of upward mobility (professionalism).

Robert Ludlum's *The Bourne Identity*—I will assume you either read the novel or saw the movie—is a suspense story shot through with the energy vitalisms of the global age: recreational psychopathy, state-of-the-art anthropotechnics, and real-sounding neuroscience—along with the performance

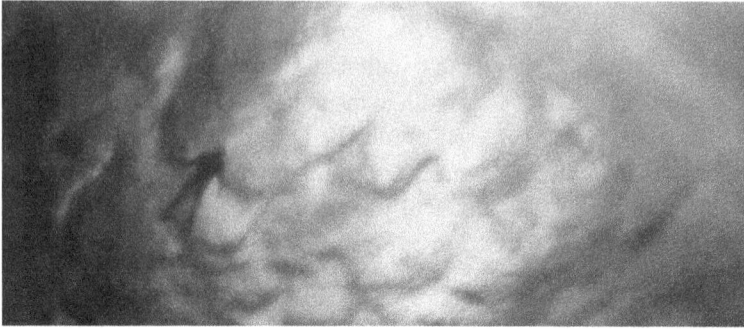

Figure 1.2. The Sea of Moods: Suspense as Aesthetic Principle (*The Bourne Identity*, dir. Doug Liman, 2002).

Figure 1.3. The Mood of Systems: Scientology in Action (*The Master*, dir. Paul Thomas Anderson, 2013).

art of exploding things. A suspended world and its acrobatics: with the aesthetics of autogenic stress as a world principle.

Here are two passages from the very start of the novel *The Bourne Identity* (with my italics), in which its aesthetics and its technics meet and fuse:

> *The trawler plunged into the angry swells of the dark, furious sea like an awkward animal trying desperately to break out of an impenetrable swamp. The waves rose to goliathan heights,* crashing into the hull with the power of raw tonnage; the white sprays caught in the night sky cascaded downward over the deck under the force of the night wind. *Everywhere there were the sounds of inanimate pain*; wood straining against wood, ropes twisting, stretched to the breaking point. The animal was dying.

He felt these things, acknowledging his own panic as he felt them. He could see his own body turning and twisting, arms and feet working frantically against the pressures of the whirlpool. *He could feel, think, see, perceive panic and struggle—*yet strangely there was peace. *It was the calm of the observer, the uninvolved observer, separated from the events. . . . Then another form of panic spread through him. . . . It would happen any second now; he was not sure what it was, but it would happen. . . . It happened. The explosion was massive. . . . Whatever it was, he had won. It happened again. And again.*

This is not exactly an allegory of the furious flows of traffic, bodies, communications, money. Nor that inner experience externalized. It is the inner experience of exteriority: an ego-technical program that combines projected pain and psychodispassionate management via its observation. (This is what Scientology programs call "exteriorization": the disinvolved self-observer as "an aware of awareness unit that functions independently of the physical body." And this suspense novel, among others, is, we will see, decidedly scientological in orientation.) Here what "it" is is what explodes, like Bourne himself. Hence the compulsive mobilities of the novel, its rapidly successive seascapes and landscapes and cityscapes, its violent eruptions, are at the same time the bioscape of Bourne's impossibly and repeatedly trained and torn and reborn body.[37]

Self-Boosterism as Worldview: Paperback Science

These are in effect reincarnation exercises: training, an ascetic practice, in repetitive self-annihilation in the service of serial self-projection. Reincarnative—but in the sense that vertical mobility (enlightenment) yields to upward mobility (professionalism), and the spiritual guide is replaced by the life-counseling industry and the personal trainer. (The direct analogues here are Scientology and its spin-offs and the related reprogramming techniques of Cold War experimental neuroscience, on both military and consumption-incitation fronts.)

The Bourne novels and films are violent thought experiments in recovering, or cognitive-mapping, interior states from the perception of external acts and their effects. The observer of Bourne's actions, in the novel or in the film version, is always a step or two behind in perceiving and processing what he senses and acts on. But so is he, as his effect on the world searches for its cause. He is literally self-taught: this is autodidactic neuroscience. Paperback scientology. It is in part a lesson in understanding media and

Figure 1.4. The Crystal World: "The Pristine Culture of Capitalism" (*The Bourne Identity*, dir. Doug Liman, 2002).

information flows or floods, the supercommodity of information, data floods on the high seas, as a sea of extroverted moods: the great transformation of substance into flow in worldwide communications, yes, but something more exact and immediate too.[38]

These personal training regimens combine "massive shocks" and "instruments of hysteria": an ascetic discipline that is a relentless training in self-disinhibition. That includes a series of what Ludlum calls "exercises": "verbal exercises," strength and endurance exercises, and, in effect, worldview exercises.

Central here are exercises in self-stressing and its observation. Or, as Bourne's personal trainer puts it: "We're combining two stresses. . . . Whenever you observe a stress situation and you have the time, do your damndest to project yourself into it." This is the idiom of the life-counseling industry and its practices: the turning of stress to self-persuasive activity, via observation and alert time management, and its re-stressing. It is the idiom of an informalized bureaucratic—or, better, bureaucratish—style, one readapted for the personal training of decidedly professional types.

This is then the hyperactivity of the official world—its ceaseless flows of capital, traffic, information, and bodies—as the lurid seascape of the thriller. (One might instance, in the wake of passages like this opening one, of the resurgent interest in "the weird" now—lurid Lovecraftian horror, for example, China Miéville's—as a rival genre of the global age, albeit presented as its alternative.) Here too something more: an immersion in the destructive element, via a program of systematic exposure, auditing, and self-clearing. These are the observation and reenactment zones, the solicited stress situations, the accelerative violence that defines such spaces and reincarnates

Figure 1.5. "The Reunification of the World through Money" (*The Bourne Identity*, dir. Doug Liman, 2002).

its reborn actors. Reenactment practices are adjusted for the conversion of what Foucault called "the care of the self" to a literalized self-boosterism. That amounts to the reprogramming of suspense as an ego-technic medium of self-production: a neon technology of autogenesis.[39]

This is a professional process indifferent to what it processes. There is a fusion of extreme formality and extreme violence, and that fusion enacts and shows an indifference to all but its own ends. It posits a systemic blindness to all but the irrational focus on an undebatably professional job well done. Suspense fiction thus provides a way of modeling an autotropic world—and field-tests, in its strict genre-fictionality, the place of the autonomous artwork in it.

Isotopias

Consider these practice zones from a different angle. If a modern society continuously stages its own conditions, that means it erects countless stages for self-referential presentation and autonomous performance. Let me outline what these staging practices look like and how they work.

The practice zone is neither a utopia nor (in the sense that Foucault gave to the term) a heterotopia: neither a no-place nor an alternative- or other-place. It is instead an isotopia: a self-conditioned reenactment space, among a proliferation of synonymous but formally demarcated spaces.[40] These make up a strangely functional continuum of self-compelling reenactment sites.

The space of the game, the scene of the crime, and the form of the work of art are today (I've suggested) the ideal-typical models of these reenactment zones. These spaces incorporate technologies that shift, moment to moment, from the backdrop to the stage and back again. They indicate the way in which the official world is not exactly the designation of a space but a way of designating spaces: positions, lines, sites, zones, communication routes, routines, impasses, and bypasses. It is a self-designating way of functioning as a function. So it has its epitomic places—the office, for example. But the office, we know, is not one place among others: stage and backstage at once, it's a switchboard of the social.

The formal dimension of these systems-internal places is crucial. Take, for example, the novelist Henry James's prescient diagnosis of one such isotopia: what he calls, around 1900, the emergence of "the amazing hotel-world." The hotel-world performs what James describes as a triumph of systematic man-agerialism: "ingenuous joy below and consummate management above." At once superfluous and autonomous, it is a "social order in positively stable equilibrium." Operating "by laws of [its] own," it is a "complete scheme of life," absolutely a "fit to its conditions" and so in "perfect adequacy to itself." The dedifferentiation of private and public life that is its premise expresses "a social indeed positively an aesthetic ideal." Autonomy, self-reference, in-ternality: an aesthetic ideal on its own.[41]

What James recognizes in a flash is the specter of what systems theorists might call death by dedifferentiation: the death of the self-distinction of the work of art which, from then on, reenters the artwork as its own theme. Yet what for James centers the crisis of the artwork in the epoch of social systems, and recasts the immanent terms of its autonomy as a "law unto itself," is the "promiscuous" spreading of these quarantine spaces.

What above all makes the hotel-world "at this supreme pitch" a copy of a social and an aesthetic ideal is the manner in which it becomes a "synonym for civilization." This is for James the real "effect of violence in the whole communication": the achievement, or promiscuous spreading, of synonymy across social scenes, the "fruit bearing action of the American example" generalized "all the world over." The basic achievement and so the real crisis, represented by the hotel-world, is the emergence and spreading of synony-mous conditions across differentiated and thus comparable institutions. The hotel is a crystal palace in a crystallizing world.

Siegfried Kracauer, writing two decades after James, extends the analysis, in his remarkable essay on the hotel lobby, and, in doing so, brings it into more proximate relation to our concerns. Here Kracauer pointedly quotes a passage from a detective novel. That's because the hotel lobby becomes, in the modern form of that genre, the counterpart of the scene of the crime. It is a space of suspended action—a space of promiscuity, stranger intimacy, and violence held in abeyance. It is a space of a synthetic civility: what Goffman will call "civil inattention" as the "surface character of public order."[42]

The scene of the crime and the hotel lobby are in effect counterpart administrative-managerial zones. In the self-depicting terms of the detective story: "once again it is confirmed that a large hotel is a world unto itself and that this world is like the rest of the larger world." In this way, it becomes possible, for Kracauer, to locate the aesthetic purposiveness without purpose that would seek and find itself in the hotel-world. It is a world unto itself, but to the very extent that it is so, a world like the rest of a scalable world. This is the crystallized space of repetitive and reenactive motion in what James elsewhere in *The American Scene* calls the extraordinary American "rotary system" of synonymous productions. That rotational system—premised on the continuous oscillation of act and representation—defines systematic management in the workplace.[43] But it defines too the sites that repeat it, in unofficial or recreational or game form. And it shapes or pressures the performativity of the work of art substituting process for product. As Kracauer expresses it, "the aesthetic that has become an end in itself pulls up its own roots." And the aesthetic pulling itself up by its own roots may then transplant itself anywhere. It makes possible what may be described as the autonomization of everything (see part V).

Take the general staging areas for reenactment that make up these isotopias. These are hyperproductive regions of compulsive motion. But they are also then iconic stations of suspended animation: at once hyperactive and inertial—like the human pyramid, a crystalized action frozen in the moment.

The academic discipline, and its rotational conference circuits, would be one working model of that. (Barbarism, we know, begins at home.) Parking structures—in the union of compulsive motion and suspended animation—another. Their correlation is one of the microsociologist Goffman's subjects, and it is a central fixation of the novelist J. G. Ballard. Ballard, an author "obsessed by car parks," is one of the great cartographers of the crystal worlds, concrete islands, high-rises, gated microclimates, no-go areas, and vast office assemblages of the late twentieth century, and their violence-pupation. There are scores of references to car parks in *Super-Cannes*, almost as many in the two other volumes (*Cocaine Nights*, *Millennium People*) of his late trilogy on situationist officialism and its internally solicited violence, from weekend fascism to corporate-recreational psychopathy. Airports, hotel lobbies, unemployment offices, shopping malls, motorways, laboratories, the proliferation of double white transit lines, yellow police tape, and "the long-term car park." *Super-Cannes*: "I thought you were writing a social history of the car park. I should. It's like Los Angeles, the car parks tend to find you, wherever you are."[44]

Here one finds too the coupling of the practico-inert—a rotational and reenactment system—and the incitations to violence that everywhere enter into Ballard's demarcation zones and atrocity exhibitions: "The city was a vast and stationary carousel, forever boarded by millions of would-be passengers who took their seats, waited and then dismounted. I thought of the bomb cutting through another temple of enlightenment, silencing the endless murmur of cafeteria conversation. Despite myself, I felt a surge of excitement and complicity."[45] This is the setting for the tanned surrealists in transit through Ballard's acceleratively lethal reenactment spaces, the outmoded space explorers overexposed to "news from the sun."[46] The stationary carousel emerges as an icon of the official world. The carousel is already, for Patricia Highsmith, in her first novel, *Strangers on a Train* (1950)—and even more emphatically in Hitchcock's film version of it (1951)—the working model of this inertial motion and for the irrational, self-induced violence that goes with it.[47] This is the rotary form of an official world intent on its own ends.

Highsmith's Pathographies

Patricia Highsmith's work epitomizes the official world. It is transfixed by the forms of violence and forms of art proper to such a world. It starkly outlines its overlit zones of action and reenactment. The relentlessly brilliant, and relentlessly narrow-cast, stagings of an autotropic order of things makes for the "strange air of captivity," the "precarious life," and the "flavour of the unearthly"—I take all three phrases from *Strangers on a Train* (the first novel Highsmith published under her own name)—that define an official world, and draw white boundary lines along its edges.

Highsmith's novels and stories are fixated on the invading realities of species life on the daily planet—albeit the life of a species apparently intent on putting an end to itself, and doing so, as Highsmith puts it, "under the weight of officialism." Highsmith's fascination, not unlike J. G. Ballard's, but generically very different, is the form of self-compelling violence in what Ballard calls "a crystal world" and what Highsmith calls "a world like an isinglass ball": a "glass cell."[48]

One of the staging areas of the official world is news from the outside. The primacy of the outside, as Peter Sloterdijk expresses it, "provides the axiom of the human sciences."[49] The great outside is its object. But this is subjected to a principle of interiority. The central drive of the official world is "to transpose the outside world into a magical immanence."[50] If a self-reporting world depends on reports on the outside, it depends not least on what the philosopher of science Thomas Nagel calls "the magical flavor of popular presentations of fundamental scientific discoveries."[51] The deliberately overanimated quality of a range of popular adaptations of science for humanities types enters into, and shapes, this magicked situation (and forms no doubt part of its charisma).[52] The allure of the great outside takes on administrative-institutional form. The refined air of these staging arenas of social life is the state of the contemporary tendency "to make nature and culture jointly into indoors affairs."[53]

This is the indoors climate of Highsmith's suspense fiction. "The name 'Patricia Highsmith,'" for Slavoj Zizek, "designates a sacred territory: she is the One whose place among writers is that which Spinoza held for Gilles Deleuze (a 'Christ among philosophers')." That territory is the self-stressed official world and its primary reenactment spaces: the scene of the crime, the space of the game, and the form of the work of art. Each designates the other, in the continuous rotation of a daily planet. These small worlds are, it turns out, scale models—diverse practice systems—of the systems epoch, but at the same time working models in it. They are not analogies to it, but analogues of it. They are, as it were, scale models of the modern social system, which is then, in effect, a life-size model of itself.

For these reasons, if Highsmith's work is the strange attractor of these pages, my primary attention is to what that work epitomizes and makes graphic and perspicuous. The intent, in part via the medium of Highsmith's suspense fiction, is to delineate the constituents of an official world. The objective in doing so is, step by step, to cast that world in relief, or to recast it in the presence of alternative, or warring, or ending worlds.

The premise of this book then is that the official world is realized in its ongoing description of its own conditions, which it then applies to itself. But the redescription of the process must then take that into account. Reflexivity, we know, is a defining attribute of modernity (a "reflexive modernity"). This means that the traps of autodescription are unavoidable in accounting for this type of society. Reflexivity or self-reference is not—to adapt Max Weber's way of expressing it—a streetcar one can step off from at the next corner if one does not like where it is going. It is not as if one were granted a legal self-exemption from the general condition one describes.

The traps of autodescription are unavoidable, but they are also nonlethal. Self-reference is not exactly the opposite of reference: it is a form of reference.

For this reason, there is more than a little melodrama in the recent return to reference from self-reference—for example, in a recent "speculative realism," the call of the wild, or at least, the weird, and to "the great outdoors" or "the outside world"—to the world as it looks without us. At the same time, there is no doubt a real fatigue with self-reference. The sense of a *Leerlaufen*, or empty running-in-place, and the plangency of zombie deconstruction (the eternal recurrence of its clichés, rotated from topic to topic, post to post). One might say of it what has been said of the city of Hong Kong: it looks like the future but there the future looks old.

No doubt the bending of reference to self-reference is one of the defining attributes of a self-legislative world (see part II). It is a part of the operating system of the official world: a social fact. It is also the defining property of the work of art in the epoch of social systems (see part V). Hence one reason for turning to the artwork—in this case, primarily, the art of fiction—in redescribing this world is that there is a distinct function of fictionality in securing this state of things as matter of fact (see part IV).

Hence, too, in the opening parts of this study, I want to set out some of the landmarks on this terrain. These landmarks include Highsmith's novels, *Strangers on a Train* and *The Talented Mr. Ripley*, and the microworlds they model. Such microworlds include the office (the architectural office, for example, in which worlds are drafted and modeled into existence); the theme park (the Kingdom of Fun, a collection of well-demarcated repeating zones—the merry-go-round, the tunnel of love, the shooting gallery, and so on—small worlds after all); the train car, a rotating and repeating place without a place; the game space (which Hitchcock literalizes, in the real-time tennis game, in his film version of *Strangers*); the scene of the crime and the returns to it; and, not least, the artwork.

Games, forensics, and the work of art everywhere indicate each other in Highsmith's fiction: they are prototypes of a unified and autistic world (see part III). These violent and reflexive zones are fractally self-similar (the emergence of comparable conditions in diverse systems is a defining attribute of modernity). And each, in turn, forms, as Highsmith puts it, "its own world, like a horrible little work of art."[54]

Stated a bit differently, these are sacrosanct precincts in which "each line, each figure, every angle—the ink itself vibrates with an almost intolerable violence."[55] These extremely formal spaces, or suspension zones, of rehearsal and reenactment incarnate the epoch of social systems. They mark the internality, autonomy, self-referentiality, and staged character of, say, the Cold War game worlds of Herman Kahn; or the floodlit interaction spaces of institutional ritual of Erving Goffman; or the insulated bureaucratic zealotry exhibited in *The Pentagon Papers*. These scenarios of premonition and preemption are familiar enough. But I ask you to consider the manner in which they epitomize too—and this is, for our purposes, the crux of the matter— the critical condition of the work of art in the systems epoch.

The aesthetic is the contemporary demarcation zone par excellence. And if aesthetics is the science of the a prioris of perception,[56] it provides something like a perceptual blueprint of this world. That is, if one takes into account how the official world blueprints itself as it goes and so, improbably and against all odds, goes on.

One art form that enters directly into Highsmith's suspense writing is the wildly popular genre (selling at one time more than fifty million issues a month) that she worked on for the first decade or so of her career as a novelist: comic books—the illuminated books of the second machine age.[57] The brutal simplifications of that art form (Highsmith worked primarily on superhero comics) encode the senses of the precarious, the captive, and the unearthly in her work. The comic-book genre provides the iterative model of an unremitting and systemic violence—a Cold War violence suspended and preemptive. It provides living diagrams of the ongoing catastrophes of modernization—and, by way of those diagrams, the intimation of counterfactual or alternate worlds, a war of the worlds, and the end of the world.

The graphic genre provides models of ego and alter—and so of alter ego—that shape Highsmith's talented killers from *Strangers on a Train* on. There is something of a likeness between the sort of superheroes, often with laboratory-induced superpowers, whose adventures Highsmith plotted at the drafting table and typewriter—Whizzer, the Human Torch, the Destroyer, Captain Midnight, Black Terror, Ghost, the Champion, Golden Arrow—and the posthuman psychopaths that populate her novels. The comic-book genre provides the laboratory conditions of Highsmith's experimental novels, their species life, and the control conditions—the humanities lab—proper to an autogenic and strictly self-conditioned world and its technical media. Or, as the psycho killer Bruno puts it in *Strangers*, "Guy and I are supermen."[58]

In the next chapter, I want first to set out in a bit more detail what I mean by the official world, and to trace its contours, via several recent experimental models of it, fictional and real. These scenes remain remarkably consistent across their different scenographies: living spaces that make life interfere with life. Life and death in those spaces take place (to adapt W. G. Sebald's formulation) "between history and natural history"—or, more exactly, take place at that turning point of collective catastrophe at which "history threatens to revert to natural history."[59] (It is of course the "between" of this duality that must be interpreted, here across a series of instances, in the sections that follow.[60]) Examining those spaces will make it possible to locate, in very preliminary fashion, what this form of life and its institutionalizations have come to look like in contemporary accounts. One might speak here of the distinction between the modern age and a modern world, the age of globalization and the global age—in that the first discovers the conditions that the second applies to itself. (More on this, in a moment, by way of the epoch-making reenactment zone, the experiment—the staging area, or dress rehearsal, of a reflexive modernity.)

TWO

BRECHT'S RABBIT

The Anthropotechnics of Suspense

> But the closer I came to these ruins, the more any notion of a mysterious isle of
> the dead receded, and the more I imagined myself amidst the remains of our own
> civilization after its extinction in some future catastrophe.
> —W. G. Sebald, *The Rings of Saturn*

We might then have begun, in approaching the logic of Highsmith's perpetual Cold War—perpetually suspended war—world, with Brecht's dictum
that "human beings learn no more from catastrophe than a laboratory rabbit
learns about biology."[1] What, after all, is the new "experimental" novel, from
Zola on, but a machine for conducting experiments?[2] One in which the species
conducting the experiment and the one submitting to it are one and the same?
The unreal reality of the perpetual postwar condition—from World War II to
World War Z—oscillates between history and natural history. These are the
coordinates of what Highsmith calls an "Imaginary Zoo" and its "glass cells."[3]

They are the presuppositions of the experimental conditions of precarious, captive, and alien life in her work. The real point is that the appeal
to either side of this distinction—history, natural history—ends up on the
other and so leads into tautology. Hence "the perspective of human history
and that of natural history are one and the same, so that destruction—and
the tentative forms of new life that it generates—work like experiments, experiments in which the life of the species is concerned."[4] For the moment,
let me outline these experiments in which species life is concerned via two
reports on the prospects, if that's the right word, for tentative forms of new
life on the daily planet.[5]

Figure 2.1. The Posthuman Pyramid (*World War Z*, dir. Marc Forster, 2013).

The Posthuman Pyramid

Consider, first, this example of a postwar form of life, one at the lower range of life and form, and so perhaps a good way to take a baseline pulse of these general conditions. Here is the opening of Max Brooks's best seller, *World War Z*, an unexpectedly compelling novel subtitled *An Oral History of the Zombie War*:

> Greater Chongquing, the United Federation of China
>
> *[At its prewar height, this regime boasted a population of over thirty-five million people. Now there are barely fifty-thousand. Reconstruction funds have been slow to arrive in this part of the country, the government choosing to concentrate on the more densely populated coast. There is no central power grid, no running water besides the Yangtze River. But the streets are clear of rubble and the local "security council" has prevented any postwar outbreaks. The chairman of that council is Kwang Jing-shu, a medical doctor who, despite his advanced age and wartime injuries, still manages to make house calls to all his patients.]*
>
> The first outbreak I saw was in a remote village that officially had no name. The residents called it "New Dachang," but this was more out of nostalgia than anything else. Their former home, "Old Dachang," had stood since the period of the Three Kingdoms, with farms and houses and even trees said to be centuries old. When the Three Gorges Dam was completed, and reservoir waters began to rise, much of Dachang had been disassembled, brick by brick, then rebuilt on higher ground. This

New Dachang, however, was not a town anymore, but a "national historic museum." It must have been a heartbreaking irony for those poor peasants, to see their town saved but then only being able to visit it as a tourist. Maybe that is why some of them chose to name their newly constructed hamlet "New Dachang" to preserve some connection to their heritage, even if it was only in name. . . . Officially, it didn't exist and therefore wasn't on any map.[6]

World War Z is, like Stoker's *Dracula* a century before, a chronicle, or better yet a chronologically ordered dossier, made up of documents, files, numbers; grids, maps, committees, officialism; the administratively located, named, and recorded—and the unnamed and unrecorded, and so officially inexistent. It has the neutrality of a series of collated reports, and so that of a foreign and unreal reality, one in which familiarity with cultural and social circumstances has been suspended, the very same familiarity on which the writing and reading of novels depends.

Hence *World War Z* lifts the distinction (as does much horror fiction) between the world as it looks to us and the world as it looks without us—as does, for example, Cormac McCarthy's novel *The Road*—and there too, "We're the walking dead in a horror film."[7] The daily planet reporter in this case is a medical officer. The coupling of biology and its administration is, of course, the mode of the experimental novel. We recall that the novelist and the doctor stand in for each other in Zola's 1880 manifesto for the experimental novel. Consider, with that, the function of fictions, or thought experiments, in the natural sciences, in pupating truth.

Here history and natural history in effect change places with each other. The account in *World War Z* compares the newly constructed, or reconstructed, to the long span of natural life (trees centuries old), and that to the yet even longer span of unnatural or social life (the Three Kingdoms, two millennia old). The Three Kingdoms and the Three Gorges Dam are in effect "floated" in relation to each other, in an ongoing comparison of what Highsmith calls "tales of natural and unnatural catastrophes."[8] This is the case because collective catastrophe marks the point where nature and history refer back to each other as two sides of a tautology. The effect is to neutralize the distinction between them. This neutralization intimates that the biological reflexes setting off both construction and destruction seem to have "long been foreshadowed by the complex physiology of human beings, the development of their hypertrophied minds, and their technological methods of production."[9]

The official world is of necessity always patrolling the dikes of made culture, and in doing so, managing the catastrophes their construction sets in motion. The unspecified "outbreak" lies then in the interval between natural and unnatural disaster, and the walking dead, like the displaced in a war zone, carry their restlessness around like a plague. (If modernity is at bottom a traffic problem, the walking dead are its sidelined, vagrant, and revenant pedestrians.)

But it is another and apparently gratuitous observation that in fact centers these opening pages and does so not in diegetic but in extremely formal terms. I am referring to the reenactment project that preoccupies the opening: the brick-by-brick disassembly and reconstruction of a small world, one irremediably in the "as-they-say" code of represented discourse ("New Dachang"). This is not exactly a constructed, or even a reconstructed, place. It is the staging of one—a life-size model of itself as a "national historic museum." The town that is not a town and place that is not a place centers this entry into the novel. Hence it is where the novel describes its own conditions; and, in doing so, frames a space of reenactment in which its own fictional reality applies. In this way, it depicts not merely a world that appears in the world, but a self-depicting one—a demarcated enclosure and the official world as observation zone.

INS

"Zombiedom," the English novelist Tom McCarthy has recently observed, "is just re-enactment without content."[10] McCarthy's novel *Remainder* (to which I return in part IV) is about reenactment, its reenactors self-ironic robots with extremely limited liability. The sponsor of these reenactments is the novel's human-like narrator, a first-person voice who is not exactly a person but, as his speaking voice puts it, a "robot or zombie," and one who is irremediably alien or "secondhand" with respect to the world.[11]

Reenactment without content. If a modern world comes to itself through staging its own conditions, then the prototype for that process is no doubt in the nature of the experiment. For one thing, the experiment is the defining form of observation, and the observation of observation, in the modern age. For another, observation via continuous reenactment, and commentary on it, are the presuppositions of the official world. That means the staging and repetition of natural processes via technical means, and the continuous alternation of observation and report, such that observing and reporting, and their repetition, may themselves be observed: "The experiment," as Hannah Arendt (following Heidegger) presents it, "repeats the natural process as though man himself were about to make nature's objects, this not for practical reasons of technical applicability but exclusively for the 'theoretical' reason that certainty in knowledge could not be gained otherwise." In Kant's terms: "Give me matter and I will build a world from it, that is, give me matter and I will show you how a world developed from it."[12]

The experiment repeats the natural process by technical means, not for practical but for formal reasons: it makes a world and shows its making.

This—reenactment without content—is the situation, as McCarthy's neo-situationism makes clear enough, the logic of the official world at its purest. Reenactments and their extreme formality take place, quite literally, under the weight of officialism and are acutely conscious of those circumstances. (Hence it's impossible to decide whether such reenactments take things to the breaking point or to the point of installation: we recall that, in Kafka, official decision makers are as shamefaced as young girls.)

McCarthy serves as general secretary of the International Necronautical Society (INS) he cofounded. (A meeting of the society is pictured in figure 2.2, featuring—of course—reenactors.) The founding manifesto of the society (1999)—an "official document" authorized by the "First Committee, INS"—sets out its mission in these terms:

We, the First Committee of the International Necronautical Society, declare the following:

1. That death is a type of space, which we intend to map, enter, colonize and, eventually, inhabit.
2. That there is no beauty without death, its immanence. We shall sing death's beauty—that is, beauty.
3. That we shall take it upon us, as our task to bring death out into the world. We will chart all its forms and media: in literature and art, where it is most apparent; also in science and culture, where it lurks submerged. . . .
4. Our ultimate aim shall be the construction of a craft that will convey us into death in such a way that we may, if not live, then at least persist.[13]

These are the contours of what I've elsewhere called death and life in our wound culture—but in the terms of a "bureaucratic comedy, trimmed out in red tape."[14]

The general secretary's report to the INS has as its ground zero, it may be noted, "Berlin: World Capital of Death." The report is replete with forensic

Figure 2.2. The Rise of the Planet of the Professionals: INS London Declaration of Authenticity, General Secretary Tom McCarthy and Chief Philosopher Simon Critchley (Reenacted; Richard Eaton/Tate). © Richard Eaton/Tate/INS.

detail, dossiers, archives, aerial surveys, sites of "marking and erasure, transit and transmission, cryptography and death."[15] It choreographs its own intent, with a hyperbolic and deadpan officialism: in its combination of a statement and a practice, it is sort of a practical joke—and the practical joke (it will be seen) is one of the dress rehearsal routines of the official world. The central place in McCarthy's account is, in fact, a place that's not quite a place, but a transit and transmission zone, and the "primary reenactment space":

> "I'd like to hire a room," I told him.
>   "What kind of room?" he asked.
>   "A space. An office."
>   "Right."[16]

IRS

Highsmith's most popular suspense novel, *The Talented Mr. Ripley*, takes off from a practical joke involving the same reenactment zone, the office—albeit in this case, one that involves the reenactment of the office space itself.

The game that Tom is playing at the start of the novel "amounted to no more than a practical joke, really. Good clean sport." The practical joke, a

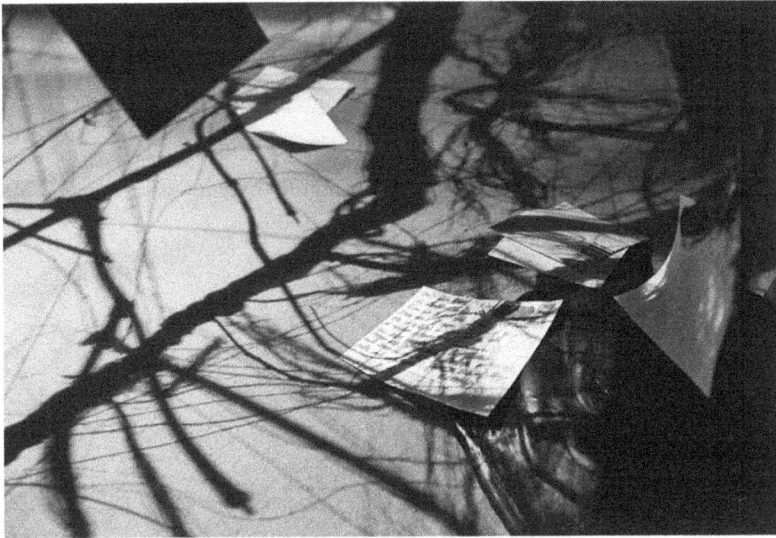

Figure 2.3. *Absolute Helligkeit,* dir. Naoko Tanaka. Courtesy of the artist.

sport or game, involves impersonating systems (that is, personating them)—in this case, not the INS but the IRS. The sport, more exactly, involves notifying strangers about back taxes they need to pay; the checks are to be made out to "McAlpin" (Tom) and sent to a mail-drop address. Tom has "a list of prospects"; "a mauve-coloured stationery box"; a "stack of various forms" he has stolen; a typewriter; "typewriter paper stamped with the Department of Internal Revenue's Lexington address"; a "supply" of carbon paper, pens, paper, stamps, numbers; a telephone directory and a telephone, and so on.[17]

The scene is thus like a diorama that might be called *Office-Dwelling Hominid in an Administrative State of Nature.* And the whole point of the joke is that Tom knows he can't cash the checks he receives: his intention is predatory but only formally so. The pleasure is in entering into and staging, writing and voicing, an impersonal system as a practical joke, a play-at-home version of the IRS, and the scale model of an official world that operates just to keep operating—and getting client-victims to play along.

Here then is the description, in *The Talented Mr. Ripley,* of what Tom Ripley's harmless sport looks like:

> He chose two forms headed NOTICE OF ERROR IN COMPUTATION, slipped a carbon between them, and began to copy rapidly the data below Reddington's name on his list. Income: $11,250. Exemptions: 1. Deductions $600. Credits: nil. Remittance: nil. Interest: (he hesitated a moment) $2.16.

Balance due: $233.76. Then he took a piece of typewriter paper stamped with the Department of Internal Revenue's Lexington Avenue address from his supply in his carbon folder, crossed out the address with one slanting line of his pen, and typed below it:

Dear Sir:

Due to an overflow at our regular Lexington Avenue office, your reply should be sent to:

    Adjustment Department
    Attention of George McAlpin
    187 E. 51 Street
    New York 22, New York

Thank you.
Ralph F. Fischer
Gen. Dir. Adj. Dept.

So much depends upon, in such modernist passages, the white spaces of the page beginning to signify—not exactly in the form of, say, Mallarmé's poetics, but like the blank spaces on official forms (which, of course, Highsmith types Tom typing). One cannot read this form, only copy it, and Tom's talent, of course, is to "copy rapidly"—and to copy uncontrollably (Bartleby—a name Highsmith borrows for her main character in her novel *A Suspension of Mercy* [1965]—but Bartleby weaponized).[18]

The administrative list-shaped control system, like the form letters that enact and copy it, is a place-value system. The modern administrative a priori, as Weber made clear early on, replaces persons with positions. More exactly, the bureaucratic form of life means that persons are shifted, or rotated, through positions. They take their place, and so take place, in the same way that the zero allows digits to take value from a position and so to function as an autonomous system. The problem is keeping up the sequence and endlessly repeating it, by rotating persons through positions.[19] (More on this in a moment.)

In case of the Ripley novels, Tom, the medium in person, takes their place. His talent is to see how place-value systems, their form and media, work—and how blindness to those systems works too. Uncontrollably reenacting, without content or character, Tom in effect turns alter into ego albeit in the form of alter ego, in this case a pale king of the IRS.

Hence Tom can take the place of Dickie, or in principle anyone else, in the same way that he can take McAlpin's position, or posit it. The Ripley novels are nothing but the possibility of that interchangeability—and the cultural techniques that enable it (the typewriter, the post, the telephone, the train, the passport, the newspaper, the telegraph, and the novel). These techniques presuppose addicts of the secondary (and their anesthetic media). Or, we might say that the epistolary novel (and Highsmith's novels are full of letters) has mutated: it now includes form letters too.[20] We may note also that, in *The Talented Mr. Ripley*, for example, the novel in places simply cedes narration to a series of letters: it pastes in letters received by Ripley or implicitly so, and reproduced in sequence, but without transition or commentary or indication of Ripley's sense of them, or relation to them. The series of letters thus effects a strict extroversion of moods and states of mind. And so they are, like form letters, detached from predictable responses of self-application or self-registration that communication by letter in novels (say, in Austen's novels or, a bit differently, James's) might, however systemic, presuppose, enact, or represent.

In short, in the reconstructed office world, and in the reconstructing official world, the act and its registration are two parts of single formation. But the parts are first separated via a legal-technical process and then recombined as, precisely, the process of administration. That combination of statement and practice here takes the form of a practical joke, a merely official world.

It is not just then that "the registration and revelation of reality make a difference to reality. [That it then] becomes a different reality, consisting of itself plus its registration and revelation."[21] The official world—that is, a modern self-generated and self-described world—is one that works via a continuous transfer of the act and its registration. It takes shape in taking into account and storing its own actions.[22]

The IRS for Highsmith is, then, like the INS for McCarthy, a sort of practical joke, but one that is at the same time a reenactment of the reenactment zone of officialism. One with, as they now say, existential consequences. The practical joke is a self-induced and self-exposed game about being taken in by games, and the observation of that process. It is a centauric form, one that combines (like the bureaucratic medium) a physics and a hermeneutics. (It is located on the switch point of the physical act, and its registration and observation, such that each indicates the other.) It does so with the intent of causing embarrassment—a sociable moment, a little space of commitment—felt on the body. Hence it provides a scale model of the interactive rituals, or drills, of the daily planet.

The practical joke is, it will be seen, one of the calisthenics of social interaction rituals by which make-believe makes belief and then discredits it, breaking what Erving Goffman calls "a socialized trance." Embarrassment or, rather, the observation of embarrassment—and its observed self-observation—is its object.[23]

The practical joke is thus a game that gives itself away in the end, since its purpose is to see whether the other person believes in the game or not. More exactly, it posits, as its formal condition, the little social system constructed "between the concealer and the concealed-from" (*IR*, 103). (It plays a game of hide-and-seek that excludes one player, from whom the game itself is hidden.) It stages a small world and then proceeds to discredit it by exposing the credulity that holds it in place—showing that one (the concealed-from one) has been taken in by taking the game as serious or real. But the point is not merely to embarrass the true believer.

The point is to show his becoming-embarrassed over his embarrassment: to mark the point "when, in short, the interactive world becomes too real for him" (*IR*, 123). The social obligation is to "keep things going." Hence, over-involvement is as much "a crime against the interaction" as dis-involvement. The interaction hero avoids both in his performance of spontaneity.

The physical symptoms of embarrassment, the "objective signs of emotional disturbance," make up a long list: they include "blushing, fumbling, stuttering, an unusually low- or high-pitched voice, quavering speech or breaking of the voice, sweating, blanching, blinking, tremor of the hand, hesitating or vacillating movement, absentmindedness, and malapropisms" and so on (*IR*, 97).

These disturbances—which are, for the most part on this account, disturbances in communication (speech and signal)—are the bodily registers by which "the standards of the little social system are maintained through the interaction" (*IR*, 106). They are means by which its rituals of self-evaluation and self-propitiation are at once represented and presented.

The self-conditioned and self-evaluative character of contemporary institutional work spaces is the normal condition of competitive socialization today, inside the "affective labor" of capitalism. As Diedrich Diederichsen narrowly expresses it: "Self-evaluation—a familiar ritual in today's universities and workplaces—is nothing other than a visible, public form of organized narcissism as higher-order repression."[24]

That's clear enough, for instance, in those games that "commemorate the themes of composure and embarrassment" (*IR*, 104), like poker or spectator sports or reality TV. The embarrassing incident tests outs how the "interaction qua interaction" is proceeding, making things "safe for the little worlds sustained in face-to-face encounters" (118).

For Goffman, it will be recalled, the matter of embarrassment in modern social situations "leads us to the matter of 'role segregation'" (*IR*, 108) or social differentiation. The scenes of embarrassment and of "joking and avoidance" that Goffman inventories are the scenes of an official and institutionally-differentiated world—office buildings, schools, hospitals. Embarrassment takes place, more exactly, at the sites of a stranger intimacy in friction with that role segregation: places of embarrassed encounter like elevators, corridors, entrances, parking garages, or the coffee machine. Hence the executive elevator, like the stratified parking facility or the freight entrance, are embarrassment-avoidance devices: the built infrastructure of what Goffman likes to call a civil inattention. The built structure of the isotopic spaces, corridors, and zones of departure, transit, and arrival: media of stopping and going, parking and trafficking. (Highsmith's *Strangers on a Train*, to which I turn in the next part of this study, centers on the technical media of a compulsively extroverted, reenactive, and blueprinted life. These media include the train, the architectural office, the stationary carousel. The violence in the novel proceeds from an accidental encounter in the transit system crisscrossing public space.)[25]

There is a good deal more to be said about the repercussive character of these situations.[26]

For now I mean to indicate the manner in which the reality tests like the practical joke, or sport, or (in fact) the artwork test out controlled and uncontrollable bodily states: these are ways to conduct social experiments, under outlined, repeated, and staged conditions, not least in the forms of identification (controlled, or uncontrollable) solicited in literary fiction. These are Highsmith's own renditions of an international necronautical society, and its demarcation zones, its games, crimes, and art. These "little worlds" epitomize the autotropic social systems of the daily planet—or what Highsmith also calls (the title of her 1958 novel) "a game for the living."

The Uncanny Valley

Highsmith's experimental novels observe the behavior and interaction of human beings in their glass cells—strange captives in an imaginary zoo.[27] These novels are clinical reports on a wound culture and its pathological states (at times, as in *Ripley's Game*, clinical reports in literal terms). They are reports on species physiology, its ouroboric reflexivity, and its bent toward technical life.[28] A certain alien way of sensing and reporting the world makes it possible to observe, for example, "the caviar [tossed in a fire], popping like little people, dying, each one a life" (*ST*, 116). To speak in terms of a character "different from . . . any other *human*" (19). To see a little turn in one's course of action as something "like the turning of the earth" (281).

An imaginary zoology is thus suspended between history and natural history, biology and its administration, unnatural and natural disasters. It includes "mermaids on the golf course." It includes an island of giant naturalist-devouring mollusks. It includes stories of "bestial affinities" (*ST*, 144)—snail keepers fascinated by the sexual life of these backyard aliens and their capacity, or talent, to move across the upturned blade of a razor (a fascination Highsmith shared); or perpetually floodlit chicken factories that generate a hothouse madness and horrific violence. It includes too an unearthly human order routinely described in terms such as these: "Some wisps of hair, darkened brown with sweat, bobbed like antennae over his forehead."[29]

The fat words "life" and "society" and "world"—especially "world"—repeat in Highsmith's writings with an unyielding abstractness. This is life viewed (the examples here are from *Strangers on a Train*), as it were, from "another planet" (54). It is viewed in terms, again and again, of "the outside world" (18), "the whole world" (132, 155, 247), "its own world" (26), "the pulse [of the] world" (232), "the new world" (38), "everything in the world" (54), "as if the crust of the world burst" (151), and so on.

But it's not hard to see the ease with which that grandness of reference overturns into grandiosity of self-reference, from "the outside world" to "someday Guy and I are going to circle the world like an isinglass ball, and tie it up in ribbon" (260), to "take on the whole world and whip it!" (262). In effect, alter and ego, "Guy and I are Superman."

Superman, who could, on a good afternoon, easily remedy worldwide problems of war, poverty, disease, and all the rest, instead divides his time between his reporting job and catching petty criminals in a big metropolis that's still then Smallville, U.S.A.[30]

There's a performance of scale here. Yet the evocation of the vastnesses of deep space or time largely functions as evocation. There is perhaps an element of the sublime in this, its apotropaic rhythm, and its countereffect of self-aggrandizement. But my sense is that this is less a matter of the sublime than of the autotropic conditioning of a modernity at once self-inciting and self-reporting, continuously reusing reference as self-reference, and so setting off the reflexes of a reflexive modernity, albeit at its meridian.[31]

Reference becomes self-reference, seeing self-seeing, observation self-observation, locating self-locating.[32]

We are in fact very familiar with this way of seeing a world or, at the least, with the diagrammatic and simplified visual techniques that lend themselves to it. A little sampling from Highsmith's *Strangers on a Train*: "the world beyond the merry-go-round vanished in a light-streaked blur" (77); "the oblique bars of shadow" (177); "two streaks of red fire that came and disappeared" (167); "a small room lined in red" (200); "Bruno's mouth a thin, insanely smiling line" (194).

A diagram and a worldview. This is the blueprinted and extroverted character of the every-guy architect Guy who draws alternate worlds into existence in his office space—"floor models" and "cartoons" of what a building or city might look like (and hangs a drawing of an imaginary zoo on his bedroom wall). And these are the lined and simplified comic-book worlds that Highsmith drafts and scripts, at the typewriter and storyboard, in hers: faces of invading and alien realities but also the look of a daily planet that is immanently unearthly. Its nonhuman figures are outlined like humans, ones who are near but also far—like strangers, with bobbing antennae, on a train. This is a stranger-intimacy with (as Bruno is introduced in *Strangers on a Train*) "a look that was eerily omniscient and hideous . . . this *thing* right in the center of [his] head." This is the alien as usual, albeit (with apologies to Tom McCarthy) more usual than usual.[33]

"A constellation of red and green and white lights hummed southward in the sky" (*ST*, 11). The constellation is not in fact the distant stars but a series of signals, a coding system, marking and reporting the moving perimeter of the zoned world (the hum of the daily planet, demarcated and encircled, the planet in effect as planetarium). There is, as it were, a condensed history of modernity in passages such as this one, or in the world vanishing behind the light-streaked blur of a rotating model of one. Suffice to say that the passage—in its shifting from the planetary to the daily planet (from constellation to a more human order of things)—invokes in order to revoke the turn to the great outside. That's what the speculative realist Quentin Meillassoux describes as the loss of the Great Outdoors—*le Grand Dehors*—and hence "the impossibility itself: *to get out of ourselves*" and our limitation to a world that "exists only on the basis of a vis-à-vis with our own existence."[34] This is the two-step by which the turn to the great outside reverts to an order of things premised on its observation. "A curious analogy," Wittgenstein notes, "could be based on the fact that the eye-piece of even the hugest telescope cannot be bigger than our eye."

In short: in Brecht's play *Galileo*, it is announced, in turning the telescope from the earth to the big sky, "January, 1610. Heaven abolished." The counterrevolution, at its limit, makes for Virginia Woolf's statement that "in or about December 1910 human character changed." (The first, a matter of the world, the second a matter of character, worldviews. The overly hasty conflation of the two—world and worldview—in recent manifestos about proliferating "literary worlds" could not be more clearly marked.) We might tentatively add that on or about January 2010, the call of the wild, the great outdoors, was heard again. That already a half century after Foucault, in the last paragraph of his archaeology of seismic and epochal shifts in *Les mots et les choses*, concluded that the brief period of the human character of things—not millennia-old but a narrow interval from the late eighteenth century to the mid-twentieth—was coming to an end: the disappearance of the face of man drawn in sand at the edge of the sea. This is a scene literalized—in the little exchange about a letter that might be written in sand on the edge of a dead ocean—in McCarthy's *The Road*. The "Anthropocene" has recently come to brand the epoch, not least in that it posits at the same time the generalization of the human-made and its incipient nullification: Brecht's rabbit holding seminars on the hopeless fix it has placed itself in.

Highsmith's work borders on this condition: on the absolute decoupling of the world as it looks to us (our "indoor" social life) and the world as it looks without us (the Great Outdoors)—and on the horrors, and pleasures, that decoupling induces. For one thing, Highsmith's narrative way of seeing—preemptive and autistic—lends to self-observation the look of omniscience and to the counterfactual the feel of objective description. For another, uncontrollable identifications determine the semantics of character and interaction in these novels. In short, we see again and again a reflexive violence that (in these reiterative terms) tears the body to pieces, and then reorders pieces into parts and parts into the two parts of a whole, the twin halves of an identity.[35]

There is a generalized failure of distinction between subject and space that is at the same time a failure of self-distinction: "The bathroom walls had that look of breaking up in little pieces, as the walls might not really have been there, or he might not really have been here" (*ST*, 200). Self-observation proceeds in just these terms (which are not metaphoric but descriptive)—such that alter enters into ego but in the form of alter ego, and so as a process of continuous "self-annihilation."

This is a refrain, for example, in *Strangers*, *The Talented Mr. Ripley*, and *Those Who Walk Away*—the disincarnations of identity that are characteristic of Highsmith's work. A state of hypertrophied reflexivity uncorrectable by external information—and so a correlate or symptom of reflexive modernity.

But to the very extent to which it is a correlate or symptom of a self-suspended world, it means the projection of individuals into extroverted life.

One must turn oneself into an anthropotechnician who turns "one's life into a project and the project into a business."[36] This is, of course, the self-designed life projected by Benjamin Franklin in his autobiographical "Art of Virtue," the projection of a workshop that is at the same time a print shop of self-invention. New ego-technic media make possible success artists such as Highsmith's talented Mr. Ripley, who sees the things that one can change about oneself as things, and so things one can acquire and make conspicuous. Hence self-projection means at the same time radical extroversion. Sampling and accessing one's own life as external data: self-enhancements, self-renewal technologies, and self-observation via a performance chart or curriculum vitae, or other signs of undebatable professionalism in personal fitness training, whatever in the world it may be. The art of virtue can then turn round to the ecumenical virtue of art: ascetic training into aesthetic conditioning to a continuous, self-stressed, virtuoso performativity.[37] Like Highsmith's acrobats or Tom McCarthy's men in space or Ballard's pilots and astronauts, gravity-defying artists.

In Highsmith's fiction, these are the intensified and denuded simplifications of character and ground that fill its self-enclosed cells. We should be familiar with these outlines. In his immensely useful account of forms of figure and ground in the art of comic books, Scott McCloud traces how, in comics "most characters were designed simply, to assist in reader-identification."[38]

Here think of the simplicity of the emoticon (or for that matter their reproduction on the faces of those viewing them, on their smartphones, for their viewers: ☺). For McCloud, they are designed to assist in identification and self-identification—"just as our awareness of our biological selves are [sic] simplified conceptualized images" (UC, 39). In short (and in terms that resonate with the account of the cellular organization of modernity I have been setting out here): "when you look at a photo or realistic drawing of a face—you see it as the face of *another* . . . the world outside of us. . . . But when you enter into the world of the *cartoon*—you see *yourself* . . . the world within" (40–41). The simplification of representation in the direction of line and outline means that "those same lines became *so* stylized as to almost have a *life* and physical presence *all their own*" (111).

McCloud's account is more complicated, but the point is that the diagrammatic in this art form lends itself to a readiness of identification, such that "we make the world over in our image": and, in this way, "we see ourselves in everything" (UC, 33).

The drive to identification here has a real counterside, however. For one thing, the intrusion of realism (a realism relative to line or diagram) interrupts

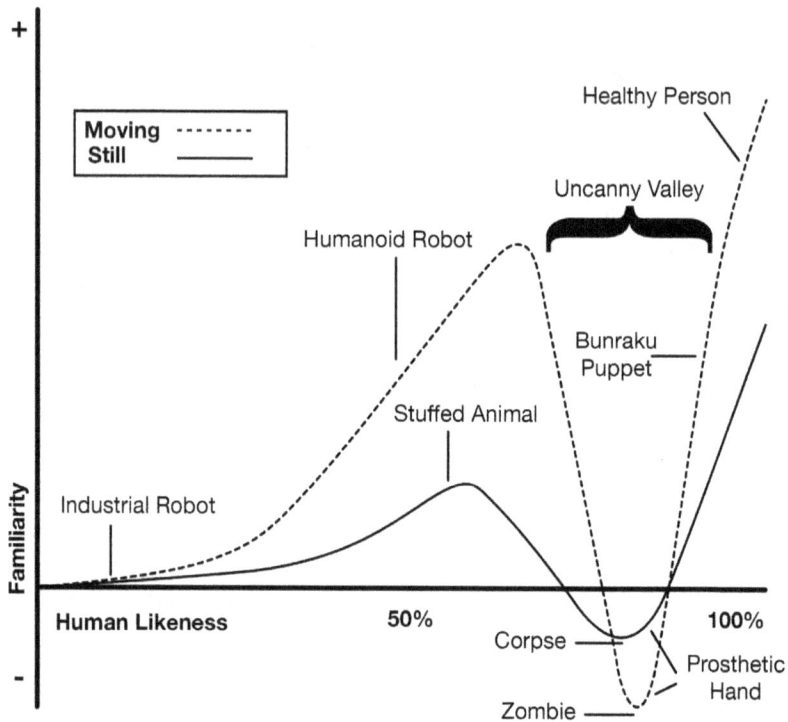

Figure 2.4. Simplified Version of Figure by Masahiro Mori, "The Uncanny Valley," *Energy* 7, no. 4 (1970): 33–35, trans. Karl F. MacDorman and Takashi Minato. © 2005 Karl F. MacDorman and Takashi Minato.

or spoils it. The deviation from line and outline into irregularity, or asymmetry, not merely interrupts but overturns that identification. This is the moment when the stylized "body-to-body analogies" that make identification possible mutate, and become images of just the opposite.

These figures inhabit what robotics engineers, from the 1970s on, call "the uncanny valley"—that abrupt transit point in realist representation at which identification with the simulation of human face or body abruptly reverses into revulsion, and the nearly human overturns into the barely human. The uncanny valley charts that moment when the incitation to identification (via say puppet or clown or doll) becomes horrific. Here it's perhaps appropriate, in the account of these living diagrams, to let the diagram stand in for a more extended explanation (figure 2.4).

The moment of the uncanny valley is the moment when overidentification turns inside out. The zombie moves and lives, or persists, at the bottom of the uncanny valley. The walking dead, motion without life, undoes the fundamental principle (as Hobbes expressed it) that "life itself is but motion." Hence the simplified analogy between bodies upon which identification is founded becomes too real to be sustained. These are the formal conditions for the uncontrollable identifications—and disidentifications—we have been setting out. They are too the preconditions for self-conditioning and autotropic practices like novel reading—and its excitations—in the first place.

Coda: The Loyalty Card

There is a party, everyone is there
Everyone will leave at exactly the same time
When this party's over, it will start again
It will not be any different, it will be exactly the same
Heaven, heaven is a place, a place where nothing, nothing ever happens.
—Talking Heads, "Heaven"

"The novel itself had found its leitmotifs in the bodies of its protagonists," Niklas Luhmann notes in *The Reality of the Mass Media*, and did so "especially in the barriers to the controllability of bodily processes." The dominance of dangerous or erotic adventures in the novel is explained, he further suggests, in that they provide ways "in which the reader can then participate voyeuristically using body-to-body analogy": the "tension in the narrative is 'symbolically' anchored in the barriers to controllability in each reader's body."[39]

It's not simply then that readers imitate characters in novels. Instead, they enter into situations of incitation and their observation—which is to say, situations of self-incitation and self-observation.[40] The complement to novel reading, on this account, is the boundary condition of bodily control to be found in the viewing of sporting events. Such events, to the extent that they are intended for spectation, provide body-to-body analogies too. The sporting event then provides not merely occasions for excitation by proxy but fitness to a reenacting, risk-driven, and self-reporting world. For example, Highsmith's novel *The Talented Mr. Ripley* turns on the model of some kind of game, as spectacle: the staging of a self-stressed structure made up of bodies, an externalization of the performance profiles of the suspense novel, and the stress-driven professionalism of the world it models, and its rotary subsystems.

In his account *On Deep History and the Brain*, the historian Daniel Lord Smail traces in some detail the emergence and spreading of autotropic commodities from the long eighteenth century on: self-stimulants such as alcohol, caffeine, chili pepper, opiates, tobacco, chocolate, sugar, gossip, sports, music, new media, religiosity, recreational drugs, sex for fun, and pornography. Last and not least—or most—is novel reading and related forms of literary leisure: what in the nineteenth century came to be called "a reading world." These are versions of what one contemporary observer calls "the controlled use of the uncontrollable."[41]

Here is the biological component of that self-incitation. Smail is entranced by the example of the snorting horse: "Horses who get bored or lonely while isolated in a paddock sometimes take pleasure in startling themselves. A lively snort causes a chemical feedback that induces a startle reflex and an exciting wash of neurochemicals." He, the horse, mimics the conditions that would naturally stimulate a startle reflex. For Smail, this feedback pleasure is like the self-stimulative history he traces, with the difference, of course, that "the horse cannot say to himself, 'I feel like getting startled,'" or report that thought to others. Hence the autotropic world is between history and natural history (at once *deep* history and deep *history*).[42]

One irony that Smail returns to is this: before the 1830s discovery of deep time and the idea of a very old earth, the general sense was that the world was about five thousand or six thousand years old, and human history five thousand or six thousand years old, less about a week, and originating in a garden traditionally located in the Middle East; after the discovery of deep time, human history is seen as beginning with the invention of writing, about five thousand or six thousand years ago in a fertile area of Mesopotamia. Despite its evocations of vast expanses of geological and planetary history, recent turns to deep time in literary studies tend to occupy the same biblical time zone. That makes sense in terms of the history of great books (from *Gilgamesh*, or the flood—the traditional "restart" of history—on). But it does not exactly make a difference in terms of a deep history. One might say that something like the same irony enters into Smail's story. The case for a deep history takes the intramural form of a disciplinary review—an internalized history of history. And that in turn devolves on a fascination with the autonomous and the self-induced or autotropic (to which my own description of the daily planet is indebted). This may indicate how acknowledging a problem may obviate dealing with it. In any case it's not hard to see how what amounts to the scaling up to the planet reversing into a scaling down to the institution, or discipline, is the pas de deux of a range of recent literary-historical studies—what I have described in terms of the "new institutionalism." It is in part the logic of such a turning outside in and its reenactments—as a defining attribute of the official world—that I have been setting out here.[43]

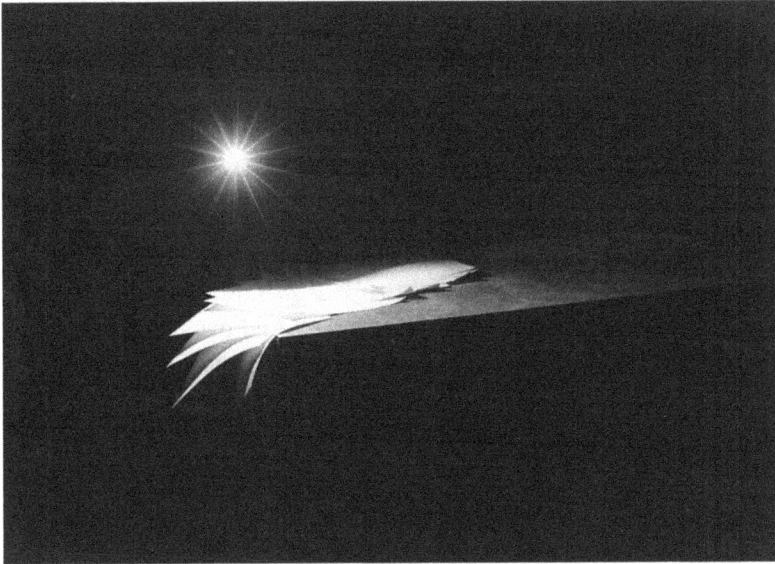

Figure 2.5. *Absolute Helligkeit,* dir. Naoko Tanaka. Courtesy of the artist.

One final introductory example of reenactment, one that I will ask you to remember next time. Since the work of one of the official world's most alert recent reporters, the novelist and choreographer of officialism Tom McCarthy, has run like a thread through these pages, it may be appropriate to give the general secretary of the INS the last word, even if it is not exactly his. This not least in that his work describes and indexes the circuitry of an auto-inciting and reenacting world. Here is a look at that world in operation: an exchange of sorts between the novel's commentator (who describes himself as a "robot or zombie") and a couple of the daily planet's actors, or reenactors (who describe themselves in the same way—"Sorry! I'm a zombie! too)—and at one of its iconic sites:

> After a while I tired of watching all these amateur performances [that is, people interacting on the street] and decided to buy a coffee from a small concession a few feet away. It was a themed Seattle coffee bar where you buy caps, lattes, and mochas, not coffees. When you order they say *Heyy!* to you, then they repeat your order aloud, correcting the word *large* into *tall*, *small* into *short*. I ordered a small cappuccino.
>
> "Heyy! Short cap," the man said. "Coming up! You have a loyalty card?"
>
> "Loyalty card?" I said.

"Each time you visit us, you get a cup stamped," he said, handing me a card. It had ten small pictures of coffee cups on it. "When you've stamped all ten, you get an extra cup for free. And a new card."

"But I'm not here that often," I said.

"Oh, we have branches everywhere," he told me, "It's the same deal." . . .

If I got all ten of its cups stamped then I'd get an extra cup—plus a new card with ten more cups on it. The idea excited me.

The loyalty card is a little technology that blueprints, comments on, and records what it does, and it reinstates itself as it goes. Not only that, it incites loyalty—that is, reenactment—in the process. And that's, as the nameless narrator puts it, "the beauty of it. It became real while it was going on."[44]

II • STATIONARY CAROUSELS AND CHAIN LETTERS

The Ego-Technic Media of the Official World

THREE

"THE PROPER STUDY
OF INTERACTION"

I have been setting out, in a preliminary way and across a developing series of accounts, how a modern society comes to itself by staging its own conditions, and how that takes the form of what I redescribe as the official world.[1] In the first part of this study I have indicated the shape of this autotropic situation. In this part, I want to shift the focus 180 degrees on its axis, in order to look more closely at the infrastructure of this type of society: its anthropotechnics and staging media.

By staging media I mean, in part, the systems of message and body transport that make it up, and the media network and its a prioris that lend unity to it. This, on the large scale, includes the histories of world traffic that define the long modernization; the self-referential motion of its accelerating practices; the applied mechanics of repetition; and the systems-immanent terms of contingency and coincidence that are defining attributes of its microclimates and enclaves. It includes the modern modes of virtual or vicarious experience that this media union selects for, reimpregnates, and reuses: forms of "vicarious life" and, it will be seen, "vicarious crime"—and their continuous rotation and correlation.[2]

The logic of vicarious life—from *vicis*, meaning "change, alternation, stead"—informs conditions of belief (that is, referred belief) and action (that is, referred action) in the official world. That provides our coordinates and commentary on the world, and so reenacts its unity. But the vicars of this world have, we know, shifted from ministration to administration. Hence the systemic and "stead" character of act and belief, and the suspended and secondhand credibility of both.[3]

This is nowhere clearer than in one of the proving grounds, or critical test sites, of modern social systems of action and belief—the novel itself. And it is nowhere clearer, I've begun to suggest, than in the suspense novel or thriller—with its transparent incitations to a gamelike and perilous, self-conditioned and autotropic form of life. It provides somatic biographies of lethal and reincarnative individuals: opportunistic, projective, stress driven. It erects, as the sets for that, the built architecture of "the auto-hypnotically closed counter-worlds"—autopoietic chambers, space capsules, high-rises, concrete islands for the anthropotechnically enhanced—the sites in which they are made and made to live. It is necessary, that is, to redescribe the medium of suspense as a worldview—and its ego-technic media, including the function of fictionality.[4] Hence my turn again to one of the suspense novel's great practitioners and strategists, Patricia Highsmith, and her "games for the living."

I ask you to go back for a moment to the manner in which a novel anchors itself in the bodies of its actors, and in doing so establishes body-to-body analogies between characters and readers—"especially in the barriers to the controllability of bodily processes."[5] This is the case not merely in the dominance of desire and self-risk but in their interincitation: the luridly explicit boundary conditions of the suspense genre.

Consider again the living schema on which the action of *The Talented Mr. Ripley* turns to violence, the human pyramid. In the self-tensed physics of the human pyramid each individual "functions in a function," which an observer may observe at a glance.[6] The quoted phrase in the previous sentence is from Michel Foucault, *Discipline and Punish: The Birth of the Prison*. Foucault's account recurrently adopts the idiom of circular causation, without quite locating its general principle. Hence principles of feedback, recursive causality, and deferred action remain occulted in the place-holding term "power." (Foucault too appeals to the model of the "continuous, individualizing pyramid" but at the same time understands this as top-down power structure, a pyramidic "hierarchy"—and so at once registers and misrecognizes the strict internality and autonomy of its operation.)

Here one is reminded that, as Gregory Bateson puts it, "many self-corrective systems were also already known. That is, individual cases were known, but the *principle* remained unknown," and that remains the case until "the various independent steps in the development of cybernetics and systems theory during and immediately after World War II."[7] One is reminded, too, as David Wellbery acutely traces, how this basic principle, has (like the paradox of Maxwell's demon) shifted from paradox to commonplace, with the emergence of the descriptive generality of systems theory.[8] (This exposition is part of what has been called "the cybernetic unconscious" of deconstructive and Foucauldian theory.)

Another version of this shift from exceptionality to commonplace might be located in relation to the sense of how words do things from person to person. Frances Ferguson usefully points to the large implications of Bentham's account of "sentence meaning," in his *Theory of Fictions*, to "capture the pressure that an ensemble of words puts on individual words," just as he "laid out plans for analyzing how social ensembles and individuals who composed them interacted."[9] We might compare this analysis to Erving Goffman's in his *Interaction Ritual* (1967): "I assume that the proper study of interaction is not the individual and his psychology, but rather the syntactical relations among the acts of different persons mutually present to one another."[10] Goffman's assumption, however, that "the proper study of mankind" is the study not of man but of interaction can have the status of an assumption in that it takes place in a social and ontological field that, from the early nineteenth century, has become incrementally sui generis in the proliferation and congregation of self-operating processes. (On the 1830s conformation of a social-technical union—the annus mirabilis is 1839—that begins to make this possible, see part III.)

"The presentation of self in everyday life," and the externality of action it involves, define, of course, Goffman's way of describing the primacy of interaction, and its presupposition of externality. The sentences leading to the human pyramid make this state of interaction absolutely explicit. Highsmith's narrative point of view is characteristically a strange impersonation of the third person: impersonation in the sense of a first-person singular in the third person, or the particularized point of view of no one in particular. But here, for a moment, there is a strictly neutral-objective third person ("They breakfasted at a café the next morning"). This is then inflected toward the internal evaluations of represented discourse (for example, in the little shifts from phrase to phrase here: "The day was cool, but not impossibly cool for swimming"). Then there is the description of other persons who are not quite (yet) persons: "a few isolated pairs of people, a group of men playing some kind of game." Pairs of people, like pairs of pants or pairs of shoes. That depersonation, in the next sentence, shifts to overly-animated personification (again, in the suspense mode's sea of moods): "The waves curved over and broke on the sand with a wintry violence." It is, in short, as if the narrative were range-finding as to the status of persons and interactions. There is a transition, the next moment, to a point of view that is explicitly a point of view ("*Now* Tom saw that the group of men were doing acrobatics") and to a view of identity via group identification: the spectacle of the human pyramid. (" 'They must be professionals,' Tom said. 'They're all in the same yellow G-strings.' ") After the performance and its thrilled observation, the pairs of people are "a couple of men," as if relation (the couple form) were precipitated by, or borrowed from, the spectacle. And it is a specific relation: it is here that the failure of self-distinction (group identity) is translated into a failure of sexual distinction ("the acrobats were fairies"). It is in these minute and incremental transitions that the pulsings of personation or impersonality, individual and group, spectation and shame, are enacted.

Seen this way, the proper study of interaction is not psychology but the relations of acts to acts. But that is to say that interaction is not a way of seeing, and a world is not a worldview (or a collection or plurality or intersection of them). Stated in very general terms for the moment, the analogues at work in moments such as these are anthropic technologies of auto-stimulation. Their systems-internalized character makes it possible for the space of the game, the scene of the crime, and the form of the work of art to refer to each other in circular fashion—and so to provide the conditions for the continuous rotation of the elements of a self-induced world. The ecumenical mode of that self-induction today, and its forms of belief and action, is no doubt the reality of the "mass media."[11]

Vicarious Life

It is not difficult to see that Patricia Highsmith's crime novels are drawn to the problem of belief, or half-belief: to the problem of making oneself and others believe. After all, her most popular killer—and for a time something of an alter ego—carried the name of this problem: "Believe it or not, old believe-it-or-not Ripley's trying to put himself to work."[12] What is perhaps less evident is how both crime and belief, in Highsmith's fiction, are bound up through and through with the reality of the mass media: with, for example, reality shows like *Ripley's Believe It or Not!*

If this is less than evident, it is by no means because the mass media in the most general sense—the modern technological media of body transport and message transport like the postal system, movies, trains, planes, telephones, dictaphones, newspapers, radio, television, or (still) novels—are "missing" from Highsmith's novels. They are everywhere. At the "Ripley-like" (*TMR*, 177) moment just glanced at, for example, Tom is talking on the telephone, about to go to American Express to get his mail, before boarding a plane, identity papers in hand, in a novel. The mass media are everywhere in Highsmith, universalized and therefore banalized, even trivialized. The media are, it seems—like the purloined letter of Poe's postal system mystery—a bit too self-evident to be seen. Or, better: in that a mass-mediated world is a self-observing world, the universalization of the media (the media a priori) is one way in which this observation may remain unobserved—and one way in which this nonobservation may itself become visible.[13]

Put simply, the mass media make up the "background" reality of this world: "A cool chill ran down Chester. This was fact. It had been on the radio. Thousands of people had heard it. 'It'll certainly be in the papers today, though.'"[14] The mass media perform this function because (in the modern world, to the extent to which it is modern) nothing else can perform this function: the function of indicating what is known and what is known to be known about.[15] They make up public reality: that is, what the public—people like you and me—know, and who, knowing that and reflecting on it, reflexively make up a public.

But if the mass media, in this sense, make up the background reality of this world, it thus seems a made up—a selected, framed, and therefore suspect—world. To say "this was fact" is to reflect on factuality and thus in part to discredit it. After all, the very dailiness of the news makes it suspect—or it is just fantastic luck that, for example, once the networks, some time ago, moved from fifteen minutes to a half hour of evening news, there has been exactly one half hour of news to report every day.[16]

In the nature of the news as news, that is, the reporting on the event becomes the event reported on. (And this always "Now more than ever!"[17]) This is not a "construction" of the mass media in the sense of a distortion to be sorted out and cast out (although there are, of course, lots of distortions and lots of things to be cast out). It is the "constructedness" of the mass media as a necessary selection and framing of what it observes (it can't show everything) and observation of what, and how, it frames and selects (it must show, in the interest of the reality it makes reference to, that it can't).

This is, we know, one of the ways in which modern society makes itself visible and opens itself to its self-conditioning. The media, that is, generates its own plausibility itself. And if the media are reflected in themselves, if they rehearse within themselves this game of deception and realization, this means that the mass media necessarily treat this self-conditioning itself, in turn, as an event.[18] This is social reflexivity at its purest. It marks a generalization of reflexivity as coextensive with the social field. But in that reflexivity is cheap—or free—today, this leads one into the confined air of

Highsmith's men and women in space. (The Cold War, after all, previewed global warming, as species-DIY end. Climate-apocalyptic fiction and film today often reenacts, in its battle plans, a Cold War nostalgia, not only for clear and present dangers, but for an ununified world that would allow one to come in from the cold.)

The characters in Highsmith's fiction endure this unremitting reflexivity like the weather: "He had had what he considered a good day."[19] Hence even the weather must be reported: "*You* look like it's raining outside" (FS, 46). There is no getting "back" of this background—and therefore no doing away with the solicitation to do just that: "The registration and revelation of reality make a difference to reality. It becomes a different reality, consisting of itself plus its registration and revelation."[20] And so on. A reading world, a mass media world, we have seen, is a self-observing world.[21]

But such equations read from right to left as well as from left to right: a self-observing world (a world that observes and observes its observing) is a mass-reading, and, now, mass-viewing, world. Whatever "democracy" may be, for instance, and whatever "the public" may be, for instance, we know (as Kittler puts it) that they are "supported by the mechanical processing of anonymous discourses."[22] That is to say, print and the public, and publicness and the mass media today, support, and expose, each other at every point. This indicates the manner in which the mass media effects and communicates the social tie—and thus makes possible vicarious life, in contemporary culture. It indicates also, then, how the mass media half-expose the social tie as nothing but an effect of communication. Consider, for example, the proliferation of scale models of this interaction—little technologies like the loyalty card (which I have already noted) or the chain letter (which I consider in a moment). These are self-processing quasi-objects that blueprint, comment on, and record what they do, and reinstate themselves as they go. Not only that, they incite loyalty—that is, reenactment—in the process, becoming real as they are going on.[23]

These special effects of the medial system provide one way of understanding the realization of reflexivity in contemporary culture, and the forms of referred belief it supports. The novel, for example, from the mid-nineteenth century on, progressively yields up its monopoly on stories of love and crime to a rivalry among media forms. The stories the novel continues to tell, in turn, turn out to be stories of vicarious life and death: that is, a vicarious life and death sponsored by, or yielded up to, the double reality of the mass media, which in this way cross-references reference as self-reference at every point.

This staging of reflexivity is nowhere clearer than in the extraordinary narrative disposition that is Highsmith's signature style of narration. The strangeness of this narrative way of seeing can yet still be more exemplified than explained. It is a form of showing and telling that only makes sense if one takes seriously the situation of the novel in a cross-referencing media rivalry and if one takes seriously the manner in which the media makes up our situation—and reports on that.

Highsmith's fiction registers this competition on a formal and not merely topical level. Here is, for example, the opening paragraph of *The Talented Mr. Ripley*:

> Tom glanced behind him and saw the man coming out of the Green Cage, heading his way. Tom walked faster. There was no doubt that the man was after him. Tom had noticed him five minutes ago, eyeing him carefully from a table, as if he weren't *quite* sure, but almost. He had looked sure enough for Tom to down his drink in a hurry, pay and get out. (TMR, 5)

In the Ripley novels, sentence after sentence begins with "Tom." This is, in part, a delimitation to Tom Ripley's point of view. It is, in part, a way of viewing Tom's view of his point of view. But such descriptions are a little misleading. In this narrative observation of the self-observed observer, a doubling takes place. In effect, "Tom" reads as "I." But if "Tom" reads as "I," then "I" reads as "Tom's" double. The effect, that is, is something like that of a first-person speaker speaking of himself and seeing himself in the third person. This is, in turn, something like an intensification, or italicization, of represented discourse—as if the desire to see oneself from the outside has been rereflected as state of seeing oneself outside oneself. In that the novel's "theme" is a violent and lethal switching between self-reference and other-reference, the form of the novel arrives as its own theme. It also indicates what the "spreading" of represented discourse in the writing of the systems epoch means, in terms of the distinction between the world as it is and the world as it is observed.[24]

Highsmith, in *Plotting and Writing Suspense Fiction*, describes the "plague" of "the first-person singular" as a narrative point of view. As she expresses it, "I don't know what was the matter, except that I got sick and tired of writing the pronoun 'I,' and I was plagued with an idiotic feeling that the person telling the story was sitting at a desk writing it. Fatal!" But the solution to this problem is not an abandonment of the first-person singular but its paradoxicalization. She defines this solution with an astonishing directness, and exactly in terms of the paradox of self-reflexivity at the level of the subject: "I prefer the point of view of the main character, written in the third-person singular."[25]

This is, of course, nothing but the talented Mr. Ripley's talent: the talent, or compulsion, of impersonation and self-impersonation, via oral and written and visual media of communication. That singular talent might more simply be called, not impersonation, but personation. Ripley (like a range of other fictional and real-life serial killers) lives in the third-person singular.[26]

The point is not to reduce such instances to a (self-evident) aesthetic or individual self-consciousness. It is necessary instead to shift the point of vantage: a slight shift perhaps but one with large consequences. It is necessary to take seriously how the recursive autonomy of art prepares the ground, as it were, for the paradoxical social structure of reflexive modernity, how the first operates as dress rehearsal for the second.

Highsmith's narrative way of seeing, in short, lends to self-observation the look of omniscience and to the counterfactual the feel of objective description. If the modern individual is the individual who can observe his or her own observation, one is then tempted to rediscover here a modernized version of the romantic conception of the double: "Nobody can know himself, unless he is both himself and an other."[27] But this is somewhat misleading too. The proliferation of doubles and doubling in Highsmith's crime writing has a different logic than that of the romantic double.

It is bound directly to the forms of life sponsored by a mass media. But these forms of life are premised on the presumption that face-to-face interaction is not merely routinely rendered impossible: it systemically presupposes its impossibility, even when, say, one is face-to-face.

The exact model for the doubling of reality and producing of doubles that mark Highsmith's crime writing is not hard to find. That model (it will be seen) is the cinema, and its viewed world. I am referring in part to the mechanized doubling of act and observation that the cinema posits as its condition and as its mode of operation (that is, it produces a world in its seeing, one in which seeing is itself seen). That mechanized doubling of observation and act reenters as the film's subject or topic, from the earliest instances of film to the present. Highsmith's novels are everywhere shot through by the media-technical reenactors of everyday life—above all, motion-repeating industries like trains, the postal service, and the movies.

These motion industries, and their relations to modern crime, remain to be elaborated. For now, it may be seen that, in the doubled reality of the mass media, reflexivity is generalized as a social and not merely (merely!) a "personal," or psychological, state. It is the general condition of an unremitting social reflexivity. (In this way social systems catch up with aesthetic and philosophical ones—hence the return of the "end of history.") This makes, we know, for an endless and violent paradox: the strict socialization and sequestration of the social order (a social order that all but makes itself from itself) requires the strictly autopoietic and autonomous individual (who makes himself from himself). But since the first mandates, and thus aborts, the second, the autopoietic autonomy "borrowed" from art opens the possibility of unremitting violence, and enters directly into the story of modern crime. Or, becomes that story.

The enduring of reflexivity and autonomy is both the talent and the sentence of Highsmith's killers and artists (who are, for that reason, often the same person). There is nothing "deeper" than the merely general reader's observing how a character observes, and how he observes, or fails to observe, that. As a character in *The Suspension of Mercy* expresses it: "everything was a matter of attitudes. . . . The attitude had been caused by his attitude."[28] As another observer puts it, in *The Cry of the Owl*: "I have the definite feeling if everybody in the world didn't keep watching to see what everybody else did, we'd all go berserk."[29] Or, as another, even more succinctly, puts it, in *Those Who Walk Away*: "Perhaps identity, like hell, was merely other people."[30]

This is, crucially, a self-observation that presupposes, as its environment, hetero-observation. It posits a viewing or listening public—and so a world scored by a continuous auditioning. It is not merely then that a media a priori enters into the interior of modern crime. (How could it be otherwise?) Vicarity is itself pathologized, even criminalized. For that reason, self-examination or self-disclosure in (for example) Highsmith's fiction takes the form of second-order observation: the interview ("If he were interviewed, he would say, '[Murder] was terrific! There's nothing in the world like it' ").[31] Introspection is conceived as an externalized and perceptible event, and interior states look like self-interviews—albeit not very revealing ones. Interaction, even face-to-face, belongs to the syntax of a system. Talking, for example, is not merely observing one's own speech act at a distance, telephonically ("For a moment he heard his own voice saying . . ."). It is like listening to an internal recording ("like a phonograph playing his head"; *TMR*, 218). Or, it is like making one ("as if he talked to an inanimate thing like a dictaphone"; *ST*, 250). The analogies here—"as if," "like"—are ways of parrying the fact that they are at once analogues and analogies: analogues that look like internal, and "inanimate," alien entities. That is to say, this is what perception looks like—and how it becomes perceptible.

The mistake would be to understand this becoming visible and general of communicative gadgets, as the situation of private and public interaction, as a fall into unreality—the invasion of a "plague of fantasies" into real life (Zizek), or, in effect, a version of what has been called "the perfect crime"—the murder of reality, without a trace (Baudrillard). The mistake, that is, would be to say that "there's nothing in the world like it," such that sheer violence ("murder") might amount to a return to "the real" and so to a real world.

It may be recalled that the phrase "real life" comes from a novel. The distinction between real and fictional reality is made from inside fiction. It is part of the narratively produced believability of the unbelievable. Here we might consider the paradoxical economy of two related truth-seeking modern fictional genres. The first is the Enlightenment genre of "the supernatural explained." The second is the more recent genre of crime writing, what might be called "the mystery revealed." In the fictional genre of the supernatural explained, ghosts, for example, may be introduced into the story in such a way as to acquire temporary plausibility, or half-credence. This can then be revoked, in the interests of an enlightened truth that excludes superstitious fiction. But, of course, the implausible is revoked precisely as a demonstration of the consistency of a larger narrative plausibility. The test of reality, the distinction between what can be treated as reality and what cannot be (the fictional), is thus made internal to the fictional system. Fiction is lifted out of fiction by fiction.[32]

This version of fictional reality, or self-induced plausibility, can be made a bit clearer by glancing at the classic form of the crime story, "the mystery revealed." Here the initial eruption of crime is taken to disrupt a normative social order, an order that is then restored when the mystery is revealed, "mere" stories (lies) exposed, and the crime solved. Fictional stories yield to the true story. But here too the distinction between truth and fiction can only be made from within fiction: that is, in the interests of the plausibility of a narrative system that must exclude, for example, rabbit-out-of-a-hat solutions as a violation of the consistency of that system.

The exclusion of such "trick" solutions is, crucially, an exclusion of a deus-ex-machina break in the order of things.[33] And the exclusion of such miracles is thus the exclusion of an inconsistency in the real—that is, in an utterly socialized and utterly secularized order of things. It marks the installation of the basic premises—the coherence of the social system, as the real order of things—via the deconstruction of a self-generated uncertainty.

But this consensus reading of classic murder stories as a return to a temporarily interrupted consensus reality is itself an instance of such an imputation of coherence. In Agatha Christie's fiction, for example—consider *Murder on the Orient Express* or *Appointment with Death* or *The Murder of Roger Ackroyd*—the basic fantasy itself is at the end exposed. It is, more exactly, theatrically and bureaucratically staged ("sit behind this table in an official position," "it was an official noise," "he spoke in an official tone"—this from a single page in Christie's *Appointment with Death*, to which I turn in part IV). It is staged, moreover, for an internal audience of characters, as proxy readers, and so then applied to the novel itself.[34]

The crucial point is this: at the end, the veridical solution is revealed but things do not stop there. At the very same time, the verdict is suspended in the interest of a false but mutually acceptable cover story. The mechanisms of an official world that comes to itself by staging and exposing its own conditions could not be more explicit. But this means that the classic crime story can scarcely be seen as a cover story that needs to be exposed. The real question, and the one that it reenacts, is rather, again: "*how* is it possible to accept information about the world and about society as information about reality when one knows *how* it is produced?"[35]

Vicarious Crime

We're taught that corporations have a soul, which is the most terrifying news in the world.
—Deleuze, "Postscript on the Societies of Control"

This is one reason why crime, true crime and false crime (crime fiction), has become a strange attractor in the pathological public sphere.[36] My focus at the moment is a different one. Here I want to unfold the coupled questions of vicarious life and the reality of the mass media centrally by way of Highsmith's inaugural crime and suspense novel, *Strangers on a Train*. But first it is necessary to put in place one final, and centering, element: what the nineteenth-century legal historian Friedrich Carl von Savigny called "vicarious crime."

Savigny describes the category of "vicarious crime" in his account of fictitious or "juristical persons" under the law. My interest for the moment is not exactly in the designation of legal or corporate-juristical persons he sets out. (The notion of "corporate persons" is by now familiar enough, albeit popularly familiar in terms of a self-dismissing reduction of its legal sense and function.) I want instead to indicate the technology of personation it designates, and how matters of crime and vicariousness are brought into that design.

Let me set out Savigny's account, albeit in very abbreviated form.[37] The juristical person, as a legal subject, is, it may be recalled, not the natural subject or individual man, "who carries his claim to Jural Capacity in his corporeal appearance" (i.e., has a body). He is, rather, an "artificial subject admitted by means of a pure fiction." Juristical persons "represent" the place of persons, and represent that place only as "feigned persons" or "mere fictions."[38] (They are institutional—artificial, weightless, suspended—bodies.)[39]

This feigning or fiction reaches its limit with respect to the matter of willing an action. The limited capacities of such a feigned person—in short, the capacity to hold, or to transfer, property—are "imputed to it, in consequence of a Fiction, as its own Will." But this is not to be confused with a "power of thinking and willing" on the part of this artificial subject. The Juristical Person is a pure fiction: one might speak of the "injured Personality" of the Juristical Person. But one can scarcely make this out to be a matter of "injured Feelings." One could no more look "back" of that fiction for the feelings or will that have not been imputed to it or made part of it than one might look at the back of a picture to see the reverse side of what it pictures.[40]

The distinction held between real and feigned persons is not hard to, as they say, undo. (Consider the deconstructive cliché that the category of the person is always already undone.) This not least given the analogies that readers of novels, and readers in them, make or enter into. The fictional person is not the fictitious person. Yet the novel's representation of character, and limited omniscience, and representation of institutions, and limited liability, are continuously "floated" in relation to each other, in the novelistic recasting of how actions are performed and how the effects of those actions may be or may not be enforceable. Hence this "mere fiction" opens to view how the distinction between natural and artificial persons is drawn into relation to dilemmas of crime and vicariousness in Savigny's mid-nineteenth-century legal history. "The Criminal Law," Savigny argues, "has to do with the Natural Man, as thinking, willing, sensible Being." The crucial premise is that the "Juristical Person, however, is nothing of this sort, but simply a Being having Property, and lies therefore completely outside the reach of the Criminal Law." Hence a Juristical Person "cannot *commit* a crime." What looks like an offense committed by a feigned person "is, in reality, always that of its members or of its Representative, and therefore, of Individual Men or of Natural Persons."[41]

Juristical Persons are thus something like "madmen and minors" under the law. They resemble persons but are "destitute of the Natural Capacity of Action"—and hence of the will to offend—"for which reason an artificial

Will is procured for them in the person of a Representative" or guardian. But, for Savigny, it would make as little sense to punish the minor or madman for the offense of his guardian as it would to impute a crime (or the will to commit one, which qualifies the criminal act as criminal and as an act) to a made-up person. "In such a case," Savigny concludes, "no one has ventured to assert the possibility of *a vicarious Crime*."[42]

That possibility has, of course, been asserted in other cases. (Vicarious crime is, for example, foundational to a conception of the world that includes the logic, and transmission, of original sin: "In Adam's Fall, We Sinned All"—and so the possibility of action or reparation by proxy.) My concern here, however, is not with a secular turn. If vicarious crime, in that otherworldly other world, meant that God held the world together by ceaselessly observing it, a world flat with its observation observes differently. It encounters a different set of problems.

The novel, as one of its observing media, adjusts for a period from an omniscient to an Asmodean perspective, and then to the internally paradoxical notion of limited omniscience. (A compromise or transitional formation—what Reinhart Koselleck would call the interval of a *Sattelzeit* or "saddle-time": limited omniscience is something like limited unlimitedness.) It moves ultimately to novels in which the limits of that omniscience are virtually unlimited, and so too the limits of liability. It adjusts critically to the understanding of character as positions in a character system or actor network, or to the received idea that "every action is a complex operation, a system." (I am quoting the reenactor of McCarthy's *Remainder*, but McCarthy's point, it will be seen, is that this is to quote anybody, to recite—that is, to reenact—the particularized words of no one in particular.)[43]

The example of "the novel" is one example, pointing to others. If vicarious crime formerly presupposed a world grasped by unremitting higher observation, the function of vicariousness today, in the redirection from vertical to upward mobility, is held by the mass media. Its providence is the reality of second-order observation.[44] If being-in-print was (as Kittler made clear) the relay point of private and public life in the writing-down network of print culture, being-in-the-media is the relay system of intimacy (stranger-intimacy) and publicness (the social network) today. Modern crime, along these lines, cannot be separated from the reality of the mass media, which enters into its interior. The mass media in turn reflexively returns to the scene of the crime as the return to the real.

Hence the possibility of vicarious life—the reality, or credibility, of the social tie—and vicarious crime, as one of its collective spectacles, solicit each other. Crime fiction is then, at the least, a good way of testing out modern distinctions between real and fictitious persons and real reality and fictional or statistical reality, and a good way of locating its modes of transmission and observation. Patricia Highsmith's suspense novel *Strangers on a Train* may be a very good way to redescribe both—in that the crisscrossing of vicarious lives and vicarious crimes forms its explicit subject.

FOUR

CHAIN LETTERS

Official Time

There is an extraordinary scene at the close of Highsmith's first novel, *Strangers on a Train* (1950), a scene that draws into relation a dense cluster of these concerns about vicarious life and vicarious crime in the official world. These are concerns, at bottom, about crime, motive, and media in an official world compulsively drawn to the scene of the crime as a way of modeling its spaces of interaction, reenactment, and outcome. This space is its official game space and internalized time zone (as Hitchcock makes as explicit as possible in the "official time" tennis game scenes that he adds to the story in his film version of the novel).[1]

The scene in the novel I want to turn to takes place in an isotopic hotel room, where Guy Haines has arranged a face-to-face meeting with his murdered wife's lover, Owen Markman. He wants to explain, or to confess, his part in that murder. He wants, in effect, to explain the gamelike plot of the novel, which is about strangers and trains:

> You see, I met Charles Bruno on a train, coming down to Metcalf. . . . I told him [my wife] Miriam's name. I told him I hated her. Bruno had an idea for a murder. A double murder. . . . My mistake was in telling a stranger my private business. . . . Bruno's idea was that we should kill for each other, that he should kill Miriam and I should kill his father. . . . The whole idea rested on the fact that there was no reason for the murders. No personal motives. (*ST*, 246)

Strangers on a Train thus not only takes on the possibility of vicarious crime: vicarious crime is the very premise and plot of the novel. Two strangers

Figure 4.1. Official Time (*Strangers on a Train*, dir. Alfred Hitchcock, 1951).

meet on a train and exchange motives and murders. This is, in short, a novel about "double murder" and about "double-track minds." That doubling involves something more than the transferences of guilt, motive, identity, and act that put the novel into motion. It involves something more than that because the transference, or doubling, of guilt, identity, and act is itself the motive—the "no-motivation scheme"—for crime.

This schema is the gamelike interaction zone of the novel, in which the suspension of individual motive means that moves are not the expression of interior states but the function of the system of locomotives, tracks, lines, and zones—think of the network system of train tracks that Hitchcock focuses on in the opening shots of his film version of the novel—the places in which they take place, and cross-track each other. (It perhaps hardly needs stating that these tracking shots are meant to depict the film they produce and so the cinematic a priori.)

Doubles, we have noted, proliferate in Highsmith's fiction. But they are only superficially versions of the romantic doppelgänger, ghosts of self-reflection. (That is, what happens when—as Kittler traces—readers, who have already been taken in by words, confuse their lives with their reading, and hallucinate print into characters like themselves.[2]) But doubling in Highsmith is not exactly that little theater of interiority: it is the register of a

Figure 4.2. The Wiring of the World (*Strangers on a Train,* dir. Alfred Hitchcock, 1951).

reflexivity gone wild. That reflexivity is inseparable from the media and mass transport technologies that double reality and produce and show doubles: for example, the strangers on trains, dressed alike, reading the same papers, sharing the same daily commute and the same daily communications, the back-and-forth of endlessly received and volleyed and returned words and things, bodies and ideas.

The face-to-face confession that ends the novel, for instance, is neither quite face-to-face nor quite a confession. Interaction and reflexive speculation are staged, and at the same time turned over to machines. The sequencing of this turnover could not be more clearly marked. Just prior to this scene, Guy has written a long confession, and what is most visible here are the primary qualities of writing and posting, its material dimensions:

> He looked at the big sleek-surfaced sheets of drawing paper. . . . Then he sat down and began to write from the upper left-hand corner across. . . . His writing blackened three of the big sheets, put them into an oversized envelope, and sealed. For a long while he stared at the envelope, wondering at its separateness now from himself. . . . This was for Anne. Anne would touch this envelope. Her hands would hold the sheets of paper and her eyes would read every word. (ST, 240–41)

Writing and printing, we know, develop possibilities of social communication without (physical or spatial) interaction.[3] Letter writing, we know, often internally reflects on the separation between messages and bodies, hallucinating the receiver/reader, her eye and hand and touch, in the form of an epistolary-sponsored love.[4]

But this is not a "scene of writing" or writing writing. (It's not, that is, a scene of externalization and recovery via self-reflection.) For one thing, this is not exactly a matter of the writing or even drawing it resembles, but covering or blackening sleek big surfaces, and doing so, they can then be folded and placed in an envelope and transmitted to a recipient, or, more precisely, transferred from one set of eyes and hands to another.

These transference effects repeat the exchange of motive and intent that makes for the crisscrossed motive and action, or reenactments, of the novel: its chain-letter effect. The letter has the formal and reenactive character of the chain letter, copied to make copies, passed on from hand to hand, such that the act of transmission and the reality of the social bond are, in keeping up the sequence, one and the same. The chain letter is vicarious life as mimetic compulsion (to borrow Roger Caillois's formulation of mimetic drives at the level of the organism). Like the selfish gene, it just wants to make copies of itself; and, if it stops, it dies.[5] The chain letter makes that its form and so arrives as its own theme.

So too does the strange face-to-face encounter with Markman that closes the novel. Guy wants to confess his part in his wife's murder to her former lover. The plan to contact Markman in person comes to Guy's mind only in the compulsive mechanism of writing: "The name had swum into his mind mechanically. He hadn't thought of Owen at all until he wrote the letter. . . . If he owed it to anyone he owed it to Markman" (ST, 242–43). Owing is nothing but, in this mechanical sequence, taking "the only step and the next step" (242): an effect of marking on paper and so owing ("Owen" and "Markman"). ("Owen Markman" is a bad play on words, if we note the words at all. The shape of the words induce and name a chain of indebtedness and so the thought of a social bond.) The insistence of the letter in the unconscious, perhaps, or communication media (as Kittler expressed it) as "the unconscious of the unconscious." But these formulations no longer seem the ways to put it.

The suspense story devolves on the apparentness of media of communication. This is not merely because media enter into, and copy, self-reflection. It is the condition, and infrastructure, of the self-denoting world's practices and operations.[6] The collective drive to auto-enclaved—and so technically

Figure 4.3. The Stationary Carousel (*Strangers on a Train*, dir. Alfred Hitchcock, 1951).

enhanced—human life submits only to the conditions it makes: on this view, technological determinism is the purest form of self-determination.

One might then attribute to Sade or to Disney "the hedonistic science of designing collective facilities that fully accommodate individual desires."[7] One might consider the individualized desires of these "voluntary prisoners of architecture." (No longer Sade's chateau or Bentham's panopticon but small worlds, after all.) These are the scientological design sites of what Norbert Wiener simply called "the human use of human beings," the contours of "control and communication in the animal and the machine." They are calculated utilitarian-hedonistic sites of autotropic violence, and what Ballard redescribes as the "bureaucracy of crime" that works to "tune up the nervous system."

There are countless examples of the "voluntary prisoners" of these stationary carousels and persons suspended in space.

Think of Zola's holiday-park/murder scene in *Thérèse Raquin*; or Highsmith's Kingdom of Fun as the scene of the crime; or the recreational intramural violence of Ballard's *Super-Cannes* or *Cocaine Nights* or *Running Wild*. Enclaves and reenactment zones of the controlled use of the uncontrollable. One rediscovers here the enhanced drive for surrogate immediacies.

That drive is coupled to complex ethnomethodologies of institutional spaces and their uses. These may take the form, for example, of the symphorophilias of the collision and the crash: "She loved accidents: any mention of an animal run over, a man cut to pieces by a train, was bound to make her rush to the spot" (Zola, *La bête humaine*); "She had originally agreed to appear naked, but on seeing the cars informed me that she would only appear topless—an interesting logic was at work there" (Ballard, *The Atrocity Exhibition*). This is the "interesting logic" of anthropotechnic-oriented violence: its excitations, its stage-set machinery, and its self-curved mode of operation.

The Autotropic Mode: Dictaphone, Answering Machine, Twitter

The practices termed "anthropotechnics" developed in the 1920s Soviet Union, as part of a scientific, or scientological, project for the remaking of persons: enhanced individuals reproduced by what we might call self-curved evolution. The concept has usefully and provocatively been extended by Peter Sloterdijk, as a way of redescribing historical and contemporary forms of "art with humans": "ego-technic media." This is to use "media" in the sense that a systems-immanent account provides, and it may be helpful, in turning to some of these ego-technical practices in *Strangers on a Train*, to very briefly summarize that sense.

Objects "become media" in their functioning as a function; the medium most visibly "becomes object" in dysfunction.[8] (The final scene of *Strangers* blueprints this situation.) On a systems-internal account, the medium is not an object, but a difference: the difference between medium and form. This is paradoxical but workable. To take a simple, and canonical, example (I draw here on Elena Esposito's account): sand, as a medium, might, depending on its grain or wetness, take the form of a footprint impressed on it. The footprint in turn might be the medium of a number of prints that takes the form of a series or trail. The trail, in turn, may be the medium that takes the form of clues in a literary detective case. That might then be read as clue to a quantitative literary history in a literary lab. Letters may be the medium that takes the form of words, which are the medium of sentence meaning, and so on. The mutual contingency of medium and form makes these operations possible. Forms cannot exist without the corresponding medium, which can be observed only via the forms assumed. Hence the media cannot be defined apart from the forms they may take; they are not causes but probabilities (eigen-objects tend to return to themselves). If then media "determine our situation," this means that the forms they enter into become more probable, and so predictable and reflexive. For example, the reality of the mass media emerges or congeals or is eclipsed as a topic or field of its own, or "the inter-disciplinary" becomes a discipline with its own narrow citation circle and its own immune system.

Nietzsche, first among philosophers to write on the typewriter, wrote that "our writing instruments enter into our thoughts."[9] No doubt they enter into our thoughts about our writing instruments too—and this not least when writing loses its monopoly over our thoughts and their transmission, and being-in-print (the identity program of print culture) yields to being-in-the-media.[10] Or, as Lacan more recently expressed these media links:

> From now on you are, and to far greater extent than you can imagine, subjects of gadgets or instruments—from microscopes to radio and television—which will become elements of your being. You cannot now understand the full significance of this; but it is nevertheless a part of the scientific discourse, insofar as discourse is something that determines a form of social cohesion.[11]

Subjects of gadgets: the relations among the social, the subjective, the scientific, and the discursive are not all secure in this portentous, even vatic, account; it implies, against its own grain, an anthropotechnic situation irreducible to discrete objects (or to the "something" formerly known as discourse).

But what then of this "form of social cohesion": this form of vicarious relation between persons with "no personal motives"? This unity of persons outside themselves? Let's say that you "cannot now understand the significance of this," but that you can understand that you can't. That these subjects confront each other like two black boxes: "Two Black Boxes, by whatever accident, come to have dealings with each other. Each determines its own behavior by complex self-referential operations within its own boundaries. Each assumes the same about the other. There, however many efforts they exert and however much time they expend, the black boxes remain opaque to one another."[12] Yet each acts on the other, and the inputs and outcomes can be observed by each of them, and cross-examined.[13]

I have in effect just summarized the plot of *Strangers*. So consider, along the lines of such a confrontation of black boxes, this example, from the closing scene of *Strangers on a Train*. The scene centers on two strangers talking to each other, or, rather, presenting words and looks, and the gadgets that enter into or stand by their interaction. This is, more precisely, a moment of face-to-face confession in which, it turns out, both the personal and the confessional are exteriorized in media doubles or instruments, such that the infrastructure of the novel and its plot index or blueprint and install each other. The scene, that is, binds an uncertain intimacy with communicative machines to "the whole idea" for murder: the whole logic of "double minds" and "double murder."

Here is what it looks like. Guy Haines has written out his confession. But, in the face-to-face encounter with Markman, he is less speaking than playing back his words ("the words, unutterable thousands and thousands of words . . . sentences and paragraphs of the confession"). Or, alternatively, he is playing back the words of his/this guy's double:[14] "he had known the last words were coming. . . . It was exactly like Bruno" (ST, 249).

The desire to confess in person at once comes up against Markman's "indifference." (Pressed on "how do you feel about the men you know who'd killed somebody," Markman beautifully responds, "Live and let live.") This indifference involves something more than stupidity or disinterest, although it involves those too. Guy "groped for a concrete idea to present to Owen. He didn't want his audience to slip away" (ST, 251). A "concrete idea" that one gropes for in order to "present": ideas then as the arrangement of things that can be presented, observed, and evaluated (just as writing before that is the counted number of words, sentences, paragraphs scoring sheets, envelopes, hands, eyes). These are relays between black boxes that include the observation of that.

A suspenseful murder story would seem enough to hold an "audience"— not least in a detective novel about a murderer who "reads too many detective stories" and featuring a detective who sounds "like a radio detective" (ST, 157). But what exactly does confessing to an audience mean? The genre of confession instanced at this moment is not hard to locate. The genre of deeply personal testimony presented to a captive, if not captivated, mass-person audience has migrated across rival media of externalization, from the novel to talk radio to confession TV. It posits an audience made up of listeners and viewers who "are included as excluded third parties, as 'parasites.'"[15] The media parasite is another name for surrogate life: the particularized point of view of no one in particular. Markham is a proxy for the media third person: the one who—at once disengaged and watchful—observes what it looks like to react to situations and to observe and to communicate about oneself: one who, in short, "listens, witnesses, and forgets."

The face-to-face interaction thus entails what Deleuze and Guattari call "the face-system." And this is nowhere clearer than in the art form that captures it. The presupposition of exteriority arrives at its truth in the medium that directly informs *Strangers*: motion pictures. The cinematic close-up, as the sociologist of social systems Dirk Baecker suggests, shows just

> how important the human face is when the shot switches back and forth from staging action to staging experience. The human face acts like the report of the previous scene and the command of the next one, never quite understanding what it reports or knowing what it commands. There is no better way to turn a situation into its experience than to shoot a face experiencing it. Remember again the faces of Ingrid Bergman and Humphrey Bogart in *Casablanca* being looked at by the face of Woody Allen in the first takes of *Play It Again, Sam*, which features Allen sitting in a cinema watching the last takes of *Casablanca*. If only in order to shoot the human face, movies would have invented people, had it not been the other way around. Actually, after having been invented by people, the movies went on to re-invent people. The human face is both receptive and inscrutable both for communication and for consciousness. And that is exactly what the movies need, and show.

The movies at once do that and show that they do: the oscillation between acting and showing is presented, "included in the world it creates": "it is their looking at them that creates them . . . everything that can be looked at by a look that creates it."[16]

Consider again the face-to-face confrontation that ends *Strangers*. The action switches between persons and communication machines in its operations: "it was as if he talked to an inanimate thing like a dictaphone in the chair, the difference that his words didn't seem to be penetrating in any way" (ST, 250). There is an ongoing comparison of the experience and its registration, as if the reality of the media were at once apparent and impenetrable. The communication of a murder with "no personal motives"—about a double murderer broken down "with letters and blackmail" (251)—is like speaking to a defective voice-recording machine or to an inanimate person.

The novel foregrounds a transitional syndrome—the problematic ubiquitization of communication and cognition devices. "A dictaphone in a chair": this is, of course, a centauric form, half person, half appliance. No doubt these techniques—a carousel of techniques that externalize and mechanize perception, duplication, speaking, answering, and memory—spread from the microtheater of the office to the macrotheater—or, better, theater chains—of the official world.

That background reality cannot be observed, in the sense that Guy can't read himself out from the trains, movies, schedules, blueprints, models, telephones, letters, dictaphones, magazines, and comic books to his motives and his acts. Yet he can experience motive and acts as coming from without, from moment to moment, as moves in a sort of game he has entered. (" 'What's your game, Bruno.' 'You know,' Bruno said quietly. 'What we talked about on the train. The exchange of victims' " [*ST*, 111].)

This is the gamelike form of the suspense novel. The suspense novel generates and dispels uncertainties strictly on its own terms: like a game, via gratuitous complication (which allows for the variety and detail of the world to enter in) and via strict self-conditioning (which means that this is, as it turns out, in service of the work's unity). In this way the little techniques that make up the background reality of this world are moves or positions in a form of game, a form of life that is the walking shadow of every move. (We are encouraged, in actor-network theory, as in action stories, to "deploy uncertainties."[17] This is the idiom of the better living through ambiguity that literary studies abides in. Action heroes, like science-in-action heroes, do the same, albeit in weaponized form.)

In very general terms, the suspense novel or film sorts some things out at the end—just as a game sorts out winners and losers at the end. So it reveals what moves meant all along. But this does not resolve the premises that gave rise to uncertainties in the first place. That's because those uncertainties are the very form of its suspense: if it was this way, it could have been another. For the mystery novel, we know there could have been other pasts. For the suspense novel, there could have been other futures. Hence the only real outcome is not to settle scores but to play again, and to see how it turns out this time too. A tight unity of form is thus made compatible with the detailed presence of alternatives, and does not sacrifice one to the other.

No doubt the suspense novel, like the mystery novel, is contrived and gimmicky—trivially systematic—in its giving and withholding of information and the staging (or the staginess) of act and observation. The suspense novel, like the mystery novel, is in this way ostensively, at times stupidly, self-referential. The real trick then is how, to the very extent that it is self-referential, it refers to a real world that works in the same way, and yet forgets that each time. We should not underestimate the real difficulty in keeping up this stupidity: "Even manifest stupidity, incidentally, cannot be taken as a simple datum: it is acquired through long training in learning-avoidance operations. Only after a persistent series of self-knockouts by the intelligence can a habitus of reliable mindlessness become stable—and even this can be undone at any time through a relapse into non-stupidity."[18]

The achievement of reliable mindlessness: a habitus, or a culture. We know that the intrications of the form of the novel and its media—from the epistolary novel as a relay of the postal system on—condition the novel's, and its readers', habitual operations. We know too, as Frances Ferguson richly articulates it, that

> the novel as it develops from the eighteenth century on has become pre-eminently the genre of social evaluation, the genre that does not merely deliver the deep texture of a society but that also (as Ian Watt has argued) renders that society in the mode of philosophical realism—by presenting the organization and hierarchization that a rationalized account of that society involves.[19]

The gamelike character of the novel (a self-organized world of act, outcome, and evaluation) and the realistic character of the novel (its "drive toward displaying . . . the sense of its social reality") are thus two sides of a single formation.[20]

My concern here is with the situation of the novel in the epoch of social systems. This does not mean a subsumption of art to sociology. The novel models and rationalizes an autonomy that a self-accountable society may then apply to itself—in that it proceeds by modeling, and rationalization in the Weberian sense of that term.[21]

Strangers on a Train, for example, takes stock of the infrastructure of this world (for example, what pieces of office equipment, like dictaphones, are dispersed about it). But there is more to it. The confession that Guy makes has been overheard by the detective who has followed him, and tapped his telephone. Yet, as the detective explains, although the phone is tapped, "There wasn't time for a dictaphone. But I heard most of it from just outside your door" (ST, 255). The dictaphone then appears, first, as a figure of speech ("as if he talked to an inanimate thing like the dictaphone in a chair") and, second, as an object in the world (but in this case not there). The speaker himself is a "voice imitator" (to use Thomas Bernhardt's way of putting it). He repeats the words of another—the words, sentences, paragraphs of his double—and knows they are coming.

The dictaphone switches properties between persons and machines, such that you can take the place of the other, and the other can take your place. The "human stupidity" of a "silent and motionless" body—one that cannot be penetrated, cannot set itself in motion, cannot register words—is set in contrast to the "intelligent silence of a live wire." The "silence" of the live wire, however, refers to its own receptivity.[22] The communicative instrument may be there or not there, on or off. But it is absolutely clear that the media a priori is already in place: the urge to confess has already turned into the desire to be interviewed.[23]

This takes us a step closer to the form of vicarious life in the novel. It is not just that Guy sees that his "mistake was in telling a stranger [his] private business" (ST, 246). Talking to strangers, in privatized public places like train cars or hotel rooms, communicates the social tie—since the social tie consists in its communication. It does so on the very model of the chain letter: "Guy had a horrible, an utterly horrible thought all at once, that he might ensnare Owen in the same trap that Bruno had used for him, that Owen in turn would capture another stranger who would capture another, and so on in infinite progression of the trapped and the hunted" (246).

The bare sociality of the chain letter indicates a social tie precipitated in the "provocations that describe it as a social tie."[24] Its mechanical transmission, endlessly reenacted, resembles contagion, and hence a transfer of pathology or criminality.[25] But the public here is a disbanding band: it is made up of strangers, those who are near but also far. Hence a second chain relation is communicated in this scene. This time the chain involves a transmission not of shared crime but of shared indifference. This is the paradox of a mutual noncommunication, and an estrangement of the publicness it effects: "What human being would inform on him. . . . Everyone would leave it for someone else, who would leave it for someone else, and no one would do it" (ST, 253). Hence the relentlessly "informed" public that is made up of those who who are near but also far, consists too—to borrow the title of one of Highsmith's later novels—of those who walk away.[26] Civil disattention.

This is what Simmel called "the negative character of collective behavior." It makes for the radically incoherent talk about "individual and society" that runs through the novel (e.g., "What business is it [murder, guilt] of mine? . . . What business? Because you—you are part of society! Well, then it's society's business. . . . Was that most people's attitude? If so, who was society? . . . Society was people like Owen, people like himself . . . people like you and me . . . so far as people go" [ST, 252]).[27] It makes for the incoherence of talk in that it leaves the "and" of this duality "individual and society" uninterpreted. Collective behavior is then enacted, so far as people go, in the crisscrossing of motives and acts that come and go: vicarious crime.

In these cases, "taking the role of the other" borders on murderous violence: a Ripley-like identification and compulsive copying to the point of "taking the place of the other." It entails an unremitting self-reflection bordering on self-violence. To the extent that the individual, in the modern sense, is one who observes his or her own observation, identity takes the extroverted form of an uncontrollable identification: a mimetic compulsion that bends reflexivity toward pathology. The actors on those printed pages are copying machines, ones that reflect on that, and, stunned and incited by it, repeat it: they are uncontrollable reenactors. This is familiar enough. But in *Strangers on a Train*, and in Highsmith's fiction generally, reflexive reenactment is explicitated as the abnormally normal idiom of relation and self-relation: "The panic in the voice panicked Bruno" (*ST*, 74); "then in response to [his] friendly grin, he smiled too" (76); "There was the sucking sound of a kiss . . . and Bruno gave it back to them" (72). That extends to the great outdoors: "As he looked, a bird flew out of the grass with a cry and wrote a fast, jagged, exuberant message with its sharp-pointed wings across the sky" (142–43). "Overhead a bird kept singing, 'Tweedledee?' and answering itself, 'Tweedle*dum!*'" (153). This is an autotropic world, one that calls and answers to itself, a messaging and twittering world.

Wrecking Our Nursery: "To Devise New Means of Destroying the World We Inhabit"

The popular technical media that systematize body and message transport and double life—media like the train or the film—form the infrastructure of this order of persons and things. The stranger—"the stranger on the train who would listen, commiserate, and forget" (*ST*, 23)—is the prototype of the second modernity's stranger-intimacy and stranger-sociality. That induces a world and enacts its unity in official time.

It is precisely in this sense that *Strangers on a Train* is about strangers and trains—and their continuous rotation. That is to take up the reality of things and images that move and vanish, return and repeat on schedule, like trains or movies.[28] It means taking up how people meet via the form and media of the motion industries, like trains and films, in a society tending toward a condition of total mobilization, and featuring mechanized motion, motives, and movies—each moving (as Highsmith puts it) along "established tracks"—a circular track or carousel. It means taking up the forms of vicarious action and vicarious crime proper to that kind of world.

Consider today the allure of end-of-the-world scenarios and the euthanasic appeal of self-extinction or "the age of extinction" or (in terms of what Ballard designates science porn) a choreographed murder by numbers on a planetary scale). The future is not merely not what or where it used to be. As Ballard expressed it, "the future is boring." Hence the antidotal call of "natural and unnatural catastrophes" (in Highsmith's terms) and the call of "cataclysms and dooms" (in Ballard's) as the contemporary call of the wild. Ballard—the great clinician of overlit spaces turned on themselves— rearticulates the manner in which the drive to build one's own world, and the drive to take it to pieces, may be two sides of the same "experimental" impulse.[29] (The logic of the experimental novel, and its pornographies of elective violence, from Zola on.) As Ballard expresses it:

> Visions of world cataclysm constitute one of the most powerful and most mysterious of all the categories of science fiction, and in their form pre- date modern science fiction by thousands of years. . . . From the deluge in the Babylonian zodiac myth of Gilgamesh to contemporary fantasies of twentieth-century super-science, there has clearly been no limit to our need to devise new means of destroying the world we inhabit. I would guess that from mankind's first inkling of this planet as a single entity ex- isting independently of himself came the determination to bring about its destruction, part of the same impulse we see in a placid infant who wakes alone in his cot and sets about wrecking his entire nursery."[30]

This is to understand cataclysm as a sort of thought experiment, and as an effect of a self-reported world (the record or "inkling" of this planet, en- thralled by its tilt). It extends the logic of Zola's experimental novel to global scale. It is to understand doom as the effect of a planetary battle between single entities, a Planet and a Superman autistic (in the root sense) and placidly annihilative. This is the self-described "superman," Bruno, in *Strangers*, "taking on the whole world and whipping it."

It is easier to see this in genres that border science fiction. But this autode- structive drive is downscaled and made part of the diurnal round in suspense fiction—in the gravity-resistant acrobatics of its men in close spaces.[31]

Take, for example, the crash, the collision, and the chase scenes that not merely run through these stories but seem to be their real story. And consider how in these scenes technology is wedded to the affections. The destructive drive is literalized, in the suspense genre, in the central- ity of chase scenes, and in the exact explicit doubling of psychopathy and transport media. Here is Hitchcock's description of his obsession with the "double chase motif": "In the ideal chase structure, the tempo and complex- ity of the chase will be an accurate reflection of the intensity of the relations between the characters. . . . Griffith was the first to exploit the possibilities of a physical chase, but I tend to multiple chases and a lot of psychology."[32]

The chase fuses the psychical and the technical. It exteriorizes (in the sci- entological sense) the first in the second. The chase "reflects" interior states in quantities of motion, such that what is moving is equivalent to a series of moves: hence a lot of chases equals a lot of psychology.

Or, think of the Bourne series (prototypical if outmoded). Here the chase scenes are an attempt to catch up with oneself, just as the crashes and leaps are stages in rebirth or, more exactly, reincarnation (scientological on this count too). Bourne is an action hero (played on screen by the all-American, typically typical, actor who also played the lookalike Tom Ripley in the remake film of Highsmith's novel). But, with respect to body-and-message transport systems, a superhero.

There are many reaction shots in these novels and films, scanning information displays, traffic, numbers, and so on, and looking at Bourne rapidly processing them. Such shots do not merely register action or Bourne's perception of it. Cognition and behavior are evoked and externalized as properties of the media. In this, such narratives (like *Strangers*) presuppose the reality of a cinema a priori and adapt to it, as they can. The reality of movies is, in short, "the reality of communication": "The movie revels in trying to find out how human emotion, which the novel and its corresponding psychologies had related back to conscious and unconscious thought, translates into, and is evoked by, mere behavior, thus triggering a different behavioral and cognitive psychology. The movie rarely, if ever, distinguishes between behavior, communication, consciousness, and situation."[33] Rapid cutting makes perspicuous Bourne's processing speed, and we can't keep up with that. It outstrips our capacity to keep up with the medium, and shows that incapacity—and so the training needed to overcome it. It compares that incapacity with the action hero's experimentally conditioned media fitness. Here again we might recall that Bourne had his externalized origin in the anthropotechnic laboratory and rebirth via that excruciated form of ascetic self-dedication called personal training sessions.

This is one of many ways in which these reincarnation stories (live, die, repeat) recombine Cold War ego-technics and the scientological.[34] The fusion of the psychical, the technical, and the reincarnative in these suspense novels is scientological on all counts, not least in its exercises of projective self-realization. Stripped of its cosmologies (such as they are), it provides models for scientology-lite movements of behavior modification (EST or its spin-offs) and for new ontogenic fitness conditioning. If not e-meter "auditing" then compulsive twittering or self-checking and metrical self-monitoring—or what are, on the LA scene, disinhibition-training sessions in actually-existing surrealism.[35] For now, simply note that Bourne ends the chase for identity or rebirth—most compelling, given Matt Damon's neotenic qualities, in the film version—by setting about wrecking a laboratory, which in this case is his own nursery.

The Train, the Carousel, and the Movies

What is it called when features of the landscape mirror the conditions of the poor fucks who live in it?
—Ben Marcus, *The Flame Alphabet*

"Genre is a minimum-security prison."
—David Shields, *Reality Hunger*

In *Strangers*, each of the killers "externalized his danger" (ST, 196) for the other. This species of externalization can take two forms. One way is to see your self outside the self as someone else, as your double. The other way is to see your self outside as the world itself, such that the outside world itself is your double. This is a version of what Spengler, in speaking of the city-as-world in *The Decline of the West*, calls a world "which suffers nothing beside itself." That way self-reference is installed as a property of the world around us.[36]

Consider, for example, the opening passage of *Strangers on a Train*:

> The train tore along with an angry, irregular rhythm. It was having to stop at smaller and more frequent stations, where it would wait impatiently for a moment, then attack the prairie again. But the progress was imperceptible. The prairie only undulated, like a vast, pink-tan blanket being casually shaken. The faster the train went, the more buoyant and taunting the undulations. (ST, 7)

Here again Highsmith's form of narration lends to fantasy the look of objective description. The overexplicitness of the personation of technological and natural topography, the train system and the prairie, makes for a psychotopography. This is at the same time a framed scene viewed from the train window. (A bit later too, and even more explicitly, and in case we've missed it: "He could sense Miriam ahead of him, not much farther now, pink and tan-freckled, and radiating a kind of unhealthful heat, like the prairie out the window" [ST, 7]).

We might understand this scenario in terms of a reversal of fantasy and reality. These are, for example, the terms drawn on in another novel about machine transport and sexual violence, J. G. Ballard's *Crash*: "In the past we have always assumed that the external world around us has represented reality, and that the inner worlds of our minds, its dreams, hopes, ambitions, represented the realm of fantasy and imagination. These roles, it seems to me, have been reversed."[37] This switching of inner and external worlds is exactly what Highsmith's form of description and narration here achieves.

But the complication here is that "what we have always assumed" and what we now assume look like assumed roles or received ideas. Take the assumption that "the media determine our situation" and that we can read the character of an age off the dominant media technology of each kind of society. That is, take the fact that these "words were coming just as they should"—as the rotation of genre-media that appear generic in the sense of generic drugs.

Strangers on a Train makes the assumption of what we had assumed as explicit as possible: " 'Ever feel like murdering somebody? . . . I do. I'm sure sometimes I could kill my father. . . . You know what my father does for a hobby? Guess. . . . He collects cookie cutters! . . . The machine age!' " (*st*, 17). "The machine age," we know, eliminates fathers. It is autogenic, and so it makes itself from itself. If it mass-produces cookie-cutter individuals, it does so via a running commentary on that. The commentary does what it says, and so, from moment to moment, reinstalls the chain-letter effect of "the machine age" and continuously reenacts it in its externalization:

> "She's what people mean when they say America never grows up, Amer- ica rewards the corrupt. She's the type who goes to the bad movies, acts in them, reads the love-story magazines, lives in a bungalow, and whips her husband into earning more money this year so they can buy on the instalment plan next year, breaks up her neighbour's marriage—"
>
> "Stop it, Guy! You talk so like a child!" (*st*, 47)

It is not merely that what we call the mass media are everywhere here: its types, love stories, movies, popular magazines, cookie-cutter commuter communities, and so on—installed via serialized life-plans The exposure of their penetration into every precinct of private and public life is spoken in the overconditioned air of an air-quoted idiom ("they say," "I read some- where people don't grow emotionally" [*st*, 47]). Here is achievement of the habitus of reliable mindlessness in action, running round a circuitous track. A culture of perfectly received ideas (Flaubert) and memeplexes (Sloterdijk). Talking of the fact that America never grows up is to talk like a child: the exposure of the mechanism at once installs it and runs it. Self- reflection is not self-exemption: it is, we are told, the reverse of that.

The same goes for the injunction to "Stop it!" Or, as the panicked off- screen voice at the close of Hitchcock's film version of the novel puts it: "Get someone to stop this thing!" Vicarious life in *Strangers on a Train* is bound up through and through with technologies of communication and transmission. The cultural techniques that mechanize images, double reality, and make up "double track" minds appear, at their simplest, as means of setting bodies, or persons, or machines in motion: as a matter of stopping or going.

The central questions, put simply, are still about what sets persons in motion, what counts as motivation, and what is the reality of things that move. These no doubt timeless questions are made timely in relation to achieved motion industries of communication and transport.[38] The motion, and motion picturing, industries are broadcast throughout the text and acted out in its practices.

That reenactment is externalized in scenes that show practices of "mere behavior" that do not distinguish between behavior, communication, transport, cognition, motion and situation-reflection. There is a continuous oscillation between going and doing and technical media. For example, one among many others, what one "was going to do" is exteriorized in the stop-and-go of motion machines: "Then he got up . . . that was coming just as it should. He felt he moved on certain definite tracks now, and that he could not have stopped himself or got off them if he wanted to. . . . He absolutely had to do what he was going to do. . . . He wanted to keep moving. He decided by the time he walked . . . it would be time to catch the train. . . . He began to think of his course of action. . . . He stopped. . . . He hailed a cab" (ST, 132–33). This is what action, decision, feeling, and self-reflection look like in the novel. Hence "point of view" is returned from its abstraction as a rhetoric of fiction and a fictional psychology. It is depsychologized and extroverted. It tracks and traces the situation of men in chronographed space.

One last thing. The thing that needs to be stopped in Hitchcock's film version of *Strangers on a Train* is a runaway merry-go-round. The stationary carousel or merry-go-round—one of the popular amusements of the machine age that couples still bodies and moving machines[39]—has a minor role in the novel. But the stationary carousel is a central character in Hitchcock's movie. It is described in these terms in the novel:

> The merry-go-round was like a lighted city in the dark woods, a forest of nickel-plated poles crammed with zebras, horses, giraffes, bulls, and camels all plunging down or upward, some with necks arched out over the platform, frozen in leaps and gallops as if they waited desperately for riders. Bruno stood still. (ST, 69)

The merry-go-round in the novel, that is, is a model of the technology of film itself: a light show in the dark, made up of stills of "frozen" motion and suspended animation; about to be set in motion to music and with the turning of the wheel; producing for stilled, immobilized, massed viewers the uncertain and fugitive reality of moving pictures.

One anecdotal account of the origin of the coupling of physiological and technical processes that makes that reality possible was the discovery that telegraph or telephone poles observed from inside the window of a moving train tended to "disappear" at the right speed, due to the psychophysiology of the eye.[40] Hence the just-so story of the discovery of the speed at which still frames might be moved to produce the mechanized images of animation and motion. This would amount to the emitting to viewers of their own processes of perception, such that act and observation fuse.[41]

One might perhaps take this a half-step further. To the extent that, by this technical means, self-observation is installed as objective description, Highsmith's narrative mode—which effects precisely that—might be said to copy these perceptual technologies: to register the installation of cinematic techniques of an everyday life that would then be a series of movies without cameras.

Consider, for example, the description of Guy Haines as he moves toward the scene of the murder he will commit, finding it "as if a curtain had lifted on a stage scene he already knew." Written and previewed plans are reenacted, such that observation and act realize, or play back, each other. Haines moves at first, "stopping and going," and "mechanically," with the "feeling of moving on established tracks." He moves finally "on certain definite tracks": "Momentum," we are told, "smoothed his movements" (ST, 133). In this astonishingly condensed description, the technical means by which momentum may smooth movements, and thus animate them—the reality of motion pictures—is at once effected and exposed. To the extent that that's the case, it becomes impossible to consider act and observation outside the mediatechnical situation of the official world, one that displays its infrastructure openly and for all to see.

The opening shot of Hitchcock's motion picture version of the novel films motion: moving feet, taxis, trains. In the scene in which Bruno and Guy talk about the no-motivation scheme of vicarious crime, the two sit at either end of the frame, which centers on the "view" outside the window of the moving train. But the view is of course a moving mirror: a film of that view "playing" on the screen/window before which the characters appear to sit. "The technology of film," as one of its first theorists put it, "must dictate its own choice of content."[42] The stopping of the merry-go-round—in a film, from the opening shots on, a chase film about stopping and going—is the stopping of the film mechanism, and film itself.[43] The mechanized doubling of act and observation—the reality of motion pictures—is installed, as the double, or motive of the crime and as its mode of operation.

Or, as Bruno puts it (in a coy recoil of the novel on itself), " 'I thought we'd do something nice. Maybe a good movie—with a murder in it—or maybe the amusement park' " (ST, 99).

The amusement park, the movies, the train, and the novel are distinct. But they are also distinct stations of the stationary carousel: the repeatable motions within those stations that are points on a self-curved space, and so the unceasing motions from station to station, and from point to point. A media circuit that approaches then a media union: and (as Guy Debord put it) one cannot go into exile in a unified world. "He broke me down," Guy says of his insanely overcommunicative alter ego Bruno, "with letters and blackmail and sleeplessness." The self-reported cause of the architect's breakdown may be dubious. But a self-reporting mood establishes a world. In the continuous suspendedness of the suspense mode of life, violently externalized and technically enhanced, sleeplessness is the professional form of wakefulness.[44]

III • "SOCIAL GAMES"

Playing Our Part in the Systems Epoch

FIVE

PARLOR GAMES

The Office and the Laboratory

The uncanny space of "the office" epitomized for a period (roughly a century) the administrative ground floor of a self-denoting world. The bureaucratic a priori—and the strange form of a life that, as many seated at them have noted, takes its name from a piece of furniture—has been mapped in detail from Weber to Adorno and C. Wright Mills and Erving Goffman to the present expositions of its architecture and media. Its operating systems have been filled in more recently by accounts of the little cultural techniques of this habitat (files, index cards, typewriters, ring binders, dictaphones, staplers, memos, carbon paper, copiers, etc., but also its counters, blinds, partitions, and passageways—an overlit realm ruled by numbers, records, and self-persuasive events. On these accounts, the microtechniques of rule by desks, paper, and screens—"the empire of the word people"—appear as epoch-making and world-transforming as the plow or stirrup.

This is not a history of the office. But a brief excursus into this uncanny space—and its projections into the surroundings it shapes and enspheres—may be useful. At the advent of its recognizably modern form, there is Flaubert's very early story (1837), written at the age of fifteen, "A Lecture on Natural History—Genus: *Clerk*": a little piece on, as it were, the anthropology, or zoology, of the office. It is premised on his "frequent trips to offices. . . . You ought to see this interesting biped in the office, copying its register."[1]

At its midpoint, consider the opening chapter of William Dean Howells's novel *The Rise of Silas Lapham* (1885).[2] The opening of the novel not merely inventories, in documentary detail, the appliances, partitions, passages, doors, occupants, moves, distinctions, and documents—the functional differentiations of persons and things, and their self-recording—that delineate this space, and make up its control climate. It makes visible the manner in which the indoor techniques of recording and self-recording become the terms and conditions of a world. The terms, that is, of a self-conditioning or air-conditioning system, constructed and calibrated to answer to, and to "perpetually assert itself against the provocation of the outside."[3]

The novel begins, it may be recalled, with an interview in an office. It begins, more exactly, with a sequence of actions, verbal, written, and physical, in an *inner private* office space set out off from the *outer public* one. Each term that I have italicized comes to indicate the distinctions of position, disposition, and situation within institutions shaped to process these distinctions. The novel likewise is a machine for processing distinctions.

The extensions of a hand, one writing, one touching; the inclination of a head, "rolled" in the direction of a desk or of a visitor; the minute shiftings from reference to self-reference, from life stories to its notation on paper and circulation in the papers; the ascetics of desk work, and the aesthetics of a form of life in which words and acts shift places. For one thing, this is an interview—for a newspaper, in a novel: an exposition that is described, recorded, and reported, as it takes place. It proceeds such that (via a back-and-forth-and-back series of cut-and-pastes in diegetic time) the event and its registration, story and storing, are folded into each other. That redoubles the event in its description, and reports that. There is, that is to say, a flattening or adequation of the world to its description and description to world, in running commentary, as the first principle of its realism.

But the real force of the official world here becomes visible in its extroversions: here not merely an indoor social life but outer space—space "indoors and out"—denotes and depicts itself too. The outside world is, it appears, everywhere a self-marking and so self-demarcating one, in one example after another, after another. Hence we find the street stones scored and "worn by dint of ponderous wheels . . . and discoloured with iron-rust from them." Hence "here and there in wandering streaks over its surface . . . the grey stain of the salt water with which the street had been sprinkled." Hence "at the end of one"—at the very edge of a self-constructing world in the very process of its construction: "block and tackle wandering into the cavernous darkness overhead." Hence, finally, this astonishing scene of self-depiction: "the spars of a vessel penciled themselves delicately against the cool blue of the afternoon sky." Everything acting is in the act of delineating itself and tracing its self-extension into heretofore unmarked space: every thing is penciling or scoring or tracing or engraving itself, performing and leaving a trace in the crystallizations of the official world, assuming and extending into definite form.

We might say that the presupposition and condition of realism then is not the description of every thing. That it is instead the description of the self-description and self-indexing of everything. If Howells's novel has been taken to epitomize a baseline realism, it does so precisely because it epitomizes a self-epitomizing world. (So much for the notion of metanarrative.) If we are meant to hear (or if by now we cannot but hear)—in the name of Howells's reporter/interviewer Bartley Hubbard—the name of the prototype office-dweller Bartleby, or its fossil record, we are meant to see not the dead zone of mechanical reproduction and bureaucratic routine. We are meant to see, beyond that, the emergence, and installation, of a ceaseless and autotropic subtitling and commentary: coterminous "indoors and out." This is the denoting and ensphering form of life that Howells calls, simply, "another world."[4]

That world looks at times like a science-fictional one, one "accomplished by forces wholly superhuman"—as Theodore Dreiser fascinatedly reports near the opening of his first novel, *Sister Carrie*. A small scene may suffice, one in which Carrie's desire to go on stage takes her to what is in effect "every managerial office in the city":[5]

> "Oh, dear!" exclaimed Carrie. "Where is his office?"
>
> He gave her the number. . . .
>
> At the Empire Theatre she found a hive of peculiarly listless and indifferent individuals. Everything ornately upholstered, everything carefully finished, everything remarkably *reserved.*
>
> At the Lyceum she entered one of those secluded, under-stair-way closets, berugged and bepaneled, which causes one to feel the greatness of all positions of authority. Here was *reserve* itself done into a box-office clerk, a doorman, and an assistant, glorying in their fine positions . . . the attitude, for that matter, of every managerial office in the city . . . lords indeed on their own ground. (SC, 277, my emphasis)

There is a live transference, in these place-value systems, from person in position, to the value of numbers determined by position. But Dreiser takes that a step further. Here "reserve" is not merely built into the design of the place. Reserve "itself" is "done into" types of individuals: a box-office clerk, a doorman, an assistant, a compartment, a gatekeeper, and auxiliary functionaries of boxing and partitioning, that function as a function.[6] In this way, the abstraction *reserve*—"done into" types of individuals—is a living diagram or live blueprint, realized in the practices that make it up: it is a real abstraction, one that (as Marx observed) "achieves practical truth as an abstraction only as a category of the most modern society."[7] That is, as a category of the systems-internal character of its world interior, reenacting and so achieving its practical truth.

That's why "I have a position" is the refrain of Dreiser's novel, an "astonished" account of the new lines and places of the official world. Carrie herself is, above all, a "carrier": the first paragraph of the novel—so flatly descriptive that it looks simply matter of fact—is in fact extremely formal: a virtual inventory of things designed to carry other things—from the suitcase or wallet or lunch box or envelope to the train car itself. Carrie in and of herself is, of course, a medium, a carrier and mode for conveying the world's longing—just as the city of Chicago itself is a place that is not exactly a place, but a premise "not so much thriving upon established commerce as upon the industries which prepared for the arrival of others" (*SC*, 11). Things hold the places of other things, and places are placeholders of a future in reserve.

Hence the administrative principle of purposive functioning that the office epitomizes expresses itself in real abstractions (or, to borrow Stephen Crane's term, "transcendental realism"). For example, the lines—the factory assembly line, the chorus line, the bread line, the streetcar line, the unemployment line, the lines of the stage script or the print newspaper, the strike line—the lines that everywhere have a place in the novel. (Is it any wonder that lines—lines of print, lines cut across landscapes and cityscapes, lines of persons—fascinate the experimental novelists of the turn of the last century— Zola, Frank Norris, Jack London, Stephen Crane, Dreiser, among them?)[8]

In this way too the types of person who enter, or hold, these places and positions in "reserved" space are, as Kracauer noted a generation later, "guests in space tout court—a space that encompasses them and has no other function than to encompass them."[9] (The hotel lobby, for Kracauer, as for Dreiser in the figure of Hurstwood, is one of these isotopic spaces; the unemployment office—the place for those who have no place: the standing and waiting reserve—is another.) Carrie herself is a "representation of the world's longing"—its longing to represent itself—done into a face.[10]

I will return to these persons in self-curved space (see part IV). For now, one more sample of the reservation, the office, this one recent, and dysfunctional or artistic: the interestingly obsessive work of the German sculptor in paper and photographer Thomas Demand. Demand constructs a paper-thin world with an uncanny massiness to it. He often works from received photographic images (for example, a postcard photo of a grotto), and constructs a life-size model of its subject in cardboard, then photographs it to scale, and subsequently destroys the model.[11] The serial-sequential movement from photograph to constructed model to photograph thus indexes a donnée redone, fabricated, depicted, and displayed.

The oscillation between installments might no doubt then be taken to indicate, as the art historian and critic Michael Fried puts it, a "redoubling of intention";[12] or, perhaps, it may indicate the excruciated intention to intend. The photograph depends upon, and insists on, the paper piece-by-piece making and assembly of its object—a Courbetian cavern interior, a news photograph of a control room, or copy shop, or a flight space simulator, or a laboratory. The doubling down on intention might then turn round to its perpetual suspension and retrieval: the hide-and-seek of a file system's systems-internal acts and reenactments.

In the circuitous transition from photograph to model to photograph, a paper scene is assembled with an exacted but strangely genericized quality. Every rock or blade of grass has been meticulously cut out and assembled, but with a realism that is derealized: control panels or signs, for example, are reproduced to scale but without the letters or numerals that normally accrue to them in the three-dimensional world. These autotropic interiors are remade to appear in denuded form—replicant and deserted. (There is an alien or "uncanny valley" effect here, but one entirely dependent on objects: human figures are absent, or subtracted.)[13]

We know that modern social systems must enact or stage their self-determination—since self-determinations, to count as self-determinations, must be recognized as such. An "indoor" social life "constitutes the conditions of possibility for its own decisions."[14] A twofold problem, or paradox, for these second-order depictions, or reenactments, emerges here. On the one side, "how to observe a world that observes itself."[15] On the other, "one cannot go into exile in a unified world." Self-description is not self-exemption. The staging of reenactments is, after all, the defining attribute of what has alternately been called the control revolution, the second industrial revolution, or (here) the epoch of social systems.[16]

Demand draws reiteratively on communication systems, postal or network news images, and other isotopias of command and control—the Fukushima nuclear plant control room; or a cruise ship at the moment of its crisis; or a flight simulator; or the laboratory, which, along with the office, is modernity's reenactment zone par excellence. These formal restagings of control sites make for a sort of secondary virginity in the artwork, with all the paradoxes that implies. The crisis of the artwork and the form games of modern social systems are twin sides of the same formation—like the two sides of a horseshoe, opposed on part of their surface, but meeting on another.

Another way of putting this is in terms of the artful, or "playful doubling," of the world. "One of the incalculable effects of Wittgenstein's philosophy," Niklas Luhmann notes, "was to raise the question of whether a concept of art can be defined":

> If the notion of play defies definition, then art should remain undefined as well. This view was widely held in the 1960s. It denies only the possibility for a definition that corresponds to the "essence" of art and holds unequivocally for all observers, however, thus leaving a loophole for the recent theory of operative constructivism [self-instating systems], which no longer raises issues of essence or of the consensus of all observers, but instead leaves the decision of what counts as art to the art system itself. . . . [Observers] must leave it to the system to determine its own boundaries. This move burdens the theory of self-describing systems with a momentous inheritance. It must salvage a highly encumbered "firm" that has been dealing in "essences" and "referring signs," for which there is no market left.[17]

It's the unfolding of this complex—the question of art and the question of play, and so the status of the art system in the systems epoch—that concerns me in this chapter.

We have seen that it is in the pages of the suspense novel that this type of "framed" reality—a situation in which interactors let the system set its own boundaries—perhaps becomes most perspicuous. We might say of novelistic fiction generally that, to the very extent that it does not (unlike, say, the epic or historical drama) depend on preexistent plot-referents, it must include the conditions of possibility for its own decisions, and posit characters who do the same. The novel (as Henry James puts it, in his prefatory remarks on his story *The Turn of the Screw*) posits a gamelikeness in that it "makes the score entirely off its own bat."[18]

That the "organization of experience" (in Goffman's terms) takes place, for example, in organizations—that these organizations resemble games practiced on, as Bourdieu has it, social fields—is perhaps too self-evident to be seen, and may then be too obvious to be ignored. Consider this institutional scene from Patricia Highsmith's novel *Ripley's Game* (1974), which is one of the focal points of this chapter. The novel begins by planning the moves in a sort of game: a dealer in art forgeries (Tom Ripley) tricks a fatally ill framer of works of art (Jonathan), into performing a series of murders. The killings are meant to simulate a mob hit; the frame-up, in turn, is designed to instigate a crime war—but one set in motion less for gain than for fun, bemused spectation. Crime scenes resembles artworks which resemble game zones. That arrangement admits the art framer into what Highsmith calls "a laboratory of the future": "the kind of place" designed for what Erving Goffman calls "frame analysis" and its "multiple versions" of the "the 'realest' reality":[19]

> The hospital was a vast assembly of buildings set among trees and pathways lined with flowers. Karl had again driven them. The wing of the hospital where Jonathan had to go looked like a laboratory of the future—rooms on either side of a corridor as in a hotel, except that these rooms held chromium chairs or beds and were illuminated by fluorescent or variously coloured lamps. There was a smell not of disinfectant but as of some unearthly gas, something Jonathan had known under the X-ray machine which five years ago had done him no good with the leukaemia. It was the kind of place where layman surrendered utterly to the omniscient specialists, Jonathan thought, and at once he felt weak enough to faint. Jonathan was walking at that moment down a seemingly endless corridor of sound-proofed floor surface.[20]

The type of society in play here could not be more clearly delineated. It indicates what death and life—or, as we now say, "existential"—situations look like in this framed and assembled world, its pathways outlined with transplants and artifact-nature.[21] This is, as it were, a working model of an antiseptic modernity and its indoor social life.

There is, first, the "vast assembly" of buildings with their endless corridors, pathways, partitions, techno-grottos, soundproofed and utterly self-conditioned. This is a corridor-world, one that coordinates at every point bodies, reports, communicative media, and spatial arrangements.[22] There is, too, the reassembling of institutional space as a laboratory for conducting experiments, and for framing, staging, or playing life and death.

Parlor Games

Can we get certain pathological phenomena as well-defined games? . . . I don't believe any game that can't be played as a parlor game.
—Martin Shubik, RAND Corporation

"'There's no such thing as a perfect murder,' Tom [Ripley] said to Reeves," opening Highsmith's *Ripley's Game*: "That's just a parlour game" (5). Yet it's not hard to see that the relation between murder and game—between real worlds and parlor games—is a good deal more complicated here. And not least in that the modern scene of the crime always resembles a "game space."[23] Three questions: What does it mean to talk about murder as a parlor game? What does it tell us about modern forms of social organization, violence, and games? And what does it tell us about their place in making up modern social systems, what they look like, and how they work?

In the pages that follow I take up these questions about game and world through a sampling of several very different scenes: initially, Highsmith's suspense novel *Ripley's Game*; next, a best seller that is in effect a popularization of systems thinking—Malcolm Gladwell's *Blink: The Power of Thinking without Thinking*; and, finally, Kazuo Ishiguro's novel about newly normal forms of death and life and the social ecologies of ignorance that go with them, *Never Let Me Go*. The focus across these scenes is first, via Highsmith, parlor games; second, via Gladwell, war games; the third, via Ishiguro, form games. These are, I mean to suggest, scenes that remain remarkably consistent across their very different scenarios. Each appears as the subset of a form that persists through its variants: encounters of a performance and a grammar. This signals, more exactly, the emergence of comparable conditions in diverse systems, which is a defining attribute of modernity. It signals, more generally, the flattening of the world and its description. These scenes then will make it possible to map these games, their rules, and their media—and the social field they at once model and realize.

Why perfect murders and parlor games, then?

For one thing, modern game theory, and the game-theoretical worldview that goes with it, takes off from John von Neumann's 1928 article, "Zur Theorie der Gesellschaftsspiele"—"On the Theory of Parlor Games." The attempt, in von Neumann's account, is to put on a mathematical basis the little games in which (unlike, say, playing dice) one is not merely playing against the odds but playing against others. This is a game in which we move against opponents whose intentions, or what look like them (bluffs), enter into the form of the game. This is, then, a complex game in that one must observe and measure and misinform self-observing observers who are doing the same. That is, one must observe what and how the observed observer can't observe— and whether he can observe that or not. It is a "social game" (the literal sense of *Gesellschaftsspiel*)—in the Weberian sense: the nature of social action is interaction. Hence one must take into account here what Goffman calls "expression games," with all their "counter-uncovering moves."[24]

In the theory of parlor games, the effects of playing the game must be included in it. The assumption (on von Neumann's or, later, Wiener's account) is a "game as played by perfectly intelligent, perfectly ruthless operators,"[25] like oneself. It is a game then along the lines of the *Kriegsspiele*, or war games, that von Neumann (a prototype for Stanley Kubrick's Dr. Strangelove) will go on to model. It is then something like a play-at-home version of the fog of war or dress rehearsal for what has come to be called the military-entertainment complex.[26]

But this is to suggest that parlor games, self-conditioned and deliberately complicated games that contain their own outcome—"social games"—are already and from the start more than that, in the epoch of social systems. "The problem," as von Neumann puts it, "is well known":

> there is hardly a situation in daily life into which this problem does not enter.... A great many different things come under this heading [the theory of parlor games], anything from roulette to chess, from baccarat to bridge. And after all, any event—given the external conditions and the participants in the situation (provided the latter are acting of their own free will)—may be regarded as a game of strategy if one looks at the effect it has on the participants.[27]

The theory of parlor games (put simply, the mathematicization of games of strategy) becomes, in von Neumann's and Oskar Morgenstern's *Theory of Games and Economic Behavior* (1947), the basis for the game-theoretical modeling of economic and other real-world behavior: "after all, any event."[28] It registers a spreading of gamelikeness, and its attribution, across the social field at the same time as it looks to model, or to monetize, that metastasis. It looks (to paraphrase Roland Barthes) to destroy the wolf by lodging comfortably in its gullet.[29]

We might say that the deficiency of this game model (at least as popularly understood) comes into view from the start—the presumption of the rationality of actors or operators—the perfectly rational and perfectly ruthless; the reliance of the model on perspicuous (if imperfect) information; on the efficiency of markets, via the tendency toward self-correcting equilibrium; and so on.[30] Or we can reverse the picture. Then we might say that the deficiency of the world, and hence the attraction of the game world, here immediately comes into view—not least for gamers looking for a better or more perfect world, or at least one that plays by the rules, and has them, and ongoingly scores the condition (or health) of one's play.[31]

We might say too then that this game outlook on life amounts to "expanding the game to the whole world" (Wark) or that a world that's like a game is thus part rules and part fiction—or "half-real" (Juul)—as two more recent, and influential, accounts of gamer theory have it.[32] But both notions—the notion of the expansion of the game to the whole world, the division of real life by halves—are too crude to do much work with. For one thing, in both the unity of the difference between game and world—the implications of the playful doubling of the world in the world—tends to be left uninterpreted. For another, so are the modern social conditions "done into" the form of the distinction in the first place.[33]

Take, for example, the film *Avalon* (2001), directed by Mamoru Oshii (director too of the anime-inspired film *Ghost in the Shell*). *Avalon* is familiar enough in the canon of reality-game films. The plot involves a potentially lethal virtual-reality war game played by addicted combatants—with the goal, it turns out, to arrive at the game stage "Class Real." There is no doubt a canonicity to the subgenre of such films—and their rehearsal, or retesting, of the distinction between the game world and the real one. But the film—like the extraordinarily powerful range of anime productions that it borders on—inquires not merely into the very problem of this distinction, but also the general conditions that sponsor it from the start.[34]

It does so in part by copying it at the level of form—the form of the cinematic medium. That is to say, in *Avalon*, the reality of the film medium—the doubling of observation and act that cinema posits as its condition and mode of operation and so makes up the reality of motion pictures—becomes plot.[35] It is not merely that we view the world viewed—the observed observer in the act of observation and so the continual reproduction of the act via its observation (the modalization of the world). Nor is it merely that this doubling continually reproduces itself via a technical process that implies a second order of vision (bringing into view everything that can be looked at by a look that creates it).[36]

The feedback loops between the human senses and the media, and between observation and act, thus take on the theme of the game/world distinction. The difference between the film world and the game world looks like the difference between the real world and a fictional one. The difference between real and fictional reality then oscillates—between discourse and story, *fabula* and *syuzhet*. This becomes visible precisely via an oscillation between media.

We know that reality—"real life"—can only be spoken of by contrasting it to something else from which it is distinguished, say, fictional (or statistical, or mathematical) reality.[37] (And it's worth remembering that the term "real life" itself comes to us from eighteenth-century fiction.) The internal articulation of reality in the film makes it possible, or necessary, to distinguish real and fictional reality: they are (again) copied into each other. Hence the paradoxical determination of "Class Real" (the real as one classification among others) itself becomes visible. And, given what appears here as the preference for violence over paradox, it is not surprising that it becomes visible as war game.

That is to say, the choice of the game enters into it: "Which is the better game? Which would you choose given the choice? The sort of game that you think you can win but can't. Or, alternatively, one that seems to be impossible, but isn't. Maintaining a delicate balance somewhere in between throughout every level of the game, that's what keeps it going."[38] The delicate and ongoing balancing between the necessary and the possible defines the self-defining space of the game.

In short, what defines the game form is its contingency, its self-conditioning, and its deliberate self-complication.[39] It's contingent in the sense that the rules of the game are neither necessary nor impossible. It's self-conditioned in that rules, measure, and outcome are defined by the "sort of game" chosen and by what's possible, or impossible, in it. It's deliberately complicated to relieve the boredom of that self-conditioning (so that the repetition of play, and the suspense it entails, are not annulled as sheer repetition).[40]

These are the "sandbox elements" that prolong the play—the gratuitous difficulties that "keep it going," and that seduce players to continue to play. This is (as Roger Caillois expresses it) "the pleasure experienced in solving a problem arbitrarily designed for this purpose"—like probing a toothache with one's tongue, and in doing so playing with one's own pain.[41]

In short, if "we lead an indoor social life,"[42] the door opens at once to the symbolic and the real. It is in this sense that the parlor game is a scale model of the modern social field—or, more exactly, of its small and sequestered, discrete but comparable, worlds. These small worlds are themselves working models of the "sequestration" of modern life—to the extent that it is modern.[43] Games such as these—parlor games, crime games, war games, and the rest—are, in short, models of a self-modeling world. They are scale models of the modern social field, which is then, in effect, a life-size model of itself.

This is not the place to rehearse the large topic of the social differentiation of modern society, set out in variant detail from Max Weber to Carl Schmitt, from Michel Foucault to Niklas Luhmann. Suffice to say that if, from the late eighteenth century on, prisons come to resemble hospitals, which come to resemble factories, which come to resemble schools, which come to resemble prisons, this is not merely because they share in common a grand theme such as discipline. These social microworlds—at once differentiated and fractally self-similar—are the genre forms of a self-realizing society: one that is "almost-completely self-reliant,"[44] one that more and more generates and dispels uncertainties itself, and "almost" on its own terms (recall Durkheim's almost sui generis society on the way to recognizing itself).

These training, educating, correcting, grading, and self-realizing institutions are the small worlds that calibrate and compare and measure and individualize individuals, and socially distribute the possibilities of personally attributable reflection, action, and evaluation. They lend incremental form to the lifestyle called a career. That is to say—and there will be more to say about this in a moment—the self-reference system of modern society, like the self-reference system of modern literature, gives itself priority over all external reference.[45] But, like the modern art system, it does so knowing that. It at every point reflexively monitors its own self-created reality—and so makes visible all the paradoxes of that self-implication.

It would not be difficult to enumerate these recursive social systems and their media, and the shift to the observation of observation—second-order observation—that each turns on. Here I will do little more than itemize what social-systems analysis has already more or less detailed: the political system (and its media of self-observation called public opinion); the legal system (which makes cases from cases and texts from texts); the scientific system (and its medium of publications, such that observations—experiments—can be observed); the art system (which leaves the determination of what counts as art to the art system itself); the erotic system (with its love and intimacy media, including novels, among many other self-stimulants: hothouse circuits communicating the uncommunicable); the education system (which discovers, or posits, the child in order to demonstrate that persons are things that can be made and measured); the economic system (with its success media, and the real "in the final instance": which, to the extent that it is a social system never finds out what real needs or real values might be, or needs to); the crime system (which, via the mass media, generalizes the scene of the crime as the demarcation zones of the modern world). And so on.[46]

In short, modernity, to the extent that it is modern, trends toward tautology. It more and more realizes a nullification, or *denudation*, of extrinsic determinations. That's one reason why the weather—from third world disasters to global warming—becomes the test case of relative modernization, of a "greenhouse effect" self-determination. (One reason too, perhaps, why the shape and function of spheres and suspended, self-curved spaces—posited in philosophical-religious practice-systems during what Karl Jaspers called "the axial age," eighth to third centuries BC—has so provocatively reemerged now across many social, aesthetic, and self-promotional fronts.) This general trending toward tautology is, as it were, rereflected in these small fenced, or paled, worlds—and reenacted by practicers, and pale kings, of a form of life who are "intent on their intramural game."[47] It is here that the game, in its contingency, self-conditioning, and purposive complication, shows itself as a working model of the self-modeling modern world—and so presents the world in the world.

The Rules of Irrelevance

The game strategist of the perfect murder in Highsmith's *Ripley's Game* is Reeves Minot, who plans the crime, as Tom Ripley puts it, "just to start the ball rolling" (*RG*, 62). In short, "he plays games" (128). Reeves, we are told, is "like a small boy playing a game he had invented himself, a rather obsessive game with severe rules—for other people" (112). The point, however, is not quite that Reeves exempts himself from the rules by determining them and so seeing through them. The real point is that seeing through the game and obsessively playing the game are not at all at odds here. For if one does not see, and see through, the rules one cannot play by the rules: seeing through the game is part of it. That is to say, again, in order for self-determinations to count as self-determinations, they have to be observed as such. In a self-validating world, its genres such as the crime story—its prolonged suspense and its predictably surprising outcome—must work the same way. It requires suspense in the sense of a self-generated uncertainty and surprise in the sense of a self-dispelled mystery. The paradox, catch, or trick, of the expected surprise is the nature of its form game.

One thing the novel allows then is for this circular causality to take the form of form.

"Word did get around, he realized" (*RG*, 23). This is how the circuits of communication and realization continually reproduce—and reignite—each other: "I'm simply telling you what Jonathan told me" (223). This is how the novel conveys information or (as Gregory Bateson frames it) "news of difference." It continually switches back and forth between act and observation, story and discourse—such that, as with the news today, the reporting on the news becomes the news reported on. "It was a matter of protecting—what had gone before" (227). The sentence's short circuit is the syntax of recursive causal systems—ongoingly feeding back outcomes into intentions, effects into causes.[48]

This is simply to observe, once again, that second-order observation is field tested in novels, which become models for trying out the modalization of the world with serious consequences. That makes for the generic preference for characters—as modal terms (self-observing observers). It also makes for the novelistic preference for affects that include their self-reflection as part of their operation: sympathy (or envy), for example, which posits the social reflection of pleasure (or pain) in the pain (or pleasure) of others, via a reciprocity of observation and self-observation.[49]

The formality of the game is in part what looks like its suspension of external reference—or what Erving Goffman calls its "rules of irrelevance." Games, for Goffman, "illustrate how participants are willing to forswear for the duration of the play any apparent interest in the esthetic, sentimental, or monetary value of the equipment employed, adhering to what might be called *rules of irrelevance.*" In this way, the real-world conditions of the game or the material that the game is made of—for example, "whether checkers are played with bottle tops on a piece of squared linoleum, with gold figures on inlaid marble, or with uniformed men standing on colored flagstones"— can be suspended.[50] Hence the "same sequence of strategic moves and countermoves" can be made nevertheless—and still "generate the same contour of excitement."[51]

Yet from another point of view the rules of the game are scarcely a suspension of the way of the world—in that the same sequestration, and so the same rules of irrevelance, mark both.

The first sentence of the first chapter of *Ripley's Game* is about murder and parlor games. The last sentences of that opening chapter are about the game Reeves is playing—if, that is, he's playing a game at all. It's not at all clear that Reeves's actions, or play, are more than strictly gratuitous—"toying" with things is the novel's repeated term for this. That is, it's not at all clear that Reeves has anything classed as real to get out of it—beyond, of course, just prolonging the play.

Here then is the astonishing passage with which the initial chapter of the novel closes:

> Reeves might gain—according to Reeves, but let Reeves figure that out, because what Reeves wanted seemed as vague to Tom as Reeves' microfilm activities, which presumably had to do with international spying. Were governments aware of the insane antics of some of their spies? Or those whimsical, half-demented men flitting from Bucharest to Moscow and Washington with guns and microfilm—men who might with

the same enthusiasm have put their energies to international warfare in stamp-collecting, or in acquiring secrets of miniature electric trains? (RG, 11–12)

The first chapter of *Ripley's Game* begins then with parlor games and ends with medial systems. But what links this antic series of activities? What draws into relation stamps, model trains, photography, information, spies, and war by other means? What makes it possible for these miniature systems of information and body-and-message transport (electric trains, stamp collections, microfilm, and so on) to make up a world? What makes it possible for these little medial systems to work as conditions and techniques of existence? To operate through scale models and working models that are at once models *of* the world and *in* it?

When, that is, did the communication of words and things become the modern medial system, before our very eyes? 1839: the annus mirabilis of the network of modern matter and message transport systems. (And the network criteria of speed, regularity, predictability, and reproducibility.) The first commercial electric telegraph, in 1839, constructed by Wheatstone and Cooke for the Great Western Railway; the first Baedeker guide (to the Rhine), 1839; and the first national railway timetable (Bradshaw's), in 1839; the invention, or congregation, of modes of photography—and its use in guidebooks, among other things—in 1839 (centrally, by Daguerre in France; and, in 1840, Fox Talbot in England; there were, of course, earlier trials of these technologies); and the first national postal system, Rowland Hill's Penny Post (based on the innovation of the prepaid stamp), in Britain, in 1840.[52]

What spreads throughout the social field, what makes up the isotopic infrastructure of the modernizing social field, is the intensified self-organization of self-operating systems and their observation and spectation. This is what the author of an article in the *Spectator* (February 1839) titled "Self-Operating Processes of Fine Art: The Daguerreotype" calls the appearance of "self-acting machines of mechanical operation."[53]

These events indicate, and index, the media genealogy of a modernizing world, one tending toward, and more and more conditioned by, speed and repeatability, and by a permanent, and asymptotically continuous, connectedness—a media union. It's possible to fill out this genealogy a bit more. First, by way of specifying how the a priorization of the media in these operations is bound to forms of observation and self-observation— and their mutual conditioning. Second, by way of locating how the distinctions of medium and form, model and scale, fundamentally structure these operations. Third, and finally, by way of sorting out what we might then make of the whimsical, half-demented, insane links—"International warfare in stamp-collecting" (!); "Acquiring secrets of miniature electric trains" (!)—that make up Ripley's game, and both modern parlor games and modern crime games.

STAMP COLLECTING

The "closing of the postal system as a system" occurs with the shift from the individual registration of letters (and their rates) to postal standards (and the mass reproducibility of stamps); with the shift from names of places to street numbers; with the appearance across the social field of systems-integral standards at every level—a working diagram for the conveyance of communications (from place to place, on time). The postal system is no longer officially person to person: "The postage stamp made the sender's presence at the postal counter just as superfluous as the recipient's presence at delivery"—the mailboxes and mail slots that are the standard inputs and outputs for sending and delivery processes, irrespective of persons.[54] The standardized post—its collection, sending, delivery—neutralizes the idea of distance (within standardized zones), just as the railroad annihilates time (standardizing those zones).

The very existence of prepaid and mass-produced stamps implies a media union: a postal system. This is the reason why we get tracking reports like this one in Ripley's Game: "He dropped the letter in a yellow box en route to his shop. It would probably be a week before he heard from Alan. . . . He thought of his letter, making its progress to Orly airport, maybe by this evening, maybe by tomorrow morning" (RG, 20). The purpose of letter writing, we know, is to mark absences—absent writers for absent readers. With the advent of a postal system, the significance of a theory of communication, and its deferrals, can then be formulated (and so deconstructed).

The second chapter of Ripley's Game opens by italicizing precisely this shift from meaning and sense to pattern and code: "So it was that some ten days later, on 22 March, Jonathan . . . received a curious letter from his good friend Alan McNear. . . . Jonathan had expected—or rather not expected—a sort of thank-you letter from Alan for the send-off party" (RG, 13). We might read this as a little lesson in the rudiments of information theory. "So it was" is then the renovated idiom of a now postally sponsored fate, keeping its appointed rounds. The postal friend then—one who is near but also far ("mcnear")—is less a subject than a position, a position in the communicative circuit. And what then makes possible the paradoxical equivalence of the expected and the not expected here is the pattern of expectations that yields the sort-of thank-you letter, its technical conditions of possibility.[55]

The epistolary novel and the detective/crime novel, the two basic forms of narrative fiction, here are braided together. In Highsmith's crime novels, there is a proliferation of letters, copied into the narrative. The love letter (which communicates the incommunicable) and the thank-you note (which says what goes without saying) approach the minimal trouble of the greeting card. In that curvature toward standardized values and the efficient regulation of mutual involvement, the channel represents itself in the channel. A typology of the postepistolary (the postal squared) novel might be set out, from, say, Stoker's *Dracula* (1897) and James's *The Turn of the Screw* (1898), both gothicized epistolary novels, to Highsmith's Ripley novels—criminalized ones.

SPIES AND SECRETS

With the advent of telegraphy and then telephony, and systems of communication that do not depend on the sending of things or bodies, the transportation of people and information divides—which allows for a period in which they (functionally, and as if nostalgically) track each other, as for a period telegraph lines ran alongside railway lines.

By then we are in the zone of the detective and suspense story, its encrypted secrets and purloined letters. "From the point of view of the cryptanalyst," as one of the founders of communications systems theory, Claude Shannon, observed, "a secrecy system is almost identical with a noisy communication system."[56] It is not merely that the modeling of transmitter and receiver, in Shannon's theory of communication, as encoder and decoder, explicitly identifies "communication with cryptanalysis."[57] Or that there are tight couplings between the takeoff of communication theory and computational analysis, on the one side, and espionage and code breaking, on the other, during World War II.[58] The inverse relation between the probability of the message and the information it gives (see n. 55) means that "the uncertainty about the value of individual bits that is called forth by interference on the channel is more or less indistinguishable from the uncertainty produced by enemy codes."[59] On that logic, the problem of modern literary interpretation—the uncertainty as to whether something is an intended/coded message or simply interference on the line (noise)—is tied to the form of the secrecy system too.[60]

In that the model of the new media—without as yet a credible account either of the media or the new—has come to look like the magical solution to the two cultures problem, we might recall what that solution looked like at the beginning of the Cold War. Warren Weaver, for example, observes in his review of Shannon's work in *Scientific American* that the analysis of communicative systems as a series of probabilistic events might be applied to

> *all of the procedures by which one mind may affect another....* This . . . involves not only written and oral speech, but also music, the pictorial arts, the theater, the ballet, and in fact all human behavior. In some connections it may be desirable to use a still broader definition of communication . . . [including] the procedures by means of which (say automatic equipment to track an airplane and to compute its probable future positions) affects another mechanism (say a guided missile chasing this airplane).[61]

Here arms and information—Norbert Wiener's groundbreaking work in recursive systems analysis via the design of antiaircraft predictors and, via that, cybernetics in general—meet and fuse.[62] The response to this is today "a nebulous unease at the over-communicative constitution of the world system," by way of telecommunications: so we can now "make one another as unhappy from afar as was once possible only among next-door neighbors."[63] What remains, we have seen, of the distances of "the daily planet" is its logo.

MINIATURES AND MODELS

No doubt the mechanical toy may excite the thrill and panic of the "self-invoking fiction." No doubt the miniature (the miniature railway, for example) may be "nostalgic in a fundamental sense"—a movement "from work to play, from utility to aesthetics." But that fiction now provides too a working model of the self-steering and self-modeling social field. The collection— stamps or trains or toys—may "replace history with *classification*," and present a "hermetic world" "self-sufficient and self-generating"; and it may provide a "narrative of interiority," one made up of the "complete number of elements necessary for an autonomous world."[64]

But for precisely these reasons its extreme formality comes to appear not as the alternative to the modern social field but as the form of the modern social field, and its small, isotopic worlds. The scale model is a matter both of modeling and of scale. It makes visible the relation of observation to itself— and so its contingent and self-referential structure.[65] It makes visible autotropic (self-turned) spaces and isotopic (self-similar) ones. And, in the search for America's next top model, it may then be well worth taking into account the way of the modern world as a self-mapping and self-modeling one.

The Switchboard of the Social

The doubling of the world in the model—the redoubling that allows the world to show in the world—means that the world can be observed in different (rival or correspondent) ways, and so be recalibrated by the existence of comparable alternatives. There are three basic consequences to this.

First, it marks the relativity of the observer, who observes himself as an observer among others. Second, one is then asked to distinguish "real" reality from other kinds (fictional or statistical, for example). Third, the matter of scale makes observation itself visible: seeing itself seen, albeit out of the corner of the eye.

The photographic—which, it seems, "permits a blow-up any scale"—epitomizes that, from the microfilmic to the big close-up of the human face: the filmic close-up is a solicitation to observe what the observed observer observes.[66] What the photographic brings into view are scales of viewing: modernity ready for its close-up. And that induces a second-order reflection, installing it as a medium and framework of perception, a cultural technique and ego-technic medium.[67]

The little models that proliferate in, and as, the world of *Ripley's Game*, for example, show the self-modeling of that world, and how it operates. Here the *historia rerum gestarum* coincides with the *res gestae*: the story of events with the events themselves. (But it will be recalled that *res gestae* refers not exactly to the event itself but instead to the coincidence of the event and its observation.[68])

The novel, *Ripley's Game*, is in effect nothing but this self-modeling and self-sampling, and, for that reason, several small and rapid examples may suffice here.

1. "His hobby was naval history, and he made model nineteenth-century and eighteenth-century frigates in which he installed miniature electric lights that he could put completely or partially on by a switch in his living room. Gerard himself laughed at the anachronism of electric lights in his frigates, but the effect was beautiful when all the other lights in the house were turned out" (RG, 47). History and model, war and game, hesitate each other here, not least in the anachronism of electric lights. (We may recall that the very notion of anachronism itself is media-dependent, an effect of the "typographical persistence" of print.)[69] The partial or complete illumination of the model—and hence the oscillation between model and world—is achieved by stage effects. The beauty of it, its aesthetic formality, is achieved by its self-illuminated and stand-alone character, distinct from its context.

2. The scale can be reversed: "Little boats bobbed gaily at anchor, and two or three boats were sailing about, simple and clean as brand-new toys" (RG, 67). These little boats are life-size and miniature at once, shifting in dimension from one to the other, and so making that visible.

3. Or, again, since the act takes shape in its recording or registration, the phatic dimension of communication (by which the channel refers to itself) is itself materialized: "He'd done little jobs for Reeves Minot, like posting on small, stolen items, or recovering from toothpaste tubes . . . tiny objects like microfilm rolls" (RG, 6). In passages such as this one, scale itself (rolls of film as "tiny objects") becomes thick and palpable—an element in the concreteness of the medium of representation.

4. Or, more generally, consider what live space (living room) looks like in *Ripley's Game*: "Jonathan carried a second cup of coffee into the small square living room where Georges was now sprawled on the floor with his cut-outs. Jonathan sat down at the writing desk, which always made him feel like a giant" (RG, 19). The geometry, the small square, of real space; the boy and his cutout models; the writing desk that scales between writing and world: all are graphs of a self-graphing world, living and lifelike at once, and so staging life in the systems epoch.

Hence the writing desk, like the light switch in the living room that turns on and off the lights of the model, is a switch point between two worlds. The model for that is the circuit switch itself:

> We do not notice that the concept "switch" is of quite a different order than the concepts "stone," "table," and the like. Closer examination shows that the switch, considered as a part of an electric circuit, *does not exist* when it is in the on position. From the point of view of the circuit, it is not different from the conducting wire which leads to it and the wire which leads away from it. It is merely "more conductor." Conversely, but similarly, when the switch is off, it does not exist from the point of view of the circuit. It is nothing, a gap between two conductors which themselves exist only as conductors when the switch is on. In other words, the switch is *not* except at the moments of its change of setting.[70]

We do not notice that the switch is an object of a different order: a quasi-object. That is, we do not notice the switch—it is anaesthetic and disappears—if it works. It appears only if it fails: "If the relation succeeds, if it is perfect, optimum, and immediate; it disappears as a relation. If it is there, if it exists, that means that it failed. It is only mediation."[71] This is the unity of the channel and its breakdowns—its interceptions and its accidents, the waves and shocks along the line.

There is of course a paradox to the insistence that (as Kittler, or his translator, posits) "the media determine our situation," but do so to the extent that we do not cease not seeing that. One can then either abide in the deconstruction of this paradox, or see how it works.[72]

One finds, across all these examples, an oscillation between model and world. The "floating" of the difference between model and world is centrally here the denudation of the distinction between game and world. ("Or was it even a game that Tom was playing? Jonathan couldn't believe it was entirely a game" [RG, 189].) This is what Poe, early on, called the "half-credences" that make believable or probable parlor games, like the murder story.[73] (It is what at the same time makes credible and see-through Poe's hoaxes, gimmicks, and tricks.) What then of the media ensembles, at once standalone and out there in the world, that make up the infrastructure of this type of society?

The object of media theory is "not an object but a difference"—the difference between medium and form (with all the paradoxes that involves). The difference between medium and form "oscillates from one side to the other [but] is never univocally defined, because each side depends on the other"—and can only be observed through the other.[74]

Take this strange, overly-literal, example: the coming to light of the medium, light itself. In *Ripley's Game*, a novel and game world so relentlessly given over to observing media of observation and self-observation, and to the conditions of what can be seen and what can't, it is not at all surprising that the medium of visibility—light—is itself depicted and arrives, as it were, in person. It would be possible to point to its fiat-lux appearances again and again in the novel. But the formal becoming-medial of the medium occurs late in the story, after Ripley has reentered the game and made it over in his own name.

Here Ripley and Jonathan, the pawn in Ripley's game, have just killed a couple of killers and are about to vaporize the bodies. At this moment Tom's body is transfigured:

> Tom's car stopped. They had gone perhaps two hundred yards from the main road in a great curve. Tom had cut his lights, but the interior of the car lit when he opened the door. Tom left the door open, and walked towards Jonathan, waving his arms cheerfully. Jonathan was at that instant cutting his own motor and his lights. The image of Tom's figure in the baggy trousers, green suede jacket, stayed in Jonathan's eyes for a moment as if Tom had been composed of light. Jonathan blinked. (RG, 210)

"Composed of light." The term "composed"—in its terminological indifference between two states, form and matter—could not be more exact. In turn object and medium, it oscillates ("blinks") between them.[75] (The easy claim that "matter matters" does the same—but then puns do that for a living.)[76]

"The important thing is that in Einstein's work, light and matter are on an equal basis," Norbert Wiener notes in *The Human Use of Human Beings*: "in his theory of relativity it is impossible to introduce the observer without also introducing the idea of message." This is the emergent unity of physics and communication. For Marshall McLuhan, light, and particularly the electric light, epitomize the distinctive characteristic of the medium:

> The electric light is pure information. It is a medium without a message, as it were, unless it is used to spell out some verbal ad or name. The fact, characteristic of all media, means that the "content" of any medium is always another medium. . . . The electric light escapes attention as a communication medium just because it has no "content."[77]

If light and matter are on the same level, there is no alternative to the modalization of the world. That modalization of the world posits the observer at every point. It's "impossible then to introduce the observer without also introducing the idea of message."[78] That means that the world and its communication are on an equal basis too.

Ripley is identified through and through with medial techniques and transformations in the series of novels that carry his name: they are the conditions of the self-conditioning that defines and empowers him. Hence, his talent. These novels operate entirely by way of technologies of body and message transport, their commutability and their self-reflection.

The coming to light of the media takes the form here (and not merely here) of a transitional syndrome. The reality of the media system flickers into view, as if suspending real reality, or wounding it. The mood of systems visibly takes on the sensational form of a wound culture and its lethal, enclosed spaces. The real of the media system is then staged and brought to light as syndrome, one that for a moment stops the world in its tracks.

The name that Highsmith gives to this syndrome is Ripley. What marks every page of the novels that bear his name is the gamelike situation by which reality must be first discredited in order to make visible that it is staged, and, second, to make what is staged real. It is self-discredited and so self-determined. This is, we have seen, the pure logic of the suspense story. It is not enough to depict its own conditions. It must expose its own conditions in order to showcase the conditions of possibility for making its own decisions its own. It can then take apart what it makes (as Demand disposes of the models he makes and photographs). These are then experiments in self-extroversion and self-extinction. Such reality tests may take on the popular form of recreational games and reincarnation exercises (live, die, repeat). Such practices in turn presuppose communicative media as ecumene.

Under the conditions of a modernizing and technogenic epoch, anthropology is transposed into history, and social-historical grounds into media techniques. Highsmith's epochal Ripley (like other serial killers, fictional and factual) is a sort of nonperson, *a man without content*.[79] He is not merely one among an indeterminate number of others, but the third person in person. One who does not exist apart from the conditions of existence provided by the impersonality of communicative and self-observing systems. The compulsively and upwardly mobile character without qualities gives those techniques a proper name, Ripley. It names a form of life too—the reality game, *Ripley's Believe It or Not!*

The Systems Turn: Art and Anthropotechnics

There's another toy in *Ripley's Game*: "The gyroscope Jonathan bought for Georges in Munich turned out to be the most appreciated toy Jonathan had ever given his son. Its magic remained, every time Georges pulled it from its square box where Jonathan insisted that he keep it." The "delicate instrument" is a scale, and working, model, of "a larger gyroscope" that "keeps ships from rolling on the sea." And, "to illustrate what he meant," Jonathan "rolled over on the floor, propped on his elbows" (RG, 139).

The embodiment, or anthropomorphization, of the little self-correcting machine is made clear enough, and not merely in the general tendency toward self-illustration (the tendency for acts to trace their own diagram) at work in this little scene. The sociologist Daniel Riesman, for example, in his 1960s best seller, *The Lonely Crowd*, had identified the gyroscope as the analogue of what he calls the "inner-directed" person:

A new psychological mechanism is "invented": it is what I like to describe as a psychological gyroscope. This instrument, once it is set in motion by the parents and other authorities, keeps the inner-directed person, as we shall see, "on course" even when tradition, as responded to by his character, no longer dictates his moves.[80]

Yet something more is at stake than the bid for scientific aura implicit in a loose coupling of sociology and mechanics, in the account of inner-directed person set in motion from without, and in effect parented by gyroscopes.

The gyroscope here is both a toy and a worldview: the gyroscope thus might be seen as a Gedenken experiment or, better, a Gedenken machine, with many forms of life. If Ripley, composed of light, is the channel or medium reflecting on itself, in this scene self-reflection is itself reflected on—by way of one of the defining instruments of the second machine age.

Hence the magical character of the little gyroscope—as toy, as model, as "psychological mechanism"—in Highsmith's novel. The gyroscope, put simply, is a mechanism that links self-governing to self-observing—and mechanizes both. The term "gyroscope" means literally "to view the turning." The gyroscope was introduced in 1852 by the physicist Leon Foucault (finding its first notable use in the device to demonstrate the earth's rotation, Foucault's pendulum). Its application to steering mechanisms took a half century to emerge (Elmer Sperry's development of the gyrostabilizer and gyrocompass for the U.S. Navy).[81]

That application is then one of the delays of the second machine age.[82] The "principle of feedback" remained like a fish out of water for a period, unable as yet to find a place to breathe.

The delay of the second machine age indicates, among other things, the delay in recognizing the significance of feedback—the "idea that circular causation is of very great importance." Here is Gregory Bateson's useful summary of the problem:

> Many self-corrective systems were also already known. That is, individual cases were known, but the *principle* remained unknown. Indeed, occidental man's repeated discovery of instances and inability to perceive the underlying principle demonstrate the rigidity of his epistemology. Discoveries and rediscoveries of the principle include Lamarck's transformism (1809), James Watt's invention of the governor for the steam engine (late eighteenth century), Alfred Russel Wallace's perception of natural selection (1856), Clark [*sic*] Maxwell's mathematical analysis of the steam engine with a governor (1868), Claude Bernard's *milieu interne*, Hegelian and Marxian analyses of social process . . . and the various mutually independent steps in the development of cybernetics and systems theory during and immediately after World War II.[83]

That is, the self-observing and self-steering instrument; the reciprocal flow of information back into a controller; the "control of a machine on the basis of its *actual* performance rather than its *expected* performance" (Wiener); the need to take into account what the machine has already said, such that effects of events can be carried all around to produce changes at the point of origin (Bateson): these escalating albeit nonvicious circles remained for a period unthinkable.[84] It was not yet possible to arrive at a theory of self-reflection that was not also a theory of subjectification.[85]

It was not yet possible, put simply, to inhabit the conditions of second-order observation: that, first, whatever is said is said by an observer; that, second, whatever is said is said to an observer; and hence that, third, reflexivity (observing the turn) is not the logical paradox on which the operation of the system founders, but, instead, the condition of possibility that founds it.[86] The modalization of the world is part of that—and the move to periodization via observing modes of seeing. So epochs appear as "turns" (in turn, the linguistic turn, the cultural turn, the affective turn)—and thus appear as bound to the distinct forms of media that steer them (from print culture to the age of technical reproducibility to digital culture). This is what it looks like to become acclimated to systems that feed back outcomes into inputs and do so by observing the turn and observing themselves doing so—hence entering into the sequestered, contingent, and self-conditioned form of Gesellschaftsspiele, and other social games.

These are the conditions of Highsmith's murder games—and what might be called Highsmith's private cold war. If there is any doubt about this, the novel makes the connection as explicit as possible. The novel does so via the figure of one of its minor "donor" characters, the facilitator of the recidivist action of the novel: Gauthier is "the art-supply man" for the dealer in art forgeries and the dealer in art frames. It is in the artwork, of course—in terms of the art system as system—that these matters of medium and form, intention and self-description appear at their purest.

This is a novel about an artificial, forged, and self-predicated world—with all its train and air and postal schedules; all its little regimes of body and message transport; its self-assessing tecchniques—from readouts of blood counts to the feedback of news reports on the murders to reports on that; its maps and "paper places" and art shops and frame stores; its "endless corridors" administered by "omniscient specialists" in life and death; and, in sum, all its observations on these modes of observing. Given all this, consider this description of "the art-supply man"—a man with an artificial eye and the kind of brain that comes with it: "Gauthier's shiny glass eye did not laugh but looked out from his head with a bold stare, as if there were a different brain from Gauthier's behind that eye, a computer kind of brain that at once could know everything, if someone just set the programming" (RG, 31). These are the anthropotechnics (art with humans) of a second order of vision, a second order of seeing and knowing via the protocols of a program: a complex system of discrete processes, and exchanges between human senses and media, that is also a differential relation of observation to itself.[87]

The novel could not be more emphatic about this. It is, for one thing, the idiom and technique of war games. In case we missed that, "A bomb through that window" is called "Unthinkable" (RG, 189). The observation of what cannot be observed—"double-think" (233)—is named. "Thinking the unthinkable" emerges as the code of Cold War thinking.[88] We might (pace Luhmann) call literary reflection on the form of modernity exasperated with the failure in its own self-description "postmodern" or "metanarrative." Or we might say that it represents something like the R&D phase of R&D.[89] This may be self-evident. But the manner in which it aligns art, war, and games is more complicated. It's to that, and to some of its new forms of life today, that I now want to turn.

SIX

THE NATURAL HISTORY
OF ARTIFICIAL LIFE

In this chapter I set out how the social games we have previewed achieve practical reality in concert with each other. In this way, they enter into the complex choreography of the epoch of social systems. In this way too, the aesthetic category of suspense opens branches throughout the social field and its institutions. So enfranchised, it becomes a way of "playing society," and doing that across the disciplinary fields of work and play, caring and learning, exchanging and creating. What emerges—in the precise terms of Kazuo Ishiguro's *Never Let Me Go*—is a radically formal way of *deferring* death and life, via a teachable, and wholesale, art with humans.

Life during Wartime

First, a modern art of war, or world of warcraft. Consider another account of a game strategy for thinking the unthinkable: the *New Yorker* writer Malcolm Gladwell's best seller, *Blink: The Power of Thinking without Thinking*. Gladwell presents a series of case studies that amount to something like a "gee whiz" version of systems theory. In this, it is directly in line with what we might call "the *New Yorker* uncanny." The same could be said about another *New Yorker* account, James Surowiecki's adept *The Wisdom of Crowds*— which might have been titled "the wisdom of systems." These case studies proceed via an italicized toggling between close-ups (little anecdotes) and pattern (the big picture) and, by way of these shifts in scale, the first, as if spontaneously, seems to give the second. A common technique. But in these cases the narrative form of that process arrives as its topic—the power of thinking without thinking, the wisdom of crowds. If this is a "house" style, it is one acclimatized to systems thinking and its popularization: to a reflexive pedagogy. In both examples, a recursive and systemic ecology of ignorance (unthinking or nonknowing) yields wisdom, or, at the least, the more trivial version of that called information. It allows for what Gladwell defines as "creating structure for spontaneity"—the paradox of a meaning that crystallizes without intention, and its implications.[1]

It is the art of war that comes into view in Gladwell's central chapter, "Paul Van Riper's Big Victory." More precisely, what comes into focus is the war gamer's way of creating form in improvisation: the surprise of thinking without thinking that makes for blink-of-an-eye "pattern recognition," and so decision, in games of strategy. Van Riper, a veteran Vietnam War battalion commander and former head of the Marine Corps University at Quantico, was recruited to play the "rogue commander" in the most expensive war game in history: Millennium Challenge '02, which cost a quarter of a billion dollars to play out, and amounted to a "full dress rehearsal for war" (that is to say, for the invasion of Iraq in 2003).

Here is the way one of his soldiers described Van Riper in action:

> He was always out in the field . . . figuring out what to do next. If he had an idea and he had a scrap of paper in his pocket, he would write that idea on the scrap, and then, when we had a meeting, he would pull out seven or eight pieces of paper. Once he and I were in the jungle a few yards from a river, and he wanted to reconnoiter over certain areas, but he couldn't get the view he wanted. . . . Damned if he didn't take off his shoes, dive into the river, swim out to the middle, and tread water so he could see downstream. (*Blink*, 100)

There is something of a resemblance between this double-entry system of observation and act, seeing and recording, and, say, Gauthier's computer eye. But there is something of a resemblance as well to the patients that Jean-Martin Charcot, in his account of fin-de-siècle maladies of energy and will ("fatigue amnesia"), described as "l'homme du petit papier": the man too depleted to remember his symptoms at the moment who arrived for sessions "with slips of paper or manuscripts endlessly listing [his] ailments"—in that he knew how he felt and what he saw only by reading about it.[2] The recording of the action enters into it, such that the act consists both of itself and its registration. What appears, in Charcot, as a modern malady of agency and intention here, in Riper, reappears as the art of thinking without thinking, and a selective adaptation to the second machine age.

A cycling between observing and recording—but the circuit of a reflexivity indifferent to self-reflection. There is, therefore, a routinized nondistinction between training and fighting ("*believe it or not* . . . we would practice platoon and squad tactics or bayonet training in the bush . . . and we did it on a routine basis" [*Blink*, 103–4, my emphasis]). The distinction between dress rehearsal and act—or between war game and war—is simply exorcized: "Sometimes when Blue Team fired a missile or launched a plane, a missile actually fired or a plane actually took off, and whenever it didn't, one of forty-two separate computer models simulated each of those actions so precisely that the people in the war room often couldn't tell it wasn't real" (104).

Model and act rotate in turn in these war game scenarios.[3] The games themselves migrate between military and entertainment modes (what Tim Lenoir calls "the military-entertainment complex"). (Millennium Challenge was not just a run-up to the war in Iraq; its engineered outcome scripted the war plan—and its embedded coverage and its marketing.) We know too the sequestration, or self-suspension, of game worlds and their rules of irrelevance: the war gamers set up shop in "huge, windowless rooms known as test bays" (*Blink*, 103) in the Joint Forces Command Building—windowless black-boxed monads (103). Thus, Van Riper notes that the "only difference" between stock traders on Wall Street and those who "played war games on computer" is that "one group bet on money and the other bet on lives" (108). These self-observations are by now familiar enough. The war game, in short, is a "management system" (119) mixing "complexity theory and military strategy" (106). But it may be useful—in setting out the terms of what I earlier described as a second-order intention and its implications—to stay a little longer with the terms that make up this worldview.

For one thing, the scenography operates, and describes its operations, in terms of a predictive and recursive guidance system—but one, we are told, without "specific guidance," intentions, or effects:

> I mean that the overall guidance and the intent were provided by me and the senior leadership . . . but the forces in the field wouldn't depend on . . . orders coming from the top. . . . I never wanted to hear the word "effects." . . . We would not get caught up in any of these mechanistic processes. (*Blink*, 118)

That Van Riper uses these terms—intent, guidance, effect—loosely is precisely the point, though it isn't, of course, his point. The war game is one of the social games in which one must observe what the opponent observes or can't observe, and whether or not he can observe that: "What my brother always says is, 'hey, say you are looking at a chess board. Is there anything you can't see? No. But are you guaranteed to win? Not at all, because you can't see what the other guy is thinking'" (*Blink*, 144).[4] It's the form and interest of these games that concerns me for the moment. This form and interest become clearest in terms of the situation of war as, in Gladwell's way of putting it, an "art form."

To understand the "internal computer" that creates structure for improvisation or spontaneity—what Gladwell calls the power of thinking without thinking—is to understand that improvisation "is an art form governed by a series of rules" (*Blink*, 113). Such an art form governed by serial rules is part of an aesthetic of Cold War modernism. One historian of Cold War brinkmanship—the "intuitive science" of thermonuclear war—lucidly sets out the protocols of analysis sponsored by the RAND corporation: "Setting the terms for gaming and man-machine simulations in the 1950s and later, RAND analysts commended these techniques for sharpening intuition, stimulating creativity, offering insight into complex fields of interaction, exploring intersubjective exchanges in an interdisciplinary research setting, instilling tolerance for ambiguity and uncertainties, and heightening sensitivity to the practitioners' own blindspots and rigidities."[5] (Who said English majors weren't being prepared for the real world?) That setting of the terms puts R&D in the orbit of an aesthetic modernism premised on ambiguity, uncertainty, and paradox (which then, via heightened self-reflexivity and sensitivity to the practitioner's own blindness and insight, can always be deconstructed).[6]

We might see this as another of the delays of the second machine age. That's to see modern literature—or literature from the standpoint of modernity—as something of a preadaptive advance on the social systems of reflexive modernity (an advance that can then be played out with real social consequences). Yet that's why it takes until the development of cybernetics for the self-evidence of autopoietic and recursive literary form to become evident, or self-evident. In this way the little game world of the poem or novel (like the little game worlds of the world) may realize modern social forms—as an exceptional and at the same time exemplary case. The nonrecognition of that may seem as strange today as the prolonged inability to understand information processing as real work (the thermodynamics paradox of Maxwell's demon) seemed yesterday.

Or, consider warcraft as a civilian game world: the online multiplayer game World of Warcraft (WOW). WOW is often referred to as a "game" but is more exactly a nonlinear and simulated world that contains games within it. The world-like and the gamelike continuously copy or solicit each other. The promise of such war games, as Alexander Galloway sets out in some detail, is not one of "revealing something as it is, but in simulating a thing so effectively that 'what it is' becomes what we make and picture."[7]

Hence it is not merely a matter of simulation but a matter of bit-by-bit construction, via a "grinding" processing of information. This suggests that wow is "not simply a fantasy landscape of dragons and epic weapons but a factory floor, an information-age sweatshop, custom tailored in every detail" (*The Interface Effect*, 44). No doubt the detailed, repetitive information gathering, token systems, reward levels, and so on betoken the self-induced and self-assessed nature of the official world today and its dispersed work spaces. (The soft work economy is familiar enough.) But the solicitation to simulate, or to re-create—such that the world becomes what we make and what we picture—is here, in its runescapes and medievalisms, not merely an instance (to borrow Habermas's term) of a playful "refeudalization" of the information age and its scenographies.[8]

The interface in wow means that at every point the act or decision is accompanied by a commentary feeding back on itself, by the screen's "thin, two-dimensional overlay containing icons, text, progress bars, and numbers" (*The Interface Effect*, 42). Yet there is too a scientological ambiance in these fusions of fitness (health), science fiction, ego-technic paraphernalia, religiosity, and the scaling of level, via exteriorized achievement. Icons, and their copying, take part, we know, in what they picture. Here we see icons in which the act, its depiction, and its outcome enter into rotation, in the form of a loyalty program: microtheaters of suspense and vertical or upward mobility, vocational ethics in ascetic repetition. (It is "my practice" in the sense that devotees of spin classes and power yoga give to monetized forms of ascetic training: a programmatic and enclaved devotion to insensitivity training, timed and calibrated fitness-survival routines, and a work-ethical self-boosterism. These are Ballardian scenarios: locally-sourced surrealisms.)

Paradoxes of a second-order intention are here reenacted and merge with its scenes. One moves, in short, from dice games to games of strategy; from the calculus of probabilities to complex systems; from the great probability salesman of the nineteenth century, Pierre-Simon Laplace, to the great cybernetics booster of the twentieth, Norbert Wiener. And so on. I have tracked elsewhere the first stage, via Poe and his advent crime story, "The Mystery of Marie Rogêt"—a story about structure and motive, in the suspense genre's calculus of probabilities.[9] The second, in these pages, via Highsmith's form games, among others. In such extraversions of the official world and its states of suspense, one can either start from the form side or from the intent side. Either way, one keeps discovering that shape and motive, form and intent, keep shifting sides. This is tautological in the same sense as another common game about intent and outcome: the very young child who plays hide-and-seek by saying, "I'm going to hide here, now you try to find me." (But one scarcely suspends the play on that count.)

In an autotropic and self-turned world, reality has to be made to appear—as it is created by the work of art itself. The world that appears in the world legislates its autonomy by remaking what it sees as what it generates, stages, and records. That makes for the paradox of the work of art, as at once exception and instance, in the systems epoch. "In explaining the work of art," as Niklas Luhmann frames it, "one frequently draws on the artist's *intention* in producing the work, but this is trivial, a tautological explanation, because the intent must be feigned, while its psychological correlates remain inaccessible."[10] The artwork can only be comprehended as intentional. But "this raises the issue of how to dissolve the tautological construct of productive intent and unfold this tautology in ways that yield intelligible representations." The work's "artificiality provokes the question of purpose" in that it displays "something unexpected, something inexplicable, or as it is often put, something new." In doing so, it creates structure for spontaneity (*AASS*, 309). In short, the artwork works as black box.

It is not merely that the demarcation zones of the artwork and the official world resemble each other in their internality and self-description. In understanding modern "art as a social system," Luhmann traces in detail, one understands that "the art system realizes society in its own realm as an exemplary case" (*AASS*, 309).[11] The autonomy in self-reflection of the artwork is exemplary in that it models a self-modeling world. That means the "theme of reflection does not define the meaning of the autonomy of art, but the meaning of the doubling of reality (*Realitätsverdoppelung*) in which this autonomy established itself" (312–13).

Perhaps such a rough redescription of reflection has by now taken on, in my account, a bit more precision. It may be worth restating premises that are now better furnished. We know that the work of art performs its self-reflexive and self-contained, internalized and stand-alone, character. We know too then, that the work of art appears as both exceptional and exemplary today. It is exceptional in its autonomous relation to the outside world. It is exemplary in that it provides the very model, a working model, of the autonomization of that world. The playful doubling of the world in the second modernity makes for what Simmel described as the emergence of "autonomous forms of sociation." These autonomous forms of social interaction resemble form games: "The more profound, double sense of 'social games' (*Gesellschaftspiele*) is that not only the game is played in *a society* (as its external condition) but that, with its help, people actually 'play' society" (Simmel, SGS, 50).

So it is perhaps worth looking at, to close this chapter on the natural history of artificial life, a recent and exceptional example of its anthropo-technical art. The final section of this part centers on the matter of "actually" playing society in relation to the situation of the work of art today. Its focus is Kazuo Ishiguro's 2005 "clone" novel, *Never Let Me Go*. This is a novel that, in the programmatic character of its secret games and narrative practices, is an experiment in how black boxes work—not least in the prefabricated worlds of the contemporary genre novel.

Secluded Education

Outside, out there, they sell everything.
—Kazuo Ishiguro, *Never Let Me Go*

The black box is a conceptual machine that makes possible "that most magical of tricks, a way of acting confidently with/from the unknown/unknowable."[12] Consider a simple example of black box theory, this one from Ross Ashby's *Introduction to Cybernetics* (1956):

> The child who tries to open a door has to manipulate the handle (the input) so as to produce the desired movement at the latch (the output); and he has to learn how to control the one by the other without being able to see the internal mechanism that links them. In our daily lives we are confronted by every turn with systems whose internal mechanisms are not fully open to inspection, and which must be treated by the methods appropriate to the Black Box.[13]

The difference between input and output means that "before and after" is a difference that makes a difference, and the causal connection between them—between internal mechanisms and external action—hidden but reliable, and workable.[14]

These black boxes are ecologies of ignorance—ways of acting confidently, and building descriptions of the world, out of the unknown, and out of "knowing about nonknowing"—since there is no alternative anyway.[15] But this does not mean the exorcism of alternatives. It means a training, an exercising, and a practicing: a learning for life.

For example, one way of making use of the seeing machine, or panopticon, set out in Foucault's account of Bentham's architectural mechanism might be to "try out pedagogical experiments":

in particular to take up once again the well-debated problem of secluded education, by using orphans. One would see what would happen when, in their sixteenth or eighteenth year, they were presented with other boys or girls; one could verify whether, as Helvetius thought, anyone could learn anything; one would follow "the genealogy of every observable idea"; one could bring up different children according to different systems of thought, making certain children believe that two and two did not make four or that the moon is a cheese, then put them together when they are twenty or twenty-five years old; one would then have discussions that would be worth a great deal more than the sermons or lectures on which so much money is spent; one would have at least an opportunity of making discoveries in the domain of metaphysics.[16]

Hence, in these experiments, one can make persons believe, say, that $2 + 2 = 5$. But this necessarily means something different than that power = knowledge. (That is, it's not $2 + 2 = 5$ in Orwell's sense.) To the extent that such experiments issue in discoveries and not simply tautologies, this means more than that "knowledge follows the advances of power."[17]

Another way of saying this is that the little experiments that Foucault here describes are games of strategy: the seeing machine must deal with what the machine has already seen and already said, and take cognizance of that. (In Luhmannese, action is lifted out of action by action.) This is not an interference with how modern social systems work. It's how they work: it is, in Simmel's sense, the principle of "autonomous forms of sociality." In short, the seeing machine, via a reflexive monitoring of action, is a black box to the very extent that the players see that too. Or, as the narrator of *Never Let Me Go* puts it, "We lost ourselves completely in our game. . . . And yet, all the time, I think we must have had an idea of how precarious the foundations of our fantasy were, because we always avoided any confrontation": "we all played our part . . . in making it last as long as possible."[18]

"Sex in the Outside World": Art with Humans in *Never Let Me Go*

The precarious prolonging of the play, in *Never Let Me Go*, is a prolongation of knowing not knowing. Ishiguro is perhaps the great contemporary novelist of the habitus of nonknowing, and its institutionalizations. (And, on that count, if no other, "Jamesian"). The novel is premised on islanded ecologies of ignorance. More exactly, its premises are the microinstitutions—gamelike, sequestered, autistic—that proliferate across the social field: that is, across the isotopic fields of working, playing, buying, selling, caring, and learning.

The small worlds of the novel—working models both of the world and in it—include the playing field and the boarding school and the ubiquitous hospital. They include "the Sales" and "the Exchanges," with their intramural "system of tokens as currency" (NLMG, 38)—which is "how we got hold of things from outside" (41). They include too, and crucially for the novel, the art world: which is to say, the system that determines what will count as art and what will not (what will be taken into the "Collection"). The art system is explicitly "like a miniature version of one of our Exchanges" (31).

Each resembles the other in that each is self-determined, autonomous, self-evaluative: each is, as Ishiguro concisely puts it, a "smart cosy self-contained world" (NLMG, 157–58). Together these self-contained, self-similar but discrete systems make up a joint world. The sales and exchanges are how we get hold of things from outside. The art system is how we get hold of things from inside: "your art will reveal your inner selves . . . what you were like inside" (254, 260).

This begins to bring into focus, from another vantage, the paradoxical situation of the work of art today: a stand-alone autonomy in an official world—one trending toward what I will call the autonomization of every-thing (see part V). *Never Let Me Go* takes this up as a sort of thought ex-periment with clones: their artificiality, their art, and their status as things designed and "grown" to be sold for parts. (Growing clones grows, in the pristine culture of capitalism, the economy.) The art world is like a miniature version of the exchanges in that the economic, like the aesthetic, domain is strictly self-conditioned: an internalized system operating in its own curren-cies, or tokens, and so within its own zones of action.

The novel, in short—and not least in the strict formalism of its exercise in "alien" point-of-view narration—sets out its relation to the strict socializa-tion of the social that is a driver of the official world. The novel does not look to get past that limit: it stages it. (As in Ishiguro's earlier novel, *A Pale View of Hills*, the view is paled: fenced and bounded.) It does so in the distinction, or withdrawal of the distinction, between bodies and institutions in what the situationists called "the overdeveloped world."[19]

The experiments in secluded education in the novel—centrally, the boarding school, Hailsham, a sort of extended nursery, that centers it—each provide something of a limit case of persons brought up according to dif-ferent systems of thought. The limit case in point resembles in part "playing in a sandpit," with all its sandbox elements. It resembles, alternatively, the playing of a "chess game" and the attempt to "teach the game." Playing it out is not exactly a matter of knowing its rules, since the chess game is both played—observed and taught—without quite understanding the rules of the game. Instead, one observed the play, or made moves, and bootstrapped the way things work from that. (The game is neither reasonable nor unreasonable, and has no grounds: "it is there, like one's life.")[20]

The novel thus proliferates maps and models of how to play its games, from "scaled down [and scaled up] versions" (*NLMG*, 66) to "life-size skeletons" (83) to "secret games" (90). It multiplies small worlds. In doing so, it proliferates scale models of a self-modeling world—and cases of defective knowledge.[21]

(One template of this game with unknown rules, and reflexive ignorance, is given relatively early on by Henry Adams, in his account of the realization of a catastrophic modernity: "Had he been consulted, would he have cared to play the game at all, holding such cards as he held, and suspecting that the game was to be one of which neither he nor any one else back to the beginning of time knew the rules or the risks or the stakes?"[22] The *Education* thus sets out, as catastrophe, the pedagogical principles of what are by now the "normal accidents" of the risk society, its acclimatizations to secondhand nonexperience and its ecologies of ignorance. For Adams, this a situation newly perspicuous and observable—and so epochal.)

The players, in *Never Let Me Go*, turn out to "play their parts" in another sense too. It turns out that these demarcated and outlined institutions, and the persons who grow up in them, are literally the parts—or, we discover, "spare parts"—of a world. The test case in making up persons according to different systems of thought is here literalized and radicalized, in that it's not quite clear whether these characters are exactly persons, or, instead, speaking body parts. Horror stories realize bodily states in external reality and literalize figures of speech in concrete form. This is a horror novel (the factory farming of human beings for parts) presented as a campus novel. Horror fiction is a literalization genre, it exteriorizes moods in the world. Here economic autonomization—the actually existing capitalism sometimes called neoliberalism—appears, as Marx expressed it, to achieve practical truth in "the most modern society" in its very indifference "towards particular kinds of labour"—here, the self-terminating labor of self-donation.[23]

The schoolchildren are, we learn—or learn that we more or less already knew, but deferred knowing—"clones—or *students*, as we preferred to call you" (*NLMG*, 261). They are grown, and sold, for spare parts. These spare parts are the "donations" that will "complete" their lives and prolong the lives of others. The "first-person" narration is spoken by one of the students, named "Kathy H." Hence she is named (without familial name) as if she were a real character in a realist novel. Or, in this case—in that she is an artificial person or clone—a fictitious or imaginary person with a real body. The narrative mode of this "first person" novel, its way of seeing and knowing, is in effect a way of not seeing and not knowing. Or, to use again one of the novel's code words, or terms of art, the mode of the narrative is a form of "deferral."

No doubt this coupling of species life and institutional forms of life lends itself to biopolitical analysis. No doubt too it epitomizes how processes of modernization stipulate the gamelike and artificial character of a social order that nonetheless posits its biological characterization. (This is by now a commonplace via the work of Roberto Esposito and Giorgio Agamben, and, of course, Michel Foucault's later work.)[24] *Never Let Me Go* is certainly a story about contemporary anthropotechnics of life and death—technologically enhanced, or subtracted, human life, or the continuous transformations of life forms into forms of life. One form this takes, in its second modernization, appears in the insulated islands of a therapeutic archipelago of pampered, or prostheticized, or harvested bodies. Or, as Pfizer Pharmaceuticals expressed it in an advertising campaign, situating these life narratives on its corporate ground floor: "Life is our life's work."

But my interest here, and the real interest of the novel, is somewhat different, and somewhat less self-evident. In *Never Let Me Go*, the problem of the artificial or biological character of persons or institutions is posed in terms of the place of art in this type of society. In this way it takes as its formal, even technical, subject, the natural history of artificial life. The art world, we have seen, is one of the artificial small worlds of the novel. But not one among others: creating "your art," and then showing it on the market, is meant to reveal "your inner self" (NLMG, 175, 254). The work of art is seen as an exchangeable, and collectible, token of personhood. It makes self-description and its observation possible, or compelling. It does so in that it is seen to make interiors available to perception and communication: it will "tell [us] what you were like inside" (260).

But how this clone art communicates, or tells, inside stories is then more complex still. Consider, for example, one character's pictures—his "imaginary animals" (the only clone art detailed in the novel):

That was when I first saw [Tommy's] animals. When he'd told me about them in Norfolk, I'd seen in my mind scaled-down versions of the sort of pictures we'd done when we were small. So I was taken aback at how densely detailed each one was. In fact, it took a moment to see they were animals at all. The first impression was like one you'd get if you took the back off a radio set: tiny canals, weaving tendons, miniature screws and wheels were all drawn with obsessive precision, and only when you held the page away could you see it was some kind of armadillo, say, or a bird. (NLMG, 187)

The body-machine complex in this multiscaled picture could not be more explicit. But the form it takes—its scale-shifting, time-shifting, trompe l'oeil effects—is densely detailed. The "scaled-down versions" are like the drawings made "when we were small." What was "seen in my mind" is not what is seen "in fact." The first impression is that one is looking at the inside of a little machine, like a radio set—but one that indifferently interweaves somatic and machinic functions (canals and tendons, screws and wheels, canalized and woven together). The drawing on the page seems at first to indicate what a special kind of machine—one that talks and plays—looks like inside. But, then, held at a distance, what this animal looks like. So it shows what these imaginary animals look like. And that what they look like is what they look like inside. In sum: a machine opened up to view, but one that talks, plays, brings news of the outside, or sings—like, say, the recorded and replayed song that gives the novel its title. It has then the look of some kind of animal (a Cartesian machine, perhaps, but one that communicates), but an animal that looks outside what it looks like inside. That releases all the paradoxes that accrue when one imagines or refers to the surface or interior of a body, or the surface or interior of a work of art.

Their art, for the students, or clones, in the novel, is to show what they are inside. In doing so, their art is to show that what they are inside is not reducible to the parts inside them: if "art bares the soul of the artist" (NLMG, 254), it shows that they have souls, and so a soul/body problem just like everyone else, or like real people. Yet what is startling and exciting about Tommy's imaginary animals is not exactly that. It's that "it's like they come to life by themselves" (178). They seem not merely lifelike but autogenic: they come alive and "grow" on their own. They have the self-propagating and magical properties of a thing that artificially comes to life, like a black box.

"The more excited he got telling me about his animals," Kathy reports, "the more uneasy I was growing" (NLMG, 179). It is not merely that growing here is uneasy because it means coming to term or "completing," in the novel's terms of art (or growing old and dying, in more generally applicable ones). As Stanislaw Lem's posthuman machine Golem expresses it to his merely human students: "When man wants to learn about himself, he must move circuitously, he must explore himself and penetrate from the outside, with instruments and hypotheses, for your genuinely immediate world is the outside."[25] Or, as the cybernetics theorist Ross Ashby expresses it, "That homo has a brain, no more entitles him to assume he knows how he thinks than possession of a liver entitles him to assume that he knows how he metabolises."[26]

See this another way. The students, or clones, in the novel are taught to believe that their works of art will show what they are like inside, bare their souls. But we don't, of course, read Ishiguro to see his inner self, any more than Ishiguro's technical experiment (the first-person narration of a nonperson) is meant to show what he's like inside. Kathy's talkative and deferring narrative, as a fictitious person, is made up of the stock of phrases and the stock ways of seeing and evaluating that she's taken in, above all, from all the novels she's read (her primary access to the outside world, but allied in the novel to TV, magazines, billboards, and plate-glass store and office displays). The students in the novel are students of the novel (Kathy is a Victorianist), writing essays that they fail to complete.

The novel then reprises the history of the novel, which from the start posits an identity between being a reader and being, or becoming, an individual. It is a communicative medium (like, say, a radio set) and an ego-technic medium. The novel is concerned, from the start, about the beneficial or pernicious effects of novel reading—its surrogate sensualities and sponsored artificialism—and the risks to behavior as an effect of print and reading. The novel as genre from the start is concerned with showing readers how they might lead their lives by showing how a life is something that can be led. For example, the career paths that lead the students in Ishiguro's novel from one stage of life to another: the shape of a career that is, however irrational, well plotted and undebatably professional, and so a self-persuasive way to plan and to spend one's life.[27]

It makes perfect, if tautological, sense then that novels have lent themselves to game theory, in that novels are working parts of social games, which include models of themselves. In game-theoretical accounts of the novel, there is often a centering on the intimacy of communication media to dangerous or erotic liaisons (from the postal system and epistolary novel on). The novel, again from the start—but perhaps not at the end (there's a last time for everything)—sets out the nature of an artificial and reading world. *Never Let Me Go* plays this out as a sort of endgame, and does so in its line-by-line explicitation of the communicative action of the novel.

In that the novel is a technical experiment in point of view (the first-person narration of a nonperson, or an imaginary one), every description of action and interaction in the novel is a self-description of its mode of depiction.[28] We expect novels to reuse reference as self-reference, as we expect novels to use the distinction between utterance and information as a way of measuring characters and placing them. (Or, as in Austen novels, to make an understanding of that distinction and reunion of utterance and information its happy outcome.) In system-theoretical terms, communication grasps a difference between the information value of the content and all the reasons for which the content is being uttered (the difference between information and utterance). Only via that distinction can the communication—and understanding—take place. The novel thematizes the distinction between information (what is said) and utterance (how or why it is said), in relation to character interaction but also in its form of narration (tone or "person"). In this way understanding or misunderstanding can be communicated about but only under the specific conditions of "the autopoiesis of the system communication":

> The utterance "You don't understand me" therefore remains ambivalent and, at the same time, communicates this ambivalence. On the one hand, it means, "You are not ready to accept what I want to say to you," and attempts to provoke the admission of this fact. On the other hand, it is the utterance of the information that communication cannot be continued under this condition of not understanding. And, thirdly, it is a continuation of communication.[29]

The novel, Ishiguro's, provides a way of dealing with these practical difficulties in communication about communication by staging them, in relation to playing society, its art and its economics. It plays out the consequences of the distinction among the three components of communication—utterance, information, and understanding—as the story itself, so that it enters the plot. When, for example, Kathy H. on the first page of the novel says, "but actually they want me to go on for another eight months," she is talking about her career as carer and not the preallocated, counted months of her life. When, on the last page of the novel, she "turned back to the car, to drive off to wherever it was I was supposed to be," she is not saying that she yet again detoured, reversed, and deferred, and that, in the self-contained zone in which she is "to be," her direction is the directive of the perfectly rational irrational system that presupposes and disposes (of) her. The perfect poise of the narrative is also the abstractness, or generic quality, of Ishiguro's locales and places, and its at once colloquial and strangely impersonal idiom. This is an idiom particular to no one in particular, as if designed for machine translation, or the conversation of media types. The surfacing of the generic lends at every moment a formal and repeating quality to every statement and action (sometimes thematized as, say, a servant's habitus of impersonality, or, here, a clone's secluded education).

The entire novel then is a sustained suspension between utterance and information and an understanding of misunderstanding that is the novel's communication about communication. The novel then could have been called *What Kathy Knew*. But it is called instead *Never Let Me Go*. The name of the novel copies the name of a song on a cassette, first an "original copy" (yes, we get it) and then another copy, to replace the first that Kathy replays. It is a love song—"Baby, baby, never let me go"—that Kathy H. mistakes as a song about mother and child.

The continuous transformation of life into forms of life, heterorestrictions into self-restrictions, is most explicit, given where the clones are coming from, in relation to the autonomization of sex, in the novel:

> We had to be extremely careful about having sex in the outside world, especially with people who weren't students, because out there sex meant all sorts of things. Out there people were even fighting and killing each other over who had sex with whom. And the reason it meant so much— so much more than, say, dancing or table-tennis—was because the people out there were different from us students: they could have babies from sex. That was why it was so important to them, this question of who did it with whom. And even though, as we knew, it was completely impossible for any of us to have babies, out there, we had to behave like them. We had to respect the rules, and treat sex as something pretty special. (*NLMG*, 84)

The world "out there" differs from the indoor world of the students, and so differs from the little game world of, "say, dancing or table tennis," in that the sex act can "mean all sorts of things"—killing, fighting, babies—distinct from or exceeding the act itself. The rules out there, that make sex special, differ from the rules in here, in which bodies are no more than exchangeable tokens, or moves, in a game or dance or marketplace.

In table tennis or dancing, interior states are irrelevant and acts and outcomes—like the prescriptive, coordinated, and reenacted movements in the systemically-managed workplace of the second modernity—don't express meaning: acts and outcomes are strictly internal to the composition of motions or moves, the self-conditioned internality, of the games in which they take place. They don't mean all sorts of things in that they don't strictly speaking mean anything. They are moves in sequence that lead to other moves.

Hence the dream the clones have to live in the outside world is, not surprisingly, the dream of working in "an open-plan office." That is, a space of planned openness, such that exteriors are repositioned and internalized: the open planned.[30] The modular and gamelike zones of the student world—the playing field or the Exchange, which is a miniature version of the economic system, or the art system, which is, we recall, "a miniature version of the Exchange"—are each ruled and self-conditioned, autonomous and formal.

The autonomization of sex from biological consequences that exceed the act is, of course, not a departure from that but the realization of that. (It is one thing to optionalize the connection between sex and reproduction, another to decouple them.) The autotropic conditions of the official world are modeled to scale in the "smart, cosy, self-contained" modular precincts of *Never Let Me Go*.

For the moment, recall that the archaic etymological root of "life"—*lib*—means what remains: what continues, or persists, particularly after battle or war, and so what goes on in its aftermath. Life, on this view, is the remainder or the remains of the day.[31] At the end of the novel Kathy goes outside, and describes that, and the ways of this world: "[I] found that I was standing before acres of ploughed earth. There was a fence keeping me from stepping onto the field. . . . I didn't know where I was. . . . I just waited a bit, then turned back to the car, to drive off to wherever it was I was supposed to be" (285). The overturned and delineated world, and its paled habitus (ruled ground, on either side of the fence), and the turning back: these are Ishiguro's subjects, from *A Pale View of Hills* on, along with the subject of art. The official world erects innumerable scored and repeating spaces. That might (as Tom McCarthy puts it) then "become about art." Which is to say, in the "autogenous atmosphere" of a greenhouse and self-growing world,[32] "maybe," as Kathy H. puts it, "the art's just one out of all kinds of different ways."

IV • SUSPENDED WORLDS

Men in Self-Curved Space

SEVEN

THE WALL OF THE WORLD

It would be difficult to deny that in our present historical circumstances we are very concerned about not simply what modern society is but how it observes and describes itself and its environment.
—Niklas Luhmann, "Deconstruction as Second-Order Observing"

He did not know that there was any outside at all. . . . Suddenly he found himself at the mouth of the cave. The wall, inside which he had thought himself, as suddenly leaped back before him to an immeasurable distance. Unlike any other wall with which he had had experience, this wall seemed to recede from him as he approached. No hard surface collided with the tender little nose he thrust out tentatively before him. The substance of the wall seemed as permeable and yielding as light. And as condition, in his eyes, had the seeming of form, so he entered into what had been wall to him and bathed in the substance that composed it. It was bewildering. He was sprawling through solidity. . . . At first, the wall had leaped beyond his vision. He now saw it again; but it had taken upon itself a remarkable remoteness. Also, its appearance had changed. It was now a variegated wall, composed of the trees that fringed the stream, the opposing mountain that towered above the trees, and the sky that out-towered the mountain . . . [it was] the wall of the world.
—Jack London, *White Fang* (1906)

Why do we play practical jokes?

Consider this prank played out toward the end of World War II, a bit of black comedy against a general background of methodical horror. The Allied air forces were launching bombing raids on German factories with a regular ferocity. The Germans came up with a plan to deceive Allied intelligence by constructing artificial wooden factories painted in industrial colors, with the intent of diverting enemy ordinance onto waste targets. In short order, the British saw through the deception and sent a single Avro Lancaster bomber to the industrial area near the city of Duisburg. The bomber's mission: to drop a wooden bomb on one of the fake factories.

The practical joke—a joke that combines a statement and a practice—may be a timeless social ritual. But it may from time to time assume new forms of life, from, say, a wooden horse and the fall of the walls of Troy to a wooden bomb.

It may take on the form too of a worldview instrument, a condition and a form. This is the case not least in a modernity marked by the stigma of contingency, and so one that plays endlessly on the status of the distinction between fictional reality and real reality. Consider, for instance, a more extended example, this time an event that at first looked to some like a practical joke: the sudden fall of the Berlin Wall, already now more than a quarter century ago.[1]

The Berlin Wall, which had divided the city for twenty-eight years, fell on a calm mid-November night in 1989. Just before midnight on November 9—in an event that seemed impossible just the day before—the checkpoints gave way to the surge of thousands of East Berliners demanding basic democratic rights and right of way. By 1 A.M. all the borders were opened, and crisis yielded to celebration: huge crowds of Berliners danced on the wall fronting the Brandenburg Gate and "cheered on an endless stream of East Berliners going west. People got together with flowers in their hands and tears in their eyes." The East German prime minister, who earlier that year maintained the wall would stand for another fifty or one hundred years, asked in bewilderment, "Who got us into this mess?" The West German chancellor, at once bewildered and joyful: "That's impossible. That's incredible."[2] The American president—George H. W. Bush, former head of the CIA—seemed as unprepared and as shocked as if Reagan's open sesame to Gorbachev had simply worked after all.

The ground was, of course, prepared for this event, an event that all seemed yet unprepared for. It followed months of crisis, the opening of Hungarian and Czechoslovakian borders, and mass demonstrations—many centered (and this was later for me very close to home), at the Gethsemanekirche in the Prenzlauer Berg district of East Berlin. All this and more made it possible, but by no means inevitable, that a little event—a press conference that contained a routine announcement about a relaxation on East German restrictions on foreign travel—could have a sudden and stunning and transformative effect, one encradled in the complicated situation of the expression of it.

Here I want to rely heavily on (and have already drawn on) the Berlin cognitive scientist Gerd Gigerenzer's concise and evocative account. I do so in part because it provides an adept sampling of events. In larger part because it relies entirely on the second-order observation of the events: an observation of observing systems. In doing so, the presentation of the present makes the staging of events concurrent with them. It indicates then the "background realities" of the staging of action, conflict, suspense, decision, and outcome that concern me here.

But "background" is then not quite the right word here. The situation borders on the elaborate framing of the practical joke—and its somatization of the interactions that compose, or discompose, social systems.

So then (via Gigerenzer), the reported event, and the explicitated media politics of the official world—its regulations, timetables, papers, guidelines, meetings, and internal self-reporting of them:

> At 6:00 P.M. Gunter Schabowski, the new secretary of the East German Central Committee for Media Politics, held an hour-long press conference, only mentioning the new guidelines at the very end. Having missed the government meeting where these had been discussed, the tired-looking and overworked Schabowski hemmed and hawed his way through an obviously unfamiliar text. . . . Attentive listeners recognized that there was not much new—East German politics as usual. An Italian journalist asked when the new regulations would be effective. Schabowski, who did not seem to know, hesitated, looked at his sheet of paper, and then said "right now, immediately." At 7:00 P.M., he ended the conference. (GF, 226)[3]

What followed the press conference—just in time for the evening news—was this: the Italian journalist, semiattentive to what had, or rather had not, happened, immediately rushed a report to his agency, which quickly spread the news that "the Wall fell." At the same time, an American journalist who did not know German, relying on a translation of the press conference, interpreted it to mean that the wall was now open. In short order, NBC broadcast that East Germans could, from the next morning on, cross without restrictions. Next West German TV "under time pressure, summarized the press conference in their own words" and then broadcast Schabowski's "right now, immediately [sofort, unverzüglich]"—setting things in rapid motion. The report ended with the onscreen headline "East Germany Opens Border."

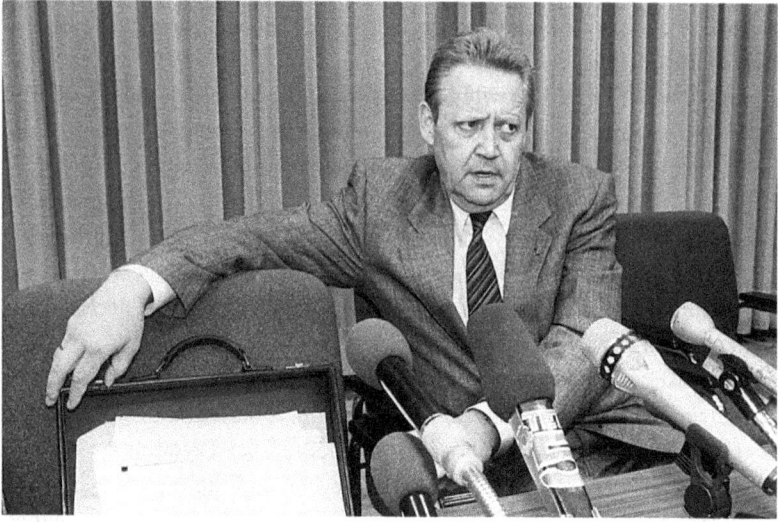

Figure 7.1. The Wall of the World.

The awareness of frames at every point enters into the report, as if it were a semantic experiment in self-grounding. Which is in turn—this is *die Wende*, the turning point—a political experiment in the same. Here one finds something like a pristine, or at least newsworthy, self-legislation of commentary—autonomy in the literal and root sense of the term. It constructs or sponsors—that hesitation is built into its self-persuasive realism—the acts that step by step begin to unfold.

Other news agencies entered this contest in wishful thinking and mistakenly reported that the border was already open. A waiter from a nearby café in West Berlin went with his guests and a tablet of champagne glasses to the perplexed border guards to make a toast to the opening of the Wall. The guards, who thought this was a bad joke [a practical joke then], refused and sent the troublemakers back. Yet the rumor spread to the West German parliament in Bonn, which happened to be meeting at the time. Deeply moved, some with tears in their eyes, the representatives stood up and began to sing the German national anthem. The East Germans who were watching West German television were more than willing to engage in the wishing thinking seeded by the news. A dream infinitely far away seemed to have come true. Thousands and soon tens of thousands of East Berliners jumped into their cars or walked to the border crossings to the West. Yet the guards had, of course, no orders to open the border.

Angry citizens demanded what they believed was their new right of way, and the guards at first refused. Yet in the face of an avalanche of citizens physically pushing at them, an officer at one crossing eventually opened the barriers, fearing that his men would otherwise be trampled to death. Soon all the crossings were open. No shot was fired, no blood was spilled. (*GF*, 227)

Wishful thinking, seeded by the news, with the thinking part installed later. And effects with the intentions put in later too: officials on both West and East sides quickly, of course, took credit for die Wende—the turning point—in German and world history.

The moral of this historical turn, for the cognitive scientist Gigerenzer, is how rumor and wishful thinking, or intuition, work as a form of knowledge and act—"gut feelings can outwit the most sophisticated reasoning." History resembles natural history (germinated seeds or the wall's fall as avalanche). Yes, no doubt. But of course what makes the account itself read like the story of a practical joke with a beautiful outcome is the sustained focus on a media union operating as it were on its own. Game and world, statement and practice, seem to change places: taking note of the fact turns into a fact-producing act, making wishes come true. Peter Jennings, anchoring ABC News in the United States, led with: "Astonishing news from East Germany. In essence, the Berlin Wall doesn't mean anything anymore." (Or, as my son commented on this statement, "That's just semantics.")

In short, what looks at first like a "bad joke" or fictional reality seems to turn into real reality, via the reality of the mass media. Yet if the segmented condition of the contemporary relies for its coordination on the describing and observing done by the mass media, that dependence on communication makes that reality suspect. In this way it resembles the reality of motion pictures; "the distinction between staging and doing is introduced by communication into a reality that is thereby produced."[4] Luhmann summarizes the situation in this way:

> What we know about the world we know from books, from newspapers, from movies, from television—be it German reunification or the living conditions of the pandas, the size of the universe or the increase of violence in Rio de Janeiro or in Los Angeles. To a large extent, mass media create the illusion that we are first-order observers, whereas in fact this is already second-order observing. All three main sectors of mass-media operations—that is, news and reports, advertisements, and entertainment—cooperate in producing a rather coherent image of the

world we are living in. We know that this is preselected information, but we do not and cannot in everyday life reflect upon and control the selectivity of this selection.[5]

The trick, as in motion pictures, is not a simple sustaining of illusion. It consists, instead, in the "rather coherent" image produced in the induced experience of second-order observation as eyewitnessing (and the spectacle of witnessing the faces on which it is registered).

The illusion of first-order observing is secured, above all, in the perpicuousness of border-crossing bodily processes. These mediagenic bodies anchor scenes of massing—its flash-lit mobs. This is the case not exclusively but not least in the scenes that most concern me here (crime, game, suspendedness: upward mobility, men in space, falling). In the instance of the night of November 9, 1989: on the one side, masses of bodies, physical pushing, trampling, pressing, jumping, singing, tears; on the other, a sheet of paper, a press conference, a bad translation, TV news and newspapers, filing deadlines and headline rivalry—and so the media-technics of reference realizing themselves. This is, in effect, a sort of practical joke in reverse, in that the stage set that has been mistaken for the real world is not exposed as a stage set to be exposed but turns out to be the real one. Here, it's not merely then that the reporting of the news becomes the news reported on. (It's not merely that Walter Cronkite—once recognized as America's foremost ontologist—signed off each broadcast with the phrase, "And that's the way it is.") Nor that once the evening news, at that time, went from fifteen minutes to a half hour nightly that there has been exactly a half hour of news every day. And it's not merely that even in the pop-up world of the practical joke.

Keep in mind that the wall did not exactly divide: it enclosed and islanded the western zone, the wall of a world. It was not a stable or a single entity. It was, in Rem Koolhaas's terms, a form of architecture, or antiarchitecture: a situation in slow-motion and uneven evolution, some of it abrupt and clearly planned, some of it improvised. Some parts forty meters tall, other parts a gesture or impromptu decision. There was, as Koolhaas saw it, a high-culture wall and a low-culture part. A first wall, "a decorative pre-wall" that was in fact building façades, empty shop windows, porticos: a Potemkin village in reverse. Behind that there was a second: a strip or moat, here and there concrete slabs; bricks or bricked-in buildings; or a sand zone, with antitank crosses on top, mines below. On Koolhaas's view, a postmodern disportment of pastiched microworlds: a Japanese garden, a minimalist sculpture field, viewing stands; a proscenium, a tourist site, a killing zone. Berlin after the wall has seemed intent on making itself a museum of its own past (Mauerpark, which translates as Wall Park—now erected on the border of Prenzlauer Berg—epitomizes that). The walled city, on this architectural view, seemed a theme park of the antiaesthetic. In places one reality detoured around another, as when a path swerved to conserve a diorama of the old normal, so that a child might bicycle to school each morning. And after the wall too—for a time—the islanded world persisted in another way. For an interval, after the wall and in the narrow interim between reunification and reoccupation as the new capital, it appeared, as Wolfgang Schivelbusch put it, as a "brand-new ghost town": for an interval, Berlin was a sort of gritty and glamorous "Brasilia in the heart of the new Europe."[6]

"A Socialized Trance": The Practical Joke

He shook with repressed laughter for a moment.
—Patricia Highsmith, *Ripley's Game*

She laughed a polite but estranging laugh. . . . She laughed with just a hint of uncontrol in the sound.
—Agatha Christie, *Murder on the Orient Express*

Why then do we play practical jokes? Or, better, how do they look and work now? What is the discrete function of the makeshift microworld of the practical joke in a type of society that realizes itself, wall to wall, by staging its own conditions?

Mystery and suspense stories, for example, often play out like practical jokes, and sometimes reflect on that. Suspense and seriality, repeated repetition, a self-conditioned and generalized autism: the form of mystery or suspense novel is a self-supporting argument for its own reality, and so one of the soliloquys of the official world.

Both Patricia Highsmith's *Ripley's Game* and the first novel of the Ripley series, *The Talented Mr. Ripley*, open with a practical joke—and then generate a worldview from it. My main focus in this chapter is on another crime fiction writer, Agatha Christie. Christie's work and its phenomenal popularity is bound up through and through with the extreme formality by which it frames an autotropic world. But let me lead into that again by way of Highsmith, and by way of a return to a scenario touched on already—the scene of embarrassment, which is, after all, the real object of the practical joke.

The motive for the pathological game that Tom Ripley plays in *Ripley's Game*, for example, is simple enough: "Tom's idea was nothing more than a practical joke, he thought." The idea of entangling an ordinary man in a murder plot—a plot that itself looks like an obsessional game with its own severe rules—was "a nasty one, but the man had been nasty to him." Or, at least, the man's remark at a little social encounter—"Oh, yes, I've heard of you"—keeps playing in Tom's mind. It induces what amounts to a recoil from face-to-face social interaction via its reflection (*he thought*). "What Tom was thinking was": "Was it worth a try? Yes, because Tom had nothing to lose." The "gain," it seems, is that "Tom was amused by his thoughts." And, in response to that internal stimulus, he "eased himself gently from Heloise, so that if he shook with repressed laughter for an instant, he wouldn't awaken her."[7]

It is not exactly that Tom is in his own world. The practical joke here in effect duplicates the world. What that means is not a duplication in the sense of imitation or copying (though it involves that mimetic faculty, or compulsion—Tom's "talent"). It means instead a redoubling of the world in another sense: in the sense that it allows for a comparison between real reality and an internally articulated or (literally) make-believe one. This distinction, we have noted, inheres in Highsmith's mode of narration ("the point of view of the main character, written in the third-person singular," as she puts it in *Plotting and Writing Suspense Fiction*). In that this view implies its own construction, it makes seeing itself seen, and opens the world to counterfactual ones.[8]

The practical joke takes on the form of this situation, its conditionality and its spotlit observation. The practical joke is a world picture in a frame. It may be worth restating its premises at this point, risking a repetition in order to reframe them.

First, the practical joke, like the mystery novel, is a self-induced and self-exposed game about being taken in by games. It is a pop-up version, a scale model, of a self-observing world, one designed for that purpose. Second, it is a framed world aware of frames: a self-posited and then self-denuded interaction ritual. Third, it is then a game about the distinction between game and world—and the reentry of that distinction into the game is its object and outcome. This distinction—via the ecology of embarrassment, one of its central components—registers on the body, its crucial observer, and (in the poker sense) its "tell."

The practice side of the practical joke goes toward the physical and toward the body—as Tom's previewed and intercepted shaking, like a filter to noise on the line, indicates. The practical joke is a joke that not merely says something but one that does something. It is a trick or game that, in practice, combines saying and doing, with the intent of causing embarrassment—a sociable moment with objective and palpable symptoms. The practical joke then is one of the calisthenics of social interaction rituals by which make-believe makes belief and then discredits it, breaking what the microsociologist of modern social systems and their interaction rituals, Erving Goffman, calls "a socialized trance."[9] It is a little theater of overcommitment. It records the moment "the interactive world becomes too real" for the entranced player. It describes then, and crucially, a function for fictionality in the little worlds sustained by these encounters.

It's possible to redescribe this ecology of interaction in somewhat different terms. The embarrassed encounter is marked by communicative break-downs and so outbreaks of interiority, such that the second (interior states) looks like a function of the first (communication). The objective symptoms of embarrassment are communicative objects: things that talk (and so may be taken to be the medium of self-exposure: in Lacanian terms, the you in you more you than you that speaks or shows). Yet in that it is "not an irrational impulse breaking through socially prescribed behavior but part of this orderly behavior itself," it is a sort of "governor" (in the cybernetic sense): it induces the pressure it adjusts.

The advantage of embarrassment, from one point of view, is that it exteriorizes off-guard states for all to see: it is a script to induce spontaneity. In that self-communication about interior states can always be deceptive or self-deceptive, or suspected to be so, the advantage of being caught off-guard is the warrant of sincerity. Put a bit differently, in that embarrassment takes the form of a rupture or slip in communication, it becomes possible to equate mistakes in communication—a slip of the tongue, an error in transcription, a stumbling over one's own words, or over one's own feet—as indexes of interior states. (It's the low road to the unconscious, as dreams are the high road to it.) In that one can then be mistaken for the other, interiority is made available for communication, via the medium of embarrassment and the forms it takes.

The awareness of observation and self-observation are central here, but ultimately to somewhat different ends. The awareness of observation and self-observation means in this case a seeing machine that is a technique for processing distinctions. It means doing so on the level of a second-order seeing. In systems terms:

On this level one has to observe not simple objects but observing systems—that is, to distinguish them in the first place. One has to know which distinctions guide the observations of the observed observer and find out whether any stable objects emerge when these observations are recursively applied to their own results. Objects are therefore nothing but the *eigenbehaviors* of observing systems that result from using and reusing their previous distinctions.[10]

We are in fact more familiar with such objects, or eigenbehaviors, than the abstraction of its statement (Luhmann-Deutsch) suggests. We are familiar with them under a newly proliferating range of names—materialized theoria, material metaphors, quasi-objects, things that talk. They are the self-referential objects of a newer media studies.[11] We may see such objects then as in the process of what Joseph Vogl calls "becoming media." Here is Vogl's elegant formulation: "media are specific, systematizable objects of study for the following reason: everything they store and mediate is stored and mediated under conditions that are created by the media themselves and that ultimately comprise those media." This is an extremely useful way of putting it. Yet its utility is also its ecumenical generalizability. To the extent that anything systematizable may become media, this opens to a general description of working social systems and how they work.[12]

Let's then for the moment simply take up the version of these magnetized objects called clues. And let's take them up by way of the form they define— the mystery novel, and by way of its most popular operator, Agatha Christie. In what follows I will turn to Christie's novel *Appointment with Death*—a novel that registers with astonishing precision the media and form of the official world. First, I want to preview that via Christie's iconic novel *Murder on the Orient Express*, relying in part on its popularity and so your familiarity with it.

Central here is the function of fictionality in the systems epoch. One example of this, one I have given elsewhere, may be worth setting out again. The working model might be the moment in the film version of *The Wizard of Oz* when the curtain is drawn back to expose the wizard and his mechanisms of illusion. His response, of course, is simply to say, "Pay no attention to that man behind the curtain!" This may be paradoxical. But it works. The fiction seen through from both sides nonetheless survives this transparency and keeps going. One gets brains, courage, heart, and home anyway.

The modern crime, mystery, or suspense story posits a world that produces the act in its recording, writing down as it writes up. And it (therefore) looks at the same time like a trick or joke or gimmick or parlor game or (in the root sense) a prestige. As Agatha Christie expresses it in her novel *And Then There*

Were None: "A practical joke, perhaps."[13] Or, as she puts it in *Murder on the Orient Express*, it's then "our business to find out how the thing was done."[14]

"Our business." Here we return to the institutional habitus of reliable mindlessness, one of the great cultural achievements of the administrative rationalization Weber described and analyzed. Bureaucracy—rule by desks, or offices—is the administrative center of what Heide Gerstenberger calls *die subjeklose Gewalt* (impersonal or "subjectless" power) of bourgeois society.[15] That business model requires insentient impersonality applied across cases and repeated from case to case. It thus institutionalizes stupidity in repeatable programs and forms.[16] Bureaucratic work ethics consist in insensitivity training via mechanical routines and meritocratic practices. Manifest stupidity, and its work-ethical installation across the stations of an acronymic empire: we have branches everywhere.

This is nowhere more clearly manifested or perfected than in the perfectly stupid novels of Agatha Christie. The best-selling writer in world history, Christie turns rule by desks or offices into suspense stories, and turns murder into database inquiry in the form of a socialized trance. This means not merely the forensic-science processing of bodies, as body-count data, by professionals. These undebatably professional types belong (as Poirot puts it) not to locales, here or there, but instead here, there, and everywhere. " 'I belong to the world, Madame,' said Poirot dramatically." We must take this literally, as a world principle: a first principle of an official world that dramatizes itself as it goes. These theatrical and entertaining extinction stories (consider Christie's eliminative novel *And Then There Were None*) may then deserve a description.

The Crystal World on Wheels: Christie's *Murder on the Orient Express*

Englobed spaces. Let me shift to another version of that, and the little worlds sustained by these encounters. Take, for example, Agatha Christie's *Murder on the Orient Express*, an isotopia erected before our very eyes, and a practical joke, perhaps, too.

We can describe the action of the novel—keeping in mind that each act, and so each word, comments on its action—in these terms. A train stranded by a winter storm is suspended in its observation: the snow-globe world of *Murder on the Orient Express*. There are discrete and concentric spheres of observers: the cast of characters, or eigen-objects, that—like the punctual characters in a sitcom—keep returning to, and reinstating, themselves. The elite of observers, the detective, observes that, and so conducts experiments on the specimen humanity—"all classes and nationalities . . . graded and placed"—that occupies its demarcation zone. The characters—this is a wound culture—are "united by a common misfortune." (First, a fire, then a storm, then a murder, then a murder story.)

Murder on the Orient Express first then explicitly lifts external conditions in order to mark and to frame the system's coherence.[17] It couples suspense and sequestration: "Did anyone pass along the corridor outside the door?"; "it was cold outside"; the "outside world." In this way the novel processes and denotes the distinctions on which its intramural reality depends. It frames the microsystems that make it up: the train carriage, the train, the station, the timetable, the railway system, the network of body and message transport systems, the economic and legal systems, and (with references to theater and fiction), the art system, which (via these self-references) includes the novel itself.[18] For an interim, it's impossible to move, wire, telephone, summon police, access files, and so on, and this is noted in detail, since in the action in the novel the world is coterminous with its denotation and commentary. ("Going over the notes" initiates the action.) The train becomes, on the model of a mobile home, a mobile office. Or, rather, a mobile but temporarily suspended and immobilized one.

Modernity has been seen as a traffic problem. *Murder on the Orient Express* or *Strangers on a Train* or *The Talented Mr. Ripley* are paperback histories of world traffic, and its universal history of coincidence and contingency taking on form. A crystal world on rails—like the crystal palaces that are also railway stations still today, these stations are places without a place, gathering together points of equal value to form images of routes, timetables and maps, vehicles and records, compulsive yet controlled and reversible movements in time and space of bodies, communications, and money.[19] It would be necessary to take this up word by word, line by line, and step by step, as the novel collates and combines them from moment to moment. It is not possible to do that here. But I will take for granted your familiarity with this text, and with Christie's great discovery of a style that presents obviousness in the form of surprise. Her writing-down machine shows us again and again that it can show us again and again.

The communicative media of the novel—functional schemas of body and message transport, moving people, money, and news around—pauses for a moment, at the start. Then it restarts on its own terms. Step by step a little society forms, and the principles of a little sociology and its interactions are set out. Its strict internality allows for a compulsive externalization of act and value, with (again) the second as the paradoxical effect of the first. That includes the function of its exercise-repeating genres, like this one.

First, "all these here are linked together—by death" (*MOE*, 26). Next, they are "graded and placed" by official monitors of gradation and placement—waiters, stewards, attendants, and so on (27). Next, "on this, the second day of the journey, barriers were breaking down. Colonel Arbuthnot was standing at the door of his compartment talking to MacQueen" (36). That is, distinction and adjacency adjust to relation, via the two-sided medium of "the communicating door" (38). Shortly, "any barriers there might have been between the passengers had now quite broken down. All were united by a common misfortune" (44). Its formal principles marked and remarked, staged and communicated, at every point. A microsociety of communicants takes form step by step, line by line—"the communal life was felt, at the moment, to pass the time better" (47). Amazing: sociality as a pastime, like reading a novel. We are to see, as business as usual, the reassembly of the social in the boxcar, with instructions on how to assemble it included in the box.

The crime to be solved, it will be recalled, is an "inside job" made to look like an "outside job." That is to say, it proceeds such that reference to "the outside world" (*MOE*, 262) makes it possible to "draw a clear circle" (310) around the inside one. (Reference turns routinely to self-reference.) Along the same lines, at first look, the crime appears "planned and staged." But, on second look, too planned and too staged. So the solution to the crime is to rotate this problem 180 degrees on its axis—and to see that the crime takes place not merely as if staged but so as to be staged.

There is thus a function of fictionality in the act itself. The mystery is the extreme coherence of the crime: it resembles an artwork in that everything in it vibrates with the meaning of the whole. The crime is planned as performance art, for the sake of jointly enacting and jointly demonstrating the concerted intention of the players. (It is a ritual revenge with a cast of players: the act exists in the service of the achieved formality of its enactment.) The dramatis personae list included with the front matter in some, but not all, editions of the novel, resembles the cast of a play. The players take the law into their own hands. This, from one point of view, substitutes vengeance for law. Christie's novels, like Greek tragedy, restage this theme of civil transition—the passage from vengeance to law—albeit, it seems, in reverse. But this is a bit misleading. The revengers, twelve in number, are a jury, but one that performs the sentence they pronounce. In taking the law into their own hands, they submit to autonomization, and act as a system.

Hence the meaning of that play list becomes clear at the end when the meaning of the list enters the plot. All this takes place leaving no time to think about it, so that the perfect unity of action and form is what Poirot then sits back and thinks about. Or, to use the bit of stage theory about the distinction between acting and act that Christie cites, and recites, from novel to novel: it "suits the action to the word."

That means every move, which is to say every sentence, in a mystery/suspense novel can be seen to report on its function. In the process, the systematizable character of the object at last emerges. Every move works to make action coterminous with commentary. (Descriptions of autotropic social situations—self-describing social situations—can then be mistaken for "allegories of reading," and so in effect miss in theory how social systems in practice work.)

Let's look simply at the "apparatus" of the novel. The novel is divided into three parts: first, "The Facts"; second, "The Evidence"; and, third, "Hercule Poirot Sits Back and Thinks." The facts ("a cry in the night," "a woman," "the body," etc.) are data that await frames. The evidence is gathered in the interview of observers as to the observation of facts that include themselves—what they tell and their noted "tells." What the novel means by "psychology" is strictly point of view, that is, point of view as viewing point, or position. Everything depends on that exteriority: who, under what circumstances and to what ends, observes, and how others do. So the third part is the move to second-order observation: not facts or evidence but form.

It takes the form of an experiment: thinking exteriorized as thought experiment. Christie's fiction experiments with simple programs, like processes of elimination (*And Then There Were None*) or fast-and-frugal decision trees. (Stanislaw Lem: "The process of elimination is the defensive reflex of every expert," an extinction program.) These tree-formed control systems substitute step-by-step decisions in real time for an exhaustive rational calculus that could not know anything unless it knew everything. It is a ruthlessly practical art with humans.

Consider Poirot's externalized and staged way of carrying conception through its stages of development, in incubating outcomes ("What an egg-shaped head he had"!):

> My friends, I have reviewed the facts in my mind, and have also gone over to [!] myself the evidence of the passengers—with this result: I see, nebulously as yet, a certain explanation that would cover the facts as we know them. It is a very curious explanation, and I cannot be sure as yet that it is the true one. To find out definitely I shall have to make certain experiments. . . . [For that] one should advance only a step at a time. (*MOE*, 258, 240)

The extroverted explanation (*in* one's mind, *to* oneself, to find *out*, one *step* at a time) must be run in real time—that is, official time—in order to run.

The Pear-Shaped Man

It is observed, in conducting these experiments, that the clues to the crime "might have been lifted bodily out of an indifferently written American crime novel. They are not *real*" (MOE, 262). That is to say, fiction is lifted bodily out of fiction by fiction. This is the torque of a fictionality anchored in the correlation of readers' bodies and fictional ones (who often are reading too). It is premised on the italicized "indifference" between lines of print and unruly bodies, on the point "where the line meets the body."[20] The semantic ambiguity is its technical condition: that is to say, it is the technical condition of the networked media, shifting between object and form. That alone, in the second modernity, can produce a common world, albeit then a continuously watchful and so suspect one.

The mass media (including novels) make it possible for an indeterminate number of others to be, as Henry James puts it in his prefatory remarks to *The Turn of the Screw*, "subject to a common thrill." That's the case even when, as James also puts it, this is a matter, at the very same time, of a strictly "literary exercise" in a world zoned and marked out as a radically formal one. When it is a matter of "playing the game, making the score, in the phrase of our sporting day, off its own bat." When it takes the explicitated form of "an annexed but independent world." This gamelike and yet annexed isotopia—a self-instating world—may then take the form of a sort of a practical joke which is, at the same time, a worldview. It is (in James's terms once again) the switching, the turns, between real and fictional reality that makes for "the finer interest" that "depends just on how it is kept up."[21]

One doesn't exactly lose oneself in fiction any more than one simply finds oneself there—no one is content just to be someone else. The process is a circular, or self-curved, one: "when individuals look at media as text or as image, they are outside, when they experience their results within themselves, they are inside, as if in a paradoxical situation; quickly, almost without losing any time, and undecidably. For the one position is only possible thanks to the other—and vice versa."[22] This is the two-sided situation of the subject who is subject to a common thrill: a description of the turning of a screw.

In short, Christie's method: observation and reenactment; depsychologization; position (place-value) systems; fast-and-frugal decision trees— thought experiments in the service of pupating truth. Poirot's method: a *poirot* is a grower of pears. Poirot is, we are told, "pear-shaped." He reinstates himself: he takes shape in the step-by-step observing, noting, storing, filing, recollecting, reenacting, and reporting of his actions. Systems thinking, through the shortcut of kitsch.

EIGHT

MARCHING IN FILES

Murder is, for Foucault, where bodies and histories cross. But the question then becomes, how does this crossing take place? And how do the genre novels that have their offices at this crossing point—the crime, mystery, or suspense novel—manage this counterintuitive duality? Here we may be reminded of the moment in the remake of the film *The Pink Panther*, in which the detective Clouseau observes, of the chalk outline of a body, "It's amazing how he fell perfectly into the drawing on the floor."[1] In this chapter I look first, from another angle, at Christie's bureaucracy of crime (centrally, her novel *Appointment with Death*), and, second, at a very different version of art, forensics, and bureaucratic zealotry (Tom McCarthy's *Remainder*). The intent is to fill in the account of how the demarcation and reenactment zones of the official world work. The suspense aesthetic stress tests and frames modes of action and art in the system epoch. More precisely, if provisionally, the distinction of action and art, in the epoch of social systems, is a matter of how the practical distinction between repeated acts and repeating acts seems framed.

In the continuous rotation of act and report in the suspense or mystery novel, the act recites itself: "'And that being so . . . we might as well shut the window. Positively it is the cold storage in here!' He suited the action to the word, and then turned his attention for the first time to the motionless figure lying in the bunk."[2] In this meticulous sequencing of statement, act, and perception (observation, storage, report), the state of being the case and the body of real things appear simply as what exists—in the simple statement of *that being so.*

This is a form of collective life that is, as the reenactor of Tom McCarthy's novel *Remainder* puts it, "marching in files."[3] Hence the disposition, retraining, and calibration of bodies in reenacted motion—the choreographics of social systems—are carried in deceptively small and ordinary techniques of officialism. These include, on a short list drawn from *Remainder*: maps, charts, timetables, diagrams, sketches, zones, programs, formats, records, commentaries, notations, pictures, imprints, plans, bills, documents, letters, arrows, notes, lines, patterns, circuits, ranks, cards, files, and, of course, lists.

A world marching in files is a zoned world. Like the sky penciled by the spars of the ship or the street scored by the wheels on the pavement in the opening chapter of Howells's *The Rise of Silas Lapham*, a world marching in files leaves a record of itself as it goes. Falling bodies, in *Remainder*, like falling leaves, imprint themselves on the pavement: " 'Leaves leave marks too, sometimes,' I said, 'outlines on the tarmac, their own skeletons. Like photos. Or Hiroshima. When they fall' " (278). That is, leaves leave leaves. The zoned world is a reenactment zone that must denote itself or die.

As Harry Braverman puts it, in his account of systematic management processes, "the process of production is replicated in paper form before, as, and after it takes place in physical form."[4] There is a paradox here too: things efficiently yet paradoxically have to be "replicated" *before* they take place— and then continuously. This is the routinization of acting as reenacting and the continuous rotation of paper forms and physical ones. In the terms of *Remainder*, the solution to the problem of keeping up the sequence and endlessly reenacting it is breathtakingly simple: "We rotate them."

The situation of the work of art in the epoch of social systems then predictably emerges as its own subject in *Remainder*. I will return to the logic of *Remainder* at the close of this chapter. Here its experimentalism may usefully frame Agatha Christie's. (McCarthy's novel, like Christie's, an experiment in stupidity, albeit to very different ends.) *Remainder* sets out a comparison of the form of the work of art and the explicitly experimental procedures of a forensic realism: its reconstructions, reenactments, and "ready-made formatted grids."[5] "Forensic procedure," the main reenactor recites, "is an art form, nothing less. No, I'll go further: it's higher, more refined than any art form. Why? Because it's real" (*Remainder*, 184). The fascination of the forensic is that it is at once, as he puts it, "extremely formal" and yet "real."

Forensic realism, on this view, is real because it is the point where the line touches the body. This is the crossing point at which things vibrate or "tingle." "Take one aspect of it—say the diagrams: with all their outlines, arrows and shaded blocks they look like abstract paintings, avant-garde ones from the last century—dances of shapes and flows as delicate and skillful as the markings on butterflies' wings" (*Remainder*, 183). The forensic epitomizes the nature, if that's the right word, of a self-delineated world. It is diagrammatic, but a living diagram, life in recordable format: "But they're not abstract at all. They're records of atrocities. Each line, each figure, every angle—the ink itself vibrates with an almost intolerable violence, darkly screaming from the silence of white paper: something has happened here, some one has died" (183). It is a strictly generic and ascetically ritualized way of proceeding: one with "rigorous rules," "gridded," "patterned," "cubistic," and "all these patterns have to be recorded": "the whole process is extremely formal."[6] Or, as Agatha Christie puts it, in relation to her own semantic experiments in the bureaucracy of crime, it is a "beautiful shining order" realized in the world.

Repeated Repeating: *Appointment with Death*

In Stephen Crane's 1890s war story "Death and the Child," the narrator describes a marching file of wounded soldiers in these words: they "were bandaged with the triangular kerchief upon which one could still see through the bloodstains the little explanatory pictures illustrating the ways to bind various wounds. 'Fig. 1.'—'Fig. 2.'—'Fig. 7.'"[7] The tendency toward a self-illustration that enters into the act is then a working model of an official world that installs itself in recording its own actions—and reports that, in this case, in a short fiction.

Along the lines of Weber's mapping of bureaucratic forms, this is a matter of positions not persons, a matter of rank and file. "The management of the modern office," as Max Weber expresses it, "is based upon written documents ('the files'), which are preserved in their original or draft form."[8] This means a reordering of the order of things and words. It marks the passage from what Roland Barthes called "the rhetorical empire" to what a historian of bureaucracy more recently calls "the empire of the word people."[9]

The reordering of the relation between words and things in an official world—the reordering of words and things that makes up an official world—means a transition from the rhetorical order to the order of the word people. The empire of the word people not merely links the act to its recording but, in putting acts on file, puts them in place and engenders their circulation: the writing down system turns res gestae into *regista* (registered things), and, in doing so, establishes a continuous feedback with its own actions. It is not merely that there is nothing in the world that is not in the files: the correlate is that there is then nothing in the files that is not in the world.[10]

It's not merely then that the world takes on the form of an "enormous file" (C. Wright Mills), of "a file that never closes" (Michel Foucault). The lag between productive capacity and communicative capabilities that makes for a crisis in control at the end of the nineteenth century—the advent of the second industrial revolution (the information age, the second modernization)—makes for a control revolution and its media-cultural techniques, with all its diagrams, timetables, lists, maps, working models, and sorting mechanisms.[11]

I have taken up some of the implications of such models and scale models in earlier parts of this study. But not merely does Christie's *Appointment with Death* denote the transition to the empire of the word people and its operations from its bureaucratic title on. It sets out in explicit terms the function of a fictionality in the systems epoch, and suspense as its dominant aesthetic category. It does so as if the novel were a program, a sequence of instructions and its execution.

The opening of the novel at once enacts and registers. Each appears as the cause of the other. The opening forms in fact a little self-organizing system. It consists in a separation of voice, writing, and act and a process for recombining them—the separation and recombination of words and acts that makes up the administrative a priori.

The opening breaks into three component parts, or moves. These are parts like the pieces of a jigsaw puzzle, or the moves of placeholder tokens on a game board (frequent analogies, or models, for her own "method" in Christie's novels). We can take them up, piece by piece, list them, and then piece them back together. A tedious process to reassemble, but a perfectly easy, even mindlessly easy, one to read.

MOVE #1

"You do see, don't you, that she's got to be killed?"

The question floated out into the still night air, seemed to hang there a moment and then drift away down into the darkness towards the Dead Sea.

Hercule Poirot paused a minute with his hand on the window catch.

Frowning, he shut it decisively, thereby excluding any injurious night air! Hercule Poirot had been brought up to believe that all outside air was best left outside, and that night air was especially dangerous to the health.

As he pulled the curtains neatly over the window and walked to his bed, he smiled tolerantly to himself.

"You do see, don't you, that she's got to be killed?"

Curious words, for one Hercule Poirot, detective, to overhear on his first night in Jerusalem.

"Decidedly, wherever I go there is something to remind me of crime!" he murmured to himself.[12]

Now it's not hard to see that this opening processes a program. It sets out a linked series of distinctions—between outside and inside, nature and culture, death and life, between the great outdoors and an indoor social life. Nor is it hard to see that, in doing so, it puts in place the cultural techniques that encode and process these distinctions, and that put everything in its place.

The explicit exclusion of the great outdoors, the sequestration of an indoor social life, is signaled in at least three ways. First, it is signaled by a syntax of reflexivity (you do see, don't you; a smiling to oneself; a self-murmuring and self-quotation). Second, it is signaled by repetition, a repeating that redoubles reality (*Realitätsverdoppellung*). It doubles the world in its recording. That reveals that reality is something that may be doubled and recorded, and so must include that. Third, a desk-ruled space that probatively links decision ("decisively," "decidedly") to a technology of reference: that, more exactly, links states of mind to the memorandum ("something to remind"). Today's minds must be made over, or reminded, for tomorrow's work.

The memorandum, of course, is the defining genre—and not merely in its ubiquity—of a modernity that connects the official character of its acts to record, file, and recall. It works by taking its own pulse, and putting it on record.[13] It is a structure of reference that is also a graphomania, one that couples the ubiquity of the media to the unhappening of the world: that is, business as usual. A novel world that says what it does and, in doing so, does what it says. That's why the details set out in Christie's novels (particularly the earlier ones) are less clues (in the sense of a trace or track or trail or symptom) than game pieces (counters moved from position to position, place markers of a danger zone).[14]

One might list the elements of this protocol (bearing in mind that the list, along with the map, the diagram, and the timetable, is one of its technical processes or abstract machines):

A. To each official action corresponds the act of putting on record.
B. Hence the act of putting on record corresponds to an official act.
C. And so the recording of facts is a fact-producing act.

These are the ABCs of an administrative a priori.[15] The list engenders a protocol: what Christie's detective Poirot everywhere calls a "method." In that act and word, event and description rotate, it is possible "to arrange the facts methodically"—and to produce the special effect that "things are straightening themselves out."[16]

For one thing, there is a voice-imitating machine at work, *der Stimmenimitator* (if not exactly in Thomas Bernhardt's sense of that mechanism). The dictaphone is a favorite media appliance, and plot device (in Christie's novels, for example, *The Murder of Roger Ackroyd* or *And Then There Were None*—among many other crime novels, from, for example, *Dracula* to *Double Indemnity* or *Strangers on a Train*).[17]

There is, from the start, the doubling of spoken words as written words, a practice that immediately records what is said, italicizes (copies) it, and then places it in quotation marks (cites it). This is the force of something "overheard"—that is, given a hearing, written down, stored, and then retrieved. It couples a little technology of reference and a little technique of registration.

Here Poirot is nothing but a finely turned receiver, detecting voices in the air, turning sounds into signs, copying, storing, and repeating them. The opening of this 1930s novel makes clear "when it becomes possible to store, retrieve, and transmit previously archived voices and sounds over the wireless."[18] The detective as voice detector is something like the wireless operator, or *marconista*, who "listened to sounds that emerged out of the static of the headset and wrote them down. The writing down of sounds was possible thanks to a relay running from the operator's ear to his or her hand, which utilized the storage possibilities of the alphabet itself."[19] The detector, the detective, records what if not written down would be irrevocably lost: hence "the necessity of constant marconigrams."[20] This means constantly writing down signs that emerge from static on live wires, amid the roar of the world, and that hang there for a moment, before they drift away down into the darkness, and toward an indistinct—dead—sea.

MOVE #2

His smile continued as he remembered a story he had once heard concerning Anthony Trollope, the novelist. Trollope was crossing the Atlantic at the time and had overheard two fellow passengers discussing the last published instalment of one of his novels.

"Very good," one man had declared. "But he ought to kill off that tiresome old woman."

With a broad smile the novelist had addressed them:

"Gentlemen. I am much obliged to you! I will go and kill her immediately!"

Poirot wondered what had occasioned the words he had just overheard. A collaboration, perhaps, over a play or a book. (*AD*, 3–4)

The official world presupposes the function of fiction. The redoubling of reality, we know, means that "real life" can only be described by contrasting it with something else (fictional or statistical or mathematical reality, for example). Hence too one everywhere finds in modern mystery or suspense writing (but not only there) the noise of unrealized plots and possible worlds. These enter into the crime story from Poe's advent story "The Mystery of Marie Rogêt" in the 1840s on. That makes for a continuous reproduction of the distinction between one kind of reality and another.

It may be said then that Umberto Eco (and Franco Moretti, following his lead) gets it exactly right in noting that everything has a reason at the end of the detective novel. But the notion that this is to be understood, above all, as a nostalgic (fictional?) restoration of an outmoded social order—is misleading on several counts. The "reasons" here are everywhere part of a self-staging system that observes and installs its operations as it goes and on its own terms.[21] There is no doubt that the crises of defective knowledge—the premise of the control revolution—are remedied by the detection method: the invisible hand is replaced by a visible one, a managerial method that inheres in the work process. But the feeding back of effects into causes expresses that control revolution—such that "things are straightening themselves out." We can say, everything in its place and a place for everything at the end—"his neatly docketed facts, his carefully sorted impressions" (*AD*, 100). But if everything is in its place at the end of a Christie novel, it is not merely that this placement looks staged, or is. Self-staging and its self-monitoring are the way of this new world, its mode and too the mood of systems.

Here we are returned, via these little in-jokes, to the complicated duality of the practical joke, and its programmatic switching between real and fictional reality. There is the story of a literary overhearing in a novel—and the astonishing presumption of the fictionality of what is overheard in real life. That presumption appears as a first thought and not a second one. In this way the distinctive modernity of Christie's self-legislative system becomes explicit, and explicitly matter-of-fact.

MOVE #3

He thought, still smiling:

"Those words might be remembered one day, and be given a more sinister meaning."

There had been, he now recollected, a curious nervous intensity in the voice—a tremor that spoke of some intense emotional strain. A man's voice—or a boy's. . . .

Hercule Poirot thought to himself as he turned out the light by his bed: "*I should know that voice again. . . .*" (AD, 4)

Thoughts are quoted—that is, thinking is self-quotation; and remembering is nothing but the retrieval of what is copied, stored, and retrieved. If a tremor speaks, then the recording of sounds joins act and sign, physics and hermeneutics, and becomes the index of an event. Italicization signals the administrative moment and its self-conditioning. What is thought, like what is said, now has the status of something given a hearing and entering the register—so that it may at some time spur a new action. The storage, or filing, of voices in the air corresponds to the latency period of information—what may yet see the light of day: office hours. Hence "we shall know the truth when they are compared with the files" (AD, 201).

That's why Poirot later recollects this moment of recollection: "I say to myself it is a voice I will know again" (AD, 100). The uncertain English that mixes tenses ("say" for "said") makes past acts present ones, still telling what is told. That registers exactly the duality of record and act, the commutability of res gestae and the *historia rerum gestarum*. Poirot still later notes "I was earlier in the day, writing down a list of printed facts" (199). The printing of the facts here paradoxically precedes its writing down. That *hysteron proteron* is the form of the writing-down empire of the word people—the continuous feeding back of record into act. (The substitutive reversal of cause and effect has been taken to betoken the rhetorical, or linguistic, moment, as such—in a deconstructive approach informed, but for the most part silently, by the cybernetic turn.)[22] The fusing of word to act lends to an official world the feel of the performative, what Elias Canetti (in *Crowds and Power*) calls "the sting of command." Hence at the close of the novel, when all is assembled to sort itself out, everything is placed "in an official position. . . . It was an official noise. He spoke in an official tone" (AD, 178). It is as if Kafka's little parable "Before the Law" has been adapted as a game show.

MOVE #4

[after a space on the page, and with my ellipses]

Their elbows on the window-sill, their heads close together, Raymond and Carol Boynton gazed out into the blue depths of the night. Nervously, Raymond repeated his former words:

"You see, don't you, that she's got to be killed?" . . .
"I know. It's getting pretty bad, isn't it?" . . .
"I know, Ray—I know." . . .
"You do agree, Carol?" . . .
Carol answered steadily. . . .
Raymond said steadily. . . .
"What's put all this into your head . . . ?"
He turned his head away, staring out into the night. . . .
He bent his head to hers. . . . (AD, 4–7)

What seems at first a flashback is instead a repetition in real time—and with that as its topic. This issues in a series of exchanges that are less transfers of information (news of difference) than a matter of repetition as its own theme: a repeated repeating that puts minds and heads together.

The first part of the first chapter thus sets in motion the administrative process, and its communicative ground of existence. The second locates the topic that will be processed. It tests the channel and attaches the voice in the air to persons. In doing so it attracts persons (and readers) to the on-going communication of communication.

This is what Roman Jakobson calls the phatic function, as the ground of sociality, and what establishes and continues it from moment to moment:

There are messages primarily serving to establish, to prolong, or to discontinue communication, to check whether the channel works ("Hello, do you hear me?"), to attract the attention of the interlocutor or to confirm his continued attention ("Are you listening? Or in Shakespearean diction, 'Lend me your ears!'—and on the other end of the wire Urn-hum!") This set for CONTACT [that is, "the physical channel and psychological connection between the addresser and addressee, enabling both to enter and stay in communication"], or in Malinowski's terms the PHATIC function, may be displayed by a profuse exchange of ritualized formulas, by entire dialogues with the mere purport of prolonging communication.[23]

Jakobson's example of this way of holding the line open is drawn from the fiction writer Dorothy Parker and consists in this he said/she said exchange: "'Well!' the young man said. 'Well!' she said. 'Well, here we are,' he said. 'Here we are,' she said. 'Aren't we?' 'I should say we were,' he said. 'Eeyop! Here we are.' 'Well!' she said. 'Well!' He said, 'well.' The endeavor to start and sustain communication is typical of talking birds." That is to say, this set on the channel is a kind of twittering. A social bond created by a mere, and merely continuous, exchange of words or sounds—by which the standards of a little social system are maintained.

The narrative proceeds in its sorting process along the lines of the "fast and frugal" decision model that "asks only a few yes-or-no questions and allows for a decision after each one."[24] The process of elimination ("and then there were none") is not merely a matter of "order and method,"[25] but a matter of counting, measuring, and listing. It is in part a matter of "list-shaped control signs":[26] "Before I go into the case . . . I would like to read to you a list of significant points which I drew up and submitted this afternoon. . . . Although I have numbered the points separately, occasionally they can be bracketed in pairs" (AD, 183). Lists, maps, diagrams, files, and timetables, and their observation. In sum, the detective's "method" is a method of placing and timing and their relation: " 'Let us now review our time-table: Thus:' " (190).

For this reason, it would be a mistake to see this point of view in terms of a psychology of the observer. Consider, for example, the railway system, its array of multiple and coordinated clocks, trains, timetables, continuous coordinations of time and space. These crisscross Christie's novels (from early novels like *The Big Four* to a late one called *The Clocks*). " 'Yes, yes, I understand that. But the *time*!' 'The time?' 'Yes, this will delay us.' 'It is possible—yes,' agreed Poirot. 'But we cannot afford delay! This train is due in at 6.55, and one has to cross the Bosphorus and catch the Simplon Orient Express on the other side at nine o'clock. If there is an hour or two of delay we shall miss the connection.' 'It is possible, yes.' "[27] The question of "the time"—clocks, distance, trains, the railway system, its concerted timetables, their connection or simultaneity—means that the coordination of the system relativizes "sides," relays and delays, and submits them to calibrations of contingency ("possibility"). "The railroad knows only points of departure and destination," as Wolfgang Schivelbusch puts it. It has "no use whatsoever of the intervening spaces."[28]

Clocks, trains, and measuring rods crisscross the great modernisms of physics as well: "The properties of time," Henri Poincaré insisted, "are therefore merely those of our clocks just as the properties of space are merely those of our measuring instruments."[29] Or, the second obvious example: "Every day Einstein stepped out of his house, turned left, and made his way to the patent office. . . . He had to walk past the great clock towers presiding over Bern. . . . 'If, for instance, I say, "That train arrives here at 7 o'clock," I mean something like this: "The pointing of the small hand of my watch to 7 and the arrival of the train are simultaneous events." ' "[30] The everyday coordination of clocks and measuring rods—the "insistence that simultaneity refer exclusively to clocks coordinated by a definite and observable procedure"[31]—prompts a series of world-altering questions: What is time? Curved space? Coincidence? Or, as Poirot puts it in *The Murder of Roger Ackroyd*, it's "a question of the relativity, is it not so?" (216).

Hearsay about modernist physics no doubt enters into Christie's official time zones (as science kitsch enters in here). Christie's forensic art is premised on the presupposition of a reality strictly relative to its observation: it is a world of aspects.[32] A grid, a format, and a form.

Here we approach the conditions of Christie's world-historical popularity as a fiction writer (the most popular human writer in world history). Take, that is, the streams of commuters, synced to the timetables of the Underground, the railway, and the office. The marching files of white-collar workers engaged in processes of typing, recording, indexing, listing, filing, storing, retrieving, transmitting, and so on—that is, in the activities of the novel itself. The rotation of commuter readers, en route to the office or back home from it, reenacting, or preenacting, the bureaucratic zealotry of a business as usual that is (as Tom McCarthy puts it) more usual than usual: at work or in reparative leisure from it, via practices that collate point by point the excitations of the official world recast as forensic zone.[33] That provides a running commentary on its moment-to-moment, step-by-step installation.

We can describe this situation as a version, or terminus, of the bourgeois convergence of being a reader and being an individual. We can describe this as a synchronization of interior states and the outside world. We can describe this is a dedifferentiation of work and play. We can describe this as a functional assimilation of the individual to the circuitry of communication and commodification in an expanded field. We can describe it, that is, as a "homogenization of inner experience and administrative communicative networks,"[34] now on 24/7—even for those of us (or earlier, for, say, Kracauer or Dreiser) who recall when being on line was not what one above all wanted in the world. We can describe this as a uniting of individuals outside themselves: an adaptive autism or what Sartre, on seriality in modern society, called the practico-inert.

Or, consider this from another, narrower, angle: in terms of a mutation in the rhetoric of fiction. In formal terms, this is the suspended state of free indirect discourse: a taut suspension between character and narrative. Or, more exactly, a suspense progressively neutralized by achieved objectivity: the sheer consistency, as they say, of received ideas. That may be seen to mark a success in socialization that has been too successful, as Franco Moretti observes (commenting on Flaubert's aesthetic objectivity). So successful that we can no longer tell the difference between a perfect novel about stupidity and a perfectly stupid novel.[35] For Moretti, this oversocialized neutralization is the bitter end of Weberian rationalization. In his lecture "Wissenschaft als Beruf" ("Science as Profession," or "Systemic Knowledge as Vocation"), Weber trenchantly describes the fields of academic vocation in terms of a systemic blindness ("a capacity to put on blinders"), or a perfect indifference, to all that is outside, that is, outside one's field ("The individual can acquire the sure consciousness of achieving something truly perfect in the field of science only in case he is a strict specialist"). This is the launching pad of an unremitting and self-persuasive professional hyperproductivity, one that produces (as Weber traces in the *Protestant Ethic*) as its pure and simple outcome only "the irrational sense of having done one's job well."[36] Hence the counterface of the irrationality of rationalization (from Bentham's utilitarianism on) is its ongoing autonomization: the self-curved spaces of an almost sui generis indoor social life, on its own terms.

Repeating Repeating: *Remainder*

[He] sounded resentful and betrayed, like a sailor who had come to the edge of a flat world.
—Ross Macdonald, *The Underground Man*

Screams spill into the air above the square as the boat rises to its apex and hangs there, undecided whether to fall back or to plough on through the zero. Its passengers, suspended, motionless . . .
—Tom McCarthy, *Men in Space*

Four musicians using their instruments like an erector set to construct a skyline that won't fall down before they're finished.
—Jonathan Lethem, on the Talking Heads

One day I got an urge to go and check up on the outside world myself. Nothing much to report.
—Tom McCarthy, *Remainder*

It is necessary, as they say, to understand the past in order not to repeat it. This is what is usually, or reflexively, repeated in defense of the study of history or perhaps modern literary history. But in McCarthy's novel the usual becomes more usual than usual. The narrative voice, or commentator, of *Remainder*—a self-described zombie or robot who resembles a character only insofar as he tonelessly repeats the sort of things that "they" say—sees this differently. He is told, "If you don't want to repeat things, you have to understand them." His response is simple enough, and oddly refreshing: "But I do want to repeat things. . . . And I don't want to understand them" (*Remainder*, 246).

This is, in part, because his reflexes and memory no longer work. An accident that takes place prior to the action of the novel—something falls on him from the air—cancels his history and his capacity to set himself in motion, and so forces him to make autonomic processes intentional ones. The accident has, in effect, abrogated the evolutionary "rule of the unconsciously efficient body."[37]

The accident, in short, deletes the commentator's memory and makes it impossible for him to do anything, like walking, say, or, to take his most extended example, picking up a carrot, without thinking about it and thinking it through. That is, without breaking down every move into its component parts, putting them back together in sequence, consciously preenacting and formatting them, and then in effect putting in practice what has been practiced again and again, so that acting is reenacting. It becomes necessary for him to systematically manage himself: to stage intentions as reenactments. With the cash settlement he receives for not recounting the accident he can't recall (in effect, if not in fact, an infinite amount of money), he then sets up a series of acceleratively violent reenactment zones, at first, annexing microworlds in the world, and last, "lifting the re-enactment out of its demarcated zone and slotting it back into the world" (*Remainder*, 265).

Here we begin to see the sense of the commentator's conflation of bodies and institutions:

> The terms of the Settlement drawn up between my lawyer and the parties, institutions, organizations—let's call them the *bodies*—responsible for what happened to me prohibit me from discussing, in any public or recordable format (I know this bit by heart), the nature and/or details of the incident (4). . . . "Given the status of these parties, these, uh, institutions, these, uh" . . . "Bodies," I said. ". . . bodies," he continued. (*Remainder*, 12)[38]

Remainder is in fact something of a send-up of the neuro-novel, and it does something more, and more interesting, than roll out all the antinomies of the mind-body problem yet once again. McCarthy, like J. G. Ballard—and McCarthy is a brilliant reenactor of Ballard's demarcated, distinctly formal, violently choreographed reenactment zones—rejects on all counts the "psychologizing," and the confessional and furtively self-assertive tone of the trauma novel. For McCarthy, as for Ballard, subjectivity works "as a kind of trajectory through space, networks, and legal systems."[39] In this way, bodies, parties, institutions, and organizations are braided together, and not least in the legal system of the corporation, and its status and nature as an artificial character system.

For one thing, legal systems are primary here (and not merely in that the primary reenactment zones of the novel are forensic spaces). For another, the novel in effect sets out an interesting comparison of "limited omniscience" and "limited liability" in the new novel. It extends the experimental novel's focus on milieu to include self-organization. It is, as it were, a neosituationism that takes as its premise that "every action is a complex operation, a system" (*Remainder*, 22). It compares the logic of actions in the novel (the acts, or reenactments, of a fictional person) and the logic of corporate-juristical actions (the acts of a fictitious one). It systemically fuses limited liability and limited omniscience, and does so most clearly in terms of crimes as acts unattributable to actors. In short, as McCarthy's reenactor expresses it, "we are not doing them: they were being done" (214).

The limitedness of the narrator's omniscience is pretty much unlimited. "Limited omniscience" is an internally paradoxical notion in itself, if you think about it (say, restricted unrestrictedness).[40] A fictitious or juristical person, the reenactor is reincarnated into the "world interior of capitalism" in its pristine form: a self-reinstating system of extremely formal, spatialized, and time-controlled operations, a choreographics and a logistics. McCarthy plays out this logic to its very end, or breaking point, with respect to persons, bodies, and institutions. These are the experimental zones and organizing premises of the novel, which the reenactor repeats by heart at its opening. Under the formal and generalized "settlement" conditions—here it is necessary to repeat what I have earlier set out—"everything solid melts into air." The decorporatization or vaporization of persons—bodies suspended in air and volatilized—realizes the status of fictitious persons in pure form. The reenactor in *Remainder* is then the fictitious or corporate or juristical person in person. He is legally immune to crime in that what he is doing is not what he has done.[41] He is immune to what Savigny argues amounts to the solecism of "vicarious crime." The acceleratively violent action of the novel gives him the sense "of being on the other side of something. A veil, a screen, the law—I don't know . . ." (*Remainder*, 241). That is to say, it at once reenacts and pierces the corporate veil, the principle of the separate and delimited personhood of the corporation. Limited omniscience ("I don't know") and limited liability ("being on the other side of something") are reciprocal functions. Hence act attribution, or irresponsibility, in these zoned spaces of action is, as he also puts it, "nonexistent" or "infinite" (which "amounts" in this case, it may now be clear, to two ways of saying the same thing [283]).

If we missed that, too, the narrator's "facilitator" in the logistics industry—Naz—coordinates his staging of the series of reenactments, funded by the enormous cash settlement the narrator has received in compensation for the reported accident. ("Choreography" and "logistics" are two of the reenactor's favorite words, along with, of course, "reenactment.") Naz, a pet name for Nazi, is a "zealot," but "his zealotry wasn't religious, it was bureaucratic" (*Remainder*, 233). Naz's bureaucratic zeal ends with a logistically perfect plan to "vaporize" all of the reenactors—a final solution that the narrator finds "beautiful" too. This programmatically makes clear, to anyone who didn't already know it, what the "enforcement" of the administered society may look like when it operates without reserve and with, for all practical purposes, and many others, unlimited money. This ascetic zealotry (and the contradictory ways in which the novel compares vertical and upward mobility, human arts and art with humans) is central to its argument, and to its limitations.

The collaboration of the concepts of limited omniscience and limited liability plays out on the very surface of the novel (and, arguably, the Novel, from mid-nineteenth century realism and the early experimental novel on). But its aesthetic implications here run in a slightly different direction, and into a series of impasses.

McCarthy observes, "Re-enactment brings about a kind of split within the act itself. . . . On the one hand it's something you do, and on the other it's not something you're actually 'doing': it's a citation, a marker for another event that this one isn't."[42] In his afterword to McCarthy's novel *Men in Space*, Simon Critchley—the chief philosopher of the International Necronautical Society that McCarthy founded—cites McCarthy's citation (in his *Tintin and the Secret of Literature* [2006]) of Paul de Man's account, in "The Rhetoric of Temporality," of the aporias of self-consciousness and authenticity: we "can know inauthenticity, but never overcome it. It can only restate and repeat it on an increasingly conscious level."[43] As Critchley adds (or subtracts), it is then "not about the overcoming of inauthenticity, but our increasing self-consciousness of its operations." Yet the real irony, repeating again, in the terms of *Remainder*, is this: we can increasingly become more and more conscious of becoming less and less conscious.

We can reframe what is at stake here by looking at a somewhat different account of reenactment, bodies, and institutions—an installation-moment of sorts of the practices of the systems epoch—and a somewhat different account of acts of repeating. Here too it is a matter of bodies suspended in air. One of these men in space is the Stylite that Mark Twain's Connecticut Yankee—the factory manager reorganizing sixth-century Arthurian England on the principles of scientific management—encounters in suspended animatedness atop a tower in the Valley of Holiness.

> His stand was a pillar sixty feet high, with a broad platform on the top of it. He was now doing what he had been doing every day for twenty years up there—bowing his body ceaselessly and rapidly almost to his feet. It was his way of praying. I timed him with a stop watch, and he made 1,244 revolutions in 24 minutes and 46 seconds. It seemed a pity to have all this power going to waste. It was one of the most useful motions in mechanics, the pedal movement; so I made a note in my memorandum book, purposing some day to apply a system of elastic cords to him and run a sewing machine with it. I afterward carried out that scheme, and got five years' good service out of him; in which time he turned out upward of eighteen thousand first-rate tow-linen shirts, which was ten a day. I worked him Sundays and all; he was going, Sundays, the same as week days, and it was no use to waste the power.[44]

The transition from the ethical work of vertical mobility to a work ethic of upward mobility is here set out in graphic terms: in short, "what was once transcendent morality becomes part of a circuit: the eternally unchanging group of ascetisms is replaced by a cybernetic optimization system."[45]

Or, put it in somewhat different terms, for the Taylorite Yankee, mindless devotion is replaced by a devotion to mindlessness: systematized purposes, noted, reenacted, recorded, convert "doing" to being done. Mindful mindless repetition or repeatedly minding the machine: intentions are extroverted both times and perspicuous only to a super-observer, or over-seer, who may be there or not. These are comparative practices in passivity, and vertical or upward mobility. The distinction then seems to be between mindfully mindless devotees and marionettes of administrative reason, iterative ascetics and irrational work ethics. The scene stages the conversion to the Taylorized work ethic, one that systematically divides cognition and motion and acts into parts, so performance and production, doing and being done, can be separated and administratively recombined.

Yet since the Stylite is doing the same thing both times, and each time, the difference between repetitions is not a property of the action. It is not exactly that the boundaries come down between mindful and mindless repetitions. Even if it is the case that (as Louis Menand once noted) academics become excited whenever boundaries are blurred. There is a continuous and shifting comparison of practices of repetition. For one thing, the suspension of intention on the part of the devotee must be intended each time, in his "disposition towards the next repetition."[46] For another, the translation of vertical mobility to upward mobility, in the workplace of a rising middle class, means that "purposing," as Twain calls it, becomes a property of systemic repetition.[47]

Hence the scene dramatizes a distinction between repeating repeating and repeated repeating.[48] "The human being is not negativity," as Sloterdijk expresses it, "but rather the point of difference between repetitions" (415). Yet even that way of putting it expresses the difficulty of locating the distinction. It is not exactly "a point of difference" between them but their continuous comparison: the ongoing suspension and precipitation—the falling or falling out—of intention, and relation to acts. This gets us a bit closer to the staging of the attempt to set repetition against repetition, which is one way of understanding the project of *Remainder* (if not the success, in practice, of the novel).[49]

That is, it gets us a bit closer to seeing in what sense an anthropotechnics, an art with humans, is an art. The distinction between repeated repeating and repeating repeating is the one that Roland Barthes obliquely but lucidly sets out in his little book on Japan, *Empire of Signs*. He poses it in terms of what he describes as the matte effect, in a range of Japanese art and daily practices, ranging from poetry to packaging, from the aesthetic arrangement of flowers to the giving of street addresses.

> If the bouquets, the objects, the trees, the faces, the gardens, and the texts—if the things and manners of Japan seem diminutive to us (our mythology exalts the big, the vast, the broad, the open), this is not by reason of their size, it is because every object, every gesture, even the most free, the most mobile, seems *framed*. The miniature does not derive from the dimension but from a kind of precision which the thing observes in delimiting itself, stopping, finishing. . . . Yet this frame is invisible: the Japanese thing is not outlined, illuminated; it is not formed of a strong contour. . . . Around it there is: *nothing*, an empty space which renders it matte.[50]

What renders it matte, we might say, is the discretion in that which appears through what Sebald calls "the shape and the self-contained nature of discrete things."[51] But Barthes is more exact: not self-contained, but self-containing. It is here again, in the distinguishing between the past and present participle (repeating repeating—delimiting, stopping, finishing; repeated repeating—

the outlined, the illuminated), that the object or gesture may enable one to "foil" (in both the sense of countering and the sense of enhancing by contrast) and so to frustrate "the conformism of his context."[52]

This is too the situation that McCarthy poses, in *Remainder*, via the uncertain distinction between the reenactment zone and the outside world (that is, an outside world made up of them). In the terms of the reenactor in *Remainder*, the drive is to make the "edge" of the demarcation zone vanish, such that a "merger" takes place. This is the ground zero of the novel: "lifting the re-enactment out of its demarcated zone and slotting it back into the world" (*Remainder*, 265). The unity of the distinction between the world and the demarcated zone is that both are seen to consist in the zoned reenactments with the properties of the intensely staged, the luxuriantly significant, and the extremely formal. In other words, these the narrator's, "Occasionally I'd let my eyes run out to the corners, looking, like the other re-enactors, for an edge, although I knew there was no edge, that the re-enactment zone was non-existent, or that it was infinite, which amounted in this case to the same thing" (283).

Remainder plays out as a sort of extended series of practical jokes, with a pratfall at the end looking like an especially elaborate and consummately lethal one. In this way, the novel (as McCarthy puts it) becomes about the conditions of the epoch of social systems and at the same time "becomes about art."[53]

Or, as McCarthy elsewhere expresses this matter: "I think there's three modes in which being in the world, being towards death and so on is most intensely staged and I'd say that's war, sport and poetry."[54] This is not exactly the three primary display modes of the official world (crime, game, and art) that I have set out. But, for the purpose at hand, close enough. The running together here of poetry with war and sport resembles the running together of "death and so on." "Being towards death" is existential. Being toward death "and so on" is zombiedom, reenactment without content. Recall that the archaic etymological root of "life"—*lib*—means the remainder: what continues, or persists, particularly after battle or war, and so what goes on in its aftermath, life as the remains of the day. A novel then, extending the line of comparison McCarthy makes between forms of intensely staged life and art, can be about art in being about art and so on.

The crisis of the artwork, in the systems epoch, is that it appears as at once exceptional and exemplary, among countless life stages in the world. (At one extreme, the exorcism of alternatives. At the other: "Maybe the art's just one out of all kinds of different ways.")[55] That in turn has become a way of posing the problem of action in systems, and, most generally, the distinction between persons and impersonal things, and the uncertain place of cognition and intent in embodied actions (an uncertainty most perspicuous in systems-repetitive ones extroverted across the social field).[56]

Consider again Barthes's way of setting out the distinction: the kind of precision that "the thing" observes in delimiting, stopping, finishing itself. There are now, we know, everywhere things that may be seen to talk, observe, move, and give direction and form to other things, and do more than they are told: the assertion, or spreading, of cognition and intent everywhere. The narrator of McCarthy's *Remainder*, in trying to be himself, erects a series of self-curved worlds, reenactment zones, forensic spaces. That becomes about art, in dioramas of form and intent (the "extremely formal" and the "intensely staged"), or in theme parks, stationary carousels, and nature reserves restocked with artificial game. Alternatively, this means seeing, at moments, as the photographer Hiroshi Sugimoto—who has photographed, among other things, the dioramas of stilled life in the American Museum of Natural History in New York—sees it: that, say and do what you will, the singularity of "art resides even in things with no artistic intentions."[57]

V • NEWS FROM THE OUTSIDE

NINE

THE TURN TURN

The great microsociologist of social interaction rituals, Erving Goffman, notes, in the opening part of his underknown collection of essays *Forms of Talk*, this little moment in the "game-like back-and-forth process" between a speaker and a respondent:[1] "In this case, [the respondent] ignores the immediately preceding sentences to which he has proudly not paid attention since his idea occurred to him, and he interrupts to present his idea despite the non-sequitur element of his sentence."[2] This is a form of talk—what Goffman calls, on the model of the "positional moves of tokens on a [game]board" (*FT*, 71), a little "reacting move"—familiar to anyone who has ever attended a talk and the response ritual after it. These are parts of what Goffman calls the "system requirements and system constraint" of talk (14). But this encounter involving talk is not merely gamelike in its turn taking and strategic moves. This is, more exactly, a case not of interaction but of turned-away, or averted, interaction. It is a moment of proud disattention. And that nevertheless civil disattention to the nominal subject of the talk is what in turn "makes things safe for the little worlds sustained in face-to-face encounters."[3]

Such a turning away and the world it models are my subjects here, as a way of drawing together the account of the official world set out so far, and testing it out, at its limits. This is, in short, the sociality of those who turn away, or what Patricia Highsmith calls the world of "those who walk away." Highsmith's *Those Who Walk Away* (1967), like Goffman's social psychology and exactly contemporary with it, couples game and pathology point by point and plays them out under "the weight of officialism."[4] That novel and, more generally, the overturned world it presents, center this chapter.

The games, in this case, are simple ones: playing tag, hide-and-seek, and cat-and-mouse—literalizations of taking turns and making moves. These are, gridded and formatted, the logistical operations of an official world—a world that, we have seen, everywhere generates life-size models of itself. One working model of that—at once exceptional and exemplary—is the crime game: the official world adrenalized by the murder plot.

Yet Highsmith's crime novel is also a ghost story of sorts, like one of the advent stories of the reflexive epoch in modern literature, Henry James's *The Turn of the Screw* (which I will touch on, very briefly, in a moment); and like Cormac McCarthy's novel *No Country for Old Men*, one that registers the violent eclipse of that epoch. (See chapter 10.) These ghost stories are stories about playing dead: that is, they are about forms of death and life in an at once gamelike, lethal, and self-reporting world. They are stories then about the end of the world—that is, the end of the world as we know it, and know that.[5] This is the cluster of concerns that I want to examine in this chapter. And, before turning to Highsmith's *Those Who Walk Away*, it will be useful to set out, or to reset, from another vantage, the imbricated elements that make up this world. These elements are, first, its mode of interaction, *away*; second, its mode of reflection, *the turn turn*; and third, its mode of world-making, *playing society*.

Away

There is a world of accumulated feeling back of the trite dramatic expression—"I am going away."

—Theodore Dreiser, *Sister Carrie*

Goffman's accounts of interaction often devolve on or designate, as the instance I have begun with indicates, tactics of noninteraction—ways, as Goffman elsewhere puts it, of being "away."[6] Awayness is a mode of sociality premised on mutual aversion or, better, mutual avertedness. It is thus the reverse of the centripetal social bond formed at the scene of the crime or at the impact point of the collective disaster: one at which witnessing is mutually witnessed, and so forms a momentary social encounter and joint world.

But the fugue-like, or centrifugal, character of this "away" response also involves an inward reflexive turn: "while outwardly participating in an activity within a social situation, an individual can allow his attention to turn from what he and everyone else considers the real or serious world, and to give himself up for a time to a playlike world in which he alone participates. This kind of inward emigration from the gathering may be called 'away'"

(*BPP*, 69). Hence, if, for Goffman, we lead an indoor social life, the alternative to that is yet a further reflexive turn.[7]

Turning away here sounds playlike or gamelike—like daydreaming, or even in the absorbed self-talk in which one is "holding a vocal or gestural conversation where the person with whom one is conversing is oneself" (or someone who just does not happen to be there; *BPP*, 72). Yet the series of examples that Goffman in fact presents goes in another direction. These are for the most part instances of institutional awayness that model the society from which one departs a bit differently. That's the case even if one takes into account the emptying-out of pleasure from the games people play—the emptying-out of what Goffman calls "fun in games"—that characterizes a range of social psychology in the postwar years.[8] (This no doubt anticipates, and conditions, the familiar designation of the workplace today as not a blue-collar or white-collar world, but a no-collar one, in which work is supposed to feel like play and so play feels a lot like work.)[9]

These self-reflexive moments of going away look less playful than pathological. There is, for example, and first, an account of a mental hospital

> when all the patients on the ninety-bed ward are herded into one of the two dayrooms in order that the other can be mopped or waxed, and thus find themselves bunched so closely together that a useful defense is to withdraw into oneself and suppress orientation to others. In these contexts the participant-observer can soon learn to disattend to incontinence or hallucinations occurring eighteen inches away. (*BPP*, 72)

Or, second, there is the cover for an observable retreat into reverie in "public eateries [that] have underwritten this practice by placing seats for lone eaters in front of a running mirror, thus allowing the patron to facilitate the away process by covertly looking at himself." Or, there is, third, "the quality of not being present" that is exhibited "for the construction of this alienated world that [is] visible to others": the construction of "elaborate doodles," building "piles of matches," or putting together "jigsaw puzzles" (*BPP*, 77). These are "toy-involvements," little gamelike projects that "in these ways pulled the whole world in on them until the circle of reality was not more than a foot in diameter around their noses" (74).

The Incrementalist Turn

The geometry of this smaller world—what Goffman calls our indoor social life, or the return of Goffman's microsociological work itself—is part of the incrementalist turn across a range of literary and cultural studies. This is a turn toward the minor and the scaled-down (in professional fields—the humanities and the social sciences—that are institutionally doing the same). Hence, for example, with respect to the novel, minor characters; with respect to affect, minor feelings; with respect to political forms, little resistances, infantile subjects, minute therapeutic adjustments; with respect to perception, the decelerated gaze and a prolonged attentiveness; and so on.[10] These forms of one-downmanship—a turn from large events to small (non) events—are the reverse side of the one-upmanship of recent academic acclimatizations to globalization.

The incrementalist turn, and these minority reports, might, along these lines, be seen in terms of what has been described as a sort of "epistemological therapeutics" by which one parries a "given" world, a world that is too much with us—and so holds at bay the givenness of the official world.[11] The distinction between that as alternative to the official world or as acclimatization or adjustment to it here is a bit hard to locate. But that may be to pose matters the wrong way. That's because a self-distancing or avertedness is a condition of modern sociality, in that reflexivity and second-order observation are the defining conditions of modernity. This a sociality premised on reciprocal distance, one that, we have seen, takes the form of a doubling of reality (the presupposition of self-registration). This is a world that consists in itself plus its registration: the official world has remade "a world elsewhere" as its slogan and its multiple-choice outlook on life (the presupposition of alterity). Hence the current turn to possible worlds, to counterfactual ones, and to the end of the world. The official world is marked by the unremitting copying of the distinction between real and fictional worlds. In Roger Caillois's terms, it is scored "by a special awareness of a second reality or of a free unreality, as against real life."[12]

There is a good deal to be said for the opening to small moments of unaccountability, and even perhaps for the uses of such an epistemological therapeutics—and the political minimalism that goes with it—in this incrementalist turn. It is, for one thing, more attuned to the institutional situation of literary and cultural forms, and their way of acting in the world, than the maximalist claims of transnational and transchronological turns, which seem at times to assume the literalism of a direct political, or emancipatory, impact on the world or even past worlds.[13]

But my concern here is a bit different. The "turns" that have proceeded in rapid series across the disciplines—the linguistic turn, the historical turn, the cultural turn, the transnational turn, the speculative turn, and so on— might simply be called the turn turn.[14] This turn taking is one of the means by which the presumption of critical and social reflexivity (a turning back on itself) periodizes—and so periodically and institutionally reignites—itself. The turn turn—the gyroscope, an instrument that views the turn and reports on it (as I've earlier set out), its model—thus stages and exposes the reflexivity that is at once the self-condition, and predicament, of the second modernity.

It is not hard to see that there is currently what might be described as something of a revulsion against that predicament and the jargon of reflexivity. The modalization of the world—via one turn after another, and the observation of that—is precisely the "correlationist" account that a speculative realism ("the speculative turn") looks to counter (in the exposure of the presumption of a correlation of the world and its human observation). That's made for something of a breakout from the prison house of self-conditioning—from a world relative to its observation, and correlative to the human measure. The move is in the direction, for example, of cognitive science, evolutionary biology, and mathematics as ontology. The turn, in all, is from an indoor social life to the great outdoors—a new Copernican turn to what is not just outside the official world but, it will be seen, "outside of everything."[15]

There is more at stake here than the bid for scientific aura (although that no doubt enters into the speculative turn in the humanities). It's part of a revulsion again reflexivity and its collation of the world to human cognition or reflection; it's a reaction against what is more and more described as secondhand nonexperience and the zombie-like afterlife of deconstruction. That idling, or empty running, is in many ways the subject and form of *Those Who Walk Away*.

The novel compulsively generates little scenes that model the reflexive turn and the perspectivism that goes with it. Take, for example, this small moment of a mingled disgust and self-reflection: "Dog dung on the pavement, in a square of light that fell from a window, looked like a deliberately vulgar display, and Ray wondered why he stared at it, until he realized it had swollen, because of the rain, to the size of human excrement. He looked away from it, and thought, 'I'm not Ray Garrett tonight'" (*T*, 117). This is a recognition scene, even if it's not pretty to think so—something like, "I am a piece of shit." The little street scene registers nothing if not a revulsion against reflexivity. The thing is displayed as if staged, looked at, and then looked away from—as if anything might solicit observation, stare, wonder, thought, realization, so long as it is "sized" to human measure and so self-recognition. Or as another character in *Those Who Walk Away* puts it with equal aversion,

"What's all this nonsense about reality? . . . All this 'perhaps,' 'I *think*'" (*T*, 40, 42, emphasis in text). The italicization of the world, its systemic self-production, becomes repellent, and so issues in self-repulsion: "he wanted his self-effacement" (*T*, 60), "I am not Ray Garrett tonight." Or, as Highsmith elsewhere expresses it, he wanted his "self-annihilation."[16] In short, the sui generis world is at the same time the suicidal one (and hence *Those Who Walk Away* begins with that terminal form of self-determination).

Playing Society

H. G. Wells, it will be recalled, compared the Jamesian novel to an overlit altar on which was displayed a broken eggshell, a piece of string, and a dead kitten. Flaubert, we know, announced the complete independence of the art of the novel from its subject matter—the novel could burn anything. Looking, showing, wondering, and realizing in Highsmith look like this: the correlationism by which the human observer is the measure of all things, not least in a novel in which hundreds of sentences have the phrases "he thought" or "he realized" attached to them. If this scene on the street is then a recognition scene, it is one that, fitting the world to human size, marks the official limits of that world.

The self-conditioned world—the world as we know it—is a version then of the parlor games, or "social games," I have earlier set out (see part IV). And it is then part of the movement of the gamelike into the social field generally, as its defining condition, or autogenous demonstration. These are ways, to adapt Simmel's phrase, of "playing society." "The expression *social game*," as Simmel sets it out in his account of "autonomous forms" of sociation, "is significant in the deeper sense to which I have already called attention. All the forms of interaction or sociation among men—the wish to outdo, exchange, the formation of parties, the desire to wrest something from the other, the hazards of accidental meetings and separations, the change between enmity and cooperation, the overpowering by ruse and revenge—in the seriousness of reality, all of these are imbued with purposive contents. In the game, they lead their own lives; they are propelled exclusively by their own attraction."[17] But the very autonomization of social forms means that these social games (Gesellschaftsspiele) model a self-modeling world: "The more profound, double sense of 'social game' is that not only the game is played in *a society* (as its external condition) but that, with its help, people actually 'play' 'society.'"[18]

Two quick examples, both forms of talk that play society. First, Goffman's lecture on that improbable institution, "the lecture." What Goffman calls "the lecture medium" is something of "a laminated affair of game and spectacle," one that links face-to-face interaction and the text brought to the lectern, a text that formally exceeds the occasion it references (FT, 167). It combines, then, reference and the process of referring, fresh talk and printed form. The magic trick is the continuous oscillation between medium and form, spectacle and game, animated print and the text in person. The use of quotation within a talk, for example, not merely brings institutionalizing credentials to the sociable encounter, but is useful to disembarrass the understanding that the speaker is merely reading—that is, quoting himself at length. It marks the distinction between print and interaction, and so includes devices for internally differentiating medium and form. Hence the framing gestures and asides that convey "the rather touching plea" that the speaker should be given credit for what he or she does not say, but could have imparted: if only there had been more time, there would have been more argument. In these ways, the external properties of the talk and the internal ones, the inside and outside of words, are systematically coupled to each other—even as that coupling can then be systematically disattended. "The lecture" thus models the turn turn it exposes. Yet this social game has a "greater" function than the intramural ones already set out. The lecturer and audience "join in affirming a single proposition": the proposition that there is, after all, "a real, structured, somewhat unitary world out there to comprehend." Its "real contract," Goffman concludes, is "to protect us from the wind": in short, to posit "that there is structure to the world, that this structure can be perceived and reported, and therefore, that speaking before an audience and listening to a speaker are reasonable things to be doing" (FT, 194–95). It allows, that is, for the transformation of hetero-determination into self-determination and so posits a unitary or autistic world, one without an exterior.

The social task of the lecturer then is not unlike the task of the storyteller. James's *The Turn of the Screw* (1898) is also a story designed to protect us from the outside, and it is about the turn turn too. The novel opens with this phrase: "The story had held us round the fire." This adult campfire story thus—whether ghost story or sexual repression story, whether real or in the narrator's head—posits a unitary world, but alternate ones. It realizes itself, as Peter Sloterdijk expresses it, in the "formal and technical construction of circles," and "rounding events," such as these opening and storied moments of thermic socialization: "just as those gathered around a hearth group freely *and* decidedly around the fireplace and its immediate advantages of warmth."[19] The circle of the sequestered country house, or the story of it, is explicit, its form homeopathic or psychopathic.

In *The Turn of the Screw*, that is, self-organization appears in pristine form: in turn, in the form of psychic hysteria or hystericized science. *Turn*, we know, continuously marks the distinction between inner and outer worlds. The distinction between utterance (self-reference) and information (hetero-reference) is remarked and reproduced at every point, and the terms of the distinction oscillate from one side to the other. It is a game, one that "makes the score off its own bat." But it solicits all the paradoxes of a game that one is "playing very hard":[20] it is a real game, a matter of life and death. The game world is "annexed but independent" with respect to the official world; and the competing themes that compel the game (the tabloid themes of sex or violence) are exchangeable parts that are, in a strict sense, moves in a game. The unity of the distinction between world and game is then the subject of *Turn*, in its testing of the presumption of reflexivity and its techniques.[21]

The official world is a world made up of the autogenic social systems that Max Weber early on described in terms of the self-documenting qualities and the self-recording processes of a modernizing world, and constitute the cultural techniques that make up its reflexive infrastructure. The official world is an "enormous file"—and if there is nothing in the world that is not in the files, then there is, conversely, nothing in the files that is not in the world.[22] This is a world that posits and endures its own self-authorization—the continuous transformation from natural life to forms of life (its "biocratic" paradigm). It is gamelike, we have seen, in its contingency, self-conditioning, and gratuitous complication. And, to the extent that it is gamelike, it is a world that presupposes its own comparative character and hence its own alterity. That makes for the strange air of captivity that marks the official world—the intimation of other worlds, a war of the worlds, and the end of the world, and these are the subjects I want now to unfold to somewhat different ends.[23]

Playing Dead

The plot of Patricia Highsmith's novel *Those Who Walk Away*—to the extent that this novel about the unhappening of the world has one—can be simply set out. Two men take turns following each other through the streets of the mazelike city of Venice, trying to kill each other. Or, more exactly, they take turns killing each other, and then resetting and "turning the tables" (*T*, 182), repeating the series of moves once more: "Very well, if it had to be done still again, it would be done again" (94–95). The game—"play dead" (55)—can simply be replayed, in that the game is independent of real life or real death:

"he would have killed you again!" (240). This is, as it were, the cartoon-like character of violence in a game world, marked by its reiteration and its inconsequentiality.

The two men are the father (Coleman, an artist) and the husband (Ray, an art dealer) of a young woman (Peggy, an artist too), who has, just before the opening of the novel, committed suicide—and the artist holds the art dealer to account for that. The death of the woman is nominally the cause of the gamelike back-and-forth process—the cat-and-mouse game: the steps, the turns, the moves—that makes up the novel. But only nominally that: these moves are annexed to this motive but seem independent of it. The death of the beautiful young woman Peggy is, it would seem, less the cause of these acts than something like a peg or game piece that circulates in them. These moves are the "steps" in a gamelike logic of composition: the series of strategic positions, step-by-step feeding back effects into causes, in an autonomous and relentlessly gamelike world.[24]

Yet what then is the status of what can only loosely be called the "game-like" itself? The game, we know, has no grounds: "The game proves its worth. That may be the cause of the game being played, it is not its ground."[25] That is, why we might like to play the game does not enter into how the game is played. But the cause of the game is not its ground too in that the game is self-causing: the language game, or the discourse/power "game is not based on grounds. It is not reasonable (or unreasonable). It is there—like one's life."[26] If what defines the game is not a set of properties but a series of acts, the point is not to ask whether these are really games. (How does one keep score in a language game? Or win one?) If the game is not a list or set of properties (or rules), but instead a way of acting (a series of acts lifted from acts), the point then is not to ask whether these are really games but what sort of actions follow from designating them games, and so entering into—that is, playing—them. The central point is this one: Why—in the spreading of game-attribution across the social field, from roughly the 1890s on—does such a range of different acts come to be called games, so as to discourage, or to lessen, the value of differentiating them?

In *Those Who Walk Away*, "playing dead" looks like a game with its own rules and one in which that autonomization—and this gamelike back-and-forth process—arrives as its own topic: "What's all this nonsense about reality" (42). The autonomization of the game means that the characters keep checking to see whether or not they are playing a game, and, if so, whether or not it's the same one. That is, they check back to make sure they are each following the same rules, and continuously cross-check positions, motives, and goals. The distinction between the gamelike and the game is not canceled: the distinction enters into the game at every point, and so must be continuously reproduced. That makes up the ambient state of the game, to the very extent that it is just "like one's life."[27]

The sui generis character of the game is what makes it simply there, like one's life. And in *Those Who Walk Away*, the sui generis and the suicidal are thus two sides of a single formation. It is no accident that for Durkheim the sociology of suicide is the take-off point for a modern sociology tout court, one that posits and analyzes the systemic character of the sui generis society.[28] The continuous transformation of hetero-determinations into self-determinations—the transformation that defines the modern epoch's paroxysmal transitions from natural life to forms of life—conjoins vital and lethal, or homicidal, tendencies: it recurrently overturns self-processing into self-annihilation. These are the mutual interferences of the bodily and the social that make up the biotechnical realities of Highsmith's writing—or what Highsmith elsewhere (in her first published novel, *Strangers on a Train*) calls "precarious life."[29] Highsmith's work everywhere rarefies the terms "life," "world," and "society"—in the name of a generalized self-defense: "life itself" is weaponized. If murder is where bodies and politics cross, this means too that the crisscrossing of natural and social life in the modern epoch is itself experienced as lethal: that the relays of biology and society, the biopolitical, devolve on the homicidal or suicidal. (Hence the mingled horror and thrill of precarious or bare life—as at once exposed life and inartificial life, and the allure of the torn body and torn world, as indexes of the real, in a wound culture.)[30]

We can begin to fill in what this looks like via several everyday passages from the novel—if we bear in mind that moves or passages, ways of getting from here to there, are at once the medium and the form of this novel of walking away. Their form, like that of the pun, devolves on literalism, and this literalism, or minimalism, marks the novel from its title on. Here then is a typical scene in this step-by-step process, midway in the novel:

> To right and left, lanes went off, dark alleys that would make it easy to give Coleman the slip. Ray went quickly into one on his right. There had been enough people on the street for him to hope Coleman had not noticed his turning, but Ray still took a left turn next, went under a sottoporto and found himself on a narrow pavement beside a canal. He paused, reluctant to go any farther, because the canal walk seemed to

lead nowhere much, and the section was dark. Ray went cautiously back the way he had come, but stopped when he saw that Coleman was advancing. Ray returned to the canal and went left on its back, running a little. He took the next lane left. A corner street light ahead showed a right turning thirty yards on. . . . Coleman was coming after him. Ray could hear his trotting footsteps. The thing to do was get back to the larger street, Ray thought. Ray took the right turn, realized he would have to go left to reach the larger street. He saw he had run into a blind alley, and started back again. (*T*, 172)

This is fast-paced, albeit in that it consists in nothing but pacing. Walking, like talking, in the novel, is a way of "getting somewhere," or, more often, "going nowhere" (*T*, 2). Taking a step is step-by-step thinking, planning, and deciding, or turning. At every point, thoughts and steps are exactly coordinated: "These thoughts went through his mind very rapidly, in a matter of a second or two, then he remembered—and slowed his steps. . . . He had to plan what to do next" (115).

Steps and turns are moves, the working parts of "an interactional perspective that recommends 'move' as its minimal unit" (*FT*, 54). Turns, steps, moves—all oscillate between the act and its reflection, between physics and hermeneutics: between the medium of the move and its form. The medium of the move is thus a complex one. The move draws into relation intention and information, decision and observation: "The move made by one participant must be attended to by the other participants and has much the same meaning for all of them" (71). In doing so, it ratifies a mutually observed commitment and hence a shared world.

The turn, that is, consists of itself plus its staging, a first and a virtual, or second, world. Steps, turns, moves resemble the positional moves of tokens, or pegs, in a game:

An arrow directed him to a vaporetto. It was when he decided to give up a certain unpromising looking street, and turned back, that he saw Coleman some thirty feet away. Coleman was looking at him, and Ray was sure had been following him. For an instant, Ray thought of approaching Coleman and telling him what he planned to do, go to the police tomorrow. But as before, in his instant of hesitation, Coleman turned round. Annoyed, Ray turned back in his original direction. (*T*, 172)

The indoor social world of the novel resembles a game board, complete with arrows directing moves: "he glanced around for one of the helpful arrows . . .

painted on the side of houses to show the way. . . . Meanwhile, he must take up the pieces of his life again. He could make a list of four or five" (*T*, 166).[31]

Arrows, pieces, moves, and lists of planned ones—these are the markers of the game space of the novel, in which space and map coincide. The arrows on the street cancel the distinction between map and territory, or, better, continuously compare them: the "American Express's tiles appeared under his feet, directing him with an arrow to their office" (*T*, 10). Venice—the iconic city as artificial and autonomous space—is the setting par excellence of such an indoor world.[32] Or, as Ray realizes, a mazelike interior, a game world, that copies itself over and over: "This little start-of-a-maze in which he stood, at La Fenice, was duplicated two hundred, three hundred times all over the city of Venice. And behind the wall of any house, really any house he walked past . . . Coleman could be hiding" (215).

These are close-ups on the moment at which, for example, one contemplates a move but hesitates before releasing the piece from the hand: moments that stage intention and decision, and their mutual observation. Intent and effect keep shifting places, such that, in the form of the game, the distinction between checking and acting is denuded or annulled: checking is a move in the game. Hence the transition to the next move, each step carving out a reference, and the live feed between observation and act: each move, via these technologies of reference, in turn retroactively unfolding the prior one and the form of its intention. Its referential afterlife, like the positional moves of tokens on a board, has no grounds but the process and form of the game itself (*FT*, 52–60, 64). Tag, cat-and-mouse, hide-and-seek, keep away, playing dead: here the sequestered or walled world of the game could not be more clearly demarcated. Things and signs—"Viale Pola, Ray read on a street sign" (*T*, 2)—are correlated at every point, flattening the distinction between them.

Officialism

This is, in short, a world "under the weight of officialism": "pen and paper were produced. The clerk sat at the side of the desk" (*T*, 184). It is a world of files, records, and filing cabinets: "This is sort of an affidavit that says you are really you" (192). It is a board-game world collating location, visibilities, and information: "For our report we must know the places at which you have been staying—and at present where you are" (191).[33]

The world under the weight of officialism is then not merely a world of observed observers, although it is that, in excruciated form:

During the next two days, Coleman more than once—in fact, three times—felt that Ray's eyes were on him. Once it was while crossing San Marco's, though in the open space maybe anybody would have felt observed, if he suspected the presence, the observant presence, of someone like Ray Garrett. She had noticed his looking. This was no place for an agoraphobe. (*T*, 104)

That's what the overlit public sphere looks like in the novel, and its media of observation and self-observation. And that's why the public reaction to Coleman's final attempt to kill Ray amounts simply and exactly to the charge "Disturbatore della quiete pubblica" (*T*, 249). This is the sign of an intramural social life and of an aversive, or averted, sociality: it is the mass public form of away.

It is too the diagram of a modern sociality that insists on, as it submits to, its own authority, and whose members have in common only that they are all on their own.[34] It consists at once of its systemicity and its self-conditioning. Via these modes of attention, or disattention, scenes and objects are folded back into the order and techniques of the observer. They are scaled to the size of the human eye and the human head. "A curious analogy," Wittgenstein notes, "could be based on the fact that the eye-piece of even the hugest telescope cannot be bigger than our eye."[35] In Cormac McCarthy's terms: "When you've said that it's real and not just in your head I'm not at all sure what it is you have said."[36] I will return to both in a moment. But I want to approach this correlationism of the world and its observation laterally, by way of the self-descriptions that make it up.[37]

One way of taking up that curious analogy appears in how, again and again in *Those Who Walk Away*, and in Highsmith's novels generally, experience is noted or recorded in its own presence: it is its own description. This has the effect not of immediacy but just the opposite: "the experience vanished as soon as he realized he was having it" (*T*, 236). Several brief examples can suffice here, in that such instances run wall-to-wall in *Those Who Walk Away*. They make visible the correlation of states of matter and states of mind in the novel: its rhetoric of reflexivity and its dead end. First: "What Coleman very much wanted to do was . . . to go to the police and say he had seen a man being rolled into the canal at about 11 P.M. on the 23rd. That would start the ball rolling nicely, Coleman thought" (195–96). Here states of matter and of mind are exactly correlated, in the oscillation between the metonymic and the metaphoric. Put simply, the physical act (the rolling of a body) turns into a move in the game (getting the ball rolling, and observing that), one that leads to another, and so runs on its own. Outside the game, what's inside the head and what's in the world look a bit different. These states are compared and collated too. Second: "He shivered partly from the cold, partly from what he was thinking, or trying to imagine" (215). Or, third: "Ray then walked for an hour in an agreeable mental fog—a fog as far as his own problems were concerned, because he simply was not thinking about them, but not a fog as far as Venice was concerned, because he felt he saw the city more sharply than ever before" (171). Here interior states are compared to outer ones, but only in terms of the outside seen from the inside. The characters in the novel enact and expose this reflexivity as if it were the unremitting bad weather of the novel. Fourth: "He was, just now, devoid of ties of any kind. That was the mechanical though not the philosophical essence. A bump from someone behind him . . . made Coleman aware that he had been standing still on the street. He walked on" (236–37). It is as if the Cartesian split between the mechanical and the philosophical, between states of matter and states of mind, were something that the characters simply take note of in passing. These moments are self-reported with a sort of stunned literalism, as if registering the matter-of-fact coming apart of the world—and as if "the only thing to do was to walk it off" (10).[38]

It is now possible to turn to the opening passage of the novel. The opening stages what the face-to-face encounter between persons has come to look like, in an unremittingly indoor, reflexive, and official world, a world under the weight of officialism. It measures how difficult it has become to posit an alternative to secondhand nonexperience—that is, an alternative to the automatic deconstruction of the very possibility of the face-to-face encounter, and to the improbability, or the paradox, of an unreported world, one without observers.

Talking and walking are reduced to their component parts. Talking is a going through the motions: Ray, we are told, "had got nowhere, trying to talk to him" (T, 2). Bodies in motion are stripped to their mechanisms and to the sounds they emit: "The pavement slanted downward. The sound of their footfalls grew higher pitched as their shoes slid a little. *Scrape-scrap-scrapety-scrape*. Ray took hardly more than one step to Coleman's two. Coleman was short and had a quick choppy gait that was at the same time rolling" (1). Highsmith's minimalism, or literalism, could not be more clearly marked.[39] It sets up a coming face-to-face with the real—an encounter that, in the recoil from just this relentless reflexivity, induces explosive violence, as if that violence were its antidote:

Ray was vaguely aware of Coleman tugging in his pocket for something. Then Coleman faced him suddenly and a shot exploded between them, rocking Ray back against a hedge, making his ears ring, so that for a few seconds he could not hear Coleman's running feet on the pavement. Coleman was out of sight, Ray did not know if a bullet had knocked him backward, or if he had fallen back with surprise. . . . Ray gasped for air, realized he had been holding his breath, then struggled forward, off the hedge to his feet. . . . He decided he was not hit. He began to walk in the direction Coleman had taken, the direction in which they had been walking. (*T*, 2)

Via minute shifts—the suspension of the immediate senses of seeing, hearing, breathing, and of knowing; the transition to realization and decision; the violence that stands in for the face-to-face encounter—the turn to the game, and to play fighting, comes about. That initiates the first round in the game, and the direction of the first move. Hence awayness enters into the given world, in a transition to second life as its everyday condition.

TEN

A POSTSCRIPT ON
THE OFFICIAL WORLD

I want, in this final chapter, to provide something of a summary account of the shape of an official world and a postscript on its suspended—that is, self-suspended—states. I will first say a bit more about the stranger sociality of *those who walk away* (by way of Highsmith), and then (by way of the stories of Cormac McCarthy, J. G. Ballard, and Karl Ove Knausgaard) turn to the current sense of a closure of the bourgeois half-millennium and the systems epoch. I mean *closure* in the twin senses carried by the recent baptism of the epoch of social systems or the world interior of capitalism as an epoch of our own: the anthropocene, the geological age of the human. That scenic designation, or charismatic naming-event (the anthropocenic), makes it possible to redescribe "the one-world state" and "world interior of capital" in epoch-geological terms. If that redescription is not entirely indifferent to the operation of social and economic systems and institutions, it is generally not attuned to their specification. It's possible to see this epoch of self-determination, and so, in effect of self-termination, along somewhat different lines: as bound up through and through with the bipolar organization of the long modernity and its stockpile, or arsenal, of image-funds.

The Autonomization of Everything

In Highsmith's *Those Who Walk Away*, "playing dead" is a game with its own rules: "he decided to play dead. . . . It was a kind of plan."[1] The game is one in which the autonomization of death and life realizes itself: hence, "What's all this nonsense about reality" (*T*, 42). In his extended study of man, play, and games, Roger Caillois describes games as calisthenics in social formation; he sets out a "sociology derived from games" that involves development of "critical reflection" and a "form of government."[2] In a brief and remarkable earlier piece, on mimicry and legendary psychaesthenia, Caillois's account of play is very different. In that case, playing is playing dead: the subject, going into hiding, is not similar to something or someone, but "just similar."[3] The relays between these two form games—playing dead and playing society—are the relays of biology and sociology in *Those Who Walk Away*.

Take, for example, the ongoing game of hide-and-seek in the novel: "I was looking for him to prove that he was alive" (*T*, 245). It is necessary to understand this as literally as possible. Hide-and-seek installs both players in a social game and so functions as "proof" of that mutual life. He was "deliberately hiding" (128). The hidden may be unintentional; hiding is intentional: "deliberately hiding" is playing the game of hide-and-seek. The difference between hiding and the hidden is the difference between social and natural life. The game of hide-and-seek involves, we know, a crisscrossing of bodily and artificial realities across an axis of self-observed observation. It is both a timeless little game and one that becomes timely as a miniature working model of processes of modernization that presuppose the gamelike character of a social order that nonetheless stipulates its biological characterization—it is, in Roberto Esposito's sense of the term, a little "biocracy." In Georg Simmel's terms, it provides a way of playing society. In his discussion of "the role of the secret in social life," Simmel notes that "the secret in this sense, the hiding of realities by negative or positive means, is one of man's greatest achievements. . . . The secret offers, so to speak, the possibility of a second world alongside the manifest one."[4] In this sense, the medium of the secret is the basic unit of sociation. It is in this transition from first to second worlds that the move to the game takes place. This is how the moves in the game—hide-and-seek, for example—take on a form felt on the body and that takes on the form of a life plan.

Hence, for Simmel, there is a distinctly autonomic and systemic character to the secret. Secrecy has the character of a quantifiable thermodynamic principle: "One could, therefore, entertain the paradoxical idea that under otherwise identical circumstances, human collective life requires a certain measure of secrecy which merely changes its topics: while leaving one of them, social life seizes on another, and in all this alternation it preserves an unchanged quantity of secrecy" (*SGS*, 335–36). The possibility of a second world alongside the first one is thus linked to the autonomization of the secret, as a social medium, and one that changes forms, or topics.

The effect of the transfer from the content of the secret to its statistical measure and form cannot be overestimated. This is the autopoietic moment, the moment at which sociation stands free of external reference, like a game, and at the same time achieves the objectivity of a social system. The game is one in which the autonomization of death and life shows or models itself ("What's all this nonsense about reality"). The first world yields to the second: it is as if reference were a foreign concept (*Fremdreferenz*) and self-reference (*Selbtsreferenz*) the default position—that is, the self-reference of the system, irrespective of persons.[5]

Here other-reference and self-reference take the form of a game of life and death. Hide-and-seek, as a cat-and-mouse game, couples homicidal and suicidal tendencies: precarious life as weaponized life targets anything that moves. It is not necessary here to rehearse once again the spreading of autonomization throughout the social body and beyond, a self-making that takes turns in changing its topics: from social systems—"autonomous forms of sociation" (SGS, 43); to psychic systems—"the *autonomy* of the field of sexuality as the field of psychoanalysis";[6] to organic ones—as Highsmith's character in *Those Who Walk Away* puts it, "the sex organs had separate existences of their own" (*T*, 87).

Nor is it necessary to rehearse the bootstrapping logic that goes with it. Coleman, we are told, is "the self-made man, blustering his way into moneyed society" (*T*, 180). Ray, we are told, is the son of "a self-made man, now a millionaire with an oil company of his own" (58). Ray lives in a house his father "might have built with his own hands. . . . Therefore there was, somehow, nothing for him to stand on" (59). The self-made man, lifting himself by his own bootstraps, has, therefore, no place to stand—for Ray, "a shattering, dumbfounding thought" (65). It is shattering—unfounding—not least in that the self-making of persons is also part of (and so merely part of) the self-making of everything.[7]

That autonomization of everything is staged and exposed too, as the topography of the novel. At the midpoint of the novel, Ray is walking in the corridor-like streets of Venice:

> Then he took a boat to San Marco and spent the latter part of the afternoon visiting the Palace of the Doges. The huge, formal council halls, the ornate emptiness of the place made him feel more calm and in command of himself. It was, somehow, the shattering purposelessness of the Palace that now made him feel so, he realized. (*T*, 131)

This is the palace described in the second section of Kant's *Critique of Judgment*, the palace that, for Kant, particularizes the "autonomization of aesthetics" and the common sense it forms. The purposelessness of an aesthetic judgment isolates "the formal" alone, and asks only to be sensible of form.[8] But here again, the autonomy of art, and its realization, appear at once exceptional and exemplary: that is to say, "the theme of reflection does not define the meaning of the autonomy of art, but the meaning of the doubling of reality in which this autonomy established itself."[9]

We find here the transference of autonomy across different registers and its serial realization condensed at this moment, in the political, the aesthetic, and the psychophysical orders of things. This autonomization of everything is at once the principle of self-shattering and the principle of self-command: the double logic of the form of life (with its different topics or media) that makes itself from itself. It is the possibility, or horror, of the autonomization of each and every thing and every one, each having a separate existence of its own.

Take the little world called the art world in *Those Who Walk Away*. The possibility of a second world is, of course, nowhere clearer than in this one. The names proposed for the art gallery Ray is about to open in New York are Gallery Zero or the Gallery of Bad Art: "people would come to laugh and start to buy, . . . in order to have something different from other people who collected only 'the best'" (*T*, 6). (Highsmith's take on the intramurality of the New York art scene makes Scorsese's film *After Hours* look something like an homage.) But the point is that this art degree zero makes evident the manner in which the art world leaves the determination of what counts as art entirely up to the art system itself.

There is, on that account, nothing deeper than cultural difference (culturalism) and competing ways of seeing (perspectivism). Take too what the artwork in the novel looks like, in the context of Highsmith's literalism or minimalism. Coleman's art is more pop than minimalist: Ray "was not fond of Coleman's current pop art phase. . . . [He] tried to imagine what Coleman's heavy black outlines and flat expanses of unvaried colour would make of Venice" (*T*, 21). But his current art phase is (as phase, or turn) an experiment in perspective and point of view—in observing the turn: "This was his new tack: the human figure seen from directly overhead. He felt this view, showing little, still showed much. . . . 'These are people?' she asked, smiling. 'Yes, seen from overhead. There's my first drawing.' He pointed, but the drawing had slipped flat from its prop against the paintbox. . . . 'I like them, don't you? These people seen from the top? . . . Angel's-eye view'" (*T*, 91, 95). Literalism here is, as it were, literalized: the terms "top" and "flat" each repeat, across different registers, in the novel, and so map this self-mapping world. That is, they graph a self-graphing world, one that is a life-size model of itself, and so one that tends toward self-modeling.

The events of the novel turn, from moment to moment, into little moments of self-illustration: excrement on the street, for example, or the view from the top: "She looked down at the pigeons bobbing on the pavement" (*T*, 29). Flatness and the view from the top are both parts of a reflexive world bound to perspective, shifts in scale, and second-order observation. The view from the top looks like omniscience, an angel's-eye view. But that omniscience is self-canceling, in that it appears as one perspective—or "prop"— among others. It is part of the turn turn. Second-order observation—the observation of observation—is the model of reflexivity, not the antidote to it. It is level with its own grounds, too.

This consists in a correlationism that makes the human eye and the human head equal to the world. The narrative makes sudden switches from Ray's point of view to Coleman's, absolutizing each in turn. Moreover, it names these turns, as if a schooling in and inventorying of perspectival techniques, and a rhetoric of fiction, were on the same level as the story: There is, for example, Coleman's view from above; there is Ray feeling "wiser, even omniscient" (*T*, 225). If this looks a bit too self-evidently like a training manual in methods, or gimmicks, such as point-of-view narration, something more is perhaps at stake. This narrative method realizes to the letter the correspondence that makes the human measure one with the given world— and rules out anything outside that. This is, we have seen, the form of Highsmith's narrative mode, her form game. Highsmith's characteristic narrative mode is a peculiar mutation in, or intensification of, represented discourse. In the Ripley novels, for example, the third-person narrative tacks so closely to a single point of view that it turns the first person inside out: the effect is something like that of first-person speaker speaking of himself and seeing himself in the third person.[10]

We have seen that Highsmith's narrative way of seeing lends to self-observation the look of omniscience and lends to the counterfactual the feel of objective description. Hence the paradoxical economy of Highsmith's narrative mode takes as given the modalization of the world: it absolutizes perspective and scale, and the reflexivity that goes with them. This makes for an endless and violent paradox: the strict socialization and sequestration of the social order (a social order that must make itself from itself) requires the strictly autopoietic and autonomous individual (who must make himself from himself). But since the first mandates, and thus aborts, the second, the autonomy "borrowed" from art opens the possibility of an unremitting violence. The enduring of reflexivity and autonomy is both the talent and the sentence of Highsmith's killers and artists (who are, for that reason, often the same person). There is nothing "deeper" than the observation of how one observes, and how he observes or fails to observe that—but that is observed too. As a character in *The Suspension of Mercy* expresses it: "everything was a matter of attitudes. . . . The attitude had been caused by his attitude."[11] As the pathological self-observer in *The Cry of the Owl* puts it, "I have the definite feeling if everybody in the world didn't keep watching to see what everybody else did, we'd all go berserk."[12] Or, as Ray thinks it, in the no-exit world of *Those Who Walk Away*: "Perhaps identity, like hell, was merely other people" (*T*, 117).

Outside the Official World

Identity is only conferred if the intention is to return to something. . . . It is with just this characteristic that a *form* develops whose inside is characterized by reusability and whose outside disappears from view . . . the "umarked space" of the rest of the world.
—Luhmann, *The Reality of the Mass Media*

Take this little sequence of return, memory, and identity, early on in the novel:

> Ray looked through a window at a green-black-and-yellow scarf. . . . A pang had gone through him at the sight of it, and it seemed that only after the pang did he see the scarf, and still a second later realized he had noticed it because it looked like Peggy . . . though in fact he did not remember a scarf of hers that was like this one. He walked on, five or six paces, then turned. He wanted the scarf. The shop was not yet open. . . . When he returned the shop was opening, and he bought the scarf for two thousand lire. (*T*, 12)

This is a sequence of actions that, with every move, marks itself as a game (one with the self-consistency of the overdescribed transaction that realizes it). The death by suicide of the young woman, Peggy, is nominally the cause of the novel's action. But the cause of the game, we know, is not its ground (the game is self-grounding). And if Peggy's death looks like the cause of the game, it turns out that Peggy is neither the ground of the game nor its cause: the scarf that "looked like Peggy," and that the two men compete for and possess in turn, is the cause. The story of the suicide, and its referential afterlife, give a feeling of pastness to the game—but do not enter into the game. We know, first, that "whatever the event does leave behind, it isn't the memory."[13] It is uncertain, second, "whether the things stored up may not constantly change their nature."[14] Memory, third, isn't a way of reexperiencing but an exercise and way of acting: "if I say rightly I remember it, the most varied things may happen, even just that I say it."[15] Hence the exactness of the description, and the sequence of acts, by which the scarf is attached to Peggy, and given "a proper setting in his memory" (*T*, 223). This is the incremental "setting" of acts and things: their stage setting in "interfacial intimate spheres," their internalization and encasement—plus the thinking of that interior.[16]

Hence too the exactness of the description indicating that the scarf does not quite stand for Peggy but is instead the cause of the action itself:

> He bought it in Venice because it *looked* like Peggy, not because—It *never* was Peggy's scarf. . . . It gave him a relief of confession, which was strange since the scarf in a way was a false prop, or object. Suddenly Ray's emotions about Peggy became unreal also, his guilt, that vast grey cyclonic form that he had been unable to deal with, seemed suddenly a thing of one dimension. . . . Peggy was not false like the scarf, yet the emotions they both caused seemed now equally unwarranted, unwarrantable. Ray shuddered, ducked his head, then deliberately sat straighter. "What's the matter?" Inez asked. "The trouble the scarf caused." (*T*, 213)

The scarf betokens Peggy but only in the sense that it betokens the unwarranted and unwarrantable relation between object (person or thing) and act, and between act and memory. It causes the trouble in that it marks the strictly contingent relation between the feeling of pastness and past experience. It oscillates between game and world, and in doing so discredits the distinction between them. And here that marks, we have seen, the turn from first to second worlds and the move into the game.

The "false prop" is the object that is the subject of circulation in a game—the game of playing dead that structures *Those Who Walk Away*. The subject of circulation in the game, like the round ball in a soccer game or the snatch of cloth in a game of flag football, is (following Serres) a quasi-object in that it designates the subject, who bears it; and it is a quasi-subject, in that it designates that, if he has it, he is "it." The game "doesn't need persons, people out for themselves"; it needs players, those "who follow the ball, and serve it." It therefore makes for a little network of relays, a simple relation (what Goffman would call an interaction ritual).[17] The scarf causes the trouble only in the sense that the game is caused by the ball: the ball that, circulating through it, conjoins the players and so forms the game. It is, like the ball, the center of the referential, in the moving game. It is a real abstraction: an object (since it is in the world) but a theoretical object (since it is nothing and of no value outside the game). The scarf, like the ball in the game, marks then the thrill/panic, even horror, of a sheer contingency ("Ray shuddered, ducked his head"), which is too the principle of sheer self-determination ("then deliberately sat straighter").

Peggy's referential afterlife is bound up with that version of the game which, in the novel, makes up an art world:

> Coleman started *towards* his jacket which hung over a chair, *towards* Peggy's picture. . . . Lately he had been in the habit of staring at it at least twice a day for several minutes; yet he knew every shade of light and dark in the photograph that made up *the flat, fleshless image called "Peggy,"* could have drawn the photograph precisely from memory, and in fact on Friday had. (*T*, 98, emphasis added)

Here a "towards" movement in the first world turns (via that small repetition) into the second.[18] The step-by-step articulation of memory and observation in this moment (like the step-by-step process by which the scarf that looks like Peggy is made her prop, and so becomes the token of the game) could not be clearer. But, in its very repleteness, this registration of the contingency of memory and its ego-technic media resembles the instructions for assembly that one finds packaged with a deceptively simple and obdurate object. Or, a folded insert setting out the rules of a dubious game.

The suicided woman is outside the game played in her name. But what does it mean to be outside the game here? And what is its relation to the official world? Peggy—the beautiful young woman and not the game called Peggy—is repeatedly described in the terms of the novel as "unrealistic" and "unworldly"—such that worldliness and the real indicate each other at every point. She is "away" from the real world, that is, the official one. If suicide is the sign, and symptom, of the sui generis society, suicide in this novel is (on the model of the big sleep) the big away. We might say then (as we have seen) that it marks the limit of the official world and so of the measure and weight of officialism. Or we might say, alternatively (as we have seen too), that it absolutizes the official world, taking as given the taking of one's life and one's death into one's own hands—the autonomization of life and death.

There's more. The problem with the world, for Peggy, isn't that it's too big for her but that it's not big enough:

> *Do you ever feel that the world is not enough?* Peggy had asked [Ray] that at least twice. Ray had wanted to find out from her how the world was

not enough, and Peggy had finally said she meant that the stars and the atoms, the systems of religion which stretch the imagination and still remain unfinished, and all painting and music—all *this* was not enough, and the human mind . . . desired more. . . . *The world is not enough, therefore I leave it to find something bigger.* (*T, 87*)

This is not exactly a matter of scale (whether the largest—the star; or the smallest—atoms). And it's not a matter of big "systems" (like religion or art) either. It's a matter of "the human mind," the imagination, taking the measure of all possible worlds and stretching beyond them. Highsmith makes it as explicit as possible: the desire of the human mind for more is here the desire for more of itself.

There is the call of the great outdoors in this notion that the world is not enough—and so one must leave it behind to find something bigger. This is the idiom of a boundless frontierism. In the self-made world of perpetual self-making, it is the idiom of America Unbound. But the paradox is that the opening to something bigger—the turn from the official world to the great outdoors—is folded back into the reflexive measure. Exploration and self-exploration (a new world and a new man: the coadvent of modernity) indicate each other at every point too, but strictly in terms of the outside projected from the inside: the human mind equal to anything.

Another way of putting this is to say that this is the difference between the unworldly and the unearthly. If the first, the unworldly, sounds like a song of (American) innocence, the second, the unearthly, sounds like the title of a horror movie. If the first is the outside of the official world, and its principle of endless expansion, the second is not just outside the worldly but "outside of everything."

Outside of Everything

I take the phrase "outside of everything" from Cormac McCarthy's novel *No Country for Old Men*. If the location of this novel is not the end of the world, you can, as they say, see it from there. *No Country* is, I've noted, like *The Turn of the Screw* and like *Those Who Walk Away*, a ghost story, and, like both too, a gamelike one. The ghost in this case is a pathological killer, and the game—"Call It": the simple toss of a coin—is bound to the sense of the utter contingency of the world, and the violence that sense of the world induces. I want to look briefly at McCarthy's terminator-version of the Western—a Western that is west of everything—and its way of marking the boundary of an official world, its laws of form, and its outside.[19]

A good deal of the novel takes place in "this outland country dead even of static from one end of the band to the other" (NC, 25). That is to say, it is outland and dead to the extent that the bandwidth of human life is taken as the boundary of life itself. Or, better, the novel engages in an ongoing comparison of the outland and the human measure, territory and map. It is full of studious moments like this one: "He pulled in at the filling station under the lights and shut off the motor and got the survey map from the glovebox and unfolded across the seat and sat there studying it. . . . He sat looking at the line he'd drawn. Then he bent and studied the terrain and drew another one. Then he just sat there looking at the map" (25).[20] The novel, in short, is replete with measures of space and time, maps, clocks, calendars, schedules, records, numbers. It sets out an official world in terms of an order of things that includes too "in what order to abandon" them (177).

That order is one of retroactive causality. The prevision of the effect shapes the act: "Chigurh stepped back to avoid the spray of ceramic chips off the tub and shot him in the face" (NC, 104). Again and again, it's said, "I knowed what you'd say fore you said it," that "you know how this is going to turn out, don't you" (184), or that, simply, "he'd seen it all before" (174). The real point is that this is not merely the foreknowledge and so foreclosure of the world but a world ruled by an unremitting reflexivity: it is populated by figures "who must think that he thought that they thought that he thought they were very dumb. He thought about that" (171). Reflexivity here is not an epistemological virtue, and it is not a form of sociological distinction. It looks, instead, like some thing held to light as if it were a curious pathogen.[21]

This retroactive and reflexive turn means not merely that one has seen it all before, but also that this is a world with its own laws of form. It is logically and temporally afterward such that "now everything can be seen at once" (NC, 178)—and the moment when everything can be seen at once is the moment of form. It is along these lines that this spare and measured novel, which draws its title from Yeats's late poem on the yielding of life to art, takes the form of form. Here we might consider, for example, this taut line, one among many others: "When you've said that it's real and not just in your head I'm not all that sure what it is you have said" (299). This is to pose the question of the correlation of the world and the human measure in the starkest terms: to pose the question of what's outside the official world—and whether that's outside of everything. But these lines do something more: they do what they say. The reflexive turn, and its laws of form, include the form of the novel too, in this exact sense: these bare hard words align the way iron filings align in a force field, assembling bits into an incipient quatrain, one that scans and rhymes:

> When you've said that it's real
> And not just in your head
> I'm not all that sure
> What it is you have said.

This is what the work of art in the epoch of systems looks like, achieving a practical form that can be seen afterward, and all at once. And here that arrives as its own theme.

The game that centers *No Country* can be called "Call It"—the instruction to toss a coin that turns out to mean life or death. That things are what they are called is the logic of constructionism, or correlationism. The novel hence poses murder as a Sadeian thought experiment on that theme. The coin is the instrument only in that "anything can be an instrument." And the identification of the necessity of contingency means that there is no unity of part and whole: "you see the problem. To separate the act from the thing. As if the parts of some moment in history might be interchangeable with the parts of some other moment. How could that be?" (*NC*, 57).[22]

Take the parts of the novel, for instance. The novel has intermittently a first-person narrator, Sheriff Bell, whose commentary chapters are italicized; and the same character is included in the plot, in other chapters, and in the third person. The officer of the law then is narratively inside but also outside the official world, acting in and reflecting on it. The killer—for the film version of the novel, the Coen brothers said they sought to cast someone "who could have come from Mars"—is the one described as "outside of everything." This is the unworldly and the unearthly again, this time set out with a mathematical precision. The senseless, machinic violence of the world means, for Bell, that there are "certain things in the world, the evidence for certain things . . . that you may very well not be equal to" (*NC*, 299). There is an abstract literalness to McCarthy's spare and outland terms. To say that there are certain things in the world you may not be equal to means, of course, that there are certain things in the world that are bigger or stronger than persons.[23] But it also means that there are certain things in the world that can't be correlated with persons and with the human measure, and hence too that the noncorrelation of what's real and what's just in your head may be the limit of reflexivity but not the limit or end of the world. Put a bit differently, if there are certain things in the world that one might well not be equal to, that's to say there are things outside that are not therefore outside of everything: things that are just there, like one's life. Or even, as McCarthy almost ends it, that "it's nice just to be here" (302).

But he actually ends it with this little fable: "And in the dream I knew that [my father] was goin on ahead and that he was fixin to make a fire somewhere out there in all that dark and all that cold and I knew that whenever I got there he would be there. And then I woke up" (NC, 307). This is the story that holds us round the fire, in James's ghost writing, and it is like, too, Goffman's little daydreams of being away from the official world. Yet can we really fault a novel of relentless violence and cold form games for having one, or two, too many happy endings? And can we fault it at all in that this dream is, after all, unfolded as the plot of McCarthy's immediately subsequent and companion novel, *The Road*? If *No Country* traces the systemic violence of a cartel one-world (the world interior of capital), *The Road*—the image of its opposite—takes up its suspension, or vanishing.[24]

"The Provocation of the Outside": "The Vanished Age of Space"

He looked at the sky. As if there were anything there to be seen.
—Cormac McCarthy, *The Road*

One day I got an urge to go and check up on the outside world myself. Nothing much to report.
—Tom McCarthy, *Remainder*

The suspended world is the "cauterized terrain" of McCarthy's apocalyptic, or revelatory, novel, *The Road*. The world has been contracted to the world interior of a father and son—"each the other's world entire"—who push down the road a battered shopping cart, containing their bare provisions, on a thoroughly consumed earth: as if going down the same road that led to the disaster in the first place. A receding world and a squandered world (to take two of the many world-descriptive terms McCarthy uses, these in *No Country for Old Men*). It is—and here I am paraphrasing Alexander Kluge's account of the devastation produced by the air war on Germany—as if the reflexes of a form of life that not merely preceded the disaster but led to it continue on in the absence of the obliterated world that was the prerequisite for them.[25]

And prerequisite for the form of the novel itself. The world of *The Road* is one virtually stripped of secondary qualities: "some cold glaucoma dimming the world." It is a world stripped of self-observation and so of news of itself. There remain only the remnant small technologies—binoculars, lamp, sextant, folded and torn "oilcompany map"—that not merely locate a way of seeing but ways of seeing: the world as it looks to us. The sudden, quenching return of color and life, in the last lines of the novel—the beauty of the brook trout "standing in the amber"; the "deep glens where they lived all things were older than man" (*R*, 287)—these appear strictly in terms of the world as it looks without us.

The Road is thus located at the crossroads of a speculative realism and a social realism. It is located, that is, at the crossroads of two worldviews, or, more exactly, a worldview and a world without a view. First, the nature of things apart from us—and apart from how we see them (cold, autistic, alien, uncoupled, implacable, a world unheard of—these are some of McCarthy's terms for this). Second, the vagrant flashes of a social realism and its prerequisite idiom of a mutually observed and self-reported world—that is, the world of the novel at its eclipse. The Beckett-like exchanges between the father and son that involve idioms shorn of their referents—"What are our long-range goals?"; "The odds are not in their favor," and so on—posit an unobserved and unobservable world, one in which there is "no one to signal to." To the extent that the novel as genre (as the way of the world) correlates the world to its observation, *The Road* indicates the world of the novel at an end: in the urge to check up on the outside oneself, there is nothing much to report.

The correlation of the world and its observation is the presupposition of social-systems theory (which collates at every point the world and its reporting, such that the reporting of the news is the news reported on). It is precisely the paradox of that correlationism that has entered into crisis today.[26] McCarthy's *dispositif* of the secondary and primary qualities of the world of the novel is another way of staging the crisis of correlation that is set out in philosophical terms most lucidly by Quentin Meillassoux, and in the uneven, and often hyperbolized or conflicted, assertions of a speculative realism more generally.

The two phrases that make up the heading of the last-but-one section of this book—"the provocation of the outside," "the vanished age of space"— are drawn, first, from the philosopher Peter Sloterdijk, and, second, from the realist novelist of the actually existing surrealism of contemporary life, J. G. Ballard. Their stories of the contemporary world interior, its logics and aesthetics, have, from very different angles, intermittently entered into the preceding accounts of self-curved space, autotropic violence and its demarcation zones, the repetition practices of modernity, our anthropotechnic exercises, and the provocation or terror of the great outside.

The title of part V of this book—"News from the Outside"—is drawn in part from two reports. The first (broached in part I) is the annunciation of the space age, Galileo's *News from the Stars* (*Sidereus Nuncius*, 1610). The second is J. G. Ballard's response, or retort, to it, his story, nearly a half millennium later, *News from the Sun*—about "the vanished age of space" and its "shabby mementos": "the rusting dish of a radio-telescope on a nearby peak, a poor man's begging bowl held up to the banquet of the universe."[27]

Both Galileo's story and Ballard's—in reporting news from the stars, or from the nearest one—are about ways of seeing, and, in its limits, about seeing itself seen. Galileo's *News from the Stars* is at once an opening to the great outside, and to its mathematization: it is on both counts about the outmoding of the postulate that, unaided by technics, the human senses are adequate to provide knowledge of the outside. Hence this extroversion has as its correlate, we have seen, a fundamental self-reference.[28] Galileo not merely sees new things, and not merely sees what he then can't see. He sees bodies suspended in empty space. As Tom McCarthy summarizes the Copernican or Galileic turn in his first novel, *Men in Space*: "Copernicus's *On the Revolutions of the Celestial Spheres* bumps Earth from the centre, sending it careening into space, making space itself infinite and uncentred and removing any single point to which objects might fall, its title naming all future revolutions."[29] The counterface of this uncentered space, its correlate, is the progressive elaboration of the modern world interior and our indoor and planned social life—and its achievement via the proliferation and coordination of its ego-technic media, from the spectacle lens and the telescope on. This is what Tom McCarthy, reenacting Ballard's reenactment zones, in *Men in Space* calls our now "cradle-to-grave relationship . . . with social institutions" (*M*, 218).

Ballard's account too is about "the first conscious experiments about time and space" and about seeing itself seen. It sets out an aesthetic science of perception and reflection not as proper to persons but as a property of matter. Hence, again and again "the darkness was filled with rotating blades." The outside scenes appear as if the effects of "a camera with its shutter left open indefinitely [such that] the eye perceived a moving object as a series of separate images." The narrator sees the last astronaut then as an iconic repeating figure, "a procession of winged men each dressed in his coronation armour"—as if the chronographs of Etienne-Jules Marey, or Hiroshi Sugimoto's photographic series "Sea of Buddhas" were encountered out there, and filling the world.[30] Yet deep space and deep time are at the same time utterly interiorized: a vision from within a collective trance, "deep fugue, an invisible dream of the great tideways of space."[31] Deep space, the primacy of the outside, is interiorized, or hallucinated, as deep fugue.

The outmoded astronaut in Ballard's story tells us, "I've started my own space program now." One might, along the same lines, start one's own religion. The goal of science fiction, L. Ron Hubbard tells us, is "to take men to the stars." This did not yet mean to take us to the Scientology Celebrity Centre in Hollywood, but it was on the way to that. It is no accident that Sloterdijk, in his expansive account of anthropotechnic training from the axial age to the present, takes up, for a moment, Scientology, and indicates (in his extended account of ascetic vertical-mobility training) that the best way of showing that religion isn't really credible—or to immunize it to parody—is to start one yourself. Perhaps, then, as Ballard suggests, in the vanished age of space, it may take the form of a space program of one's own. Freelance reporting, freelance space programs, freelance religion: self-suspension and self-projection programs.

Scientology brings not merely news from the stars: it brings personal trainers to the stars. It combines (as Sloterdijk and Lawrence Wright note) science fiction, psychology fiction, and religion fiction, the great outside and ascetic-technical exercises in cosmic ego-boosterism.[32] The central program, we recall, is the extroversion of reflexivity via record and monitoring machines (the electropsychometer, or E-meter, in scientological auditing). It is a reincarnation program: "Live, Die, Repeat" (as the announcement for the film *Edge of Tomorrow*, starring the world's foremost Scientologist, Tom Cruise, puts it).

The suspense genre—a form game of the suspension system of modernity—is about encapsulated persons in space, "parts of a modulating system which you had to watch as though from outside, or above, or somewhere else" (*M*, 3). The modular operating systems and protocols of the official world: I have been setting out some of its principal reenactment programs and experimental zones.

These are live blueprints, "like some living algorithm . . . drawn on the ground in chalk" (*M*, 139, 46), the loyalty cards and passports and switchboards and report cards of the official world, "making the world by moving through it" (33). These are its air-conditioned enclosing spaces, its anthropotechnics, its forms of reporting and self-reporting, its everyday and autotropic violence, its mood systems, its wish and terror plasmas or flood tides, its reincarnation exercises, its hystericized self-boosting and its work ethics—self-devotional personal training as an irrational end in itself. The program is reenacted on numerous stages, with, here and there, the extreme formality of the game, the forensic grid, or the iconic work of art. It takes shape and keeps in shape in the antigravity exercises and suspension practices—in the turning and modeling and observing and stressing, in the talented and protean and relentless shaping—of a self-shaped and self-turned world.

The Anatomy and the Atlas: Knausgaard's *Mein Kampf*

1. *The Heart.* "For the heart, life is simple: it beats for as long as it can. Then it stops." This is the opening of the first volume of the Norwegian writer Karl Ove Knausgaard's improbable event of a novel, *My Struggle* (*Min kamp*, 2009).[33] The novel goes on to describe the physical changes that occur within the body after the heart stops, some of which may be seen without: "Sooner or later, one day, this pounding action will cease of its own accord, and the blood will begin to run towards the body's lowest point, where it will collect in a small pool, visible from outside as a dark, soft path on ever whitening skin" (*I*, 7). Yet, and with a barely perceptible transition, the life history of inner physiological processes migrates to the outside, in another sense. It migrates from natural processes to world historical ones, disclosing in a body interior a world interior, and, exposing, through that, the history of the making and the unmaking, or dereliction, of a modern world.

This secondary terrain takes form in the clinical description of biological changes:

> changes that occur so slowly and take place with such inexorability that there is something almost ritualistic about them, as though life capitulates according to specific rules, a kind of gentlemen's agreement to which the representatives of death also adhere, inasmuch as they always wait until life has retreated before they launch their invasion of the new landscape. (*I*, 7)

The rules of invasion of the new landscape are relayed through two distinct but strangely comparable systems: a bodily interior and a global interior. An anatomy and a map, or atlas, are folded into each other: a new territory, and its exploration and devastation. The heart stilled, the microbial yet "enormous hordes advance on the Havers Channels, the Crypts of Lieberkühn, the Isles of Langerhans. They proceed to Bowman's Capsule in the Renes, Clark's Column in the Spinalis, the black substance in the Mesencephalon" (*I*, 8). At last, the body, deprived of "the activity to which end its whole construction was designed," resembles an abandoned "production plant" at the edge of a great forest, lines of equipment stilled, "from which the workers have fled in haste" (*I*, 8).

One begins to see in this advance into new islands, channels, and landscapes, and design of a new and newly abandoned world, a history of the long modernity: a history (as Sebald, too, traces) in the complex physiology of human beings indissociable from their technological methods of production and social organization. Let's say the epoch of exploration, invasion, settlement, clearing, and unearthing coming to its designed ends, and end: "the stationary vehicles shining yellow against the darkness of the forest, the huts deserted, a line of fully loaded cable-buckets stretching up the hillside" (*I*, 8). This is a Ballardian scenario of an advanced modernity in dereliction: like a deserted stage at the end of a performance, or the abandoned pieces of a giant sculpture, or (yet again) a now-stationary and action-suspended carousel.

This cleared or deserted landscape is the real terrain of Knausgaard's battle or struggle: a struggle felt on the body, such that somatic and kinetic forces become tensions for a system-epoch, a world interior. That tension system—a suspense world—opens to view, in this case, the reactionary antimodernism that appears here and there in the novel. It runs through it as a sort of provocation, one that could not be clearer from its title—*Min kamp* (or, in German, *Mein Kampf*)—on. This is a reaction, above all, to the outgrowth of the epoch of social systems: to what is seen as the unifying and leveling enclosure acts of the official world. One reencounters here the bipolar organization and image-funds of the long modernity: the planned and alienated world, "our indoor social life"—but as soon-to-be deserted stages struck and set against the "dark" and "alien" great outdoors. I want to close by looking at this extreme mise-en-scène in a little more detail.

2. *The Systems State.* First, the planned life. The madness, cruelty, and death of his father centers the first volume of *My Struggle.* His schoolteacher father was, we are told, a child of

> the first post-war generation, which in many ways represented something new, not least by dint of their being the first people in this country [Norway] to live in a society that was, to a major degree, planned. The 1950s were the time for the growth of systems—the school system, the health system, the social system, the transport system—the public departments and services too, in a large scale centralization that in the course of a surprisingly short period would transform the way lives were led. (*III*, 9)

The transformation of the way lives are led with the growth of centralizing systems means, for Knausgaard, a deadly homogenization, which he expresses in familiar terms. As he reports it, "not human uniqueness but equality . . . not cultural uniqueness, but multicultural society" (*II*, 374). This is a society in which diversity is a disguised form of homogeneity: it makes for a proliferation of identity-planning kits and autogenic regimes, and local cultures "now encapsulated as small museums in a culture that was no different from the one you had left or the one that you were going to" (*II*, 70).

The growth of systems is, here, the spread of scripted and prescriptive isotopias. At the heart of the planned society, there is the installation and the ubiquitization of planned life and life-plans: its curricula and training practices, its exteriorization regimens, and its self-realization step systems. There is the replacement of singularity by difference, universal multiculturalism, and rise of the "culture-creating middle class" (self-loathing is Knausgaard's dominant mood).

Knausgaard's critique of the metastasis of systems-equality is explicitly a reaction against liberal democracy. It expresses an open fascination with "classic antiliberal cultures" (*II*, 126) and with counter-modern writers such as Yukio Mishima and, particularly, Ernst Jünger, the great theorist of fascism from the inside. Knausgaard samples Jünger's account of a reduced-to-zero democratic future. This is what, for Jünger, amounts to "something approaching a world state": "and this movement, what else is it *at heart*, if not nihilistic . . . the nihilistic world is in essence a world that is being increasingly reduced . . . with the movement toward a zero point" (Knausgaard citing Jünger, *II*, 100, my emphasis). "Or, as Jünger writes, 'Little by little all areas are brought under this single common denominator, even one with its residence as far from causality as the dream.'" "This is," Knausgaard adds, "where our night is" (*II*, 100).[34]

Hence, if the opening passage of the novel is, at once, life story and world history, it is an encryption of the bourgeois half-millennium, internal to a single life, at the end of its day. It is "my struggle"—in the sense given to the phrase by the psychopathic reactionary technomodernist from whom Knausgaard takes his title—as synonymously it is a world struggle. The choice of worlds is set out in the most uncompromising or most reductive form, and so presents the systems-internal world and its dream states—and the alternatives to it—in high definition.

3. *Half-Educated Men*. There is yet another and revelatory tie along just these lines. His father, Knausgaard tells us, was

> a member of the new educated middle class, he was also well-informed about the wider world, which came to him every day via the newspaper, radio, and television . . . he was not an expert at anything . . . but he knew a little bit about everything . . . all the necessary systems have been put in place. (*I*, 14, 15)

In a brief piece on what he calls Hitler's "novel" *Mein Kampf*, J. G. Ballard describes its author in these terms: "Hitler was one of the rightful inheritors of the twentieth century—the epitome of the half-educated man." Ballard's brief literary history of novels of the 1920s compares the Austrian writer to an unlikely counterpart and his ostensible archenemy:

> Wandering about the streets of Vienna shortly before the first World War, his head full of vague artistic yearnings and clap-trap picked from popular magazines, whom does he most likely resemble? Above all, Leopold Bloom . . . wandering around Joyce's Dublin about the same time, his head filled with same clap-trap and the same yearnings. Both are the children of the reference library and the self-improvement manual, of mass newspapers creating a new vocabulary of violence and sensation. Hitler was the half-educated psychopath inheriting the lavish communications systems of the 20th century.[35]

Ballard may here be drawing on Theodor Adorno's "theory of half-education" (*Halbbildung*)—put simply, the unreflected internalization of information via media systems of socialization ,"the culture industry" (say, knowing a little bit about everything via newspaper, radio, television, and incorporating the reality and dreamlife of the mass media).[36] This is a way of making sense of the struggles of the half-educated to grapple with the information overflow that threatens to drown them: what we now routinely refer to as data saturation.

But, for Ballard, the concern is not exactly half-education as a ruse of the culture industry. It is, more exactly, a direct symptom of the segmental differentiation, and modular or enclaved character, of the systems epoch. This was reflected institutionally in what C. P. Snow, in the mid-twentieth century, called "the two cultures." That designation by now seems a quaint way of describing the proliferating cultures and sciences that have entered into an ecumenical "ecology of ignorance."[37] (In this artificial ecology, academic fields may relate to each other almost as eco-tourists in rapid transit through a fictional country called "interdisciplinarity.")

Knausgaard's psychopathic educator-father (whose discipline ultimately dissolves into an alchoholism that the novel describes in excruciating detail) seems, on this account, the epitome of what Adorno called "the half-educated man"—in his perfect conformity to the systems-planned life, a strict functionary of officialism in its expanded field. Hence

> the meaning of his days was not concentrated in individual events but spread over such large areas that it was not possible to comprehend them

in anything other than abstract terms. "Family" was one such term, "career" another. Few or no unforeseen opportunities at all can have presented themselves in the course of his days, he must always have known in broad outline what they would bring and how he would react. (*I*, 14)

The father who terrorized him personates the planned-life in its inculcated abstraction, its latent violence, and its nascent madness. Like Highsmith's Ripley, or Ludlum's Bourne, this is the half-educated citizen of the modular risk society, its multiple-choice courses of life, and built-in drive to match, in broad outline, present futures and future presents so that there is nothing unplanned or unforeseen. (For the child, Knausgaard, the father is a daily terror, and the novel is, of course, no more uninterested in the cant of working-through that than it is in self-realization therapies or planned parenthood or lifestyle coaches.)

This is, in short, the brutal and textbook disciplinarian as "well-informed" interdisciplinarian: as an undebatably professional product of the browsing and data-scanning half-education system, and an embodiment of the growth of the professional-managerial server systems of an official world. It—and he, more generally—is a function of well-scripted and widely informed interdisciplinary life: its pallid institutions and extending archipelagoes of support and teaching, and training and counseling, systems of an encapsulating modernity. Knausgaard's horror story.

4. *Bathing in Totality.* The alternative to half-education and its cross-referencing institutions, for Knausgaard, is what he calls "bathing in the totality" (*III*, 302). *My Struggle* repeatedly switches between the minute descriptions of all the days of his life that occupy most of the book's pages, and such a bathing in totality: an immersion, or bathos, that in effect holds the place of a great outside. On one level, Knausgaard simply sees himself as suspended between two worlds: a Viking with a pram. But, on another, the world is in a suspended state, tensed between the systems-internal one-world state of the overforeseen life, and an alien-natural grandeur experienced as transcendence or a dissolving—a dissolution—in totality. This is how he stages the struggle between world self-determination and so self-termination, the life and death of the individual and the life and extinction of a world.

The counter to the growth of an indoor social life and death is starkly the great outdoors—or at times its high or weird romanticization (in, I am tempted to say, Leni Riefenstahl's "blue light" or "destiny of the mountain" mode). As Knausgaard frames it, "If there were a world I turned to in my mind, it was that of the sixteenth and seventeenth centuries, with its enormous forests, its sailing ships . . . its explorers and inventors" (*II*, 68). This is the advent of the long modernity, as nature-adventure story, "when the sea was full of whales, the forests full of bears and wolves, and there were still countries so that were so alien no adventure story could do them justice" (*II*, 67). It is, in part, the dream of a premodern world of black forests, blue mountains, teeming wildlife, and open seas.

Yet this is not exactly a dream of how the alien world looked without us. It is, more exactly, the coupling of an adventure story and a venture capital one, and so bound up through and through with the bipolar explorations of the age of world-discovery and world-invention.

Hence, it is how it looks to the explorers and inventors when (in the terms of the great seventeenth-century epic of modernity as a lost paradise) *the world was all before them*—and about to enter (as Milton's angel previews) into the forming of a global human history. That marks the transition, for Knausgaard, to a worldwide and globally replicable ego-technics, by which death and life were, to a major degree, planned and fundamentally transformed. This may be seen as the simple heart, the systole and diastole, of the anthropocenic mise-en-scène—a self-turned world. It's in small the cleft organization of a life-world at once venture story and its nullification, the opening and vanishing of the great age of space.

5. *Self-Determination and Self-Termination.* Bathing in the totality— transcendence or bathos—means explicitly, for Knausgaard, ongoing adolescent dreams of "our teenage years": a "preoccupation with existential issues" that is a turning away from the euphemistic services and servers performing on the administrative ground floor of the anthropocene [*II*, 99]).[38] The term "existential" has now largely replaced the phrase "matter of life and death" in a wall-to-wall self-reporting culture, a replacement that is, in miniature, what Knausgaard reports on and reacts to. That may take on the form of the struggle between the one-world state and world dissolution. That is, in turn, one way to stage the coming to terms of the self-determination of the human epoch and so the logic of its termination or self-extinction. It is one way to understand the logic of men in encapsulated spaces: the aesthetics of suspense and suspended worlds, and an extraordinary and captivating art with humans. It is one way, too, to understand the current fascination with processes of elimination (*And Then There Were None*) and countless, thrilled spectacles of self-elimination. Or as Knausgaard puts it: our extinction is now "something we are drawn to and will happily pay to see" (*I*, 5).

ACKNOWLEDGMENTS

This book was thought of in Berlin, largely written in Los Angeles, and changed by Tokyo. The book is in many ways shaped by these places, which enter into its stories of self-curved worlds. I am at every moment of the study indebted to UCLA, for great students and wonderful colleagues, a salary and a workplace, and an administrative zeal that makes official business as usual more usual than usual: hence this book.

My thanks to many friends and colleagues—in, among other places, New York, New Haven, Chicago, Los Angeles, Palo Alto, Providence, Princeton, San Juan, London, Berlin, Cologne, Bonn, Uppsala, Rio de Janeiro, Sydney, Beijing, Hong Kong, Tokyo, and Seoul—for inviting me to try out pieces of the book, and for the good challenges and good advice that helped make it better.

Here I want to name just a few who contributed with timely kindness, and remarkable keenness, and real generosity to the situation of its writing: Mark McGurl, Michael North, Sianne Ngai, Bill Brown, Kate Marshall, Frances Ferguson, Hanjo Berressem, and Ken Wissoker.

The book is for two people whose names are not, for me, on any list, even a short one.

For my dearest friend, for her loveliness and bravery and love, and her so special way of carrying a tune.

For my son, for his strength of heart, wondrous wit and intelligence, and everything he has given me for the better part of my life.

Earlier versions of pieces of this book have appeared in *Critical Inquiry* (2009, 2011); *Archiv für Mediengeschichte* (2010); and the online journal *Post45* (2013). I am grateful for permission to include the material here.

1. Introduction to the Official World

1. Clive Barker, introduction to Neil Gaiman, *The Doll's House* (DC Comics, 1990; reprint, New York: Vertigo, 2010), not paginated. (*The Doll's House* is the second volume of Gaiman's remarkable serial graphic novel, *The Sandman*.)

2. Jacob Burkhardt, *The Civilization of the Renaissance in Italy* (1860; New York: Dover, 2010), 172–99.

3. On the "Galileic turn"—the opening to the great outside—and its contemporary foreclosure, see the concluding section of part V.

4. Niklas Luhmann, *Theories of Distinction: Redescribing the Descriptions of Modernity*, ed. William Rasch (Stanford, Calif.: Stanford University Press, 2002), 105.

5. G. Spencer Brown, *Laws of Form* (New York: Julian, 1972), xxiv.

6. Vladimir Nabokov, *Speak, Memory* (New York: Vintage, 1989), 19.

7. The anthropotechnic turn is the subject, in part, albeit to very different ends, of my earlier attempts to get at the body-machine complex and its effects, particularly the books *Bodies and Machines* (1992, reprint, New York: Routledge, 2015), and *Serial Killers: Death and Life in America's Wound Culture* (New York: Routledge, 1998). My extended use of the term here is inflected by and indebted to Peter Sloterdijk's accounts of the techniques of training and self-training on "the planet of the practicing," in his *In the World Interior of Capital*, trans. Wieland Hoban (Cambridge: Polity, 2013), and, especially, *You Must Change Your Life*, trans. Wieland Hoban (Cambridge: Polity, 2013).

8. Cormac McCarthy, *The Crossing* (New York: Vintage, 1995), 203.

9. I will return to McCarthy's contractions of history and natural history—and his restaging of the ways in which the presumption of a world correlated to its communication and reporting shapes the form and history of the novel.

10. See Dirk Baecker, "The Reality of Motion Pictures," *MLN* 111, no. 3 (1996): 560–77.

11. The turn turn signals the rise of the planet of the professionals: the professors of the official world and its self-turned (autotropic) signaling practices and rotational systems.

12. The distinction between vertical mobility and upward mobility, and its continuous reenactment, is a fleeting but crucial one. On that working distinction, and how it designates contemporary forms of reenactment or repeating—repeated repeating and repeating repeating—see part IV. Anthropotechnics describes a system of practices, and that is its utility in defining the conditions of the official world. It might be compared to the charismatic periodization, the Anthropocene. That, paradoxically, reasserts an anthropocentrism and annuls it—designating a species designed to bring about its own end. On that view, one might say of the human epoch what Roland Barthes said of literature: that, like phosphorous, it burns brightest at the moment it is about to die. But the news of a self-reporting modernity, from Galileo's "News from the Stars" (1610) on— starring "man" at the moment of his decentering—is a double discourse from the start. On this, see Jorge Luis Borges's little essay "Pascal's Sphere," on Giordano Bruno's joy and Pascal's horror in the discovery of an infinite universe. As Borges—for whom universal history may be the history of the various intonations of a few metaphors—points out, "for one man, Giordano Bruno, the breaking of the stellar vaults was a liberation," for another, Pascal, an uncertain horror. Pascal in writing of an "*infinite* sphere," seems, in his manuscript, to have started to write the word *effroyable* ("a *frightful* sphere"), before canceling it. Borges, "Pascal's Sphere," in *Borges: Selected Non-fictions*, trans. Eliot Weinberger (New York: Penguin, 2000), 351–54. See also Sloterdijk's trilogy *Spheres*, for a provocative rediscovery of the ensphered shape of things, and its implications today.

13. The description is Alexander Kluge's, "Deutsches Kino," in *Bestandsaufnahme: Utopie Film: Zwanzig Jahre neuer deutscher Film/Mitte* (Frankfurt am Main, 1983), 141–94.

14. We can punctually date the emergence of a self-describing society with the appearance of its scribes: the advent of official self-description in the rise of sociology and the first sociologists, the field reporters of a daily planet. On self-describing modernity, see, for example, Niklas Luhmann, "Deconstruction as Second-Order Observing," in *Theories of Distinction*, 94–112.

15. Stanislaw Lem, *Imaginary Magnitude*, trans. Mark E. Heine (Orlando, Fla.: Harcourt Brace Jovanovich, 1984), 131.

16. Roland Barthes, *The Empire of Signs*, trans. Richard Howard (New York: Hill and Wang, 1982), 80.

17. See Cornelia Vismann, *Files: Law and Media Technology*, trans. Geoffrey Winthrop-Young (Stanford, Calif.: Stanford University Press, 2008).

18. It is autonomous in the root sense of the term: auto-nomos, self-legislative, a law unto itself.

19. See the elaboration of this argument in part V.

20. I draw here directly on Niklas Luhmann, *Art as a Social System*, trans. Eva M. Knodt (Stanford, Calif.: Stanford University Press, 2000). The question then, of course, is whether the consideration of "art as a social system" is adequate to the consideration of the work of art or to accounting for the crisis of the artwork in the epoch of social systems. The large question then, on another level, is whether social-systems theory provides a good account of these matters or a good symptom of them. Systems theory is very good at describing self-organization and it is very weak on describing how systems relate to each other. The emergency notion of their "structural coupling" (as Luhmann frames it) names rather than resolves the problem. Network theory, on the contrary, is good at describing relations but weak on indicating how self-consistency is then possible (in that, as Henry James put it, relations stop nowhere). Nor will it do to split the difference between the two. Form theory (and here I draw on Dirk Baecker's work) may provide a better description, albeit one with its own trapdoors. See Dirk Baecker, "Systems, Networks, and Culture," *Soziale Systeme: Zeitschrift für soziologische Theorie* 15 (2009): 271–87. On some of the limitations of systems theory, with particular reference to literary examples, see also Mark Seltzer, "The Crime System," in *True Crime: Observations on Violence and Modernity* (New York: Routledge, 2007), 57–90.

21. On the manner in which social systems stage their own unity, and its implications, see Dirk Baecker, ed., *Problems of Form*, (Stanford, Calif.: Stanford University Press, 1999); and Elena Esposito, "The Arts of Contingency," *Critical Inquiry* 31, no. 1 (autumn 2004): 7–25.

22. Baecker, "The Reality of Motion Pictures," 562.

23. I am indebted to the account of the significance of this distinction, and its hesitation, in contemporary accounts of reflexivity, provided by Sloterdijk, *In the World Interior of Capital*.

24. On the chain letter, see part II. On the phatic function, with the twittering of birds as one of its models, see part IV.

25. See Jean-Paul Sartre, *Critique of Dialectical Reason*, vol. 1, trans. Alan Sheridan-Smith (London: Verso, 1976), 271. The heroine of Dreiser's novel, Carrie, is a carrier, a medium, of the world's longing, its struggle to express itself. In this case, the medium is the face: what Georg Simmel, writing at the advent of motion pictures and so the discovery of the medium of the close-up, called "the aesthetic significance of the face." Mirrors are not recent ego-technic devices, but their ubiquitization is: it takes, as it were, the reality of motion pictures to launch the regular compulsion of visual self-externalization.

26. I am indebted here to the sense of a "world of effects" set out in Frances Ferguson's *Pornography, the Theory: What Utilitarianism Did to Action* (Chicago: University of Chicago Press, 2004). On "news from the outside," see the final section of part V, below.

27. Dirk Baecker, "The Form Game," in *Problems of Form*, 106. There is a good deal more to be said about the gamelike structure of these operations (see part III).

Just as in spectator sports, one must repeatedly reenact the distinction between the inside and the outside of the game, which is then copied into the game. It is necessary to distinguish between what is inside and outside the lines: to take note at every moment of what is, say, inside and outside the zone, between time in and time out, between live and dead balls, between game space and spectation space, between act and record, score and standings, and so on. These are its strike zones of demarcation and reenactment. Administrative zones, it is true. But the administrative a priori must then be understood in expanded, open-plan form. The real question is whether, as, for example, Tom McCarthy's *Remainder* (New York: Vintage, 2007), 283, puts it, these demarcation zones are now "nonexistent" or "limitless"—which would, of course, amount to the same thing.

28. Ralph Waldo Emerson, "Circles," in *Essays and English Traits*, vol. 5 (New York: P. F. Collier and Son, 1909–14).

29. Patricia Highsmith, *The Talented Mr. Ripley* (1955; reprint, London: Vintage, 1999), 86.

30. On pornography and, in effect, a systems outlook on action, see Ferguson, *Pornography, the Theory.*

31. Rem Koolhaas, *Delirious New York* (New York: Oxford University Press, 1978).

32. See C. Wright Mills, "White Collar," as quoted in Alan Delgado, *The Enormous File: A Social History of the Office* (London: John Murray, 1979), 5.

33. Highsmith, *The Talented Mr. Ripley*, 165.

34. The compulsive externalization and objectification of interior states consist in countless practices that are, on the one side, practical and objectivist, and, on the other, deliberately useless, superfluous, and willfully simulated acts. In sum, performance art that in turn resembles games that resemble bureaucratic pyramids and systemic work processes that in turn resemble art scenes. The formation of the human pyramid may then look like the practice zone for capitalist ideology and its training in the systemic differentiation of labor. Or it may look like the hyperbolic and superfluous exertion, self-referential motion, and crystallized performativity of an art scene turned from product to process. (See Sloterdijk's brief assessment, in similar terms, albeit to different ends, in *You Must Change Your Life*, 360–64.) But it's necessary to recall that the real innovation of systematic management (from Taylorization on) becomes visible in the incorporation of the description, representation, and recording of the work process into the work process itself—or, better, the incorporation of the presentation of the work process *as* the work process itself.

35. Franco Moretti, in *The Bourgeois: Between History and Literature* (London: Verso, 2013), points to this passage; and his larger study approaches, via Ibsen's work, these system-internal protocols, albeit in terms of the collapse of the "irreconcilable" contradictions of bourgeois life. The terminus of the bourgeois, for Moretti, is the installation of immanence, the "changing [of] a variable here and there, to see what happens to the system": the erection of a doll's house, a

play pen, the closed space of the modern living room, and irrational vocation of sheer professionalism. Yet this may be seen less as terminus than installation moment. Werner Sombart captures the tautological blindness by which the self-incarnative (and so self-destructive) entrepreneur "dreams the dream of the successful issue of his undertaking," whatever that may be. See Moretti, *The Bourgeois*, 169–87; Werner Sombart, *The Quintessence of Capitalism* (New York: E. P. Dutton, 1915), 91–92.

36. Robert Ludlum, *The Bourne Identity* (New York: Bantam, 2010), 54.

37. The sea as the modality of these reincarnation rites is nowhere clearer than in the novels of Yukio Mishima (in the image-funds, for example, of *The Temple of the Golden Pavilion* [1956], or plot-realized, for example, in *The Sailor Who Fell from Grace with the Sea* [1963]). And it is nowhere more relentlessly applied and institutionalized than in the practices of Scientology and its Sea Organization under the command of its founder, "Commodore" L. Ron Hubbard. Lawrence Wright's study of Hubbard and Scientology, *Going Clear: Scientology, Hollywood, and the Prison of Belief* (New York: Alfred A. Knopf, 2013), and the recent documentary film version of it which has the same title; and Paul Thomas Anderson's film *The Master* (New York: Weinstein Company, 2012), which approaches Scientology, and Hubbard, are instructive on how the sea mood-organization of these projective or exteriorization states looks and feels. I turn to a neosituationist version of this sea mode, the International Necronautical Society, in a moment. A fuller account of "the scientological turn" in science-oriented humanities culture today is a subject of my forthcoming work.

38. Just as kitsch in art is a shortcut to the grand passions, science kitsch is the shortcut to news from the outside. (See Sloterdijk's comments on what might be called performative science, *In the World Interior of Capital*.) Bourne must then learn who he is from the outside, by observing the reflexes and impact of his unconsciously efficient body. Here our real outside is our own body: as Stanislaw Lem's Golem puts it, "When man wants to learn about himself, he must move circuitously, he must explore himself and penetrate from the outside, with instruments and hypotheses, for your genuinely immediate world is the outside world. . . . That body of yours, which to some extent obeys you, says nothing and lies to you. . . . It hides and defends itself against you, alert to the environment with every sense and yet opaque and mistrustful toward its owner." Lem, *Imaginary Magnitude* (Orlando, Fla.: Harcourt, Brace, Jovanovich, 1984), 175.

39. But, as the opening sequence of the novel exemplifies, or melodramatizes, and as this instruction on combining inner and outer stresses explains, this is not simply about "transference" or "correlation" between inner and outer worlds. Its protocol is the continuous rotation of observation and action. Via sets of instructions, time-management regimens, and the exercise of a continuous self-monitoring, the inside and outside of the act are observed, separated by analytic description, and then recombined as a process of autogenesis. (In the eponymous Bourne stories, from novel to novel or from film to film, this is all

but explicitly, in its scientological bent, a process of reincarnation.) One might compare these death and rebirth scenarios to the extraordinary and popular anime of the 1990s, for example, *Neon Genesis Evangelion* (1995–96, directed by Hideaki Anno), or its film continuation *Death and Rebirth* (1997, directed by Hideaki Anno and Kazuya Tsuremaki).

40. Isotopia: I adapt this term from A. J. Greimas's semiotic notion of isotopy: an internal synonymy or semic homogeneity, in the interpretive direction taken by the text.

41. Henry James, *The American Scene*, in *Collected Travel Writings* (New York: Library of America, 1993).

42. Siegfried Kracauer, "The Hotel Lobby" (1922–25; 1963) in *The Mass Ornament: Weimar Essays*, ed. and trans. Thomas Y. Levin (Cambridge, MA: Harvard University Press, 1995), 173–85; subsequent citations are to this text. Erving Goffman, *Relations in Public* (New York: Harper and Row, 1972), 385.

43. On systematic management in the workplace as a rotation of act and representation, see my *Bodies and Machines*, esp. part V.

44. J. G. Ballard, *Super-Cannes* (London: Flamingo, 2000), 111.

45. J. G. Ballard, *Millenium People* (New York: Norton, 2005), 147.

46. On Ballard's story "News from the Sun" and its implications, see part IV.

47. It would in fact be possible to do a slideshow of the carousel as image-fund, from the 1950s on: whether Highsmith/Hitchcock's merry-go-round as small world (see part II); or the reincarnation carousel in the 1970s film *Logan's Run*; or the remarkable episode (2007) of the television series *Mad Men*, in which the carousel as slideshow is achieved as the actual thing. The advertising man Don Draper, in introducing the Kodak Carousel slide-projector, at a product presentation, expresses its science-fictional power: "This device is not a spaceship. It's a time machine." He presents, in the demonstration, a description of the device coupled to slides of his own life, such that the device is installed in the (televised) world it installs. The action and its description, and the observation of the action and its description, are thus observed. The show (the serial, at that very moment) tells and shows its own story, Kodak Carousel moments, and so shows that. In doing so, the advertised device "does the thing" and makes a world that it at the same time exasperates: "He had been getting some news of the art of advertisement," Henry James writes in his own time machine, the novel *The Ambassadors* (1903). "Advertising scientifically worked presented itself thus as the great new force. 'It really does the thing, you know. . . . So it's an art like another, and infinite like all the arts . . . With the right man to work it, *c'est un monde*.' " Henry James, *The Ambassadors* (1903; Oxford: Oxford University Press, 1985), 431.

48. Patricia Highsmith, *The Glass Cell* (Garden City, N.Y.: Doubleday, 1964); J. G. Ballard, *The Crystal World* (New York: Farrar, Straus and Giroux, 1988). On crystallized capitalism, see Peter Sloterdijk, "The Crystal Palace," *Public*, no. 37 (2008). Highsmith's depictions of violence aesthetics, like Ballard's, is bound to a bioeconomics of enclosed structures, albeit in a very different mode, one bor-

dering on crime fiction (with its aesthetics of the aftermath), the other on science fiction (with its future-casting). Ballard's fiction, however, is not space age but part of what he calls "the vanished age of space"—an aftermath, and part of a temporally closed structure. For Ballard, as he expresses in his introduction to his novel *Crash*: "We have annexed the future into the present, as merely one of those manifold alternatives open to us. Options multiply around us, and we live in an almost infantile world where any demand, any possibility, whether for life-styles, travel, sexual roles and identities, can be satisfied instantly." This rotational system of possibilities exteriorizes fantasy. It means that individuals access their own inner lives as constantly externalized information. If one is to "lead" one's life, then this is necessarily a stress-driven, premonitory, and extroverted situation or condition. Hence if the future has been annexed to the present, "the roles," as Ballard puts it, of "fantasy and reality . . . are reversed." For Ballard, "The most prudent and effective method of dealing with the world around us is to assume that it is a complete fiction." Highsmith's Ripley adapts this assumption to his own criminal ends, in the discovery that the fictionality of the world is its working reality. Hence his "talent" for self-projection becomes a career option, and a lethal one. For Ballard, this discovery, at the turn of the millennium, appears as well, in his own speculative thrillers, bound to the enclosed self-conditioned spaces that, spaces of the official world, take form via what he calls (in *Cocaine Nights*) the "bureaucracy of crime." Highsmith and Ballard, near contemporaries (Highsmith is born in 1921, Ballard in 1930) but generic worlds apart, thus provide alternative cartographies of the official world and its systemic forms of death and life.

49. Sloterdijk, *In the World Interior of Capital*, 23.

50. Ibid., 168.

51. Thomas Nagel, "What Is It Like to Be a Bat?" *Mortal Questions* (Cambridge: Cambridge University Press, 1987), 166.

52. The allure of neuroscience in literary studies today—what Tom McCarthy calls "the glib wholesale transferal of the logic of neuroscience to the realm of culture"—is, from this perspective, an emergent form of this interdisciplinary magic. Tom McCarthy, Simon Critchley, and Nicolas Bourriaud, *The Mattering of Matter: Documents from the Archive of the International Necronautical Society* (Berlin: Sternberg, 2013), 273.

53. See Sloterdijk, "The Crystal Palace."

54. Patricia Highsmith, *Strangers on a Train* (1950; reprint, New York: Norton, 2001), 26.

55. McCarthy, *Remainder*, 185.

56. I am borrowing from Bernhard Siegert, "There Are No Mass Media," in *Mapping Benjamin: The Work of Art in the Digital Age*, ed. Hans Ulrich Gumbrecht and Michael Marrinan (Stanford, Calif.: Stanford University Press, 2003), 38.

57. See Joan Schenkar, *The Talented Miss Highsmith: The Secret Life and Serious Art of Patricia Highsmith* (New York: St. Martin's, 2009), 157.

58. Highsmith, *Strangers on a Train*, 261. My thanks to Tom Perrin for reminding me that Bruno is a reader of comic books (see *Strangers on a Train*, 14).

59. See W. G. Sebald, "Between History and Natural History," in *Campo Santo*, trans. Anthea Bell (New York: Modern Library, 2005), 65–96; and Sebald, *On the Natural History of Destruction*, trans. Anthea Bell (New York: Modern Library, 2004). What is set out in Sebald's account is not a biological explanation for social forms of life (or their "naturalization") but instead the incoherence of the antinomy in the first place. That incoherence becomes explicit above all in episodes of catastrophic modernization—episodes in which, as Kluge puts it, those affected "could not have devised practicable emergency measures . . . except with tomorrow's brains." Alexander Kluge, *Neue Geschichten: Unheimlichkeit der Zeit* (Frankfurt: Surhkamp, 1977), 53.

60. The presumption of the reciprocal conditioning of each by the other (positive feedback)—generalized now to mean sort of "everything is connected"—has lessened interpretive pressure on the dilemmas the duality is designed to address. (Hence it has generated terms, like "intersectionality" or "relationality" or "connectedness," that name or brand-name what is in effect a black-boxed business as usual.) The coalescence of many of these issues of social and natural history around the large term "affect" has made for similar naming events. (My sense of these matters has been inflected by the brilliant installation/performance work of Naoko Tanaka, including *Absolute Helligkeit*, presented at Performance Platform: Body Affects, Berlin, July 5–8, 2012.)

2. Brecht's Rabbit

1. Brecht, as cited (loosely) in W. G. Sebald, "Between History and Natural History," in *Campo Santo*, trans. Anthea Bell (New York: Modern Library, 2005), 89.

2. Zola's program for the experimental novel in the Rougon-Macquart series makes this explicit, from the descriptive subtitle of the series on—*Histoire naturelle et sociale d'une famille sous le Second Empire* (Émile Zola, *Oeuvres complètes*, ed. Henri Mitterand (Paris: Cerce du livre précieux, 1966). The fusion of histories and bodies in naturalism tends toward pornographies of violence, and the bent of the experimental novel may be reconsidered in the context of more recent "interdisciplinary" fusions of the humanities and the sciences. J. G. Ballard, for example, calls *Crash* a novel about "science and pornography": "the first pornographic novel based on technology." As Ballard notes in *Love and Napalm: Export USA* (New York: Grove, 1972), 83: "Science is the ultimate pornography, analytic activity whose main aim is to isolate objects or events from their contexts in time and space. This obsession with the specific activity of quantified functions is what the sciences share with pornography . . . On the autopsy table science and pornography meet and fuse." More exactly, as Ballard expresses it in his *News from the Sun*: "A widespread taste for pornography means that nature is alerting us to some threat of extinction."

Consider, on this view, recent science-humanities projects, such as a "poetics" of extinction. The aesthetics adduced here is, to be sure, largely limited to genre classification and lists (what Zola, already in his manifesto-essay "The Experimental Novel," declared as the outmoded taxonomies of Linnaeus and Buffon, work blind to the experimental milieu that Zola promotes as his own modern mode of investigation). Yet, for Ballard, it is perhaps this very regression to lists and quantities that makes visible a new scientological pornography. In that the current "sixth extinction" is in effect *assisted* extinction—that is, *extermination* (the epochal impact of human action)—a poetics of *extinction* is a "poetics of *extermination*": list-shaped stories of serial murder by numbers on a planetary scale. Ballard's measure of self-righteous environmentalisms is clear enough (not least in his novel *Rushing to Paradise* [New York: Harper Collins, 1994]). In brief: "decadence takes the form not of libertarian excess, but of the kind of over-the-top puritanism we see in political correctness and the assorted moral certainties of physical fitness fanatics, New Agers, and animal-rights advocates" ([London] *Daily Telegraph* [1993]). I will return to extinction-allure in the final section of part V, by way of the work of Karl Ove Knausgaaard.

3. The first phrase appears in Patricia Highsmith, *Strangers on a Train* (1950; reprint, New York: Norton, 2001), 143; subsequent references, *st*, in text. For the second, see Highsmith's captivity (or self-captivity) narrative *The Glass Cell* (Garden City, N.Y.: Doubleday, 1964).

4. Sebald, "Between History and Natural History," 77. One finds too, in Sebald's divagating and searching fiction, something like the pathos of the search engine, with all its safaris and explorers, and sites of lost or sought things. This may be one of the secondary attractions of Sebald's work today. We might compare here the sense of taking stock of a used world in Cormac McCarthy's *The Road*. (Or even recession reality shows like *Antiques Roadshow*, in its lost-and-found revelations of history and value.) On *The Road*, see the final section of part V, chapter 10.

5. It would be necessary, in a fuller account, to pressure not merely the presumption of social constructionism that's currently going out of vogue but also the counter-turn to biology in the humanities and social sciences that's coming into it. The return to biology and natural history in literary and social studies today has taken on an optative, even peppy tone: at its weakest, species life as the family of man. This tone often amounts to the evocation of deep time and space as mere evocation—and in the service of a strictly intramural conservativism. In this way (it will be seen) evocation of the deep history of the planet programmatically overturns into microhistories of literary institutions. The institution of literature thus appears as something like a little house on the cosmic prairie. Along these lines, the Great Outdoors is invoked but in effect as a circular detour that returns us to our indoor life: reference into self-reference, seeing into self-seeing, location into self-location. (I am here drawing on Joseph Vogl's "Becoming-Media: Galileo's Telescope," *Grey Room*, no. 29 [fall 2007]: 14–25.

See also note 40 below.) This is the reflex of an autotropic and official world. I have set out what this looks like (with particular reference to speculative realism, and the work of Quentin Meillassoux) in "Die Freie Natur," *Gefahrensinn: Archiv für Mediengeschichte*, ed. Lorenz Engell, Bernhard Siegert, and Joseph Vogl, 127–39 (Paderborn: Wilhelm Fink, 2009). Here we may simply note that one need not evoke deep time and vast space in order to see, for example, high modernity and the hunting-and-gathering stage of species life side by side: one might instead, say in Berlin or Tokyo on a day in 1945, or in Sendai several years ago, just step outside.

6. Max Brooks, *World War Z: An Oral History of the Zombie War* (New York: Three Rivers, 2007), 4–5. I thank my teenage son for directing my attention to this novel. On the spread of zombiedom in the humanities, and culture at large, see Mark McGurl, "The Zombie Renaissance," *n+1*, no. 9 (spring 2010); and Deborah Christie and Sarah Juliet Lauro, eds., *Better Off Dead: The Evolution of the Zombie as Post-human* (New York: Fordham University Press, 2011).

7. On McCarthy's *The Road*, and its *dispositif* of the novel as the way of the world come to an end, see the final section of part V.

8. This is the title given to Highsmith's collection of short stories first published in 1987: *Tales of Natural and Unnatural Catastrophes* (London: Bloomsbury, 1987).

9. Sebald, "Between History and Natural History," 95. Or, as Sebald expresses it elsewhere, in *On the Natural History of Destruction*, trans. Anthea Bell (New York: Modern Library, 2004), 66: "Is the destruction not, rather, irrefutable proof that the catastrophes which develop, so to speak, in our hands and seem to break out suddenly are a kind of experiment, anticipating the point at which we shall drop out of what we have thought for so long to be our autonomous history and back into the history of nature?"

10. See Clodagh Kinsella, "The Radical Ambiguity of Tom McCarthy" (interview), *Dossier* (July 25, 2009).

11. "Re-enactment brings about a kind of split within the act itself. . . . On the one hand it's something you do, and on the other it's not something you're actually 'doing': it's a citation, a marker for another event that this one isn't." Tom McCarthy, quoted in Simon Reynolds, *Retromania: Pop Culture's Addiction to Its Own Past* (London: Faber and Faber, 2011), 54. This citation—this one— reminds you that events are possible, and only because they happened before. In his afterword to McCarthy's novel *Men in Space*, Simon Critchley cites McCarthy's citation (in his *Tintin and the Secret of Literature* [2006]) of Paul de Man's "The Rhetoric of Temporality": we "can know inauthenticity, but never overcome it. It can only restate and repeat it on an increasingly conscious level." Simon Critchley, afterword to Tom McCarthy, *Men in Space*, updated ed. (New York: Vintage, 2012), 287. The irony is that that way we can, in effect, become more and more conscious of becoming less and less conscious.

12. "Gebet mir Materie, ich will eine Welt daraus bauen! Das ist, gebet mir Materie, ich will euch zeigen, wie eine Welt daraus entstehen soll." See Kant's preface to

his *Allgemeine Naturgeschichte und Theorie des Himmels: Erweiterte Ausgabe* (1755; reprint, Hamburg: Tradition Classics, 2013). Hannah Arendt, *The Human Condition* (Chicago: University of Chicago Press, 1998), 295.

13. International Necronautical Society, "Manifesto," accessed November 16, 2012, http://www.necronauts.org/manifesto1.htm.

14. See Saul Bellow, *Dangling Man* (1944; reprint, New York: Penguin, 1998), 10.

15. On the reconstruction of Berlin in these terms, see my "Berlin 2000: 'The Image of an Empty Place,'" in *After-Images of the City*, ed. Joan Ramon Resina and Dieter Ingenschay (Ithaca, N.Y.: Cornell University Press, 2003), 61–74.

16. McCarthy, *Remainder*, 93.

17. Patricia Highsmith, *The Talented Mr. Ripley* (1955; New York: Vintage, 1999), 14–15.

18. Highsmith, *The Talented Mr. Ripley*, 20. For a very short review of the office century, see the opening of part III.

19. "I have a position" is the refrain of Dreiser's novel of the new lines and places of the official world, *Sister Carrie* (1900). Carrie herself is above all a "carrier": the first paragraph of the novel is a virtual inventory of things designed to carry other things—from the suitcase or wallet or lunch box or envelope to the train car itself. And Carrie is of course a medium, a carrier and mode of conveying the world's longing—just as the city of Chicago itself is a place that is not exactly a place, "not so much thriving upon established commerce as upon the industries which prepared for the arrival of others." Theodore Dreiser, *Sister Carrie* (New York: Norton, 1970), 11. Things hold the places of other things, and places are placeholders.

20. Tom's reenactive violence is a form of serial violence. On some of the relays between that form of reenactment and its copy machines, see my *Serial Killers: Death and Life in America's Wound Culture* (New York: Routledge, 1998).

21. See Dirk Baecker, "The Reality of Motion Pictures," MLN 111, no. 3 (1996): 561.

22. See Cornelia Vismann, "Out of File, Out of Mind," in *New Media/Old Media: A History and Theory Reader*, ed. Wendy Hui Kyong Chun and Thomas W. Keenan (New York: Routledge, 2005): "files display a rather complicated duality"; hence "the simple equation between files and the world, between the physicality of storage and the existence of data in the order of signs" (119–28).

23. See Erving Goffman, "Embarrassment and Social Organization," in *Interaction Ritual: Essays on Face-to-Face Behavior* (Chicago: Aldine, 2005), 97–112 (subsequent references to *Interaction Ritual*, IR, appear in text). I return to the practical joke and its implications in part IV.

24. See Diedrich Diederichsen, "Radicalism as Ego Ideal: Oedipus and Narcissus," trans. James Gussen, *E-Flux*, no. 25 (May 2011).

25. Kate Marshall, in her book *Corridor: Media Architecture in American Literature* (Minneapolis: University of Minnesota Press, 2013), provides a superb account of how such built structures work.

26. I take up these matters in the context of an account of the games, forensics, and art in the writings of Agatha Christie in "Die Freie Natur."

27. Ripley goes to the bar called the Green Cage at the start of *The Talented Mr. Ripley*; near the close of *Strangers on a Train*, the detective Gerard "poked a finger between the bars and waggled it at the little bird that fluttered in terror against the opposite side of the cage" (215). The novel *The Glass Cell*, about imprisonment and its aftereffects, names her world.

28. The reference to Ouroboros is to Plato's *Timaeus* and the animal "made in the all-containing form of a sphere. . . . He moved in a circle turning within himself."

29. This last is Bruno in *Strangers on a Train* (19). "Mermaids on the Golf Course" is a short story, included in a collection with the same title (New York: Penzler Books, 1988), 11–26. Two of the lethal snail stories are "The Snail-Watcher" and "The Quest for *Blank* Caveringi," both included in Highsmith, *Eleven: Short Stories* (London: Heineman, 1970). The snail-fixated murder novel is *Deep Water* (New York: Harper, 1957). The story of factory-farmed chickens gone wild is "The Day of Reckoning," originally published in Highsmith's *The Animal-Lover's Book of Beastly Murder* and reprinted in *The Selected Stories of Patricia Highsmith* (New York: Norton, 2001), 84–97. Hitchcock, it may be noted, invents and interpolates Bruno's little speech about "life on Mars" in the party scene of his film version of the novel. He stops short of the sentence John Carpenter gives to Natasha Henstridge in his *Ghosts of Mars*: "As soon as I get back I'm going to tell my superiors all about this fucked-up planet."

30. See Umberto Eco, "The Myth of Superman," in *The Role of the Reader: Explorations in the Semiotics of Texts* (Bloomington: Indiana University Press, 1979), 107–27. Eco's account locates Superman in part in terms of what David Riesman, in *The Lonely Crowd*, called the "other-directed" as opposed to the inner-directed individual—what Eco calls "a model of 'heterodirection'" David Riesman, Nathan Glazer, and Reuel Denney, *The Lonely Crowd: A Study of the Changing American Character*, rev. ed. (New Haven, Conn.: Yale University Press, 2001). In these rapid alternations between the inside and outside of worlds, and between self-reference and hetero-reference, we return to Lem's statement that "your genuinely immediate world is the outside world"—"that body of yours, which to some extent obeys you, says nothing and lies to you." Stanisław Lem, *Imaginary Magnitude*, trans. Mark E. Heine (Orlando, Fla.: Harcourt Brace Jovanovich, 1984), 175. Or, as Sharon Cameron articulates it, in her indispensable commentary on Emerson's *Nature*, "Emerson's Impersonal": "Nature is not outside of us. If we can't oversee nature, that is not because it is alien but is rather because it is internal." Cameron, *Impersonality: Seven Essays* (Chicago: University of Chicago Press, 2007), 98.

31. The performance of scale (evocations of big space and deep time that do not proceed beyond the evocative) functions in much the same way in a range of recent literary history—in the service of disciplinary self-reflection. In this way the discovery of deep history, for example, is folded back into the history of institutions, or into the reflexive history of history. Here one might consider

what art critics have described as "the New Institutionalism." This refers in part to what Wolfgang Kemp has called the "Betriebssystem Kurator"—the curator as operating system. (Nowhere more in evidence than in the recent *Documenta 13*, 2012.) These operations, in turn, mark the turn to the institution as a cross-referencing system (what is sometimes described as "interdisciplinarity"). Hence the curator as operating system "aims at stimulating discussion and dialogue with other fields of knowledge and is committed to . . . radical exhibition strategies." In this way reference becomes cross-reference, and cross-reference becomes self-reference, in curating a world. All under the banner of "political engagement" and "expanded programming." See Wolfgang Kemp, "Betriebssystem Kurator," *Kunst*, June 2012, 6–11, part of the special issue "God Is a Curator." For an alternate account of this institutional turn in the art world, see Diedrich Diederichsen, *On (Surplus) Value in Art* (Berlin: Sternberg, 2008). (I briefly return to this New Institutionalism in the final section of this chapter, in part by way of Daniel Lord Smail's *On Deep History and the Brain*.)

32. I am here paraphrasing Vogl, "Becoming-Media." The turn from reference to self-reference is both the subject and form of Vogl's instructive piece (as it is in a range of media studies that turns from the object to the form of its observation). Or in the terms of the systems theorist Heinz von Foerster (who described himself as Wittgenstein's "honorary" nephew), "reality appears as a consistent reference frame for at least two observers." Heinz von Foerster, *Observing Systems* (Seaside, Calif.: Intersystems, 1981).

33. The current rediscovery of counterfactual and alternative worlds, in history and fiction, locates but narrowly localizes such moments in the ordinary life of the daily planet, which continuously involves acts recast by the presence of alternatives.

34. See Quentin Meillassoux, *After Finitude: An Essay on the Necessity of Contingency*, trans. Ray Brassier (London: Continuum, 2008), 7, 27.

35. See my *True Crime: Observations on Violence and Modernity* (New York: Routledge, 2007), 111–32, and part II of this study.

36. Peter Sloterdijk, *You Must Change Your Life*, trans. Wieland Hoban (Cambridge: Polity, 2014), 329.

37. I return to this style of reenactment-management in part IV, the final section of chapter 8.

38. Scott McCloud, *Understanding Comics: The Invisible Art* (New York: William Morrow, 1994), 44. Subsequent references as UC in text.

39. Niklas Luhmann, *The Reality of the Mass Media*, trans. Kathleen Cross (Stanford, Calif.: Stanford University Press, 2000), 59.

40. Embarrassment and its self-observed observation epitomize those situations of self-incitation and self-observation that correspond most closely to everyday life; one cannot imagine the first two centuries of the European novel without it—what Edith Wharton, in *The House of Mirth*, calls the "art of blushing at the right time."

41. Daniel Lord Smail, *On Deep History and the Brain* (Berkeley: University of California Press, 2008), 161–85; quotation, 169. See also Wolfgang Schivelbusch, *Tastes of Paradise: A Social History of Spices, Stimulants, and Intoxicants* (New York: Vintage, 1993).

42. Smail, *On Deep History*, 127, 144.

43. Diedrich Diederichsen, "Living in the Loop," *Fillip*, no. 14 (summer 2011).

44. McCarthy, *Remainder*, 52, 115–16, 296. I return, briefly, to McCarthy's work—which also includes a book on comic books: *Tintin and the Secret of Literature*—in part IV.

3. "The Proper Study of Interaction"

1. An earlier, substantially different, version of this chapter appeared as the outlier, and so the preview, of this study, in my *True Crime: Observations on Violence and Modernity* (New York: Routledge, 2007).

2. That correlation will make it possible to draw out the relays between a version of media studies attentive to, even transfixed by, technology, on the one side, and a version of social-systems theory, on the other, relatively indifferent to it. The attention to form—what George Spencer Brown called the "laws of form"—in systems theory has made for, until recently, relative disattention to cultural techniques. For Kittler, technology is the blind spot of deconstructive media theory. The same could be said of systems-theoretical accounts—centrally, Niklas Luhmann's—of "the reality of the mass media."

3. On such models of referred belief—what Poe referred to as "half-credences"—in modern society, see my "The Crime System," *Critical Inquiry* 30, no. 3 (spring 2004): 557–83, a version of which appears in *True Crime*.

4. My approach to Highsmith's suspended and boundaried worlds has a range of referents and I want to note several here. The immediate referent (again) is to the fiction of J. G. Ballard, whose exhibitions of the autotropic violence proper to self-enclosed, or self-curved, space are crucial to its understanding. On this, I am returning then to the examinations of "lethal spaces" begun in my earlier accounts of a wound culture and pathological public sphere (accounts, too, persistently directed by cartographies of contemporary violence, through media technologies wedded to the affections). See my "Wound Culture: Trauma in the Pathological Public Sphere," *October* 80 (spring 1997), 3–26; and the chapter "Lethal Spaces" in *Serial Killers: Death and Life in America's Wound Culture* (New York: Routledge, 1998). The present pages are also instructed by Peter Sloterdijk's descriptions of these modern, or modernized, anthropotechnical practices and his accounts of "spheres" and other "auto-operatively curved spaces." (The quoted phrase "auto-hypnotically closed counter worlds" is from Sloterdijk's *You Must Change Your Life*, trans. Wieland Hoban [Cambridge: Polity, 2014], 391.) The idiom for describing these repeating enclaves is inflected as well by Tom McCarthy's reenactments, on Ballardian premises, as delineated spaces of accelerative violence, in the novels *Men in Space* and *Remainder*.

These sources are, among other things, useful counters to the retrivialization of repetition that the eternal recurrences of the clichés of deconstruction have amounted to.

5. Niklas Luhmann, *The Reality of the Mass Media*, trans. Kathleen Cross (Stanford, Calif.: Stanford University Press, 2000), 59.

6. Michel Foucault, *Discipline and Punish: The Birth of the Prison*, 2nd ed., trans. Alan Sheridan (New York: Vintage, 1995), x.

7. See Gregory Bateson, *Mind and Nature: A Necessary Unity* (New York: Dutton, 1979), 117.

8. Hence Wellbery indicates that the "greatest weakness of Foucault's theory, however, is that his veiled use of cybernetic concepts invites their distortion in the sense of pseudopolitical romanticism. Unhinged from their utterly trivial cybernetic significance, terms like *control* or *constraint* take on an aura of malevolence. They invite a romantic, self-aggrandizing myth of critical inquiry as revolutionary gesture." David Wellbery, "The General Enters the Library: A Note on Disciplines and Complexity," *Critical Inquiry* 35, no. 4 (January 1, 2009): 982–94.

9. Frances Ferguson, *Pornography, the Theory: What Utilitarianism Did to Action* (Chicago: University of Chicago Press, 2004), 3.

10. Erving Goffman, *Interaction Ritual: Essays on Face-to-Face Behavior* (New York: Pantheon, 1982), 2.

11. In what follows I use the phrase simply to indicate media not premised or dependent on interaction among those orally or visibly copresent, and in fact indifferent to that presence. I don't mean the presumptive implantation of mass psychology by technical means. On this, see Bernhard Siegert, "There Are No Mass Media," in *Mapping Benjamin: The Work of Art in the Digital Age*, ed. Hans Gumbrecht and Michael Marrinan, 30–38 (Stanford, Calif.: Stanford University Press, 2003).

12. Patricia Highsmith, *The Talented Mr. Ripley* (1955; reprint, London: Vintage, 1999), 150, subsequent references in the text, abbreviated *TMR*; Andrew Wilson, *Beautiful Shadow: A Life of Patricia Highsmith* (New York: Bloomsbury, 2004), 194–96.

13. Here we might compare Kittler's account and Luhmann's. On Kittler's account, this media dependency goes on in that it does not cease not seeing itself. Hence media, on this account, become "anaesthetic" and imperceptible, and continue insofar as they do. For Luhmann, the paradoxical reality of the mass media is a paradox but a working, observable, and knowable one: the question, rather, is that how the trick is done is open to see: "How is it possible to accept information about the world and about society as information about reality when one knows how it is produced?" The explicitation of the media—its perspicuous reflexivity—is then a property of its operations, not the self-conferred privilege of critique. (My sense is that Sianne Ngai's recent work on "the literary gimmick" is in part an unfolding of these paradoxes.)

14. Patricia Highsmith, *The Two Faces of January* (New York: Atlantic Monthly Press, 1964), 63.

15. On the function of the mass media as the background reality of modernity, see Luhmann, *The Reality of the Mass Media*; and Friedrich A. Kittler, *Literature, Media, Information Systems*, ed. John Johnston (Amsterdam: Routledge, 1997). I am in what follows tracing some of the implications of these rival accounts of the modern media a priori and testing out these rival idioms of analysis.

16. The contemporary form of this half-credence as to the constructed reality of the mass media means that, as Samuel Weber expresses it, "the paranoic element and the realistic element seem to work in tandem, reinforcing each other without providing any alternative sort of mediation." See Hent de Vries and Samuel Weber, "Theory on TV: 'After-Thoughts,'" in *Religion and Media*, ed. Hent de Vries and Samuel Weber (Stanford, Calif.: Stanford University Press, 2001), 99. Yet if this "tandem" structure is irreducible, it may be possible to specify it beyond a generalized, or overly rapid theorization of, "mediation."

17. It is striking the extent to which deconstructive media theory has adopted this tabloid temporal urgency—"Today, more than ever before . . ." See, e.g., Jacques Derrida, "Artifactualities," in Jacques Derrida and Bernard Stiegler, *Echographies of Television*, trans. Jennifer Bajorek (Oxford: Polity, 2002), 5. This urgency is coupled to its opposite: deconstructive media theory hesitates to attribute any deep difference at all to different materialities of communication (any new media appliance "reveals" a writing-in-general always already at work—albeit always now more than ever before). This coupling of urgency and timeless sameness indicates at the least a certain stalling in deconstructive media theory—or, as Kittler more severely puts it, "technology is the blindspot of poststructuralism" (see Kittler, *Literature, Media, Information Systems*, 8).

18. The notion of media "spin," that is, does not exhaust the panic/thrill that (as the ad for endless news puts it) "the world keeps spinning while you are sleeping you know." On the systemic structure of media self-conditioning and self-exposure, see Luhmann, *The Reality of the Mass Media*, 53–54, 33, et passim. I am in these pages drawing generally on Luhmann's account. That account is at once limited in the range of media it discusses and sketch-like in places (*Reality of the Mass Media* is a posthumous gathering of short pieces). But it's productive in its testing out—if not quite showing—whether mass media forms can operate autopoietically, and, if so, by what means and to what ends. (The auxiliary term "anthropotechnics" may be useful here, but it too is more optative than descriptive.)

19. Patricia Highsmith, *Found in the Street* (New York: Atlantic Monthly Press, 1986), 6, subsequent references in text, abbreviated FS.

20. Dirk Baecker, "The Reality of Motion Pictures," *MLN* 111, no. 3 (1996): 561.

21. On the emergence of a crime-centered mass-print media in the 1840s, see my "The Crime System," in *True Crime*. It is a world marked, that is, by second-order observing and secondhand nonexperience—just as a walk-on waitress in

a late J. G. Ballard novel, *Super-Cannes* (London: Flamingo, 2000), for example, wears a T-shirt with quotations from Baudrillard printed on it. One scarcely needs the 101st conference on the work of art in the age of mechanical copying to report on that. But one can then look into the strange attraction of the media (as vicarious life) and crime (as vicarious performance and transferred guilt) that structures that novel, among others. Ballard's late novels are thesis novels about the relays between media and crime, or more exactly about autotropic violence and its ego-technical media—and, at the same time, about that thesis as "paperback sociology." J. G. Ballard, *Cocaine Nights* (London: Flamingo, 1996), 121. It is part of Ballard's archaeology of knowingness, by which we see that "media speculation is today's crucible of accepted truth," and accept it (as with the Baudrillard T-shirt) in the claws of quotation marks. J. G. Ballard, *Millennium People* (London: Flamingo, 2003), 290.

22. Kittler, *Literature, Media, Information Systems*, 63.

23. See part I; I return to McCarthy's *Remainder* in part IV.

24. Recent returns to ontology—reactions against the correlation of the world to its observation—tend to tell this story in the genre of the horror story (particularly the story that usefully, as in Lovecraft, provides quotable summaries of its themes, which can then be quoted). Highsmith takes up these matters in extremely formal ways. Her posthuman psychopaths, cold and alien, make visible the situation in which the autopoietic autonomy and closure of social systems (and its art systems) is perceived and so pathologized. The ontological turn has turned from the world as it looks to us to the world as it looks without us. But the real horror story is perhaps not exactly the world as it looks without us—in the dust of this planet—but the world as it looks to us, but to us as one thing among others. Highsmith's killers—for whom the distinction between self-reference and other-reference does not hold—are not merely similar to one person or another, whose place they take. They are (pace Caillois) just similar. The horror—Highsmith's posthuman psychopath is alien and everyday at once—is neither long ago nor far away, but, like that of the stranger, one who is (as Simmel expressed it) near but also far. This is the situation of the stranger on a train, whose hair bobbed like antennae over his forehead.

25. Patricia Highsmith, *Plotting and Writing Suspense Fiction* (New York: St. Martin's, 1983), 88. Hence the person telling the story sits at a desk and types about Ripley, sitting at a desk writing and typing, making believe and making himself up. And, in real life, Highsmith, having written about this story of two persons—"one of whom kills the other and assumes his identity"—received the Mystery Writers of America award for the novel. She recalls that on that award document, "I lettered 'Mr. Ripley and' before my own name, since I think Ripley himself should have received the award. No book was easier for me to write, and I often had the feeling Ripley was writing it and I was merely typing" (*Plotting*, 75–76). (She would go on to "forge" Ripley's name on other documents, and checks, as well.)

26. See my *Serial Killers*.

27. Friedrich Schlegel, "Über Lessing," cited in Niklas Luhmann, *Art as a Social System*, trans. Eva M. Knodt (Stanford, Calif.: Stanford University Press, 2000), 287.

28. Patricia Highsmith, *A Suspension of Mercy* (1965; reprint, New York: Norton, 2001), 235, 155.

29. Patricia Highsmith, *The Cry of the Owl* (London: Heinemann, 1963), 7–8.

30. Patricia Highsmith, *Those Who Walk Away* (New York: Atlantic Monthly Press, 1967), 117.

31. Patricia Highsmith, *Strangers on a Train* (1950; reprint, New York: Penguin, 1979), 96, hereafter abbreviated ST.

32. I am here drawing on Niklas Luhmann, "A Redescription of 'Romantic Art,'" *MLN* 111, no. 3 (1996): 506–22.

33. In Highsmith, this is routinely the figure of a dea ex machina—the angelized woman—Anne in *Strangers on a Train*, or the suicided wife in *Those Who Walk Away*, for example. On the gender marking of the boundaries of modern technical, information, and media systems, see Friedrich A. Kittler, *Discourse Networks 1800/1900*, trans. Michael Metteer with Chris Cullens (Stanford, Calif.: Stanford University Press, 1990); and, with respect to the American scene, my *Bodies and Machines* (New York: Routledge, 1992) and *Serial Killers*.

34. I have taken up Christie's fiction, in "Die Freie Natur," in *Gefahrensinn: Archiv für Mediengeschichte*, ed. Lorenz Engell, Bernhard Siegert, and Joseph Vogl, 127–39 (Paderborn: Wilhelm Fink, 2009); and, to other ends, in part IV of this book.

35. Luhmann, *The Reality of the Mass Media*, 122.

36. See my *True Crime*.

37. Carl Friedrich von Savigny, *System des heutigen romischen Rechts* (1840); *System of Modern Roman Law*, vol. 2 (reprint, Madras: J. Higginbotham, 1867), 206, 176.

38. Savigny, *System of Modern Roman Law*, 179, 210. For instance, the institution of the university, or the corporation, or "the greatest and most important of all Juristical Persons: the Fiscus, that is to say the State itself" (182).

39. In part IV, and by way of Tom McCarthy's *Remainder*, I want to take up these questions in terms of the interesting combination of "limited liability" and "limited omniscience" in the recent novel. Making explicit the ties that bind these limit cases together makes it possible for McCarthy to compare the logic of actions in the novel (the acts, or reenactments, of a fictional person) and the logic of corporate actions (the acts of a fictitious one)—and to do so in terms of crimes as acts unattributable to actors. In short, "we are not doing things, they are being done." This is the case "'given the status of these parties, these, uh, institutions, these, uh . . .' 'Bodies,' I said. 'bodies,' he continued, 'almost anything's enforceable.'" Tom McCarthy, *Remainder* (New York: Vintage, 2007), 12. We will see that McCarthy plays out this logic to its very end: in that,

under these corporatist conditions, and as everyone who has attended the first meeting of a course on Marxism and culture knows, "everything solid melts into air." The disincorporation or volatilization of persons—bodies suspended in air and "vaporized"—realizes the logic of fictitious persons to the letter. The transubstantiations of the pristine culture of capitalism are business as usual. The aesthetics and forensics of such persons and acts are the subjects of Agatha Christie's or J. G. Ballard's or here Highsmith's reports on what playing out this interim logic looks like in the official world, and the institutional-administrative structure of a "bureaucracy of crime," solicited in and by the novel.

40. Savigny, *System of Modern Roman Law*, 232, 231. And it is worth recalling that the concept of personhood is itself "juristical" from the start: "Up until the early modern period, personhood remained an attribute mostly for legal relationships (but also relevant for existence as *civis* in a society) . . . Only in the eighteenth century was the concept of the individual tailored to persons, a refinement that transformed the concept of person at the same time." Niklas Luhmann, "The Mind and Communication," in *Theories of Distinction: Redescribing the Descriptions of Modernity*, ed. William Rasch (Stanford, Calif.: Stanford University Press, 2002), 183.

41. Savigny, *System of Modern Roman Law*, 231–33. The term "commit" means both to do something deliberately and to assign responsibility to another person. The two are not incompatible: to do something deliberately would be to assign responsibility to oneself as in effect to another. It is a model of being accountable to oneself. On this self-bookkeeping, and the administrative a priori, see part IV.

42. Savigny, *System of Modern Roman Law*, 234–35.

43. On McCarthy's presentation of action, reenactment, and the money-crime-liability complex, and its implications for art in the epoch of social systems, see part IV.

44. Second-order observation means observing not just one's observation but observing the mode of observing.

4. Chain Letters

1. My thanks to Kate Marshall, for reminding me, by way of Christian Marclay's film *The Clock*, of this scene—and so its explicit collation of game space, official time, and a temporary suspension of suspense.

2. See Friedrich Kittler, "Romanticism, Psychoanalysis, Film: A Story of Doubles," in *The Truth of the Technological World: Essays on the Genealogy of Presence*, trans. Erik Butler (Stanford, Calif.: Stanford University Press, 2014), 69–83; and Kittler, *Gramophone, Film, Typewriter*, trans. Geoffrey Winthrop-Young and Michael Wutz (Stanford, Calif.: Stanford University Press, 1999). See also my "The Crime System," *Critical Inquiry* 30, no. 3 (March 1, 2004): 557–83.

3. See, for example, Elena Esposito, "The Arts of Contingency," *Critical Inquiry* 31, no. 1 (autumn 2004): 7–25.

4. See Bernhard Siegert, *Relays: Literature as an Epoch of the Postal System*, trans. Kevin Repp (Stanford, Calif.: Stanford University Press, 1999).

5. In fact, the first, the chain letter, has been used to heuristically model the second, genetic replication. See Charles H. Bennett, Ming Li, and Bin Ma, "Chain Letters and Evolutionary Histories," *Scientific American*, June 2003. See also Richard Dawkins, *The Selfish Gene* (New York: Oxford University Press, 1976). (Dawkins's account, it may be added, is a strictly autotropic one, in that the argument with respect to evolution is that no extrinsic cause to answer the question, "Why are people?" need be posed.)

6. I take this up, in a more detailed way, via the fiction of Agatha Christie, in part III.

7. Rem Koolhaas, Madelon Vreisendorp, Elia Zenghelis, and Zoe Zenghelis, *Exodus, or the Voluntary Prisoners of Architecture* (New York: Museum of Modern Art, 1972), http://socks-studio.com/2011/03/19/exodus-or-the-voluntary -prisoners-of-architecture/.

8. For a lucid summary of this "becoming-media," see Joseph Vogl, "Becoming-Media: Galileo's Telescope," *Grey Room*, no. 29 (fall 2007): 14–25.

9. Friedrich Nietzsche, letter to Peter Gast (1882), cited by John Johnston, introduction to Friedrich Kittler, *Literature, Media, Information Systems* (Amsterdam: GB Arts International, 1997), 13.

10. There is a dense clustering of writing, recording, communicative media in the final pages of *Strangers*, and, it will be seen, in mystery and suspense novels and films generally. Such a drawing into relation of the becoming-visible of recording (the materialization of writing and the data stream, the writing of writing, and so on) and graphic violence is more or less canonical from the later nineteenth century on. On this radical entanglement of writing writing and modern violence—word counts and body counts—see my *Serial Killers: Death and Life in America's Wound Culture* (New York: Routledge, 1998).

11. Jacques Lacan, *Encore: Le seminaire, livre XX*, ed. Jacques Alain Miller (Paris: Editions du Seuil, 1975), 76.

12. See Ranulph Glanville, "A (Cybernetic) Musing: Ashby and the Black Box," *Cybernetics and Human Knowing* 14, no. 2–3 (2007): 191, quoting Niklas Luhmann, *Social Systems*, trans. John Bednarz, Jr. with Dirk Baecker (Stanford, Calif.: Stanford University Press, 1995), 109.

13. Do we need to posit a cooperation gene or mirror neuron solution to this situation? (Or does that trade one black box for another?) Would we not need to observe and to evaluate that too, from its (or our own) actions, speech acts, and otherwise?

14. Which is to say, Guy is, of course, like an indeterminate number of guys; or as Bruno puts, "I meet a lot of guys—but not many like you" (*ST*, 27).

15. Niklas Luhmann, *The Reality of the Mass Media*, trans. Kathleen Cross (Stanford, Calif.: Stanford University Press, 2000), 60. Luhmann is here drawing on Michel Serres's notion of the parasite, which he extends in these terms: "This

consequently means that the mass media themselves are second-order parasites, parasites which live parasitically on the parasiticality of their viewers." That is, if one depathologizes parasitism—and the addiction to the secondary.

16. Dirk Baecker, "The Reality of Motion Pictures," MLN 111, no. 3 (1996) 560–77. One might say then that the real dream of an autotropic world is one of movies without cameras. At the same time—and this may be one way of understanding the accelerative violence of these reenactments—that's one application of the anthropotechnical logic of the principles of scientific management from the start. The cinema, as Bernhard Siegert has traced, has its origins not in photography but in the scientific laboratory: in the labs of Etienne-Jules Marey or Frank and Lillian Gilbreth, for example, time, motion, and bodies are cut into pieces and reassembled in the interest of military effectiveness and industrial productivity, Weberian work ethics fused to body-machine complexes.

17. See Bruno Latour, *Reassembling the Social: An Introduction to Actor-Network Theory* (Oxford: Oxford University Press, 2007).

18. Peter Sloterdijk, *You Must Change Your Life*, trans. Wieland Hoban (Cambridge: Polity, 2014), 408.

19. Frances Ferguson, *Pornography, the Theory: What Utilitarianism Did to Action* (Chicago: University of Chicago Press, 2004), 30–31.

20. These two sides are perhaps not quite brought together in Ferguson's account, which focuses on how Bentham's utilitarian schemes provide the blueprint for that genre of social evaluation of exteriorized acts and outcomes. That account adapts Foucault's Bentham, but powerfully readjusts the focus from disciplinary suspicion to liberal individualism and its systemic presentation. But there is a certain anachronism in this account, and not merely that always involved in precursor-attribution. The little systems of act, outcome, and evaluation that Bentham blueprints are not definitive of the social field before the control and information revolutions of the second modernization make that operating system operational. And not until the emergence of self-operating technical systems in the 1830s—the annus mirabilis year is 1839—are even the questions for these answers in place (on the 1839 memeplex, see part III). Foucault finds it necessary to add that Bentham's panopticon is not a "dream machine," and does so via the "command and control" idiom of a cybernetic systems outlook that informs his account but is not taken into account (see also chapter 3, note 8, above). But this is necessary to add not exactly because Bentham's models are not yet built but because the proposition of a self-modeling world is not yet a social fact. The realism of the novel and its gamelike character are two sides of the same formation only when the "almost sui generis" character of modern social systems are social facts—ones that, across the social field, blueprint themselves as they go and so go on.

21. The distinction between art and nonart is continuously reprocessed by the modern art world as its self-definition. It must make the distinction, and do so via the commentary and ranking institutions of the art system (which provide

its indispensable writing on the wall). It's this condemnation to autonomy that Highsmith takes up in her art-world novel *Those Who Walk Away* (see part IV), and that makes for her description of the autistic unity of a character's inner world as "like a horrible little work of art." The artwork here keeps finding little models of itself in the world—microworlds like itself. This is nowhere clearer than in Hitchcock's adaptation of *Strangers on a Train*, in which the tennis game, the amusement park—the Kingdom of Fun—and its merry-go-round, and even the artfully arranged little landscape beneath the sewer plate (a tiny landscape Hitchcock obsessively rearranged) provide models of the film itself.

22. These mechanically doubling machines are part of a self-reflexive media network—that is, one that describes itself as a media network. The prototype of this apparently gratuitous but structurally determinate media machine is perhaps the daguerreotype apparatus in Hawthorne's *The House of the Seven Gables* (1852)—a novel that involves strangers and trains, vicarious life and vicarious crime, too. There, in a scene of stopped narrative, a daguerreotype image is made of the dead body. But it is made with no clear diegetic purpose, in a moment of something like photography for photography's sake. Yet it sets the narrative back in motion. Here too an apparently "extra" piece of technology, just there, seems to determine the situation. But why? What, more exactly, does this machine paradox indicate?

For one thing, the image apparatus, as everyone by now knows, records death (the trace of what had been). Here, in doing so, it immediately generates something like a "modern" sphere of privacy and intimacy. This is an intimacy then bound from the start to a reflexive doubling via mechanical representation. This is something like the first "Kodak moment." Vicarious life through the media is bound to, that is, the mechanical operators of motion and stillness (in this novel, train, telegraph, daguerreotype). These mechanical doublers undo the identification of (natural) life with motion and generate (machinic) life.

But there is more. The uncertain agency of the photograph in this scene is absolutely central to its functioning. It is not merely that the photographic act, in Hawthorne, immediately seems to evoke the by now canonical relation between death and recording. The givenness of that relation conceals something else. This is the (temporal) uncertainty as to whether the photographic—the "it was"—exteriorizes a timeless relation between death and the media or marks a timely and media-specific one. The undecidability of this question does not settle the question. We can only communicate about and reflect on the media through media of communication and reflection. Hence the attempt to periodize media forms is itself bound to the question of the media. The question as to the periodization of the media returns periodically whenever "new media" enter the scene. But in that the media operate via rather than despite that paradoxicality, the media question is not exhausted in its being "put in question" (that is, its deconstruction). The question concerning the media concerns how the media—that is, the media a priori, the media as system—enters into a circuit of self-determination. That is, what appears here—in the paradox of the gratuitously determinate dictaphone or camera—is the media paradox: the self-generating but also self-exposing, and so self-installing, system of the media..

23. The uncertain effect of media technologies here is, as we say, no accident. The difference between media analogy and media a priori is the difference between media "revealing" our situation, on the one side, and media "determining" our situation, on the other. (If the first roughly corresponds to the accounts of, say, Derrida or Stiegler, the second roughly corresponds to Kittler's.) This might be seen in terms of the difference between analogy (we are like the machines we make) and cause (that's because we are made by them). But this tension is self-supporting and so recitative. In *Strangers* the social tie is flat with its communication and the plot is its recoil. This is named too in many other crime and suspense novels, such as Jim Thompson's *Recoil*, or Raymond Chandler's *Playback*, or James M. Cain's *The Postman Always Rings Twice* or *Double Indemnity*.

24. See Friedrich Kittler, *Literature, Media, Information Systems* (Amsterdam: GB Arts International, 1997), 53.

25. That style of social bond is necessarily an unbinding tie, an asocial sociality. The paradox of sociality in the pathological public sphere means that the "acme of the 'sympathetic' relationship with others is simultaneously the ultimate nonrelationship with others": each imitates the 'every man for himself' of the others, here assimilation is strictly equivalent to a disassimilating dissimulation." Mikkel Borch-Jacobsen, *The Emotional Tie: Psychoanalysis, Mimesis, and Affect*, trans. Douglas Brick (Stanford, Calif.: Stanford University Press, 1992), 33, 9.

26. On *Those Who Walk Away*, see part V.

27. See Georg Simmel, "The Negative Character of Collective Behavior," in *The Sociology of Georg Simmel*, trans. and ed. Kurt H. Wolff (Glencoe, Ill.: Free Press, 1950), 396–401.

28. See Baecker, "The Reality of Motion Pictures." On the psychic technology of film, from Munsterberg to Deleuze, see Kittler, *Gramophone, Film, Typewriter*; and Bernard Stiegler, *Technics and Time, 1: The Fault of Epimetheus*, trans. Richard Beardsworth and George Collins (Stanford, Calif.: Stanford University Press, 1998). Let me add that Deleuze's commentary on the transition from the movement image to the time image may be seen to register the transition to second-order observation, on the level of the system of images, that I am taking up here.

29. On such "lethal spaces," in Zola and Ballard, among others, see my *Serial Killers*.

30. See J. G. Ballard, "Cataclysm and Dooms," in his collection of short essays, *The User's Guide to the Millennium* (New York: St. Martin's, 1996), 208–9.

31. Perhaps the purest novel of this concept of lethalized space in suspense fiction is Tim Krabbé's novel *(The Vanishing) Het Gouden Ei* (Amsterdam: Uitgererij Bert Bakker, 1984), trans. Claire Nicholas White, under the title *The Vanishing* (New York: Random House, 1993). The novel intensifies the conditions of englobed and vanished space as its plot, one that combines scenes of interment with fantasies of encapsulated persons suspended, in a golden egg, in alien space.

32. Cited in Donald Spoto, *The Dark Side of Genius: The Life of Alfred Hitchcock* (New York: Ballantine, 1983), 90.

33. Baecker, "The Reality of Motion Pictures," 561.

34. On Scientology, see especially Lawrence Wright, *Going Clear: Scientology, Hollywood, and the Prison of Belief* (New York: Knopf, 2013); and, collaterally, Paul Thomas Anderson's film *The Master* (New York: Weinstein Company, 2012). Sloterdijk's account of Scientology's founder, L. Ron Hubbard, in *You Must Change Your Life*, 94–105, emphasizes how Hubbard "decisively increased our knowledge about the nature of religion, even if largely involuntarily" (94).

35. Lululemon's founder-guru credits one spin-off, Landmark Forum—along with Ayn Rand—for the success of his yoga-based miracle about money. See Amy Wilson, "Chip Wilson, Lululemon's Guru, is Moving On," *New York Times Magazine*, Feb. 2, 2015. http://www.nytimes.com/2015/02/08/magazine/lululemons -guru-is-moving-on.html?_r=0

36. This not least in the artificial microworlds—like the amusement park, the Kingdom of Fun, the site of the first murder—that proliferate in the novel, and the gamelike spaces that Hitchcock adds to it—the soundproof booth, viewed by an internal audience as if viewing a silent film; the "real-time" tennis game, with its crowd transfixed by the back-and-forth crisscross of the ball; the runaway carousel and its spectators (including the play-fighting boy riding on it, who does not make the distinction between real and game worlds, either).

37. J. G. Ballard, introduction to the French edition, *Crash* (New York: Vintage, 1974), 5.

38. And, along these lines, the panic of uncertain agency and the panic/thrill of the body-machine complex become indissociable. On this, see my *Bodies and Machines* (1992; reprint, New York: Routledge, 2015), esp. part I.

39. On the merry-go-round in the machine age, see Bill Brown, *The Material Unconscious: American Amusement, Stephen Crane, and the Economics of Play* (Cambridge, Mass.: Harvard University Press, 1997).

40. See Wolfgang Schivelbusch, *The Railway Journey: The Industrialization of Time and Space in the Nineteenth Century* (Berkeley: University of California Press, 1986), 124.

41. On this "fusion" of act and observation—the technical form of second-order observation—see (in addition to Baecker and Kittler) Mark Hansen, *Embodying Technesis: Technology beyond Writing* (Ann Arbor: University of Michigan Press, 2000); Stiegler, *Technics and Time, 1*; and Bernard Stiegler, "The Discrete Image," in *Echographies of Television: Filmed Interviews* (Cambridge: Polity, 2002), 147–63. One might consider too the range of psychoanalytic film theory by which psychic and filmic apparatus are taken to double each other (hence making film and its media specificity simply redundant). Or one might consider, alternately, the visual history of "absorption and theatricality" that Michael Fried has so compellingly traced. Here the techniques of the observer, and the techniques for observing nonobservation, provide another way of under-

standing the media history of the forms of second-order observation, in an art history.

42. Paul Wegener, *Die Kunstlerischen Moglichkeiten des Films* (1919), cited in Kittler, "Romanticism, Psychoanalysis, Film," 97.

43. The modern psychology of doubling—Otto Rank's Freudian account *The Double: A Psychoanalytic Study*, ed. Harry Tucker (Chapel Hill: University of North Carolina Press, 1971)—takes most of its examples (as Kittler traces) from films, without noticing it is going to the movies (just as the word *Kino*—movies, cinema—never appears in Freud's published writing). At the same time, the film engineer Munsterberg puts in place the psychotechnology of film, which relies on a neurological precision that cannot be accessed "either by consciousness or language. Munsterberg assigns every single camera technique to an unconscious, psychical mechanism: the close-up to selective attention, the flashback to involuntary memory, the film-trick to day-dreaming, and so forth" (Kittler, "Romanticism, Psychoanalysis, Film," 100).

44. Hence the last word of the *Bourne Supremacy* is a piece of collegial advice, a sort of practical joke framed by the window, the telescope, and the telephone, about that: "Get some rest, Pam. You look tired." I will return to such practical jokes, and their institutional significance, in part IV.

5. Parlor Games

1. Gustave Flaubert, "A Lecture on Natural History—Genus: *Clerk*," in *Early Writings*, trans. Robert Griffin (Lincoln: University of Nebraska Press, 1991), 45–49.

2. William Dean Howells, *The Rise of Silas Lapham* (Edinburgh: Davis Douglas, 1885).

3. Peter Sloterdijk, *Bubbles: Spheres, Volume 1,* trans. Wieland Hoban (Los Angeles: Semiotext(e), 2011), 46.

4. All references to the first chapter of the novel.

5. Theodore Dreiser, *Sister Carrie* (New York: Norton, 1970), 2, 277; subsequent references, SC, in text.

6. This realization of an extremely formal new order of things takes place in "every managerial office in the city": in the makeshift of Kafkaesque office spaces, secluded under stairways, in backstage prop rooms, in reserves of self-persuasive rules, that rule on "their own ground."

7. I am quoting Karl Marx, *Grundrisse: Foundations of the Critique of Political Economy,* trans. Martin Nicolaus (1973; reprint, London: Penguin Classics, 1993), 23. Marx here continues: "The example of labour shows strikingly how even the most abstract categories, despite their validity—precisely because of their abstractness—for all epochs, are nevertheless, in the specific character of this abstraction, themselves likewise a product of historic relations, and possess their full validity only for and within these relations." It is the specific character of this autonomy and the shape of its practices—its practices of self-exposition and self-exposure—in the epoch of social systems that concerns me in these

pages. My thanks to Sianne Ngai for pointing me to this passage and so for suggesting its pertinence to my argument.

8. On this fascination, see my *Bodies and Machines* (1992; reprint, New York: Routledge, 2015), e.g. 224–25.

9. Siegfried Kracauer, "The Hotel Lobby," in *Rethinking Architecture: A Reader in Cultural Theory*, ed. Neil Leach, 51–57 (London: Routledge, 1997); see also Kracauer's remarkable account, "On Employment Agencies: The Construction of a Space," in *Rethinking Architecture*, 57–62.

10. Carrie is in all these senses then what Alfred Sohn-Rethel calls an "abstract thing." The abstract thing par excellence: as Dreiser puts it, "She was capital." (*Sister Carrie*, 296.) Alfred Sohn-Rethel, *Intellectual and Manual Labor: A Critique of Epistemology* (Atlantic Highlands, N.J.: Humanities Press, 1978), 45. That may be seen as dialectical witchcraft or as the form of self-organizing systems that achieve practical form in lifting action out of action. For Dreiser it is a world of carriers, lines, placeholders, and the bipolar force of self-comparison—an "innate trend of mind" reenacted on a multiverse of stages, and across an improbable continuum of diverse scenes and new lines of work. Medial work: Carrie's prompter in the later part of the novel is the inventor Ames, and the "line" that he is in is the invention of a "new kind of light." Light, for Dreiser, as for McLuhan, is the ideal-typical medium (the medium without "content").

11. Demand's space-simulators may be viewed at http://artblart.com/tag/thomas -demand-space-simulator/.

12. Michael Fried, *Why Photography Matters as Art as Never Before* (New Haven, Conn.: Yale University Press, 2008).

13. The experiment, we have seen, reenacts natural or social processes by technical means. "In this way"—in the overfamiliarized but exact terms Heidegger provides in "The Question Concerning Technology"—"the impression comes to prevail that everything man encounters exists only as it is his construct. The illusion gives rise to the one final delusion: it seems as though man everywhere and always encounters only himself." (*The Question Concerning Technology and Other Essays*, trans. William Lovett [New York: Harper, 1977]), 27.

14. Niklas Luhmann, *Art as a Social System*, trans. Eva Knodt (Stanford, Calif.: Stanford University Press, 2000), 204.

15. Luhmann, *Art as a Social System*, 91.

16. Luhmann, "Self-Description," in *Art as a Social System*, 224–315.

17. Luhmann, *Art as a Social System*, 244.

18. This is James's self-description of his novel *The Turn of the Screw*. The characterization of framed experience is clearest in the space of the game, the scene of the crime, and the form of the work of art. *Turn of the Screw* is, of course, all three.

19. Goffman's *Frame Analysis: An Essay on the Organization of Experience* appeared in 1974, as did *Ripley's Game*. Goffman's accounts of interaction as a property of systems, not individuals—the syntactical relations among the acts of different persons—describe the gamelike structures of Highsmith's plots.

See, for example, Goffman's description of what generates human "contact," in *The Presentation of Self in Everyday Life* (New York: Anchor, 1959): "Whatever it is that generates the human want for social contact and for companionship, the effect seems to take two forms: a need for an audience before which to try out one's vaunted selves, and a need for teammates with whom to enter into collusive intimacies. . . . The performance is something the team members can stand back from, back far enough to imagine or play out simultaneously other kinds of performances attesting to other realities. Whether the performers feel their official offering is the 'realest' reality or not, they will give surreptitious expression to multiple versions of reality, each version tending to be incompatible with the others" (206–7). This description of the "official offering" of the "'realest' reality" concisely describes the collusive stranger-intimacies of the official world. It is too an exact description of Ripley's "talent"—and of the comparative realities it entails. The difference is that Goffman's accounts are premised on the mutual presence to each other of the players, and Highsmith's on the presence of techniques of communication that no longer require (or tolerate) that. Action in Highsmith depends on and presupposes techniques of communication that no longer need or admit copresence. Ripley's "talent" is to know how that works and to know whether opponents know that too, or know that they don't. He can in this way monetize the controlled use of the uncontrollable, in the back-and-forth that belongs to his games, and so stage and enter into the "realest" versions of official offerings. This is Ripley's "prestige" (in the sense of the term that the director Christopher Nolan unfolds in his film of that title). Ripley's practical jokes or parlor games or gimmicks or tricks—each one calls attention to itself and yet causes something to work. This is institutional self-exposition as a kind of performance art (familiar to anyone who has worked at a large public university, for instance).

20. Patricia Highsmith, *Ripley's Game* (1974; reprint, New York: Vintage, 1999), 59. Subsequent references, *RG*, in the text.

21. I take up the natural history of artificial life—via Kazuo Ishiguro's novel *Never Let Me Go*—in the final section of chapter 6.

22. See Kate Marshall's account of the corridor as medium in the second modernity in her recent *Corridor: Media Architectures in American Fiction* (Minneapolis: Minnesota University Press, 2013).

23. This is not merely in that the observed scene of the crime—a demarcated and ruled zone of motive and act, outcome and information—resembles the game scene. I am here picking up from the postscript to my *True Crime: Observations on Violence and Modernity* (New York: Routledge, 2007).

24. As Goffman summarizes it: "if the observer is to inform himself effectively it will behoove him to conceal the fact that he is doing anything more than accepting the subject at face value—else he will put the latter on guard and discredit his own show of ingenuousness. This makes the observer a concealer too. Similarly, if the subject aims to conceal well then he will be advised actively to

try to uncover whether or not there are suspicions concerning him; this makes him a searcher too. However, here no real symmetry of role obtains since the points at which each player takes on a function like the other's are restricted to particular nexes in the expression game in progress." Erving Goffman, *Strategic Interaction* (Philadelphia: University of Pennsylvania Press, 1969), 70–71. Not surprisingly, such accounts have lent themselves to applications of game theory to novels, in particular the expression games in the novels of Jane Austen and Henry James. But the syntax of face-to-face interaction, to which Goffman confines his account, then excludes precisely the reality of mass media premised on the condition in which not only is such copresence "effectively and *visibly* rendered impossible"; also and beyond that, the success of communication no longer depends on it. Here one may speak of "success" itself as a medium. See Niklas Luhmann, *The Reality of the Mass Media*, trans. Kathleen Cross (Stanford, Calif.: Stanford University Press, 2000), 16. Letters are, of course, the transitional medium in the case of the novel. The use of game theory in contemporary literary studies, centering on character, or character decisions, tends toward an account of game theory as expression game. The novel—to the very extent that it yields character to system in terms of what Alex Woloch calls the "character-system" may then continue to work as a sort of paramnesic symptom of the reality of ego-technic media irreducible to psychology or point of view.

25. Norbert Wiener, *Cybernetics: Or the Control and Communication in the Animal and the Machine*, 2nd ed. (Cambridge, Mass.: MIT Press, 1965), 159. See Peter Galison, "The Ontology of the Enemy: Norbert Wiener and the Cybernetic Vision," *Critical Inquiry* 21, no. 1 (autumn 1994): 228–66.

26. Timothy Lenoir, "All but War Is Simulation: The Military-Entertainment Complex," *Configurations* 8, no. 3 (2000): 289–335.

27. John von Neumann, "Zur Theorie der Gesellschaftsspiele," *Mathematische Annalen* 100 (1928): 295–320; for an English translation, see "On the Theory of Games of Strategy," in *Contributions to the Theory of Games*, vol. 4, ed. A. W. Tucker and R. D. Luce (Princeton, N.J.: Princeton University Press, 1959), 13–42.

28. John von Neumann and Oskar Morgenstern, *Theory of Games and Economic Behavior* (1947; reprint, Princeton, N.J.: Princeton University Press, 2007).

29. Roland Barthes, *Empire of Signs*, trans. Richard Howard (New York: Hill and Wang, 1982). The point, for Barthes, is that the rational is only one system among others. An alternative way to parry the reflexive character of second-order observation is via reassertions of "radical" (that is, conservative) undecidability or paradoxicality as such (routinized deconstruction).

30. For a useful summary of game theory and its discontents, see William Poundstone, *Prisoner's Dilemma: John von Neumann, Game Theory, and the Puzzle of the Bomb* (New York: Doubleday, 1992), 167–78. The "prisoner's dilemma" has emerged as the paradox on which such "rational choice" accounts are clearly seen to founder. The popular understanding, however, simplifies a notion of rationality that is itself more complex in game theory. The capacity to forecast that

future presents will look like present futures is premised on the sharing of those presumptions among other actors—that is, on their decision to behave like economic actors, or economists, are supposed to behave. But the positing of rationality in game theory is thus nontrivial and reflexive too. As Oskar Morgenstern expresses it, "To determine optimal, or 'rational' behavior is precisely the task of the mathematical theory of games. *Rational behavior is not an assumption of that theory*; rather, its identification is one of its *outcomes.*" Morgenstern, "Game Theory," in *Dictionary of the History of Ideas*, ed. Philip P. Wiener (New York: Charles Scribner's Sons, 1968), 267. "Clearly, if more and more players act rationally," as Morgenstern elaborates it, "there will be shifts in actual behavior and in real events to be described. This is an interesting phenomenon worth pointing out. It has philosophical significance: progress in the natural sciences does not affect natural phenomena, but the spread of knowledge of the workable social sciences changes social phenomena via changed individual behavior from which fact there may be a feedback into the social sciences." Cf. Oskar Morgenstern, "Vollkommene Voraussicht und wirtschaftliches Gleichgewicht," *Zeitschrift für Nationalökonomie* 6, no. 3 (1935): 337–57. The fact of the evolution of this "interesting phenomenon" into a banality is here the interesting one. One now knows that social systems have emerged once there are sociologists. There is a rapid transition in this period from the perception of feedback as a curious, if interesting, phenomenon to its central place in understanding the behavior of complex systems. In systems-theoretical terms, one operates ongoingly on imperfect information—and only on that basis: a world that contains decision makers has an uncertain future, since it depends on what is decided in the present. Cf. Elena Esposito, Lecture, "Probability and Fiction in Science and Economics," Facoltà di Scienze della Communicazione, Università di Modena e Reggio Emilia, Italy, June 21, 2006. If this recursive rationality seems implausible, one might consider how the academic archipelago of disciplines—the sequestration and reciprocal ignorance on which the differentiation and mutual opacity of disciplines depends—keeps on going anyway. And not least by ongoingly reflecting on the fact that they do (the stationary carousel of the academic conference circuit, for example). These self-conditioned social microfields are premised on reciprocal *rules of irrelevance*–codes of *civil inattention* or *involvement shields*—by which self-generated and self-dispelled uncertainties can be processed with relative and "indoor" independence. Rules of irrelevance, and the ignorance management they enable. (The italicized phrases are drawn from Erving Goffman's description of behavior in public places and its interaction rituals. In adapting them, I mean to suggest that such descriptions might be extended to the relative continence of the social microworlds, and disciplines, that concern me here—to their self-conditioning and so to their ways of managing uncertainty and ignorance or nonknowing. Learning avoidance, and secluded education, as a protocol of disciplines is the subject of chapter 6, by way of Ishiguro's campus novel, *Never Let Me Go*.)

31. The return of "altruism," in accounts of evolutionary biology that appeal to game theory, is one response to the ruthless simplifications of behavorial self-advantage in its "classical" applications to group or social behavior. The response is beset by its own problems, not least an idealization of the neurosciences, a neuroscientism, often tautological or loosely metaphoric (the selfish gene vs. the mirror neuron, for example). Pertinent here is what the philosopher Thomas Nagel describes as the magical flavor of popular representations of recent scientific discoveries, and, for example, the hyperbolically animated character of these representations. (On the scientological quality in such fusions of popularized science, science fiction, and psychology fiction, see part V.) The same goes for a strain of "affect" theory, which, differentiating affect from emotion in terms of the distinction between the impersonal and quantitative (the quantity of intensity), on the one side, and the personal, recognized, conscious, on the other (the quality of experience) in effect reinstates the mind-body problem on another level. (The lucid critiques of the neuroscientific turn and affect theory in the humanities and social sciences offered by Ruth Leys make this case most strenuously.) My own concern here is more limited: it is a concern with the autotropic and self-descriptive character of modern social systems and the manner in which that autotropy is registered and parried in a range of recent work. Consider, for instance, the opening of Richard Dawkins's highly influential account of evolutionary biology, *The Selfish Gene* (New York: Oxford University Press, 1976): "Intelligent life on a planet comes of age when it first works out the reason for its own existence. If superior creatures from space ever visit earth, the first question they will ask, in order to assess the level of our civilization, is: 'Have they discovered evolution yet?'" (1). That is to say, the strict internality and autonomy of self-evolving systems is the Darwinian response to the question, "Why man?" Yet this is also (as Smail traces), the self-induced character of a self-assessing modernity, here seen from space.

32. See McKenzie Wark, *Gamer Theory* (Cambridge, Mass.: Harvard University Press, 2007); Jesper Juul, *Half-Real: Video Games between Real Rules and Fictional Worlds* (Cambridge, Mass.: MIT Press, 2005).

33. The games I am considering here are pathological games—"funny games" in the sense that Michael Haneke gives to violent play in his film of the same name. In a 1952 letter to Norbert Wiener, Gregory Bateson observed, "What applications of the theory of games do, is to reinforce the players' acceptance of the rules and competitive premises, and therefore make it more and more difficult for the players to conceive that there might be other ways of meeting and dealing with each other. . . . Von Neumann's 'players' differ profoundly from people and mammals in that those robots totally lack humor and are totally unable to 'play' (in the sense in which the word is applied to kittens and puppies)." Or, as Herbert Marcuse expressed it, RAND gamers "arrange games with death and disfiguration in which fun, team work, and strategic planning mix in rewarding social harmony. . . . [RAND] reports such games in a style of

absolving cuteness." Marcuse, *One-Dimensional Man: Studies in the Ideology of Advanced Industrial Society* (Boston: Beacon, 1964), 80–81. Yes, no doubt. But it's not just that Highsmith and RAND are kitten- and puppy-free zones. These pathological games (like Haneke's) are staged for the sake of their observation, reported and recorded, with a psychodispassionate distance between the little planning world (and its models), and the larger planned one (with its working models too). The fun of that, as opposed to, say, the play-fighting of kittens, is a bit harder to locate, and not exactly my concern here. But it's joined in these cases to the self-exempting and self-administering and overlit microworlds of, say, Sade or Bentham, Highsmith or Foucault—and bound to the differentiation and autonomous validity of modern social systems. It's linked to what training and measuring and comparing and assessing in these institutions come to look like, and feel like. And it depends on the a priorization of the media as condition of existence (the doubling of reality, via, e.g., the graphomanias of Sade or Highsmith; the observer-recorder worlds of Bentham or Foucault, or Luhmann). That there are many disparate disciplinary approaches to explain these links is a version of the same differentiation (here, of pleasure principles). As Roger Caillois notes, near the close of his *Man, Play, and Games*, trans. Meyer Barash (Urbana: University of Illinois Press, 2001), "It is not merely [in defining the domain of play] a question of different approaches arising from the diversity of disciplines. The facts studied in the name of play are so heterogeneous that one is led to speculate that the word 'play' is perhaps merely a trap, encouraging by its seeming generality tenacious illusions as to the supposed kinship between disparate forms of behavior" (162). We might then take this "diversity" of self-observed capsule worlds into account as a component, or condition, of modern pathological games.

34. My interest for the moment is strictly in the media rivalry that the game spaces of this film posit, and how that stages and shows the reality of communication as the reality produced, a reality "anchored in its own ambivalence." Dirk Baecker, "The Reality of Motion Pictures," MLN 111, no. 3 (1996): 562. The graphic extraversions of psychic and somatic states in technics, and the lurid-violent depictions of an alien sociology fused to technology, in manga and anime, are directly pertinent at this point. One might consider, among many others, the natural history of artificial life and death in the superb anime series *Serial Experiments: Lain* (Ryūtarō Nakamura, dir., and Chiaki J. Konaka, author [Tokyo: Triangle Staff, aired from 1998]); the provocation of other worlds, and species extinction as staged games of assisted evolution, in *Bokurano* (Ours; Hiroyuka Morita, dir., and Mohiro Kitoh, author [Tokyo: SUN-TV and TOKYO-MX, aired from 2007]); or the fashionable annihilative character of techno-fascism (the terms for "fashion" and "fascism" are pronounced nearly identically in Japanese) in *Kill la Kill* (Hiroyuki Imaishi, dir., and Kazuki Nakashima, author [Tokyo: Trigger, aired from 2013]); and, of course, the mainstreamed wiring of the world in *Ghost in the Shell* (Mamoru Oshii, dir. [Tokyo: Production I.G,

from 1995]). On the last, see Wendy Hui Kyong Chun, "Orienting Orientalism, or How to Map Cyberspace," in *Asian American.net: Ethnicity, Nationalism, and Cyberspace*, ed. Rachel C. Lee and Sau-ling Cynthia Wong (New York: Routledge, 2003), 3–36. The matters of "the Anthropocene" and the contemporary allure of extinction scenarios are continuously depicted and tested in such anime series. Such extroversions of psychology and bodily states in ego-technic media are examined in detail in my current work on practices of suspense. At the moment my limited concern is with its prerequisite: the emergence and generalization of cultural techniques that make for the capacity to "play society" and its form games.

35. See Baecker, "The Reality of Motion Pictures," 561.

36. On such a becoming-medial as a cultural technique (tacitly on the model of Deleuze's "becoming-machine"), see Joseph Vogl, "Becoming-Media: Galileo's Telescope," *Grey Room*, no. 29 (fall 2007): 14–25.

37. For example: historical reality (singular persons and events that are real but accidental and inessential); fictional reality (persons and events that are unreal but representative or essential); and real—that is, mathematical or statistical— reality (numbers are, of course, the first virtual reality). The coemergence of the realistic novel (fictional reality) and the calculus of probabilities and statistics is well known. So too is the collateral emergence of the fictional and the historical turns (not least in the rise of historical fiction). As Niklas Luhmann concisely states it, "Modernity has invented probability calculations just in time to main- tain a fictionally created, dual reality. . . . What are we to make of the fact that the world is now divided into two kinds of reality—a world of singular events and a world of statistics (or of inductive references), a reality out there and a fic- tional reality?" Luhmann, *Observations on Modernity*, trans. William Whobry (Stanford, Calif.: Stanford University Press, 1998), 70; Luhmann, *Art as a Social System*, 175.

38. Here the player commenting on the game is also its designer. The paradox would seem to be that the arbiter of the game enters into it—and how can the player play the arbiter? Yet the paradox, at the level of plot, is the principle, at the level of structure: a world designed to have designs of its own must include its designer. In this way the aesthetic problem of form and intention is recast in terms of the systems epoch.

39. I am drawing here on Dirk Baecker, "The Form Game," in *Problems of Form*, ed. Dirk Baecker, trans. Michael Irmscher and Leah Edwards (Stanford, Calif.: Stanford University Press, 1999), 99–106. On the contingent as that which is neither necessary nor impossible, see Luhumann, *Observations on Modernity*: "Anything is contingent that is neither necessary nor impossible. The concept is therefore defined by the negation of necessity and impossibility" (45). On the implications of a contingency defined by that simultaneous double negation, see Mary Ann Doane, *The Emergence of Cinematic Time: Modernity, Contingency, the Archive* (Cambridge, Mass.: Harvard University Press, 2002), 231–32. For an intralogical account of the necessity of contingency itself, see Quentin Meil-

lassoux, *After Finitude: An Essay on the Necessity of Contingency*, trans. Ray Brassier (London: Continuum, 2008).

40. Similarly, the formulism of genre fiction—mystery novels, for example—has to cultivate variousness amid typified and garden-variety redundancies. Think of Hercule Poirot's vegetable marrows in *The Murder of Roger Ackroyd* then as narrative self-description, the cultivation of one's own plot.

41. Roger Caillois, *Man, Plan and Games*, 29.

42. Goffman, *The Presentation of Self in Everyday Life*, 244.

43. See Anthony Giddens, *Modernity and Self-Identity: Self and Society in the Late Modern Age* (Stanford, Calif.: Stanford University Press, 1991), 144–80.

44. Luhmann, *Observations on Modernity*, 17. See also, on how this is conditioned by "the over-communicative constitution of the world system," Peter Sloterdijk, *In the World Interior of Capital: Towards a Philosophical Theory of Globalization*, trans. Wieland Hoban (Malden, Mass.: Polity, 2013), 13.

45. Luhmann, *Observations on Modernity*, 21; and Luhmann, *Art as a Social System*, 244, 312–13.

46. On the legal system, see Cornelia Vismann, *Files: Law and Media Technology*, trans. Geoffrey Winthrop-Young (Stanford, Calif.: Stanford University Press, 2008); and Niklas Luhmann, *Law as a Social System*, ed. Fatima Kastner and Richard Nobles, trans. Klaus Ziegert (Oxford: Oxford University Press, 2008); on public opinion, see Elizabeth Noelle-Neumann, *The Spiral of Silence: Public Opinion, Our Second Skin* (Chicago: University of Chicago Press, 1993); on the economic system, and the autonomization of financialization, see, for instance, Joseph Vogl, *The Specter of Capital* (Stanford, Calif.: Stanford University Press, 2014); and Dirk Baecker, "The Form of the Firm," *Organization: The Critical Journal on Organization, Theory and Society* 13, no. 1 (2006): 109–42; on crime as social system, see my "The Crime System," *Critical Inquiry* 30, no. 3 (spring 2004): 557–83. See centrally, for a quick inventory, Luhmann, *Observations on Modernity*, 16, 59–60. One can either describe this as the coming-to-term of the reflexive turn, or—as the recent "speculative turn" would have it—its death throes. That is, if for Goffman, "we lead an indoor social life," for Meillassoux the call is then to "the great outdoors" (Meillassoux, *After Finitude*, 7).

47. Ross Macdonald, *The Underground Man* (New York: Knopf, 1971), 172.

48. In the following section I take up how the delay in recognizing feedback makes for endless rehearsals of the form/intent paradox with respect to artificial, and artful, objects.

49. The affective turn today reproduces exactly this preference for affects that incorporate their self-reflection (or consist in it). I have in mind here the provocative work, for instance, of Brian Massumi, Rei Terada, and especially Sianne Ngai. I have in mind too work building on in part the earlier social-psychological work of Silvan Tomkins and Erving Goffman (on the latter, especially Heather Love's work on stigma). Second-order affect theory trades in derivatives of feeling in the same way that hedge funds trade in derivatives of financial products. See

particularly Goffman's splendid account of the communicative structure of the "little social system" of embarrassment in his "Embarrassment and Social Organization," in *Interaction Ritual: Essays on Face-to-Face Behavior* (Chicago: Aldine, 2005), 97–112. The current affective turn in academic criticism is on some fronts a return to sensibility criticism, at times groundbreaking, at times arguably amounting to a methodologically concealed conservatism. (Hence the perpetual redemonstration of the end of "the Cartesian subject," its deconstruction playing on an endless loop.) It is, unarguably, a retrofitting to the world systems of second-order observation. Such a retrofitting is embedded in the very notion of the turn—the linguistic turn, the cultural turn, the affective turn—as a way of marking historical epochs. This is an extraordinary vehicle of periodization: what amounts not merely to the modalization of history but to its self-observation.

50. Huizinga, in *Homo Ludens*, cites "the popular Dutch saying to the effect that 'it is not the marbles that matter but the game.'" That is, as he terms it, "Play is a thing by itself." Johan Huizinga, *Homo Ludens: A Study of the Play Element in Culture* (1949; reprint, London: Routledge, 1998), 49. Yet it is precisely the perspicuous autonomization of functionally differentiated systems, as things in themselves, that in effect suspends the world-suspension of play as set out in these terms. If *serious* is *not playing, playing* then, in the systems epoch, appears as higher-order *seriousness*. The art work that Henry James, in his experiment with autonomous reenactment zones—*The Turn of the Screw*—calls "playing very hard."

51. Erving Goffman, *Encounters: Two Studies in the Sociology of Interaction* (New York: Penguin, 1972), 19.

52. And, in the early 1840s, the first scheduled oceanic steamship service; the first railway hotel (in New York), along with railway station bookshops; the earliest department stores; the first modern urban system for the separate circulation of water and sewage (Chadwick in Britain); the first "package" tour—Thomas Cook's, between Leicester and Loughborough. And so on. For a useful summary of these systems tending toward total mobilization and systems-internal unities, see John Urry, *Mobilities* (Cambridge: Polity, 2007), 3–16. See also James R. Beniger, *The Control Revolution: Technological and Economic Origins of the Information Society* (Cambridge, Mass.: Harvard University Press, 1986). It should be clear that "1839" is then a relay point, not a point of origin, of a self-observing media union.

53. See Joel Snyder, "Res Ipsa Loquitur," in *Things That Talk: Object Lessons from Art and Science*, ed. Lorraine Daston (New York: Zone, 2004), 195–221.

54. I am directly indebted here to Bernhard Siegert, *Relays: Literature as an Epoch of the Postal System*, trans. Kevin Repp (Stanford, Calif.: Stanford University Press, 1999), 110, 109 et passim.

55. "The more probable the message, the less information it gives. . . . The transmission of information is impossible save as a transmission of alternatives. If only one contingency is to be transmitted, then it may be sent most efficiently

and with the least trouble by sending no message at all." Norbert Wiener, *The Human Use of Human Beings: Cybernetics and Society* (New York: Doubleday, 1950), 12.

56. Claude Shannon, "Communication Theory of Secrecy Systems," in *Claude Elwood Shannon: Collected Papers*, ed. N. J. A. Sloane and Aaron D. Wyner (New York: Wiley-IEEE Press, 1993), 113. Cf. also Wiener, *The Human Use of Human Beings*, chapter 7, "Communication, Secrecy, and Social Policy."

57. See Paul N. Edwards, *The Closed World: Computers and the Politics of Discourse in Cold War America* (Cambridge, Mass.: MIT Press, 1996), 201.

58. Consider, to take two obvious fictional examples, its rehearsals in Thomas Pynchon's novel of war and information, *Gravity's Rainbow* (1973), or Neil Stephenson's about war games and Turing machines, *Cryptonomicon* (1999).

59. Siegert, *Relays*, 262.

60. James Gleick, *Information: A History, a Theory, a Flood* (New York: Vintage, 2012), provides a useful overview.

61. Claude Shannon and Warren Weaver, *The Mathematical Theory of Communication* (Urbana: University of Illinois Press, 1949), 95, my emphasis—but the extension of field of communication could not be more emphatic.

62. For Wiener, predicting the future in the coming together in space of a missile and a target is like playing poker: "If the action were completely at the disposal of the pilot, and the pilot were to make the sort of intelligent use of his chances that we anticipate in a good poker player, for example, he has so much opportunity to modify his expected position before the arrival of a shell that we should not reckon the chances of hitting him to be very good. . . . On the other hand, the pilot does *not* have a completely free chance to maneuver at his will" (*Cybernetics*, 5). On the aesthetics of such encounters, see my "The Art of the Collision," in *Speed Limits*, ed. Jeffrey T. Schnapp (Milan: Skira, 2009).

63. Sloterdijk, *In the World Interior of Capital*, 13.

64. I am here invoking the incisive account of Susan Stewart, *On Longing: Narratives of the Miniature, the Gigantic, the Souvenir, the Collection* (Durham, N.C.: Duke University Press, 1993), 57, 58, 151, 159, 158, 152. The miniature, moreover, provides the elements of a self-induced world not exactly from its scale but from its framed, or better self-framed, quality. As Roland Barthes expresses it, "the miniature does not derive from the dimension but from a kind of precision which the thing observes in delimiting itself, stopping, finishing." Barthes, *Empire of Signs*, trans. Richard Howard (New York: Hill and Wang, 1982), 43. It conveys, that is, a precision in space that frustrates context. (See also chapter 8.) The becoming-significant of scale in recent literary interpretation is one sign of that, albeit with a tendency to overturn the grandeur of distance even as it is evoked: hence "every point on the earth is the top, the *present* is the form of all life." Arthur Schopenhauer, *The World as Will and Representation*, vol. 1, ed. Judith Norman, Alistair Welchman, and Christopher Janaway (Cambridge: Cambridge University Press, 2010).

65. In systems-theoretical terms, it turns to second-order observation—the observation of the field of observation—and so to a second order of vision.

66. See Barbara Rose, "Blow Up—the Problem of Scale in Sculpture," *Art in America* 56 (1968): 80–91. The notion of the photograph as scale-free network is (as Michael North's *Camera Works: Photography in the Twentieth Century* [Oxford: Oxford University Press, 2005] reminds us) misleading, given that observing operations actually need to take place. The blow-up makes visible the distinction between medium and form and uses it. On the problems with assumptions of scale-free systems, see Evelyn Fox Keller, "Revisiting 'Scale-Free' Networks," *BioEssays* 27, no. 10 (2005): 1060–68. On the microfilmic, see Jonathan Auerbach and Lisa Gitelman, "Microfilm, Containment, and the Cold War," *American Literary History* 19, no. 3 (2007): 745–68.

67. See Joseph Vogl, "Becoming-Media"; and Bernhard Siegert, "Cacography or Communication? Cultural Techniques in German Media Studies," *Grey Room*, no. 29 (fall 2007): 26–47.

68. In making up the reality of the mass media, that "coincidence" must be referenced and dramatized, or staged, at every moment and at all costs. Consider the voice delay of news commentary that is, paradoxically, to signal the hard-won simultaneity, over distance and time, of the scene-of-the-event and its reporting. Scale-shifting literary studies, detecting hard-won simultaneities or family resemblances over deep space or time, may tend to do the same.

69. See Jack Goody and Ian Watt, "The Consequences of Literacy," in *Literacy in Traditional Societies*, ed. Jack Goody (Cambridge: Cambridge University Press, 1968), 27–68; and Elizabeth L. Eisenstein, *The Printing Revolution in Early Modern Europe* (Cambridge: Cambridge University Press, 1993).

70. Gregory Bateson, *Mind and Nature: A Necessary Unity* (New York: Bantam, 1980), 120–21.

71. Michel Serres, *The Parasite*, trans. Lawrence R. Schehr (Minneapolis: University of Minnesota Press, 2007), 79.

72. On this deconstructive *Leerlaufen*–empty-running: an idling engine—with respect to media-cultural techniques, see my "Die Freie Natur," in *Gefahrensinn: Archiv für Mediengeschichte*, ed. Lorenz Engell, Bernhard Siegert, and Joseph Vogl (Paderborn: Wilhelm Fink, 2009).

73. See my *True Crime*, 57–90.

74. See Elena Esposito, "The Arts of Contingency," *Critical Inquiry* 31, no. 1 (2004): 7–25. On the media/form distinction in systems theory on which Esposito's lucid account draws, see Niklas Luhmann, *Die Gesellschaft der Gesellschaft* (Frankfurt am Main: Suhrkamp, 1997), vol. 1, 190–201. I have been setting out samples of this double unity and how it works. David Wellbery provides further exposition in his entry on "Systems," in *Critical Terms for Media Studies*, ed. W. J. T. Mitchell and Mark B. N. Hansen (Chicago: University of Chicago Press, 2010).

75. That "terminological indifference" (see Vismann, *Files*, xii) is the crux of a series of media studies that center on cultural techniques—for example, file, post,

index—that are at once object and act: they say what they do and so appear to do what they say. These relations (to adapt Deleuze's phrase) are real but abstract—in effect, living diagrams. This, in effect, magnetizes relays—and so lends to administration the feel of the performative.

76. "The Mattering of Matter" is the title given to a collection of pieces by the members of the International Necronautical Society, including pieces by Simon Critchley and Tom McCarthy.

77. Marshall McLuhan and Lewis H. Lapham, *Understanding Media: The Extensions of Man* (Cambridge, Mass.: MIT Press, 1994), 8–9.

78. Wiener, *The Human Use of Human Beings*, 20. For Wiener, it may be noted, this is a "returning the emphasis of physics to a quasi-Liebnitzian [*sic*] state, whose tendency is once again optical" (20). That baroque turn is well marked in recent media studies. So too is the systems-theory turn to matters of first-order and second-order observation. One finds in a range of recent "Kittlerian" media studies—on which account the "media determine our situation"—something of a migration to a systems theory outlook. I have in mind, for example, Bernhard Siegert's "Cacography or Communication? Cultural Techniques in German Media Studies"—with its emphasis on observation, recursivity, contingency, and on how media "process distinctions"; or Joseph Vogl's "Becoming-Media: Galileo's Telescope" with its emphasis on "a relativized observer who observes him- or herself as an observer." The turn would in part seem to be from a history of media objects (gramophone, film, or typewriter, say) to systems-internal operations. But these "objects" themselves are already (in Heinz von Foerster's formulation) "tokens for Eigenbehaviors"—recursively stabilized and so self-referential processes. See von Foerster, "Objects: Tokens for [Eigen]Behaviors," in *Observing Systems* (Seaside, Calif.: Intersystems, 1981), 273–85.

79. The italicized phrase is drawn from Giorgio Agamben, *The Man without Content*, trans. Georgia Albert (Stanford, Calif.: Stanford University Press, 1999).

80. David Riesman, Nathan Glazer, and Reul Denny, *The Lonely Crowd: A Study of the Changing American Character* (1961; reprint, New Haven, Conn.: Yale University Press, 2001), 16. The gyroscope is, however, already quasi-outmoded, for Riesman, as a model for persons. What Riesman traces is a shifting from the inner-directed to the "outer-directed" person: for the second, "the control equipment, instead of being like a gyroscope, is like a radar" (25). On radar and on the black boxes of a "radar philosophy," see chapter 6.

81. See Beniger, *The Control Revolution*, 302–7.

82. See Hans Sachs, "The Delay of the Machine Age," *Psychoanalytic Quarterly* 2 (1933): 404–24. The problem of that delay involves, in part, why, for example, the Greeks of the axial age, adept at making little devices like toy steam engines, never thought of adapting these toys to do real work.

83. Bateson, *Mind and Nature*, 117. See also Otto Mayr, *The Origins of Feedback Control* (Cambridge, Mass.: MIT Press, 1970). One can add to this list the pre-adaptive advance that modern literature (or literature from the standpoint of

modernity) represents. On the ties between the visual arts and systems theory, see Pamela Lee, *Chronophobia: On Time in the Art of the 1960s* (Cambridge, Mass.: MIT Press, 2004); and Alexander R. Galloway, *Protocol: How Control Exists after Decentralization* (Cambridge, Mass.: MIT Press, 2004).

84. See Wiener, *The Human Use of Human Beings*, 151, 24; Bateson, *Mind and Nature*, 116. These self-steering mechanisms (Wiener's term "cybernetics" is, of course, derived from the Greek word for steersman) involve "a method of controlling a system by reinserting into it the results of its past performance." Feeding back outcomes into input, it involves, that is, "the unpurposeful random mechanism which seeks for its own purpose through a process of learning" (Wiener, *The Human Use of Human Beings*, 38).

85. It was unthinkable until it became possible—to put it in the idiom of the Cold War theorist Herman Kahn—to think the unthinkable. On that short-circuiting of reflexivity and self-reflection, and its larger context, I am indebted to Siegert, *Relays*. There is a return to phenomenology in new media studies. There is some tendency in that work toward something of an uneven adjectival drift—an entailment drift, from materiality to body to embodiment to experience. Along these lines, reflexivity becomes embodied reflection which becomes human embodiment which becomes richly embodied human experience. Consider Bruno Latour's critique of such tendencies: "Most often inspired by phenomenology, these reform movements have inherited all its defects: they are unable to imagine a metaphysics in which there would be other real agencies than those with intentional humans, or worse, they oppose human action with the mere 'material effect' of natural objects which, as they say, have 'no agency' but only 'behavior.' But an 'interpretative' sociology is just as much a sociology of the social than [*sic*] any of the 'objectivist' or 'positivist' versions it wishes to replace. It believes that certain types of agencies—persons, intention, feeling, work, face-to-face interaction—will *automatically* bring life, riches, and 'humanity.'" Bruno Latour, *Reassembling the Social: An Introduction to Actor-Network Theory* (New York: Oxford University Press, 2007), 61. I discuss the "principle of scarcity with respect to agency" and its implications in a range of realist and naturalist fiction and science studies (including Latour's) in *Bodies and Machines*.

86. See Ranulph Granville, "A (Cybernetic) Musing: Ashby and the Black Box," *Cybernetics and Human Knowing* 14, no. 2–3 (2007): 189–96.

87. Gauthier, the art supply man, is the relay of anthropotechnics in and for the novel. He supplies matter and information: he effects, at his art shop, the meeting of Ripley and the framer; he forwards Ripley's game in relaying misinformation that Ripley, as a practical joke, inputs into the social network, just to see what will happen; he is killed in a hit-and-run accident that is uncertainly accidental, and reenters Ripley's plot as a counterplot that turns on that.

88. Thinking the unthinkable is of course epitomized and renamed by a Cold War novel, *Catch-22* (written 1954–61), with "22" as the ordinance of double-think. The trick, or catch, of catch-22 logic is, again and again, the continuous reentry

of outcomes into intents, results into causes. A sort of stand-up version of basic systems theory.

89. The Cold War think tank—the operations center of contemporary war gaming—is, of course, the RAND Corporation, and RAND, of course—in what Marcuse called our administrative "syntax of abbreviation"—is an acronym for research and development.

6. The Natural History of Artificial Life

1. Malcolm Gladwell, *Blink: The Power of Thinking without Thinking* (New York: Little, Brown, 2005), 99. Subsequent references, *Blink*, in text. It's of course the case that the popularization of styles of systems thinking—from pop psychology and self-help to ecological/planetary studies—is extensive and extending. My momentary focus on Gladwell here—at the risk of overburdening that account—is opportunistic: to rehearse, inventory, and take the measure of that spreading of a systems outlook, and the notion of "art" that goes with it. One might compare Gladwell's account with one of its primary sources, the incisive work of the cognitive scientist Gerd Gigerenzer, particularly *Gut Feelings: The Intelligence of the Unconscious* (New York: Viking, 2007); I will be drawing on Gigerenzer's work in part IV, albeit to different ends.

2. On Charcot, see Anson Rabinbach, *The Human Motor: Energy, Fatigue, and the Origins of Modernity* (New York: Basic Books, 1990), 160. I examine these pathologies of agency and maladies of will in *Serial Killers: Death and Life in America's Wound Culture* (New York: Routledge, 1998), 74–81. The reentry of observation into act is the real innovation of the managerial/control revolution: the observation and registration of the work process enter into the work process, or, better, emerge as the work process itself. On the cultural techniques that make it possible for checking and acting to alternate and switch places, and the worldview in self-description it entails, see also part IV.

3. That is, the "gee whiz" effect in these reality games is—*Believe it or not!*—constitutive. The construction of reality and the reality of construction—a chiasmic routine in a range of literary theory—routinely go on in and through each other. The connection between the name Ripley and the reality show is, again, explicit, and explicitly enacted, in *The Talented Mr. Ripley*. Put a bit differently, it poses the question: if we know that make-believe makes belief, can we still believe it? The self-exposing character of modern social systems—their self-exposition and so self-persuasive character—is thus bound to this trick of belief detouring through disbelief. The trick is not exactly that one sees through it and it works anyway. (On this structure of a world of "half-credences," as Poe put it, see my "The Crime System," *Critical Inquiry* 3, no. 3 [spring 2004]: 557–83.) The real trick is in how self-exposition officially functions in a world that comes to itself by staging its own conditions.

4. Or, in the terms of *Ripley's Game*: "How much did the enemy know?" (167), and "Was it even a game?" (189).

5. Sharon Ghamari-Tabrizi, *The Worlds of Herman Kahn: The Intuitive Science of Thermonuclear War* (Cambridge, Mass.: Harvard University Press, 2005), 170; see also Sharon Ghamari-Tabrizi, "Simulating the Unthinkable: Gaming Future War in the 1950s and 1960s," *Social Studies of Science* 30, no. 2 (April 2000): 190–213.

6. See Paul de Man, "Form and Intent in the American New Criticism," in *Blindness and Insight: Essays in the Rhetoric of Contemporary Criticism* (Minneapolis: University of Minnesota Press, 1983), 20–35.

7. Alexander R. Galloway, *The Interface Effect* (New York: Polity Press, 2012), 13.

8. It may be worth noting that Habermas's account of "the refeudalization of the public sphere" in his *The Structural Transformation of the Public Sphere: An Inquiry into a Category of Bourgeois Society* (originally published 1962, as *Strukturwandel der Öffentlichkeit. Untersuchungen zu einer Kategorie der bürgerlichen Gesellschaft*) was provocatively anticipated in Thorstein Veblen's *The Theory of the Leisure Class: An Economic Study of Institutions* (1899); Veblen presents both an account of "refeudalized" institutional architectures and a prescient diagnosis of the emergent play-work economy that today fascinates arts commentators on aesthetic /economic crossplay, and at times cosplay.

9. The crime story, with its dependence on the topoi of motive and surprise, is of course the happy hunting ground of intention (the motive of the crime) and outcome (the form of its surprise). Hence it provides an economical way of dramatizing the feedback loops between structure and spontaneity—and the tautological repetition that secures the genre as genre. For Poe, for example, "accident forms part of the superstructure." The reinhabiting of intentions is a way of apprehending the criminal by reverse engineering the plot. But this from the start appears as a trick or paradox. In "The Murders in the Rue Morgue," for example, the doubling of motive and act means entering into the motives of an actor who cannot properly have motives or perform acts (an orangutan: providing a version of what Poe elsewhere calls "motive not motivirt"). On Poe, in this regard, see my "The Crime System," *Critical Inquiry* 30, no. 3 (March 1, 2004): 557–83.

10. Niklas Luhmann, *Art as a Social System*, trans. Eva Knodt (Stanford, Calif.: Stanford University Press, 2000), 68, subsequent references, AASS, in text.

11. This is to raise the question of art "as" social system, not to posit their identity. For Luhmann, society consists in communications and nothing else. But the notion that art "makes perception available for communication" and the notion of art as social system (and so distinct from perceptual systems) remain in tension or paradox in Luhmann's account. That account is relatively uninterested in the cultural techniques via which media take form. How those cultural techniques enter into and register perception is part of what I broach here.

12. See Ranulph Glanville, "A (Cybernetic) Musing: Ashby and the Black Box," *Cybernetics and Human Knowing* 14, no. 2–3 (2007): 189–96.

13. Ross Ashby, *Introduction to Cybernetics* (London: Chapman and Hall, 1956), 86.

14. On the concept of the black box, see also Norbert Wiener, *Cybernetics: Or the Control and Communication in the Animal and the Machine*, 2nd ed. (Cambridge, Mass.: MIT Press, 1965), xi, 27, 108. The earliest use of the designation in this sense is attributed to James Clerk Maxwell, in his *Theory of Heat* (1871). Peter Galison points out that the term became popular in "radar philosophy" during World War II—in the use of common black-speckled boxes to encase radar equipment. Peter Galison, "The Ontology of the Enemy: Norbert Wiener and the Cybernetic Vision," *Critical Inquiry* 21, no. 1 (October 1, 1994): 247. If the gyroscope anticipates such equipment, the gyroscopic model of personhood—the "inner-directed" person—gives way in the Cold War period to another model: for Riesman, as we have seen, the "control equipment" of the "other-directed person" is a form of radar. On all counts, black boxes are "boxes with unspecified interiors," which report back "their *performed* action on the outer world, and not merely their *intended* action." Norbert Wiener, *The Human Use of Human Beings: Cybernetics and Society* (New York: Doubleday, 1950), 27.

15. On modernity's "ecology of ignorance," see Niklas Luhmann, *Observations on Modernity*, trans. William Whobrey (Stanford, Calif.: Stanford University Press, 1998), 75–112. See also Lars Qvortrup, "Luhmann Applied to the Knowledge Society: Religion as Fourth-Order Knowledge," *Cybernetics and Human Knowing* 14, no. 2–3 (2007): 11–27. The contemporary differentiation and segmentation of disciplines, and their rival media of communication—and, too, the extreme narrowness of the "interdisciplinary" citation loops designed to solve that—make this clear enough. Disciplinary ecologies of ignorance—necessarily building descriptions of the world, like this one, out of "knowing about nonknowing"—are in this sense black boxes, or black-speckled ones.

16. Michel Foucault, *Discipline and Punish: The Birth of the Prison*, trans. Alan Sheridan (New York: Vintage, 1995), 204. On this view it is possible to align Wittgenstein's language games and Foucault's power-discourse games as disciplines in the sense of forms of life, and not (as Sloterdijk notes) as "a self-repression that doubles an external repression." That is to say, self-techniques (as set out in Foucault's later work) that are not just subtle mendacities impregnating everyday life and the routines of culture with "power"—and so calling for a perpetual mea culpa. On this connection between Wittgenstein's language games and Foucault's truth games, in terms of a more "general disciplinics," see Peter Sloterdijk, *You Must Change Your Life*, trans. Wieland Hoban (Cambridge: Polity, 2014), 132–59. The earlier work of Foucault, as Sloterdijk notes, "was the point of highest imitability that triggered academic success, because in both cases it constituted the point of most suggestive misunderstandability"—"anarcho-criticistic kitsch" (154). The aesthetic of this earlier work (as traced in my *Henry James and the Art of Power* [Ithaca, N.Y.: Cornell University Press, 1984]) already carried within it the meaning of a form of life that is irreducible to discipline in the narrow sense, albeit without as yet the idiom to describe it. (The word "power" took the place and held the place

for such an account.) Hence the need for an analysis that makes it possible to describe a reflexivity without interiority, and so to set out a form of reflection—an aesthetic reflexivity or an anthropotechnics—that is not, in itself, illiberally repressive or liberally subversive.

17. Foucault, *Discipline and Punish*, 204.

18. Kazuo Ishiguro, *Never Let Me Go* (New York: Knopf, 2005), 47, 52. Subsequent references, NLMG, in text.

19. I will return, from another vantage, to the conflation of bodies and institutions, in Tom McCarthy's story of fictitious persons, *Remainder*, in chapter 8.

20. See, on this Wittgensteinian view of the game, part V.

21. The novel thus tacks closely to the genre of the bildungsroman, with its secluded microsocieties—and their "miniaturization" in the "aesthetic harmony of the individual." See Franco Moretti, *The Way of the World: The Bildungsroman in European Culture*, trans. Albert Sbragia (London: Verso, 1987), 36. It tacks closely to its history of a self-modeling on a model-picture (*Bild*), with the difference that the genre here epitomizes itself: it is a bildungsroman told from the standpoint of a clone, or picture model. The microsociety of the novel is a society that sees itself as self-constituting and, therefore, self-observing, by way of career "carers" and "donor" figures—death, and life, thus making up the dark side of a career. In short, the novel continues to play out the semantic vocation of the bildungsroman after its story of social and individual harmonization has been officially abandoned.

22. Henry Adams, *The Education of Henry Adams: An Autobiography* (1907; reprint, Boston: Houghton Mifflin, 1918), 4.

23. See Karl Marx, *Grundrisse: Foundation of the Critique of Political Economy*, trans. Martin Nicolaus (1973; reprint, London: Penguin Classics, 1993): "The simplest abstraction, then, which modern economics places at the head of its discussions, and which expresses an immeasurably ancient relation valid in all forms of society, nevertheless achieves practical truth as an abstraction only as a category of the most modern society. One could say that this indifference towards particular kinds of labour, which is a historic product in the United States, appears e.g. among the Russians as a spontaneous inclination. But there is a devil of a difference between barbarians who are fit by nature to be used for anything, and civilized people who apply themselves to everything" (105). Here the devil of a difference melts into air: in the story of students who are, by design, "fit by nature" to be used *for* anything and so are used by civilized people who apply themselves *to* everything.

24. As Michel Foucault observed early on, in *The Order of Things: An Archaeology of the Human Sciences* (New York: Vintage, 1970), 127–28: "the pattern of knowledge that has been familiar to us for a hundred and fifty years is not valid for a previous period. . . . If biology was unknown there was a very simple reason for it: that life itself did not exist. All that existed is living beings, which were viewed through a grid of knowledge constituted by *natural history*" (127–28).

The history looks different in Foucault's later work on the practices and exercises of the self, the life techniques and sets of disciplines not so easily open to "interdisciplinary" fusings of biology and power.

25. Stanislaw Lem, *Imaginary Magnitude*, trans. Mark E. Heine (Orlando, Fla.: Harcourt Brace Jovanovich, 1984), 175.

26. Ross Ashby, "Aphorisms," in *The W. Ross Ashby Digital Archive*, 2008, http://www.rossashby.info/aphorisms.html.

27. The life-counseling industry readapts these narratives into self-realization training courses: staging ascetic retreats from everyday life—weekend monasticism or weekday practice sessions—and awakening as a business model. I will take up life-planning systems, in part through Karl Ove Knausgaard's novel series *My Struggle*, in the final chapter of this book. Novels, of course, propose learning from novels, not least how not to learn from them, or to mistake them for life. Howells's novel *The Rise of Silas Lapham*, for example—itself a "rise" story—takes in, and instances how-to books, self-transformation models, a detailed comparison of (religious) vertical mobility and (capitalist) upward mobility, and proposes an algorithm ("the economy of pain") that combines the distinct economic, legal, religious, erotic, and aesthetic domains that have systemically differentiated such that what they above all have in common is their autonomy relative to each other. *The Rise of Silas Lapham* is an experiment in actually existing interdisciplinarity.

28. In this it is akin to the emergent genre of the novel that Kate Marshall has identified as "novels by aliens."

29. Niklas Luhmann, "What Is Communication?" in *Theories of Description: Redescribing the Descriptions of Modernity*, ed. William Rasch (Stanford, Calif.: Stanford University Press, 2002), 159.

30. The program of deconstruction was the anticipatory program of the open-plan office: its project was, put simply, the continuous redescription of differences between as differences within.

31. Here we may think not merely of Ishiguro's novel, but of Tom McCarthy's very different *Remainder* (see part IV). For McCarthy, as I take up in the next part, the reenactment zones of the intensely staged game or the discrete act of violence, in the systems epoch, resemble artworks which resemble them too.

32. See Peter Sloterdijk, *Bubbles: Spheres Volume I: Microspherology*, trans. Wieland Hoban (Los Angeles: Semiotext(e), 2011), 45–46.

7. The Wall of the World

1. My take on the event here—directed, it will be seen, by Gerd Gigerenzer's report on it—centers on how the reporting of the event enters into it, such that it borders on the complicated duality of the practical joke.

2. See Gerd Gigerenzer, *Gut Feelings: The Intelligence of the Unconscious* (New York: Viking, 2007), 224–29; subsequent references, GF, in text.

3. See also Elizabeth Pond, *Beyond the Wall: Germany's Road to Reunification* (Washington, D.C.: Brookings Institution Press, 1993), 1–7.

4. Dirk Baecker, "The Reality of Motion Pictures," MLN 111, no. 3 (1996) 560–77.

5. Niklas Luhmann, "Deconstruction as Second-Order Observing," in *Theories of Distinction: Redescribing the Descriptions of Modernity*, ed. William Rasch (Stanford, Calif.: Stanford University Press, 2002), 107–8. See also Niklas Luhmann, *The Reality of the Mass Media*, trans. Kathleen Cross (Stanford, Calif.: Stanford University Press, 2000), 1: "Whatever we know about our society, or indeed about the world in which we live, we know through the mass media. This is true not only of our knowledge of society and history but also of our knowledge of nature. What we know about the stratosphere is the same as what Plato knows about Atlantis: we've heard tell of it."

6. Wolfgang Schivelbusch, *In a Cold Crater: Cultural and Intellectual Life in Berlin, 1945–48*, trans. Kelly Barry (Berkeley: University of California Press, 1998), 6.

7. Patricia Highsmith, *Ripley's Game* (1974; reprint, New York: Vintage, 1999), 11, 10.

8. On this self-implication, see Joseph Vogl, "Becoming-Media: Galileo's Telescope," *Grey Room* 29 (fall 2007): 14–25.

9. Erving Goffman, *Interaction Ritual: Essays on Face-to-Face Behavior* (New York: Pantheon, 1982), 113. Subsequent references, IR, in text. I am in these paragraphs in part reprising, and so reframing, in the hope that this will work for a reader. If not, what Roland Barthes said of reading interludes of landscape descriptions in novels—skip them—may.

10. Luhmann, "Deconstruction as Second-Order Observing," 99. In this way objects and behavior indicate each other: eigen-objects, again, are "tokens" for perceptual regularities—eigenbehaviors—that lend them stability.

11. The medium is then, in Michel Serres's terms, a quasi-object. Like the ball on the field of play, or the posted letter, it is not an ordinary object: the letter, or ball, is "the subject of circulation; the players [passers, senders and receivers] are only the stations and relays." The quasi-object, the letter or the ball, is also then a quasi-subject, "since it marks or designates a subject who, without it, would not be a subject": it, "when being passed, makes the collective, if it stops, it makes the individual"—the witness of relays. See Michel Serres, *The Parasite*, trans. Lawrence R. Schehr (Minneapolis: University of Minnesota Press, 2007), 225–26. Brian Massumi cogently adapts Serres's ball game to an account of "the political economy of belonging" and its media events, in *Parables for the Virtual: Movement, Affect, Sensation* (Durham, N.C.: Duke University Press, 2002), 71–81.

12. Joseph Vogl, "Becoming-Media." That is to say, it repeats that social systems consist in and reproduce themselves through communication.

13. Agatha Christie, *And Then There Were None* (1940; reprint, New York: St. Martin's, 2001), 113.

14. Agatha Christie, *Murder on the Orient Express* (1934; reprint, New York: Berkley, 2000), 80. Subsequent references, MOE, in text.

15. Heide Gerstenberger, *Impersonal Power: History and Theory of the Bourgeois State*, trans. David Fernbach (Chicago: Haymarket, 2009).

16. It should be clear that the term "stupidity" is here used, as Elaine Scarry uses it, in *The Body in Pain: The Making and Unmaking of the World* (New York: Oxford University Press, 1987), in a technical and nonjudgmental sense, as "literal designation rather than as dismissive label" (278)—here, the designation, in institutional settings, of an insentient, meritocratic, impersonality.

17. On such framing moves, see Niklas Luhmann, *Art as a Social System*, trans. Eva Knodt (Stanford, Calif.: Stanford University Press, 2000), 283.

18. These discrete but coupled microsystems are coordinated on their own terms: in terms of the self-grounding, planning, staging, and reenacting of the series. (The programmed and serial zones of the transport system are featured here.) This seriality is the case in that we can no longer appeal to a microcosm/macrocosm unity or even to what Kierkegaard called "dialectical witchcraft" to perform this function.

19. On traffic in modernity, see Peter Sloterdijk, *In the World Interior of Capital: Towards a Philosophical Theory of Globalization*, trans. Wieland Hoban (Cambridge: Polity, 2013), with particular reference to Jules Verne, pp. 36–39. See also John Urry, *Mobilities* (Cambridge: Polity, 2007).

20. Stephen Crane, *The Red Badge of Courage*, in *Crane: Prose and Poetry*, ed. J. C. Levenson (New York: Library of America, 1984), 79–213.

21. Henry James, preface to *The Turn of the Screw*, ed. Robert Kimbrough (New York: Norton, 1966).

22. Luhmann, *The Reality of the Mass Media*, 115.

8. Marching in Files

1. My thanks to Hanjo Berressem for reminding me of this moment, and its pertinence to my argument.

2. Agatha Christie, *Murder on the Orient Express* (1934; reprint, New York: Berkley, 2000), 68. Subsequent references, *MOE*, in text.

3. Tom McCarthy, *Remainder* (New York: Vintage, 2007), 252; subsequent references, *Remainder*, in text.

4. Harry Braverman, *Labor and Monopoly Capital: The Degradation of Work in the Twentieth Century* (New York: Monthly Review Press, 1998), 84.

5. I take up, along different lines, the relays between forensic realism and forms of art and architecture today—for example, the status of "reconstructions and reenactments" (from the remodeling of urban space in Berlin to synthetic and interactive models of the scene of the crime)—in "Berlin 2000: 'The Image of an Empty Place,'" in *After-Images of the City*, ed. Joan Ramon Resina and Dieter Ingenschay (Ithaca, N.Y.: Cornell University Press, 2003).

6. Forensic investigation "was laid out in paragraphs headed by numbers, then by capital letters, then by roman numerals, then by lower-case letters as they indented further and further from the left-hand margin. Each indentation

corresponded to a step or half-step in the chain of actions you must follow when you conduct a forensic search. The whole process is extremely formal: you don't just go ahead and do it—you do it slowly, breaking down your movements into phases that have sections and sub-sections, each one governed by rigorous rules. You even wear special suits when you do it, like Japanese people wearing kimonos as they perform the tea ritual" (*Remainder*, 186). This is Poirot's—or Ripley's—way of proceeding at its purest. And it is a deadpan description worthy of Goffman and a user's guide to Robbe-Grillet. The forensic method "turns space hollowed out by action into solid matter." Like a Rachel Whiteread sculptural cast of negative space, these reenactments are the recasting of the world.

7. Stephen Crane, "Death and the Child," in *Stephen Crane: Prose and Poetry*, ed. J. C. Levenson (New York: Library of America, 1984), 947.

8. Max Weber, *Economy and Society: An Outline of Interpretive Sociology*, trans. Ephraim Fischoff et al., ed. Guenther Roth and Claus Witich (Berkeley: University of California Press, 1978), 2: 957. I am here indebted to John Guillory, "The Memo and Modernity," *Critical Inquiry* 31, no. 1 (autumn 2004): 108–32; and especially, at this point and elsewhere, to Cornelia Vismann, *Files: Law and Media Technology*, trans. Geoffrey Winthrop-Young (Stanford, Calif.: Stanford University Press, 2008). As Vismann traces in detail, this means "the evolution of an administration that increasingly linked the official character of its acts to their recording" (49); "administrative acts, decisions and rules are formulated and recorded in writing, even in cases where oral discussion is the rule or is even mandatory" (91).

9. Roland Barthes, "The Old Rhetoric: An *Aide-Mémoire*," in *The Semiotic Challenge*, trans. Richard Howard (Berkeley: University of California Press, 1994); "the empire of the word-people," cited in Vismann, *Files*, 103.

10. See Vismann, *Files*, 103. See also Vismann, "Out of File, Out of Mind," in *New Media/Old Media: A History and Theory Reader*, ed. Wendy Hui Kyong Chun and Thomas W. Keenan (New York: Routledge, 2006): "files display a rather complicated duality"; hence "the simple equation between files and the world, between the physicality of storage and the existence of data in the order of signs," 119–28. Here I am doing little more than summarizing Vismann's incisive account of an administrative a priori, albeit bending it from its Derridean premises—instances of archive fever—toward a systems distinction between medium and form.

11. See James R. Beniger, *The Control Revolution: Technological and Economic Origins of the Information Society* (Cambridge, Mass.: Harvard University Press, 1986). For Gilles Deleuze "machines are social before being technical"—that is, if we understand by "the social" the abstract and informal diagrams that the concrete machine assembles. Deleuze, *Foucault*, trans. Sean Hand (Minneapolis: University of Minnesota Press, 1988), 34. The rifle, for example, exists as a tool only in the sense that it is "a machinery whose principle would no longer be the mobile or immobile mass, but a geometry of divisible [and compos-

able] segments." And if Remington (after the American Civil War) retools its factories from gun production to typewriter production, these principles of segmentation, replication, and composition are already in place.

12. Agatha Christie, *Appointment with Death* (1938; reprint, New York: Berkley, 1984), 3. Subsequent references, *AD*, in text.

13. See Guillory, "The Memo and Modernity." See also Friedrich A. Kittler, "Dracula's Legacy," in *Literature, Media, Information Systems*, ed. John Johnston (Amsterdam: Routledge, 1997).

14. These game pieces figure as jigsaw puzzles (*Murder on the Orient Express*, for example) or mah-jongg tiles (*The Murder of Roger Ackroyd*) or the line of little figurines eliminated one by one by one (*And Then There Were None*). The pieces are grouped and regrouped, listed and put in place, relisted and replaced—such that what is put in place takes place and things sort themselves out.

15. See, again, Vismann, *Files*.

16. Agatha Christie, *The Murder of Roger Ackroyd* (1926; reprint, New York: Berkley, 2000), 106, 316.

17. Its continuations appear too in the extradiegetic voice-overs that structure crime films, from *Sunset Boulevard* to *True Romance*, and beyond.

18. See Timothy C. Campbell, *Wireless Writing in the Age of Marconi* (Minneapolis: University of Minnesota Press, 2006), xi.

19. Campbell, *Wireless Writing in the Age of Marconi*, xiv.

20. Agatha Christie, *The Big Four* (1927; reprint, New York: Berkley, 1984), 9.

21. See Franco Moretti, "The Slaughterhouse of Literature," *Modern Language Quarterly* 61, no. 1 (March 2000): 207–27.

22. See Paul de Man, *Allegories of Reading: Figural Language in Rousseau, Nietzsche, Rilke, and Proust* (New Haven, Conn.: Yale University Press, 1982).

23. See Roman Jakobson, "Linguistics and Poetics," in *Selected Writings*, ed. Stephen Rudy (Berlin: Mouton, 1985), 18–52. Bernhard Siegert instructively draws on Jakobson's account in "Cacography or Communication? Cultural Techniques in German Media Studies," *Grey Room*, no. 29 (fall 2007): 26–47.

24. Gerd Gigerenzer, *Gut Feelings: The Intelligence of the Unconscious* (New York: Viking, 2007), 173.

25. Christie, *The Big Four*, 2.

26. Vismann, *Files*, 7.

27. Christie, *Murder on the Orient Express*, 13–14.

28. Wolfgang Schivelbusch, *The Railway Journey: The Industrialization of Time and Space in the 19th Century* (Berkeley: University of California Press, 1987), 38.

29. Poincaré, quoted in Peter Galison, *Einstein's Clocks and Poincaré's Maps: Empires of Time* (New York: Norton, 2003), 301.

30. Galison, *Einstein's Clocks and Poincaré's Maps*, 18–19.

31. Galison, *Einstein's Clocks and Poincaré's Maps*, 24.

32. It produces, along these lines, a system for processing perspectives—a place-value system that, first, makes clear that signs may be absent from their place;

second, finds what is then missing but invisibly present—the symbolic or systemic order of these scattered things; and, third, puts the pieces together—or, more exactly, puts in place the conditions of administration that allow things to take their places and so to right themselves. See Siegert, "Cacography or Communication?"

33. It would be possible to take this up from another side. Roger Caillois takes note of the peculiar recreational attitudes of an "industrial civilization" in terms that are by now (and in fact were by then) familiar enough: "Industrial civilization has given birth to a special form of *ludus*, the hobby, a secondary and gratuitous activity, undertaken and pursued for pleasure, e.g. collecting, unique accomplishments, the pleasure in billiards or inventing gadgets, in a word any occupation that is primarily a compensation for the injury to personality caused by bondage to work of an automatic and picayune character. It has been observed that the hobby of worker-turned-artisan readily takes the form of constructing *complete* scale models of the machines in the fabrication of which he is fated to cooperate by always repeating the same movement"; *Man, Play and Games*, trans. Meyer Barash (Urbana: University of Illinois Press, 2001), 32. The second industrial revolution no doubt continues these forms of play. (One might think of the machine hobbyist obsessed with his little repeating machines—the narrator/killer in Christie's *The Murder of Roger Ackroyd*, or Poirot's own hothouse pleasures.)

34. Jonathan Crary recounts such descriptions in *24/7: Late Capitalism and the Ends of Sleep* (London: Verso, 2014), 98. These descriptions are by now more or less memetic.

35. This is another way of understanding "manifest stupidity." Or Poirot's basic English as an incipient world language. We may recall that the detective fiction writer Raymond Chandler called Poirot a "half-wit," and his handling of cases something "like assembling an egg-beater."

36. I am indebted to Franco Moretti for this connection. See *The Bourgeois: Between History and Literature* (London: Verso, 2013). For a counterhistory of these immunity systems, their practices, and the contours of capitalist systematicity, closer to the one I set out here, see Peter Sloterdijk, *In the World Interior of Capital: Towards a Philosophical Theory of Globalization*, trans. Wieland Hoban (Cambridge: Polity, 2013).

37. Stanisław Lem, *Imaginary Magnitude*, trans. Mark E. Heine (Orlando, Fla.: Harcourt Brace Jovanovich, 1984), 175.

38. We may recall here that a "record" refers back to the heart as the scene of memory (*recordari*—to restore by heart); and it was originally, as Johan Huizinga traces, then, a drawing into relation of body, game, and denotation: "Naturally a certain play-element had entered into business competition at an early stage. Statistics stimulated it with an idea that had originally arisen in sporting life, the idea, namely, of trading records. A record, as the word shows, was once simply a memorandum, a note which the inn-keeper scrawled on the walls of

his inn to say that such and such a rider or traveller had been the first to arrive after covering so and so many miles." Huizinga, *Homo Ludens: A Study of the Play-Element in Culture* (London: Routledge and Kegan Paul, 1949), 200.

39. Clodagh Kinsella, "The Radical Ambiguity of Tom McCarthy" (interview), *Dossier*, July 22, 2009, http://dossierjournal.com/read/interviews/the-radical -ambiguity-of-tom-mccarthy/.

40. Limited liability and limited omniscience are network repeaters in what McCarthy calls "the wiring of the world," receiving, retransmitting, and reshaping its signals. They cosponsor the world in and of the novel. This wiring of the world is also a "ritualizing [of] the cradle-to-grave relationship . . . with social institutions" that Tom McCarthy traces in *Men in Space* (New York: Vintage, 2012), 218.

41. On the juristical person's immunity to crime, recall the discussion of what Savigny calls the impossibility of "vicarious crime," part II.

42. Tom McCarthy, quoted in Simon Reynolds, *Retromania: Pop Culture's Addiction to Its Own Past* (London: Faber and Faber, 2011), 54.

43. Simon Critchley, afterword to McCarthy, *Men in Space*, 287.

44. Mark Twain, *A Connecticut Yankee in King Arthur's Court* (New York: W. W. Norton, 1982), 171.

45. Peter Sloterdijk, *You Must Change Your Life*, trans. Wieland Hoban (Cambridge: Polity, 2014), 389.

46. Sloterdijk, *You Must Change Your Life*, 407.

47. In McCarthy's *Men in Space*, this distinction between repetitions, and the disposition toward them, is placed in relation to the difference between devotional art, on the one side, and the art market under the wall-to-wall universalization of market conditions, on the other. In short, the novel is fascinated by the comparison of the icon (the icon painter's repeating devotional work, the practice or exercise of painting again and again the same received image) and the forgery (the forger copying art for the market).

48. Here, in this distinction between the past participle and the present participle of repeat, I draw directly on Sloterdijk, on "exercises and misexercises" (*You Must Change Your Life*, 404–35), and, to related but ultimately different ends, Roland Barthes, *The Empire of Signs*, trans. Richard Howard (New York: Hill and Wang, 1982).

49. These distinctions between exercises and practices become more difficult, given the franchising of locally sourced surrealisms. When the power-yoga devotees of L.A.'s solar cults, and the body worshippers of Venice's Silicon Beach refer, self-thrilled, to "my practice," the conflation of vertical and upward mobility is perspicuous. When a very intelligent student at UCLA referred to her Venice Beach yoga workout studio, Yoga Works, as the Mecca of Buddhism, the syncretism was breathtaking, if not at just that moment a matter of conscious breathing. Or, as J. G. Ballard puts it, in his no-prisoners story about the capitalist-spiritual merger of work exercises and leisure practices in a unifying world, "The Largest Theme Park in the World" (1989): "The cult of physical perfection had gripped

everyone's imagination. . . . The new evangelism concealed behind the exercise and fitness fads of the 1980's now reappeared. A devotion to physical perfection ruled their lives more strictly than any industrial taskmaster. Out of necessity, leisure had moved into a more disciplined phase. . . . Brigades of handsomely tanned men and women drilled together as they faced the sun." Ballard, "The Largest Theme Park in the World," in *The Complete Stories of J. G. Ballard* (New York: Norton, 2009), 1143–44. The academic disciplines have entered into a more disciplined phase too. Luhmann, noted, some time ago, the ways in which recycled deconstruction resembled "dancing around the golden calf while knowing that a qualifiable god has already been invented," and notes, too, the remarkable brevity of its "span of attention"—an "almost one-word discussion"—which yet "captures some elements of the 'spirit of our times,'" in the self-organization of its own dance. Niklas Luhmann, "Deconstruction as Second-Order Observing," in *Theories of Distinction: Redescribing the Descriptions of Modernity*, ed. William Rasch (Stanford, Calif.: Stanford University Press, 2002), 98. That "almost one-word discussion" has spread generally with the necessarily short attention-span of interdisciplinary scanning and reporting, as disciplines overview each other and advise on "how to brand and re-brand themselves" and how to "elaborate and frame regenerative strategies" and narratives. The quotations are from Tom McCarthy's *Satin Island: A Novel* (New York: Alfred A. Knopf, 2015), 15. McCarthy more concisely captures this spirit-of-the-times choreography—the work ethic of the new server economy— in *Remainder*. Here's a little two-step interaction that takes place in the iconic foodie/media-type franchise, the Blueprint Cafe: " 'Did you serve us here before?' I asked the waiter. He stepped back and looked at me. 'Possibly, sir,' he said. 'I'll remember you next time'" (247).

50. Barthes, *Empire of Signs*, 44.
51. W. G. Sebald, *Austerlitz*, trans. Anthea Bell (New York: Modern Library, 2001), 76–77.
52. Barthes, *Empire of Signs*, 43.
53. Kinsella, "The Radical Ambiguity of Tom McCarthy." Forensic science as higher art because it's real is, again, the reenactor's central example: "There were pages of detailed diagrams. . . . Three men were drawn in outline with numbers inside the outlines, like you get in children's colouring books. There were arrows indicating movement and direction. The longer I stared at these pictures, the more intense the tingling in my upper body grew. . . . My whole head was tingling. The diagrams seemed to be taking on more and more significance" (*Remainder*, 192).
54. Kinsella, "The Radical Ambiguity of Tom McCarthy."
55. Kazuo Ishiguro, *Never Let Me Go* (New York: Knopf, 2005).
56. The INS formulates the larger problem as "the mattering of matter" and the documents it presents show, among other things, how hard it is to avoid the clichés of deconstruction. Tom McCarthy, Simon Critchley, and Nicolas Bour-

riaud, *The Mattering of Matter: Documents from the Archives of the International Necronautical Society* (Berlin: Sternberg, 2013).

57. Hiroshi Sugimoto, http://www.sugimotohiroshi.com/.

9. The Turn Turn

1. Erving Goffman, *Forms of Talk* (Philadelphia: University of Pennsylvania Press, 1981), 73; subsequent references, *FT*, in text.

2. Patricia Clancy, "Analysis of a Conversation," *Anthropological Linguistics* 14, no. 3 (1972): 78–86, as quoted by Goffman, *Forms of Talk*, 28, where Goffman misquotes, as "proudly," Clancy's term "probably."

3. Erving Goffman, *Interaction Ritual: Essays on Face-to-Face Behavior* (New York: Pantheon, 1967), 118.

4. Patricia Highsmith, *Those Who Walk Away* (1967; reprint, New York: Atlantic Monthly Press, 1988), 191; subsequent references, *T*, in text.

5. "Away" in *Those Who Walk Away* is about the desire to get away from ourselves. The novel then previews, in the mode of "away," what has come recently to be dreamt of (in speculative realisms) as "the world as it looks without us"— but as the dream-realism of self-extinction. This is, in Ballard's terms, "the unlimited dream" of the autotropic world interior (universal capitalism), a self-determining and so self-terminating world, one in which extinction—self-extinction—is in vogue and something we will pay to see. On the logic of self-determination and self-termination, see the final sections of chapter 10, which focus on the novels of Cormac McCarthy and Karl Ove Knausgaard's series of novels, *Min kamp* (*Mein Kampf*, or *My Struggle*).

6. See Erving Goffman, *Behavior in Public Places: Notes on the Social Organization of Gatherings* (New York: Free Press, 1966), 69–75; subsequent references, *BPP*, in text.

7. Along the same lines, it's crucial to see that Goffman's sociological model is the strictly intramural one of face-to-face interaction. Hence communicative media premised on the exclusion, or impossibility, of face-to-face interaction ("mass" media) are admitted only to the extent to which they devolve on its simulation.

8. See Erving Goffman, "Fun in Games," in *Encounters: Two Studies in the Sociology of Interaction* (1961; reprint, Harmondsworth: Penguin, 1972). See also Eric Berne's best seller, *Games People Play: The Basic Handbook of Transactional Analysis* (New York: Ballantine, 1964): "the use of the word 'game' should not be misleading. . . . It does not necessarily imply fun or even enjoyment. . . . The same applies to the word 'play,' as anyone who has 'played' hard poker or 'played' the stock market over a long period can testify" (50–51). The extension of the meaning of game and play to areas of life that require this sort of explanation is part of a general spreading of game attribution to domains or actions that do not seem proper to it. One must include here too Wittgenstein's language games and Foucault's truth/power games, among these form games, as practiced disciplines. (That is, disciplines in the expanded sense of repeated or repeating practices, as set out in part IV.)

9. See Andrew Ross, *No-Collar: The Human Workplace and Its Hidden Costs* (Philadelphia: Temple University Press, 2003). See also Luc Boltanski and Eve Chiapello, *The New Spirit of Capitalism*, trans. Gregory Elliot (London: Verso, 2005).

10. See, for example, Alex Woloch, *The One vs. the Many: Minor Characters and the Space of the Protagonist in the Novel* (Princeton, N.J.: Princeton University Press, 2003); Anne-Lise François, *Open Secrets: The Literature of Uncounted Experience* (Stanford, Calif.: Stanford University Press, 2008); Sianne Ngai, *Ugly Feelings* (Cambridge, Mass.: Harvard University Press, 2005); Rei Terada, *Looking Away: Phenomenality and Dissatisfaction, Kant to Adorno* (Cambridge, Mass.: Harvard University Press, 2009). Sloterdijk's "microspherologies" are perhaps the most comprehensive accounts of this geometry of small worlds and their bubble-like and fragile yet encapsulating power. See also, on the calibrations of the scaled-down, Yves Alain-Bois, "Slow (Fast) Modern," and Mark Seltzer, "Collision," both in Jeffrey Schnapp, ed., *Speed Limits* (Milan: Skira, 2009).

11. See Terada, *Looking Away*, 71. See also McKenzie Wark, *Gamer Theory* (Cambridge, Mass.: Harvard University Press, 2007).

12. Roger Caillois, *Man, Play and Games*, trans. Meyer Barash (Urbana: University of Illinois Press, 2001), 10.

13. My sense of scale in this—and the pertinence of terms such as maximalist and minimalist in describing this scalar dimension—are directly indebted to Mark McGurl's work on postwar fiction, and particularly to his essay, "Ordinary Doom: Literary Studies in the Waste Land of the Present," *New Literary History* 41, no. 2 (2010): 329–49.

14. My thanks to Bernhard Siegert for pointing me in this direction.

15. The speculative turn is most incisively articulated in Quentin Meillassoux's *After Finitude: An Essay on the Necessity of Contingency*, trans. Ray Brassier (London: Continuum, 2008)—the turn from an indoor world (reflexive modernity) to "the great outdoors"; on its implications for the form of the novel, see my "Die Freie Natur," in *Gefahrensinn: Archiv für Mediengeschichte*, ed. Lorenz Engell, Bernhard Siegert, and Joseph Vogl (Paderborn: Wilhelm Fink, 2009): 127–39.

16. See Patricia Highsmith, *The Talented Mr. Ripley* (1956; reprint, London: Vintage, 1999), 110.

17. Georg Simmel, *The Sociology of Georg Simmel*, trans. and ed. Kurt H. Wolff (Glencoe, Ill.: Free Press, 1950), 49–50.

18. Simmel, *The Sociology of Georg Simmel*, 50. One burden of systems theory has been to deitalicize such statements and to move them into descriptions of how these social forms work. Compare the autonomization, or "perfect continence," of gamelike forms of life in this account with one of the primary texts of systems theory, George Spencer Brown's *Laws of Form* (New York: Julian, 1972); and compare the negation of external grounds in social games with another generative systems account, Heinz von Foerster's *Observing Systems* (Seaside,

Calif.: Intersystems, 1981). Von Foerster's thinking is in turn directly linked to that of (his "honorary" uncle) Wittgenstein—with respect to memory, game, and form; both enter into the pages that follow.

19. Peter Sloterdijk, *Bubbles: Spheres Volume 1: Microspherology*, trans. Wieland Hoban (Los Angeles: Semiotext(e), 2011), 79.

20. Henry James, *The Turn of the Screw*, ed. Robert Kimbrough (New York: Norton, 1966), 29.

21. Henry James, *The Art of the Novel* (New York: C. Scribner's Sons, 1934), 169–77.

22. See Cornelia Vismann, *Files: Law and Media Technology*, trans. Geoffrey Winthrop-Young (Stanford, Calif.: Stanford University Press, 2008).

23. A reminder on other worlds in Highsmith: Highsmith, a scriptwriter for superhero comic books at the same time as she wrote her first novels, was no stranger to interplanetary thinking, and this comic book geist of alter egos and other worlds enters directly, we have seen, into the idiom of her novels. Alter (other-reference) is converted into ego (self-reference), albeit in the form of alter ego. This is the logic of the double, and "the otherworldly," in Highsmith's work. Highsmith's extended (seven-year) experience writing stories for adventure and superhero comic books is detailed in Joan Schenkar's biography, *The Talented Miss Highsmith: The Secret Life and Serious Art of Patricia Highsmith* (New York: St. Martin's, 2009).

24. Poe's "Philosophy of Composition," it will be recalled, proceeds in "steps," "step-by-step," and via "step-ladders." In "Murders in the Rue Morgue," there are stepping-stones (*Kopfsteine*—street stones the size of a human head) via which Dupin reads off his walking companion's thoughts: what he calls a "stereotomy" that coordinates headstone and the human head. This step-by-step process, in practice, correlates what's in the head and what's in the world, hermeneutics and physics. This is the incremental and continuous distinction between physics and signs that makes up the gamelike world of the crime story and how it is played.

25. Ludwig Wittgenstein, *On Certainty*, trans. Denis Paul, ed. G. E. M. Anscombe and G. H. von Wright (New York: Harper and Row, 1972), § 474, 62e.

26. Wittgenstein, *On Certainty*, § 559.

27. Wittgenstein's term for game is of course *Spiel*, a term meaning both game and play and without an exact English equivalent. The notion of language game and the notion of family resemblance ("like the world") are thus elaborated together, and so mark at every point the unity of the distinction between what enters into the game and what does not. Here the account of language game borders on that of habitus (as set out by Pierre Bourdieu) or discipline in the sense of a general disciplinics (as set out in the later work of Foucault). The work of Peter Sloterdijk, particularly *You Must Change Your Life* and the *Spheres* volumes, represents a remarkable, if awry, attempt to redescribe what this fascination with closeness, internalization, and encasement looks like,

when self-organization is not scientistically hystericized as the prison house of language ("discursive" regimes) or as militarized social construction ("strategies of containment"), but seen as the collaborative intimacy of *arrondissements*, or rounded worlds.

28. See my "Statistical Persons," *Diacritics* 17 (fall 1987): 82–98; reprinted and expanded in *Bodies and Machines* (New York: Routledge, 1992; new edition, 2015).

29. Patricia Highsmith, *Strangers on a Train* (1950; reprint, New York: Norton, 2001), 4. In this way, reflexivity overturns into self-reflexivity, and self-reflexivity into self-consciousness. If Highsmith's formulation ("precarious life") anticipates some recent "biocratic" accounts of bare life (the work of Giorgio Agamben, Judith Butler, and, centrally, Roberto Esposito), the rapport is a bit deceptive. There is a tendency in this recent work tonally to restore the "anthropological machine" it critically dismantles. In these cases, what might be described (with apologies to David Wellbery) as "the presupposition of interiority" is reinstated. Wellbery develops the concept of a "presupposition of exteriority," recalcitrant to internalization, in his indispensable foreword to Friedrich A. Kittler, *Discourse Networks 1800/1900*, trans. Michael Metteer and Chris Cullens (Stanford, Calif.: Stanford University Press, 2000), xii. If, for example, "Man is nothing other than technical life" (Bernard Stiegler, in David Barison and Daniel Ross, dirs., *The Ister* [film; Black Box Sound and Image, 2004]), if "man is the animal who must recognize itself as human to be human" (Giorgio Agamben, *The Open: Man and Animal*, trans. Kevin Attell [Stanford, Calif.: Stanford University Press, 2004], 26), "man is" is the operating code of that anthropological machine, one premised on self-recognition, and hence on the rolling out of antinomies..

30. On such a remodeling of Foucault's biopolitical analysis, see Roberto Esposito, *Bios: Biopolitics and Philosophy*, trans. Timothy Campbell (Minneapolis: University of Minnesota Press, 2008). I am here redirecting the account of a wound culture set out in my *Serial Killers: Death and Life in America's Wound Culture* (New York: Routledge, 1998).

31. The novel is replete with such lists, numbered and lettered ones (ABCs): e.g., "But he realized the difficulty of finding Americans who (a) had a flat or a house in Venice and (b) would be Bohemian enough to take in a stranger" (*T*, 57). On the multiple-choice and counterfactual outlook on life, in the context of the literature of reflexive modernity, see my *True Crime: Observations on Violence and Modernity* (New York: Routledge, 2007). On Highsmith's astonishing obsession with lists, maps, charts, and diagrams—including, for example, detailed charts comparing lovers—see Schenkar, *The Talented Miss Highsmith*, 2–4, 23, and appendix 3.

32. As Henry James expressed it, in *The Aspern Papers* (1888): "Without streets and vehicles, the uproar of wheels . . . the little winding ways where people crowd together as if in the corridors of a house . . . the place has the character of an immense collective apartment." James, *"The Aspern Papers" and Other Stories*, ed. Adrian Poole (1888; reprint, Oxford: Oxford University Press, 1983), 93–94.

33. The "weight of officialism" in this case is "the policial," in the expanded sense that Jacques Rancière, amending Foucault, sets out. See Rancière, *Disagreement: Politics and Philosophy* (Minneapolis: University of Minnesota Press, 1999), 29. Yet that "expansion" may in effect pathologize the interiority of the social as such.

34. In Mikkel Borch-Jakobsen's terms, "Each imitates the 'every man for himself' of the others." See Borch-Jakobsen, *The Emotional Tie: Psychoanalysis, Mimesis, and Affect*, trans. Douglas Brick (Stanford, Calif.: Stanford University Press, 1992), 8–9. See also, Esposito, *Bios*, 66.

35. Ludwig Wittgenstein, *Culture and Value*, trans. Peter Winch (Chicago: University of Chicago Press, 1984), sec. 17b.

36. Cormac McCarthy, *No Country for Old Men* (New York: Knopf, 2005), 299.

37. It is perhaps worth noting that the current turn to scale—both scaling down (the incrementalist turn) or scaling up (distant reading, the turn to big time or deep space) is not exactly a break with correlationism or perspectivism. It is not a break from it in that scale—scaling down and up, like a continuous rotation of aspects—is instead something like its motorization.

38. The steps and moves of those who walk away are then a continuous restaging of mechanical and philosophical states, bodies, and acts; or as Wittgenstein expresses this correlation, "I walk about, as it were, to prove to myself that I can walk as I like." Ludwig Wittgenstein, *Philosophical Occasions, 1912–1951*, ed. James Carl Klagge and Alfred Nordmann (Indianapolis: Hackett, 1993), 438.

39. My appeal to these terms is indebted to Michael Fried's accounts of "literalist" art. The theatricality of socially observed games and of the presentation of the self in everyday life appear along parallel lines, in the discrete worlds of 1960s art criticism and Goffman's social psychology in the notions of absorption (away) and theatricality (presentation). There is perhaps a link in the mutual appeal to Wittgenstein's investigations—to what Goffman calls "some 'game' or other in the peculiar sense employed by Wittgenstein" (*FT*, 24).

10. A Postscript on the Official World

1. Patricia Highsmith, *Those Who Walk Away* (1967; reprint, New York: Atlantic Monthly Press, 1988), 55; subsequent references, *T*, in text.

2. Roger Caillois, *Man, Play and* Games, trans. Meyer Barash (1958; Urbana: University of Illinois Press, 2001), 100; subsequent references, *MPG*, in text.

3. See Caillois, *Man, Play and Games*; and Roger Caillois, "Mimétisme et psychasténie légendaire," in *Le mythe et l'homme* (Paris: Gallimard, 1937), 101–43. In the first, this kind of play is a pathological preadaptation, a melting or mottling into place; in the the second (*Man, Play and Games*) play is a form of normalization—what I have described in terms of the spreading of the gamelike across the social field. Caillois reassesses the first and the second in these terms: "Unfortunately, this [earlier] study treats the problem with a perspective that today seems fantastic to me. Indeed I no longer view mimetism as a disturbance of space perception

and a tendency to return to the inanimate, but rather, as herein proposed, as the insect equivalent of human games of simulation" (*MPG*, 178).

4. Georg Simmel, *The Sociology of Georg Simmel*, trans. Kurt H. Wolff (Glencoe, Ill.: Free Press, 1950), 330; subsequent references, *SGS*, in text.

5. On self-reference and other-reference (Fremdreferenz) in systems theory, see Albrecht Koschorke and Cornelia Vismann, eds., *Widerstände der System-theorie: Kulturtheoretische Analyse zum Werk von Niklas Luhmann* (Berlin: Akademie-Verlag, 1999).

6. Jean Laplanche, *Life and Death in Psychoanalysis* (Baltimore: Johns Hopkins University Press, 1976), 122.

7. Bruno Latour pressures the paradox of the self-made society (modeled on the paradox of the self-made man)—its flatness with respect to its own grounds, and the feedback loops of an endless self-creation. As Latour puts it: "we don't want to confuse the cause and the effect, the explanandum with the explanans"; Bruno Latour, *Reassembling the Social: An Introduction to Actor-Network Theory* (Oxford: Oxford University Press, 2007), 63; subsequent references, *RS*. And one version of that confusion is what he calls "the archaic and magical ghost"—"a self-generated, self-explicative society" (*RS*, 86). Yet Latour's response—the joy of the endless reassembly of the social—is not exactly at odds with what Ian Hacking calls this "looping effect of human kinds." See Ian Hacking, "The Looping Effect of Human Kinds," in *Causal Cognition: A Multidisciplinary Approach*, ed. D. Sperber, David Premack, and Ann James Premack (Oxford: Oxford University Press, 1995), 351–83. What Latour advocates—"learning to feed off controversies" and uncertainties (*RS*, 21)—is another way of entering into these feedback loops, that is, the eternal recurrence of self-making. Latour's procedure—multiplying kinds of "uncertainties" and gamelike "moves"—has its limit, for example, in his response to the principle of scarcity with respect to agency (its restriction to persons). Here the agency problem is parried by extending agency to everything; as Latour expresses it, "objects too have agency" (*RS*, 63). But this flat world is not an alien or even unfamiliar one in literary studies, or even in its "conventional methods." We might say that literary studies tend to borrow back from Latour the metaphorics of looping effects, spiraling uncertainties, and better living through ambiguity that he has in effect borrowed from literary studies. Hence this significant redescription of the agential tends to yield back to a buoyant and deliberately overanimated idiom of some recent literary studies synced to the sciences, or to the scientological idiom. See Rita Felski's "Context Stinks!" *New Literary History* 42, no. 4 (2011): 573–91, which "draws on the work of Bruno Latour to question conventional methods of 'historicizing' and 'contextualizing' works of art."

8. I allude here to the distinction between a sociology of art and the aesthetic as a form of life, in Jacques Rancière, "The Aesthetic Dimension: Aesthetics, Politics, Knowledge," *Critical Inquiry* 36, no. 1 (autumn 2009): 1–19; and Rancière,

"Thinking between Disciplines: An Aesthetics of Knowledge," *Parrhesia* 1, no. 1 (2006): 1–12.

9. See Niklas Luhmann, *Art as a Social System*, trans. Eva M. Knodt (Stanford, Calif.: Stanford University Press, 2000), 312.

10. See also my *True Crime: Observations on Violence and Modernity* (New York: Routledge, 2007), esp. 112–17.

11. Patricia Highsmith, *A Suspension of Mercy* (1965; reprint, New York: Norton, 2001), 235, 155.

12. Patricia Highsmith, *The Cry of the Owl* (London: Heinemann, 1963), 13.

13. Ludwig Wittgenstein, *Remarks on the Philosophy of Psychology* (Chicago: University of Chicago Press, 1980), par. 220.

14. Ludwig Wittgenstein, *Notes of 1935/6*, quoted in David G. Stern, "Models of Memory: Wittgenstein and Cognitive Science," *Philosophical Psychology* 4, no. 2 (1991): 204.

15. Ludwig Wittgenstein, *Philosophical Grammar*, ed. A Kenny, trans. R. Rhees (Oxford: Blackwell, 1974), 42.

16. See Peter Sloterdijk, *Bubbles: Spheres Volume 1: /Microspherology*, trans. Wieland Hoban (Los Angeles: Semiotext(e), 2011).

17. For Michel Serres, "the quasi-object that is a marker of the subject is an astonishing constructor of intersubjectivity. We know, through it, how and when we are subjects and when and how we are no longer subjects. . . . The 'I' in the game is a token exchanged. And this passing, this network of passes . . . weaves the collection"—and so the collective; Michel Serres, *The Parasite* (Minneapolis: University of Minnesota Press, 2007), 227.

18. "That flat fleshless image called 'Peggy' ": the image is "flat" in that it is literal, and pertains to the flatness of the medium (the drawing and its photographic referent); it is "fleshless" in that it registers the transition from the body to its doubling and self-reflection; it is an "image" in that it is bound to its copy; it is "called" Peggy in that, in order for determinations to be recognizable as self-determinations, they must be seen as such; and it is called "Peggy" in that the girl is the peg or game piece in the social game that makes up the plot of the novel.

19. Cormac McCarthy, *No Country for Old Men* (New York: Knopf, 2005); subsequent references, NC, in text. I take "west of everything" from Jane Tompkins's history of the Western, *West of Everything: The Inner Life of Westerns* (New York: Oxford University Press, 1993).

20. Or this one, numbering the world (in that the world is "dead even" in the strictly mathematical sense too): "Hoskins over in Bastrop County knowed everybody's phone number in the whole country by heart" (NC, 64). Or this one, collating its media: "In the room he sat on the bed with the map spread out. . . . A TV was playing somewhere" (100). Or this one, putting map and terrain in an absolute physical proximity: "He got a city map at the quickstop and spread it out on the seat of the cruiser while he drank coffee out of a Styrofoam cup. He traced this

route on the map with a yellow marker from the glovebox and refolded the map and laid it in the seat beside him and switched off the domelight and started the engine" (125).

21. This is to see such moments of "correlationism" in terms of what Highsmith calls "the glass cell" and what Quentin Meillassoux describes as a "transparent cage." Yet the "provocation of the outside" thus evoked appears at the same time as its other side: what Ballard calls "the vanishing age of space." In the last pages of this book I take up, the coupling of provocation and vanishing and its implications—and its relation to the aesthetics and practices of suspense today.

22. In the introduction to the *Critique of Judgment* (section VI), Kant sets out the waning of pleasure in the grasp of unity and a sense of the general: "It is true that we no longer feel any noticeable pleasure resulting from our being able to grasp nature and the unity in its division into genera and species that alone makes possible the empirical concepts by means of which we cognize nature in terms of its particular laws. But this pleasure was no doubt there at one time, and it is only because even the commonest experience would be impossible without it that we have gradually come to mix it with mere cognition and no longer take any special notice of it." Immanuel Kant, *Critique of Judgment*, trans. Werner S. Pluhar (Indianapolis: Hackett, 1987), 27. The shift from noticeable pleasure in the unity of the distinction to its mere cognition—the shift from pleasure to technique—may then be countered by pleasure in the perception of unity in aesthetic form. But what then does it mean when form—such as the form ex machina of the crime novel—appears as a self-exposing game, with its own generic set of techniques, or parlor tricks? In popular crime fiction such as Agatha Christie's, as I set out, this appears as a practical joke, and the job is to see how this trick is done. The effect is to magic the official world and its genres. In Highsmith, the trick is that the autonomization of the game does not distinguish it from the world but exemplifies the world. The effect this time is the special notice of mere cognition, reflexivity, on its own and so pathologized (in both Kantian and colloquial senses). In McCarthy's at once outland and formal world, mere cognition targets life itself.

23. One of those things is the killer, the Martian Chigurh, who is therefore " 'pretty much of a ghost.' 'Is he pretty much or is he one?' 'No, he's out there. . . . I guess if he was a ghost you wouldn't have to worry about him.' " The ghost story is here then (as in *The Turn of the Screw*) a story about making a distinction between self-reference and hetero-reference, what's in your head and what's out there.

24. Cormac McCarthy, *The Road* (New York: Vintage, 2007); subsequent references, *R*, in text.

25. The Miltonic cadence—"each the other's world entire"—evokes the transition from paradise lost to a paradise within, happier far: albeit in a "coldly secular" world, it is turned toward an unrepentant familialism.

26. This not merely in officially speculative fiction—for example, in its alien, Lovecraftian, and outlandishly explicit modes—but in novels such as *Remainder* or

The Road, or, along very different lines, Sebald's testing of the boundary lines of history and natural history, or in quasihistorical fiction like *The Rings of Saturn*, or quasifictional history like *Campo Santo*. Its paroxysms make up, we have seen, Highsmith's depictions of a self-stressed daily planet.

27. J. G. Ballard, *News from the Sun* (London: Interzone, 1982, unpaginated). Reprinted in *The Complete Stories of J. G. Ballard* (New York: Norton, 2010), 1010–36.

28. See, again, Joseph Vogl, "Becoming-Media: Galileo's Telescope," *Grey Room*, no. 29 (fall 2007): 14–25.

29. Tom McCarthy, *Men in Space* (New York: Vintage, 2012), 247; subsequent references, *M*, in text. In this context, the epigraph, on the outside, I have repeated in this section perhaps now looks a little different. The plot, such as it is in *Men in Space*, centers on the forging for sale on the black market, in Eastern Europe at the precise moment of the collapse of alternatives to the world interior of capitalism, of a religious icon: a breathtakingly simple iconization of the distinction between repeating repeating (the devotional repetition of icon painting) and repeated repeating (its copying for the market), and their continuous comparison.

30. Sugimoto's "Sea of Buddhas" images may be viewed at his website, at http://www.sugimotohiroshi.com/buddha.html.

31. Ballard, *News from the Sun*, and *The Complete Stories of J. G. Ballard*, 1030–36, et passim. "The old astronaut could once again see himself suspended in space" (1013). My thanks to Kate Marshall for literally putting this story in my hand. Another of Ballard's stories of the Galileic turn and its interiorization is "The Dying Fall"—about the toppling of the Leaning Tower of Pisa, "this unbalanced mass of masonry sustained for so many centuries": that is, the toppling of the site of Galileo's gravity experiments.

32. Lawrence Wright, *Going Clear: Scientology, Hollywood, and the Prison of Belief* (New York: Knopf, 2013).

33. Karl Ove Knausgaard, *My Struggle*, trans. Don Bartlett (New York: Archipelago Books, 2012), 7. I will, in what follows, be referencing this first volume and the second and third volumes of *My Struggle/Min kamp*: *My Struggle Book 2: A Man in Love*, trans. Don Bartlett (New York: Archipelago Books, 2013), and *My Struggle Book 3: Boyhood*, trans. Don Bartlett (New York: Archipelago Books, 2014). Subsequent references to the volumes, *I* (*My Struggle*), *II* (*My Struggle Book 2*), and *III* (*My Struggle Book 3*), are given in the text, with page number preceded by volume number.

34. Liberal "common denominator" social organization is, of course, the very antithesis of the classic antiliberal cultures represented by Mishima (the explosive postwar Japanese novelist of extremities of violence and tradition, Kabuki playwright, and nationalist warrior-suicide) or the novelist and philosopher Jünger (who, in an active life that spanned the twentieth century, wrote about, among many things, "the storm of steel," "war as inner experience," and the modern soldier as "the day-labourer of death").

35. J. G. Ballard, "Alphabets of Unreason," in Ballard, *A User's Guide to the Millennium: Essays and Reviews* (New York: Picador, 1996), 221–23.

36. Theodor W. Adorno, "Theorie der Halbbildung" (1959). In Adorno, *Gesammelte Schriften*, Band 8 (Darmstadt: Wissenschaftliche Buchgesellschaft, 1998), 93–121. My thanks to Martin Roussel for discussions about this pedagogical adaptation.

37. On the ecology of ignorance, see Niklas Luhmann, *Observations on Modernity*, trans. William Whobrey (Stanford, Calif.: Stanford University Press, 1998), 75–112.

38. Think here of the performance art of Ripley's IRS, McCarthy's INS, and so on. And compare Knausgaard's teenage visions—and his boyhood absorption in adventure novels and superhero comics—to the speculative experiments of Japanese anime (genres of the teenage years that, put simply, stage life-encapsulating systems and life-planning institutions at their limits and in terms of a war of moods physically instantiated in world-epochal form).

BIBLIOGRAPHY

Adams, Henry. *The Education of Henry Adams: An Autobiography*. 1907. Reprint, Boston: Houghton Mifflin, 1918.

Adorno, Theodor W. *Negative Dialectics*. New York: Continuum Publishing Group, 1973.

———. "Theorie der Halbbildung" (1959). In Adorno, *Gesammelte Schriften*, Band 8. Darmstadt: Wissenschaftliche Buchgesellschaft, 1998.

Agamben, Giorgio. *The Man without Content*. Translated by Georgia Albert. Stanford, Calif.: Stanford University Press, 1999.

———. *The Open: Man and Animal*. Stanford, Calif.: Stanford University Press, 2004.

Anderson, Paul Thomas, dir. *The Master* (film). New York: Weinstein Company, 2012.

Arendt, Hannah. *The Human Condition*, 2nd ed. Chicago: University of Chicago Press, 1998.

Ashby, W. Ross. "Aphorisms." *The W. Ross Ashby Digital Archive*. 2008. http://www.rossashby.info/aphorisms.html.

———. *Introduction to Cybernetics*. London: Chapman and Hall, 1956.

Auerbach, Jonathan, and Lisa Gitelman. "Microfilm, Containment, and the Cold War." *American Literary History* 19, no. 3 (September 21, 2007): 745–68. doi:10.1093/alh/ajm022.

Baecker, Dirk. "The Form Game." In *Problems of Form*, edited by Dirk Baecker, translated by Michael Irmscher and Leah Edwards, 99–106. Stanford, Calif.: Stanford University Press, 1999.

———. "The Form of the Firm." *Organization: The Critical Journal on Organization, Theory and Society* 13 (June 1, 2006): 109–42.

———. "The Reality of Motion Pictures." *MLN* 111, no. 3 (1996): 560–77. doi:10.1353/mln.1996.0032.

———. "Systems, Network, and Culture." *Soziale Systeme: Zeitschrift für Soziologische Theorie* 15 (June 9, 2009): 271–87.

Ballard, J. G. "Alphabets of Unreason." In *A User's Guide to the Millennium: Essays and Reviews*, 221–23. New York: St. Martin's, 1996.

———. *The Atrocity Exhibition*. London: Jonathan Cape, 1970.

———. "Cataclysms and Dooms." In *A User's Guide to the Millennium: Essays and Reviews*, 208–9. New York: Picador, 1996.

———. *Cocaine Nights*. London: Flamingo, 1996.

———. *The Complete Stories of J. G. Ballard*. New York: Norton, 2010.

———. *Crash*. London: Vintage, 1995.

———. *Crash: A Novel*. New York: Picador, 2001.

———. *The Crystal World*. New York: Farrar, Straus and Giroux, 1988.

———. "The Largest Theme Park in the World." In *The Complete Stories of J. G. Ballard*, 1139–44. New York: Norton, 2009.

———. *Love and Napalm: Export U.S.A.* New York: Grove, 1972.

———. *Millennium People*. London: Flamingo, 2003.

———. *News from the Sun*. London: Interzone, 1982.

———. *Super-Cannes*. London: Flamingo, 2000.

Barison, David, and Daniel Ross, dirs. *The Ister* (film). Black Box Sound and Image, 2004.

Barker, Clive. Introduction to Neil Gaiman, *The Sandman*, vol. 2: *The Doll's House*. DC Comics, 1990. Reprint, New York: Vertigo, 2010.

Barthes, Roland. *Empire of Signs*. Translated by Richard Howard. New York: Hill and Wang, 1982.

———. "The Old Rhetoric: An Aide-Mémoire." In *The Semiotic Challenge*, translated by Richard Howard, 11–94. Berkeley: University of California Press, 1994.

Bateson, Gregory. Letter to Norbert Wiener, quoted in William Poundstone, *Prisoner's Dilemma: John von Neumann, Game Theory, and the Puzzle of the Bomb*. New York: Doubleday, 1992.

———. *Mind and Nature: A Necessary Unity*. New York: Bantam, 1980.

Bellow, Saul. *Dangling Man*. 1944. Reprint, New York: Penguin, 1998.

Beniger, James R. *The Control Revolution: Technological and Economic Origins of the Information Society*. Cambridge, Mass.: Harvard University Press, 1986.

Bennett, Charles H., Ming Li, and Bin Ma. "Chain Letters and Evolutionary Histories." *Scientific American*, June 2003. http://www.scientificamerican.com/article/chain-letters-and-evoluti/.

Berne, Eric. *Games People Play: The Basic Handbook of Transactional Analysis*. New York: Ballantine, 1964.

Borch-Jacobsen, Mikkel. *The Emotional Tie: Psychoanalysis, Mimesis, and Affect*. Translated by Douglas Brick. Stanford, Calif.: Stanford University Press, 1992.

Borges, Jorge Luis. "Pascal's Sphere." In *Borges: Selected Non-fictions*, edited by Eliot Weinberger, translated by Esther Allen and Suzanne Jill Levine, 351–54. New York: Penguin, 2000.

Brooks, Max. *World War Z: An Oral History of the Zombie War*. New York: Three Rivers, 2007.

Brown, Bill. *The Material Unconscious: American Amusement, Stephen Crane, and the Economics of Play*. Cambridge, Mass.: Harvard University Press, 1997.

Brown, G. Spencer. *Laws of Form*. New York: Julian, 1972.

Burckhardt, Jacob. *The Civilization of the Renaissance in Italy*. Mineola, N.Y.: Dover, 2010.

Caillois, Roger. *Man, Play and Games*. Translated by Meyer Barash. Urbana: University of Illinois Press, 2001.

———. "Mimétisme et psychasthénie légendaire." In *Le mythe et l'homme*, 101–43. Paris: Gallimard, 1937.

Cameron, Sharon. *Impersonality: Seven Essays*. Chicago: University of Chicago Press, 2007.

Campbell, Timothy. *Wireless Writing in the Age of Marconi*. Minneapolis: University of Minnesota Press, 2006.

Carpenter, John, dir. *Ghosts of Mars* (film). Hollywood, Calif.: Storm King Productions, 2001.

Christie, Agatha. *And Then There Were None*. New York: St. Martin's, 1940.

———. *Appointment with Death*. New York: Berkley, 1938.

———. *The Big Four*. New York: Berkley, 1984.

———. *The Murder of Roger Ackroyd*. 1926. Reprint, New York: Berkley, 2000.

———. *Murder on the Orient Express*. New York: Berkley, 1934.

Christie, Deborah, and Sarah Juliet Lauro, eds. *Better Off Dead: The Evolution of the Zombie as Post-human*. New York: Fordham University Press, 2011.

Christov-Bakargiev, Carolyn, Guillermo Faivovich, and Nicolás Goldberg. *Documenta 13: Catalog III/3, the Guidebook*. Ostfildern: Hatje Cantz, 2012.

Chun, Wendy Hui Kyong. *Control and Freedom: Power and Paranoia in the Age of Fiber Optics*. Cambridge, Mass.: MIT Press, 2008.

———. "Orienting Orientalism, or How to Map Cyberspace." In *Asian American .net*, edited by Rachel Lee and Sau-ling Wong, 3–36. New York: Routledge, 2003.

Clancy, Patricia. "Analysis of a Conversation." *Anthropological Linguistics* 14, no. 3 (March 1972): 78–86.

Crane, Stephen. "Death and the Child." In *Stephen Crane: Prose and Poetry*, edited by J. C. Levenson, 947–63. New York: Library of America, 1984.

———. *The Red Badge of Courage*. In *Crane: Prose and Poetry*, edited by J. C. Levenson, 79–213. New York: Library of America, 1984.

Crary, Jonathan. *24/7: Late Capitalism and the Ends of Sleep*. London: Verso, 2014.

Critchley, Simon. Afterword to Tom McCarthy, *Men in Space*, updated ed. New York: Vintage, 2012.

Dawkins, Richard. *The Selfish Gene*. New York: Oxford University Press, 1976.

Deleuze, Gilles. *Foucault*. Translated by Sean Hand. Minneapolis: University of Minnesota Press, 1988.

Deleuze, Gilles, and Félix Guattari. *A Thousand Plateaus: Capitalism and Schizophrenia*. Translated by Brian Massumi. Minneapolis: University of Minnesota Press, 1987.

Delgado, Alan. *The Enormous File: Social History of the Office*. London: John Murray, 1979.

Derrida, Jacques. "Artifactualities." In Jacques Derrida and Bernard Stiegler, *Echographies of Television: Filmed Interviews*, translated by Jennifer Bajorek, 1–28. Cambridge: Polity, 2002.

Diederichsen, Diedrich. "Living in the Loop." *Fillip*, no. 14 (summer 2011). http:// fillip.ca/content/living-in-the-loop.

———. *On (Surplus) Value in Art*. Rotterdam: Sternberg, 2008.

———. "Radicalism as Ego Ideal: Oedipus and Narcissus." Translated by James Gussen. *E-Flux*, no. 25 (May 2011). http://www.e-flux.com/journal/radicalism-as-ego -ideal-oedipus-and-narcissus/.

Doane, Mary Ann. *The Emergence of Cinematic Time: Modernity, Contingency, the Archive*. Cambridge, Mass.: Harvard University Press, 2002.

Dreiser, Theodore. *Sister Carrie*. Edited by Donald Pizer. New York: Norton, 1970.

Eco, Umberto. "The Myth of Superman." In *The Role of the Reader: Explorations in the Semiotics of Texts*, 107–24. Bloomington: Indiana University Press, 1979.

Edwards, Paul N. *The Closed World: Computers and the Politics of Discourse in Cold War America*. Cambridge, Mass.: MIT Press, 1996.

Eisenstein, Elizabeth L. *The Printing Revolution in Early Modern Europe*. Cambridge: Cambridge University Press, 1993.

Emerson, Ralph Waldo. *Essays and English Traits*, vol. 5. The Harvard Classics. New York: P. F. Collier and Son, 1909–14; Bartleby.com, 2001. www.bartleby.com/5/.

Esposito, Elena. "The Arts of Contingency." *Critical Inquiry* 31, no. 1 (autumn 2004): 7–25. doi:10.1086/427300.

———. "Probability and Fiction in Science and Economics." Lecture, Facoltà di Scienze della Communicazione, Università di Modena e Reggio Emilia, Italy, June 21, 2006. https://www.lse.ac.uk/collections/informationSystems /newsAndEvents/2006events/Esposito.htm.

Esposito, Roberto. *Bios: Biopolitics and Philosophy*. Translated by Timothy Campbell. Minneapolis: University of Minnesota Press, 2008.

Felski, Rita. "Context Stinks!" *New Literary History* 42, no. 4 (2011): 573–91. doi:10.1353/nlh.2011.0045.

———. "Latour and Literary Studies." *PMLA* (forthcoming). http://www.academia .edu/10210939/Latour_and_Literary_Studies.

Ferguson, Frances. *Pornography, the Theory: What Utilitarianism Did to Action*. Chicago: University of Chicago Press, 2004.

Flaubert, Gustave. "A Lecture on Natural History—Genus: *Clerk*." In *Early Writings*, translated by Robert Griffin, 45–49. Lincoln: University of Nebraska Press, 1991.

Foerster, Heinz von. *Observing Systems*. Seaside, Calif.: Intersystems, 1981.

Foucault, Michel. *The Birth of the Clinic: An Archaeology of Medical Perception*. Translated by Alan Sheridan. London: Tavistock, 1973.

———. *Discipline and Punish: The Birth of the Prison*, 2nd ed. Translated by Alan Sheridan. New York: Vintage, 1995.

François, Anne-Lise. *Open Secrets: The Literature of Uncounted Experience*. Stanford, Calif.: Stanford University Press, 2008.

Fried, Michael. *Why Photography Matters as Art as Never Before*. New Haven, Conn.: Yale University Press, 2008.

Gaiman, Neil. *The Sandman*, vol. 2: *The Doll's House*. 1991. Reprint, New York: Vertigo, 2010.

Galilei, Galileo. *Sidereus Nuncius, or The Sidereal Messenger*. Chicago: University of Chicago Press, 1989.

Galison, Peter. *Einstein's Clocks and Poincaré's Maps: Empires of Time*. New York: Norton, 2003.

———. "The Ontology of the Enemy: Norbert Wiener and the Cybernetic Vision." *Critical Inquiry* 21, no. 1 (October 1, 1994): 228–66.

Galloway, Alexander R. *Protocol: How Control Exists after Decentralization*. Cambridge, Mass.: MIT Press, 2004.

Gerstenberger, Heide. *Impersonal Power: History and Theory of the Bourgeois State*. Translated by David Fernbach. Chicago: Haymarket, 2009.

Ghamari-Tabrizi, Sharon. "Simulating the Unthinkable: Gaming Future War in the 1950s and 1960s." *Social Studies of Science* 30, no. 2 (April 1, 2000): 163–223. doi:10.1177/030631200030002001.

———. *The Worlds of Herman Kahn: The Intuitive Science of Thermonuclear War*. Cambridge, Mass.: Harvard University Press, 2005.

Giddens, Anthony. *Modernity and Self-Identity: Self and Society in the Late Modern Age*. Stanford, Calif.: Stanford University Press, 1991.

Gigerenzer, Gerd. *Gut Feelings: The Intelligence of the Unconscious*. New York: Viking, 2007.

Gladwell, Malcolm. *Blink: The Power of Thinking without Thinking*. New York: Little, Brown, 2005.

Glanville, Ranulph. "A (Cybernetic) Musing: Ashby and the Black Box." *Cybernetics and Human Knowing* 14, no. 2–3 (2007): 189–96.

Gleick, James. *The Information: A History, a Theory, a Flood*. New York: Vintage, 2012.

Goffman, Erving. *Behavior in Public Places: Notes on the Social Organization of Gatherings*, reissue ed. New York: Free Press, 1966.

———. *Encounters: Two Studies in the Sociology of Interaction*. 1961. Reprint, Harmondsworth: Penguin, 1972.

———. *Forms of Talk*. Philadelphia: University of Pennsylvania Press, 1981.

———. *Frame Analysis: An Essay on the Organization of Experience*. Cambridge, Mass.: Harvard University Press, 1974.

———. *Interaction Ritual: Essays on Face-to-Face Behavior*. Chicago: Aldine, 2005.

———. *The Presentation of Self in Everyday Life*. New York: Anchor, 1959.

———. *Relations in Public*. New York: Harper and Row, 1972.

———. *Strategic Interaction*. Philadelphia: University of Pennsylvania Press, 1969.

Goody, Jack, and Ian Watt. "The Consequences of Literacy." In *Literacy in Traditional Societies*, edited by Jack Goody, 27–68. Cambridge: Cambridge University Press, 1968.

Greengrass, Paul, dir. *The Bourne Supremacy* (film). Hollywood, Calif.: Universal Pictures, 2004.

Greimas, A. J. *Structural Semantics: An Attempt at a Method*. Lincoln: University of Nebraska Press, 1983.

Guillory, John. "The Memo and Modernity." *Critical Inquiry* 31, no. 1 (September 1, 2004): 108–32. doi:10.1086/427304.

Hacking, Ian. "The Looping Effect of Human Kinds." In *Causal Cognition: A Multidisciplinary Approach*, edited by Dan Sperber, David Premack, and Ann James Premack, 351–83. Oxford: Oxford University Press, 1995.

Hansen, Mark B. N. *Embodying Technesis: Technology beyond Writing*. Ann Arbor: University of Michigan Press, 2000.

Highsmith, Patricia. *The Cry of the Owl*. London: Heinemann, 1963.

———. "The Day of Reckoning." In *The Selected Stories of Patricia Highsmith*, 84–97. New York: Norton, 2001.

———. *Deep Water*. New York: Harper and Brothers, 1957.

———. *Eleven: Short Stories*. London: Heinemann, 1970.

———. *Found in the Street*. New York: Atlantic Monthly Press, 1986.

———. *The Glass Cell*. Garden City, N.Y.: Doubleday, 1964.

———. "Mermaids on the Golf Course." In *Mermaids on the Golf Course: Stories*, 11–26. New York: Penzler, 1988.

———. *Plotting and Writing Suspense Fiction*. New York: St. Martin's, 1983.

———. *Ripley's Game*. 1974. Reprint, New York: Vintage, 1999.

———. *Strangers on a Train*. 1950. Reprint, New York: Norton, 2001.

———. *A Suspension of Mercy*. 1965. Reprint, New York: Norton, 2001.

———. *The Talented Mr. Ripley*. 1955. Reprint, London: Vintage, 1999.

———. *Those Who Walk Away*. 1967. Reprint, New York: Atlantic Monthly Press, 1988.

———. *The Two Faces of January*. New York: Atlantic Monthly Press, 1964.

"Hiroshi Sugimoto." Accessed April 7, 2015. http://www.sugimotohiroshi.com/.

Howells, William Dean. *The Rise of Silas Lapham*. Edinburgh: David Douglas, 1885.

Huizinga, Johan. *Homo Ludens: A Study of the Play-Element in Culture*. London: Routledge and K. Paul, 1949.

Imaishi, Hiroyuki, dir., and Kazuki Nakashima, author. *Kill la Kill* (anime series). Tokyo: Trigger, 2013.

International Necronautical Society. "Manifesto." Accessed November 16, 2012. http://www.necronauts.org/manifesto1.htm.

Ishiguro, Kazuo. *Never Let Me Go*. New York: Knopf, 2005.

———. *A Pale View of Hills*. New York: Vintage, 1990.

Jakobson, Roman. *Roman Jakobson: Selected Writings. VII. Contributions to Comparative Mythology, Studies in Linguistics and Philology, 1972–1982*, ed. Stephen Rudy. Berlin: Mouton, 1985.

James, Henry. *The American Scene*, in *Collected Travel Writings*. New York: Library of America, 1993.

———. *"The Aspern Papers" and Other Stories*. Edited by Adrian Poole. Oxford: Oxford University Press, 1983.

———. *The Art of the Novel*. New York: C. Scribner's Sons, 1934.

———. *The Turn of the Screw*. Edited by Robert Kimbrough. New York: Norton, 1966.

Johnston, John. Introduction to Friedrich Kittler, *Literature, Media, Information Systems*, 1–26. Amsterdam: GB Arts International, 1997.

Juul, Jesper. *Half-Real: Video Games between Real Rules and Fictional Worlds*. Cambridge, Mass.: MIT Press, 2005.

Kant, Immanuel. *Allgemeine Naturgeschichte und Theorie des Himmels: Erweiterte Ausgabe*, 1755. Reprint, Hamburg: Tredition Classics, 2013.

———. *Critique of Judgment*. Translated by Werner S. Pluhar. Indianapolis: Hackett, 1987.

Keller, Evelyn Fox. "Revisiting 'Scale-Free' Networks." *BioEssays: News and Reviews in Molecular, Cellular and Developmental Biology* 27, no. 10 (October 2005): 1060–68. doi:10.1002/bies.20294.

Kemp, Wolfgang. "Betriebssystem Kurator." *Kunst*, June 2012, 6–11.

Kinsella, Clodagh. "The Radical Ambiguity of Tom McCarthy" (interview). *Dossier*, July 22, 2009. http://dossierjournal.com/read/interviews/the-radical-ambiguity -of-tom-mccarthy/.

Kittler, Friedrich. *Discourse Networks, 1800/1900*. Translated by Michael Metteer. Stanford, Calif.: Stanford University Press, 1990.

———. *Gramophone, Film, Typewriter*. Translated by Geoffrey Winthrop-Young and Michael Wutz. Stanford, Calif.: Stanford University Press, 1999.

———. *Literature, Media, Information Systems*, edited by John Johnston. Amsterdam: Routledge, 1997.

———. "Romanticism, Psychoanalysis, Film: A Story of Doubles." In *The Truth of the Technological World: Essays on the Genealogy of Presence*, translated by Erik Butler, 69–83. Stanford, Calif.: Stanford University Press, 2014.

Kluge, Alexander. "Deutsches Kino." In *Bestandsaufnahme: Utopie Film: Zwanzig Jahre neuer deutscher Film*, 141–94. Frankfurt am Main: Zweitausendeins, 1983.

———. *Neue Geschichten: Hefte 1–18: Unheimlichkeit der Zeit*. 1. Aufl., Erstausg edition. Frankfurt am Main: Suhrkamp, 1977.

Knausgaard, Karl Ove. *My Struggle (Min kamp)*. Translated by Don Bartlett. New York: Archipelago Books, 2012.

———. *My Struggle Book 2: A Man in Love*. Translated by Don Bartlett. New York: Archipelago Books, 2013.

———. *My Struggle Book 3: Boyhood*. Translated by Don Bartlett. New York: Archipelago Books, 2014.

Koolhaas, Rem. *Delirious New York: A Retroactive Manifesto for Manhattan*. Paris: Oxford University Press, 1978.

Koolhaas, Rem, Madelon Vreisendorp, Elia Zenghelis, and Zoe Zenghelis. *Exodus, or the Voluntary Prisoners of Architecture*. Drawings, watercolors, and collage. New York: Museum of Modern Art, 1972. http://socks-studio.com/2011/03/19 /exodus-or-the-voluntary-prisoners-of-architecture/.

Koschorke, Albrecht, and Cornelia Vismann, eds. *Widerstände der Systemtheorie: Kulturtheoretische Analyse zum Werk von Niklas Luhmann.* Berlin: Akademie-Verlag, 1999.

Krabbé, Tim. *The Vanishing (Het Gouden Ei).* Translated by Claire Nicholas White. New York: Random House, 1993.

Kracauer, Siegfried. "The Hotel Lobby." In *The Mass Ornament: Weimar Essays.* Edited and translated by Thomas Y. Levin, 173–85. Cambridge, Mass.: Harvard University Press, 1995.

————. "On Employment Agencies: The Construction of a Space." In *Rethinking Architecture: A Reader in Cultural Theory.* Edited by Neil Leach, 57–62. London: Routledge, 1997.

Lacan, Jacques. *Encore: Le Séminaire, Livre XX.* Edited by Jacques Alain Miller. Paris: Editions du Seuil, 1975.

Laplanche, Jean. *Life and Death in Psychoanalysis.* Baltimore: Johns Hopkins University Press, 1976.

Latour, Bruno. *Reassembling the Social: An Introduction to Actor-Network Theory.* Oxford: Oxford University Press, 2007.

Lee, Pamela M. *Chronophobia: On Time in the Art of the 1960s.* Cambridge, Mass.: MIT Press, 2004.

Lem, Stanisław. *Imaginary Magnitude.* Translated by Mark E. Heine. Orlando, Fla.: Harcourt Brace Jovanovich, 1984.

Lenoir, Tim. "All but War Is Simulation: The Military-Entertainment Complex." *Configurations* 8, no. 3 (2000): 289–335. doi:10.1353/con.2000.0022.

Leys, Ruth. "The Turn to Affect as Critique." *Critical Inquiry* 37 (spring 2011): 434–72.

Liman, Doug, dir. *The Bourne Identity* (film). Hollywood, Calif.: Universal Pictures, 2002.

Ludlum, Robert. *The Bourne Identity.* New York: Bantam, 2010.

Luhmann, Niklas. *Art as a Social System.* Translated by Eva Knodt. Stanford, Calif.: Stanford University Press, 2000.

————. "Deconstruction as Second-Order Observing." In *Theories of Distinction: Redescribing the Descriptions of Modernity,* edited by William Rasch, 94–112. Stanford, Calif.: Stanford University Press, 2002.

————. *Die Gesellschaft der Gesellschaft.* Frankfurt am Main: Suhrkamp, 1997.

————. *Law as a Social System.* Edited by Fatima Kastner and Richard Nobles. Translated by Klaus Ziegert. Oxford: Oxford University Press, 2008.

————. *Observations on Modernity.* Translated by William Whobrey. Stanford, Calif.: Stanford University Press, 1998.

————. *The Reality of the Mass Media.* Translated by Kathleen Cross. Stanford, Calif.: Stanford University Press, 2000.

————. "A Redescription of 'Romantic Art.'" *MLN* 111, no. 3 (1996): 506–22. doi:10.1353/mln.1996.0038.

————. *Theories of Distinction: Redescribing the Descriptions of Modernity.* Edited by William Rasch. Stanford, Calif.: Stanford University Press, 2002.

———. "What Is Communication?" In *Theories of Distinction: Redescribing the Descriptions of Modernity*, edited by William Rasch, 155–68. Stanford, Calif.: Stanford University Press, 2002.

Macdonald, Ross. *The Underground Man*. New York: Knopf, 1971.

Man, Paul de. *Allegories of Reading: Figural Language in Rousseau, Nietzsche, Rilke, and Proust*. New Haven, Conn.: Yale University Press, 1982.

———. "Form and Intent in the American New Criticism." In *Blindness and Insight: Essays in the Rhetoric of Contemporary Criticism*, 2nd ed., 20–35. Minneapolis: University of Minnesota Press, 1983.

Marclay, Christian. *The Clock* (film). London: White Cube, November 14, 2010.

Marcuse, Herbert. *One-Dimensional Man: Studies in the Ideology of Advanced Industrial Society*. Boston: Beacon, 1964.

Marshall, Kate. *Corridor: Media Architectures in American Fiction*. Minneapolis: University of Minnesota Press, 2013.

Marx, Karl. *Grundrisse: Foundations of the Critique of Political Economy*. Translated by Martin Nicolaus. 1973. Reprint, London: Penguin Classics, 1993.

Massumi, Brian. *Parables for the Virtual: Movement, Affect, Sensation*. Durham, N.C.: Duke University Press, 2002.

Maxwell, James Clerk. *Theory of Heat*. London: Longmans, 1871.

Mayr, Otto. *The Origins of Feedback Control*. Cambridge, Mass.: MIT Press, 1970.

McCarthy, Cormac. *The Crossing*. New York: Vintage, 1995.

———. *No Country for Old Men*. New York: Knopf, 2005.

———. *The Road*. New York: Vintage, 2007.

McCarthy, Tom. *Men in Space*, updated ed. New York: Vintage, 2012.

———. *Remainder*. New York: Vintage, 2007.

———. *Satin Island: A Novel*. New York: Knopf, 2015.

———. *Tintin and the Secret of Literature*. Berkeley, Calif.: Counterpoint, 2008.

McCarthy, Tom, Simon Critchley, and Nicolas Bourriaud. *The Mattering of Matter: Documents from the Archive of the International Necronautical Society*. Berlin: Sternberg, 2013.

McCloud, Scott. *Understanding Comics: The Invisible Art*. New York: William Morrow, 1994.

McGurl, Mark. "Ordinary Doom: Literary Studies in the Waste Land of the Present." *New Literary History* 41, no. 2 (2010): 329–49. doi:10.1353/nlh.2010.0002.

———. "The Zombie Renaissance." *n+1*, no. 9 (spring 2010).

McLuhan, Marshall, and Lewis H. Lapham. *Understanding Media: The Extensions of Man*. 1964. Reprint, Cambridge, Mass.: MIT Press, 1994.

Meillassoux, Quentin. *After Finitude: An Essay on the Necessity of Contingency*. Translated by Ray Brassier. London: Continuum, 2008.

Mitchell, W. J. T., and Mark B. N. Hansen, eds. *Critical Terms for Media Studies*. Chicago: University of Chicago Press, 2010.

Moretti, Franco. *The Bourgeois: Between History and Literature*. London: Verso, 2013.

———. "The Slaughterhouse of Literature." *Modern Language Quarterly* 61, no. 1 (2000): 207–27.

———. *The Way of the World: The Bildungsroman in European Culture*. London: Verso, 1987.

Morgenstern, Oskar. "Game Theory." In *Dictionary of the History of Ideas*, edited by Philip P. Wiener. New York: Charles Scribner's Sons, 1968.

———. "Vollkommene Voraussicht und wirtschaftliches Gleichgewicht." *Zeitschrift für Nationalökonomie* 6, no. 3 (June 1, 1935): 337–57. doi:10.1007/BF01311642.

Morita, Hiroyuka, dir., and Mohiro Kitoh, author. *Bokurano* (anime series). Tokyo: SUN-TV and TOKYO-MX, 2007.

Nabokov, Vladimir. *Speak, Memory: An Autobiography Revisited*. New York: Vintage, 1989.

Nagel, Thomas. *Mind and Cosmos: Why the Materialist Neo-Darwinian Conception of Nature Is Almost Certainly False*. Oxford: Oxford University Press, 2012.

———. "What Is It Like to Be a Bat?" In *Mortal Questions*, 165–80. Cambridge: Cambridge University Press, 1987.

Nakamura, Ryūtarō, dir., and Chiaki J. Konaka, author. *Serial Experiments Lain* (anime series). Tokyo: Triangle Staff, 1998.

Neumann, John von. "Zur Theorie der Gesellschaftsspiele." *Mathematische Annalen* 100, no. 1 (December 1, 1928): 295–320. doi:10.1007/BF01448847.

Neumann, John von, and Oskar Morgenstern. *Theory of Games and Economic Behavior*, 60th anniversary commemorative ed. Princeton, N.J.: Princeton University Press, 2007.

Ngai, Sianne. *Ugly Feelings*. Cambridge, Mass.: Harvard University Press, 2005.

Noelle-Neumann, Elisabeth. *The Spiral of Silence: Public Opinion, Our Social Skin*, 2nd ed. Chicago: University of Chicago Press, 1993.

North, Michael. *Camera Works: Photography in the Twentieth Century*. Oxford: Oxford University Press, 2005.

Oshii, Mamoru, dir. *Ghost in the Shell* (anime series). Tokyo: Production I.G., 1996.

Plato. *Timaeus and Critias*, rev. ed. Edited by Thomas Kjeller Johansen. Translated by Desmond Lee. London: Penguin Classics, 2008.

Poe, Edgar Allan. *The Complete Poetical Works of Edgar Allan Poe*. Edited by R. Brimley Johnson. Oxford: Oxford University Press, 1909.

Pond, Elizabeth. *Beyond the Wall: Germany's Road to Reunification*. Washington, D.C.: Brookings Institution Press, 1993.

Poundstone, William. *Prisoner's Dilemma: John von Neumann, Game Theory, and the Puzzle of the Bomb*. New York: Doubleday, 1992.

Pynchon, Thomas. *Gravity's Rainbow*. New York: Viking, 1973.

Qvortrup, Lars. "Luhmann Applied to the Knowledge Society: Religion as Fourth-Order Knowledge." *Cybernetics and Human Knowing* 14, no. 2–3 (2007): 11–27.

Rabinbach, Anson. *The Human Motor: Energy, Fatigue, and the Origins of Modernity*. New York: Basic Books, 1990.

Rancière, Jacques. "The Aesthetic Dimension: Aesthetics, Politics, Knowledge." *Critical Inquiry* 36, no. 1 (autumn 2009): 1–19. doi:10.1086/606120.

———. *Disagreement: Politics and Philosophy*. Minneapolis: University of Minnesota Press, 1999.

———. "Thinking between Disciplines: An Aesthetics of Knowledge." *Parrhesia* 1, no. 1 (2006): 1–12.

Rank, Otto. *The Double: A Psychoanalytic Study*. Edited by Harry Tucker. Chapel Hill: University of North Carolina Press, 1971.

Reynolds, Simon. *Retromania: Pop Culture's Addiction to Its Own Past*. London: Faber and Faber, 2011.

Riesman, David, Nathan Glazer, and Reuel Denney. *The Lonely Crowd: A Study of the Changing American Character*, rev. ed. New Haven, Conn.: Yale University Press, 2001.

Rose, Barbara. "Blow Up: The Problem of Scale in Sculpture." *Art in America* 56, no. 4 (1968): 80–91.

Ross, Andrew. *No-Collar: The Human Workplace and Its Hidden Costs*. Philadelphia: Temple University Press, 2003.

Sachs, Hans. "The Delay of the Machine Age." *Psychoanalytic Quarterly* 2 (1933): 404–24.

Sartre, Jean-Paul. *Critique of Dialectical Reason, vol. 1: Theory of Practical Ensembles*. Translated by Alan Sheridan-Smith. London: Verso, 1976.

Savigny, Friedrich Carl von. *System of Modern Roman Law*, vol. 1. 1840. Reprint, Madras: J. Higginbotham, 1867.

Scarry, Elaine. *The Body in Pain: The Making and Unmaking of the World*. New York: Oxford University Press, 1987.

Schenkar, Joan. *The Talented Miss Highsmith: The Secret Life and Serious Art of Patricia Highsmith*. New York: St. Martin's, 2009.

Schivelbusch, Wolfgang. *In a Cold Crater: Cultural and Intellectual Life in Berlin, 1945–1948*. Translated by Kelly Barry. Berkeley: University of California Press, 1998.

———. *The Railway Journey: The Industrialization of Time and Space in the 19th Century*. Berkeley: University of California Press, 1986.

———. *Tastes of Paradise: A Social History of Spices, Stimulants, and Intoxicants*. Translated by David Jacobson. New York: Vintage, 1993.

Schnapp, Jeffrey T., ed. *Speed Limits*. Milan: Skira, 2009.

Schopenhauer, Arthur. *The World as Will and Representation, vol. I*. Edited by Judith Norman, Alistair Welchman, and Christopher Janaway. Cambridge: Cambridge University Press, 2010.

Scott, Tony, dir. *True Romance* (film). Burbank, Calif.: Warner Bros. Pictures, 1993.

Sebald, W. G. *Austerlitz*. Translated by Anthea Bell. New York: Modern Library, 2001.

———. "Between History and Natural History." In *Campo Santo*. Translated by Anthea Bell, 65–96. New York: Modern Library, 2005.

———. *On the Natural History of Destruction*. Translated by Anthea Bell. New York: Modern Library, 2004.

———. *The Rings of Saturn*. Translated by Michael Hulse. London: Harvill, 1998.

Seltzer, Mark. "The Art of the Collision." In *Speed Limits*, edited by Jeffrey T. Schnapp, 84–92. Milan: Skira, 2009.

———. "Berlin 2000: 'The Image of an Empty Place.'" In *After-Images of the City*, edited by Joan Ramon Resina and Dieter Ingenschay, 61–74. Ithaca, N.Y.: Cornell University Press, 2003.

———. *Bodies and Machines*. 1992. Reprint, New York: Routledge, 2015.

———. "The Crime System." *Critical Inquiry* 30, no. 3 (March 1, 2004): 557–83. doi:10.1086/421162.

———. "The Daily Planet." *Post45*, December 18, 2012. http://post45.research.yale .edu/2012/12/the-daily-planet/.

———. "Die Freie Natur." In *Gefahrensinn: Archiv für Mediengeschichte*, edited by Lorenz Engell, Bernhard Siegert, and Joseph Vogl, 127–39. Paderborn: Wilhelm Fink, 2009.

———. *Henry James and the Art of Power*. Ithaca, N.Y.: Cornell University Press, 1984.

———. *Serial Killers: Death and Life in America's Wound Culture*. New York: Routledge, 1998.

———. "Statistical Persons." *Diacritics*, no. 17 (fall 1987): 82–98.

———. *True Crime: Observations on Violence and Modernity*. New York: Routledge, 2007.

———. "Wound Culture: Trauma in the Pathological Public Sphere." *October* 80 (April 1, 1997): 3–26. doi:10.2307/778805.

Serres, Michel. *The Parasite*. Minneapolis: University of Minnesota Press, 2007.

Shannon, Claude Elwood. "Communication Theory of Secrecy Systems." In *Claude E. Shannon: Collected Papers*, edited by Aaron D. Wyner and Neil J. A. Sloane, 84–143. New York: Wiley-IEEE Press, 1993.

Shannon, Claude Elwood, and Warren Weaver. *The Mathematical Theory of Communication*. Urbana: University of Illinois Press, 1949.

Siegert, Bernhard. "Cacography or Communication? Cultural Techniques in German Media Studies." *Grey Room*, no. 29 (fall 2007): 26–47. doi:10.1162/grey.2007.1.29.26.

———. *Relays: Literature as an Epoch of the Postal System*. Translated by Kevin Repp. Stanford, Calif.: Stanford University Press, 1999.

———. "There Are No Mass Media." In *Mapping Benjamin: The Work of Art in the Digital Age*, edited by Hans Gumbrecht and Michael Marrinan, 30–38. Stanford, Calif.: Stanford University Press, 2003.

Simmel, Georg. *The Sociology of Georg Simmel*. Translated by Kurt H. Wolff. Glencoe, Ill.: Free Press, 1950.

Sloterdijk, Peter. *Bubbles: Spheres Volume I: Microspherology*. Translated by Wieland Hoban. Los Angeles: Semiotext(e), 2011.

———. "The Crystal Palace." *Public*, no. 37 (January 1, 2008). http://pi.library.yorku .ca/ojs/index.php/public/article/view/30252.

————. *Globes: Spheres Volume II: Macrospherology*. Translated by Wieland Hoban. Los Angeles: Semiotext(e), 2014.

————. *In the World Interior of Capital: Towards a Philosophical Theory of Globalization*. Translated by Wieland Hoban. Cambridge: Polity, 2013.

————. *You Must Change Your Life*. Translated by Wieland Hoban. Cambridge: Polity, 2014.

Smail, Daniel Lord. *On Deep History and the Brain*. Berkeley: University of California Press, 2008.

Snyder, Joel. "Res Ipsa Loquitur." In *Things That Talk: Object Lessons from Art and Science*, edited by Lorraine J. Daston, 195–222. New York: Zone, 2004.

Sohn-Rethel, Alfred. *Intellectual and Manual Labor: A Critique of Epistemology*. Atlantic Highlands, N.J.: Humanities Press, 1978.

Sombart, Werner. *The Quintessence of Capitalism: A Study of the History and Psychology of the Modern Business Man*. Edited and translated by M. Epstein. New York: E. P. Dutton, 1915.

Spoto, Donald. *The Dark Side of Genius: The Life of Alfred Hitchcock*. New York: Ballantine, 1983.

Stephenson, Neal. *Cryptonomicon*. New York: Avon, 1999.

Stern, David G. "Models of Memory: Wittgenstein and Cognitive Science." *Philosophical Psychology* 4, no. 2 (January 1, 1991): 203–18. doi:10.1080/09515089108573027.

Stewart, Susan. *On Longing: Narratives of the Miniature, the Gigantic, the Souvenir, the Collection*. Durham, N.C.: Duke University Press, 1993.

Stiegler, Bernard. "The Discrete Image." In *Echographies of Television: Filmed Interviews*, 145–63. Cambridge: Polity, 2002.

————. *Technics and Time, 1: The Fault of Epimetheus*. Translated by Richard Beardsworth and George Collins. Stanford, Calif.: Stanford University Press, 1998.

Tanaka, Naoko. *Absolute Helligkeit* (installation and performance). Berlin: Body Affects, July 5, 2012.

Terada, Rei. *Looking Away: Phenomenality and Dissatisfaction, Kant to Adorno*. Cambridge, Mass.: Harvard University Press, 2009.

Tompkins, Jane. *West of Everything: The Inner Life of Westerns*. New York: Oxford University Press, 1993.

Tucker, Albert William, and Robert Duncan Luce, eds. "On the Theory of Games of Strategy." In *Contributions to the Theory of Games*, vol. 4, 13–42. Princeton, N.J.: Princeton University Press, 1959.

Urry, John. *Mobilities*. Cambridge: Polity, 2007.

Vismann, Cornelia. *Files: Law and Media Technology*. Translated by Geoffrey Winthrop-Young. Stanford, Calif.: Stanford University Press, 2008.

————. "Out of File, Out of Mind." In *New Media, Old Media: A History and Theory Reader*, edited by Wendy Hui Kyong Chun and Thomas Keenan, 97–124. New York: Routledge, 2005.

Vogl, Joseph. "Becoming-Media: Galileo's Telescope." *Grey Room*, no. 29 (fall 2007): 14–25. doi:10.1162/grey.2007.1.29.14.

———. *The Specter of Capital*. Stanford, Calif.: Stanford University Press, 2014.

Vries, Hent de, and Samuel Weber. "Theory on TV: 'After-Thoughts.'" In *Religion and Media*, edited by Hent de Vries and Samuel Weber, 94–111. Stanford, Calif.: Stanford University Press, 2001.

Wark, McKenzie. *Gamer Theory*. Cambridge, Mass.: Harvard University Press, 2007.

Weber, Max. *Economy and Society: An Outline of Interpretive Sociology*. Edited by Guenther Roth and Claus Wittich. 2 vols. Berkeley: University of California Press, 1978.

Wellbery, David E. Foreword to Friedrich Kittler, *Discourse Networks 1800/1900*, vii–xxxiii. Stanford, Calif.: Stanford University Press, 1992.

———. "The General Enters the Library: A Note on Disciplines and Complexity." *Critical Inquiry* 35, no. 4 (January 1, 2009): 982–94. doi:10.1086/599588.

Wharton, Edith. *The House of Mirth*. New York: Penguin, 1993.

Wilder, Billy, dir. *Sunset Boulevard* (film). Hollywood, Calif.: Paramount Pictures, 1950.

Wiener, Norbert. *Cybernetics: Or the Control and Communication in the Animal and the Machine*, 2nd ed. Cambridge, Mass.: MIT Press, 1965.

———. *Human Use of Human Beings: Cybernetics and Society*. New York: Doubleday, 1950.

Wilson, Andrew. *Beautiful Shadow: A Life of Patricia Highsmith*. New York: Bloomsbury, 2004.

Wittgenstein, Ludwig. *Culture and Value*. Translated by Peter Winch. Chicago: University of Chicago Press, 1984.

———. *On Certainty*. Edited by G. E. M. Anscombe and G. H. von Wright. Translated by Denis Paul. New York: Harper and Row, 1972.

———. *Philosophical Grammar*. Edited by Anthony Kenny. Translated by Rush Rhees. Oxford: Blackwell, 1974.

———. *Philosophical Occasions: 1912–1951*. Edited by James Carl Klagge and Alfred Nordmann. Indianapolis: Hackett, 1993.

———. *Remarks on the Philosophy of Psychology*. Edited by G. E. M. Anscombe and G. H. von Wright. Translated by G. E. M. Anscombe. Chicago: University of Chicago Press, 1980.

Woloch, Alex. *The One vs. the Many: Minor Characters and the Space of the Protagonist in the Novel*. Princeton, N.J.: Princeton University Press, 2003.

Wright, Lawrence. *Going Clear: Scientology, Hollywood, and the Prison of Belief*. New York: Knopf, 2013.

Zola, Émile. "The Experimental Novel." In George Joseph Becker, *Documents of Modern Literary Realism*. Princeton, N.J.: Princeton University Press, 1967.

———. *La bête humaine*. Paris: G. Charpentier, 1890.

———. *Oeuvres complètes*. Edited by Henri Mitterand. 10 vols. Paris: Cercle du livre précieux, 1966.

———. *Thérèse Raquin*. Paris: A. Lacroix, Verboeckhoven, 1867.

Note: Italic page numbers indicate figures.

bildungsroman genre, 242n21

biocracy, 179

black boxes, 67–68, 114, 115–16

Blink (Gladwell), 90, 109–12

Bourne Identity, The (film), 13, *14, 16, 17,* 75–76

Bourne Identity, The (Ludlum book), 13–15, 197

Brecht, Bertolt, 25, 37, 38

Brooks, Max, 13, 26–28

Burkhardt, Jacob, 3

Bush, George H. W., 128

Caillois, Roger, 93, 166, 178–79, 231n33, 248n33

Canetti, Elias, 149

carousels, 20, 22, 78–79, 194, 206n47

car parks, 19–20, 35

Casablanca (film), 69

cataclysms, 73–76

chain letters, 8, 52, 64, 72, 77

Charcot, Jean-Martin, 110

chase scenes, 74–75

Christie, Agatha, 57, 133, 136–40, 141, 142, 143, 144–52. *See also specific works*

Clocks, The (Christie), 151

Cocaine Nights (Ballard), 65, 207n48

Cold War novels, 10–11, 22, 25, 75, 107, 238–39n88

comic-book genre, 23, 39

confession genre, 67–68

Crane, Stephen, 86, 144

Crash (Ballard), 76–77, 207n48, 208n2

crime novels, 56, 57–60, 142, 240n9

Critchley, Simon, 29, 156

Cry of the Owl, The (Highsmith), 55

cryptoanalylsis, 99

daily planet, 20, 21, 35, 37, 213n33. *See also* official world

Daily Planet (fictional newspaper), 3, *4*

"Death and the Child" (Crane), 144

Decline of the West, The (Spengler), 76

deep space/deep time, 36, 191

deep time, 42

Deleuze, Gilles, 21, 57, 68

de Man, Paul, 156

Demand, Thomas, 86–87

depersonation, 49

destructive drive, 16, 74

dictaphones, 71–72, 147

Diederichsen, Diedrich, 34

Discipline and Punish (Foucault), 48, 115–16

disidentifications, 38–40

Doll's House, The (Gaiman), 3

double-think, 108

doubling, 54, 62–63, 74, 78, 80, 88, 92, 101, 114, 225n43

Dracula (Stoker), 27, 99

Dreiser, Theodore, 8, 85–86, 164

Durkheim, Émile, 6, 172

Eco, Umberto, 148

education, secluded, 115–16, 117, 195

ego-technics, 9, 39, 48, 66, 75, 101, 121, 185, 191, 198

embarrassment, 33–35, 133–35, 213n40, 233–34n49

emoticons, 39

Empire of Signs (Barthes), 158

epistolary novels, 99

Esposito, Roberto, 179

exteriority, 8, 9, 15, 20–21, 68–69, 140, 254n29

externalization, 9, 41, 55, 69, 75, 76–78, 80, 138, 140, 203n25, 204n34, 207n48

extinction/self-extinction, 25, 73, 137, 197, 198, 208–9n2, 232n34, 251n5

face-system, 68–69

feigned persons, 58

Ferguson, Frances, 49, 71

fictional reality, 56, 232n37

Flaubert, Gustave, 83, 168

Forms of Talk (Goffman), 163

Forster, Marc, 26

Foucault, Léon, 106

Foucault, Michel, 4, 17, 38, 48, 115–16, 142, 145, 242–43n24

Franklin, Benjamin, 39
Fried, Michael, 87

gadgets, 67
Gaiman, Neil, 3
Galileo, 190–91
Galileo (Brecht), 37
Galloway, Alexander, 112–13
games, 4; exteriority in, 9; form, 90, 113–14;
    hide-and-seek, 34, 114, 179–80; inside/
    outside, 204n27; in mystery novels, 146;
    paradoxes in, 95, 113; parlor, 89–95, 168;
    pathological, 230–31n33; real vs. fictional
    in, 92–93; rules of irrelevance in, 96, 111,
    229n30; in suspense novels, 22, 48, 70, 71,
    89–90, 107; theory, 90, 121, 228–29n30,
    228n24, 230n31; use of term, 171–72,
    253n27; war, 22–23, 90, 91–93, 109–15. *See
    also* play
Gedenken machine, 105–6
Gigerenzer, Gerd, 129, 131
Gladwell, Malcolm, 90, 109–10, 112
globalization, 4, 5, 24
Goffman, Erving, 7, 9, 19, 22–23, 33–34,
    35, 49, 89, 90, 96, 163, 165, 166–69,
    227–28n24, 233–34n49
Gravity (film), 13
Great Outdoors, 37–38, 190, 191
Guattari, Félix, 68
gyroscopes, 105–6

half-educated men, 195–97
Haneke, Michael, 230n33
heart, in modern world, 193–94
"Heaven" (Talking Heads), 41
hetero-reference, 170, 212n30, 258n23
Highsmith, Patricia, 4, 10–11; on alien
    realities, 37; on artwork, 22, 88–89; belief,
    use of, 50; carousel, use of, 20, 78–79,
    206n47; on cataclysm, 73–74; chain-letter
    effect, 64; comic books, 23, 253n23; on
    decoupling, 38; doubling, use of, 54,
    62–63, 78; on experience, 175; on games,
    22, 48, 89–90, 107, 113–14; on laughter,
    133; letters, use of, 99; narrative point of

view, 49, 53–55, 76, 78, 79; pathographies,
    20–23; practical jokes, use of, 30–35; on
    precarious life, 172; self-observation and,
    182–83; on spectacle, 41; on violence
    aesthetics, 206–7n48; on walking away,
    163. *See also specific works*
Hitchcock, Alfred, 20, 61, 62, *62*, 63, *65*, 74,
    77–79, 206n47
Hitler, Adolf, 196
horror novels, 118
hotel-world, 18–19
Howells, William Dean, 83–85, 243n27
Hubbard, L. Ron, 192, 205n37
human pyramid, 11–13, 48, 50, 204n34
Human Use of Human Beings, The
    (Wiener), 104

Ibsen, Henrik, 204n35
icons, 113
improvisation, 112
industrial civilization, 248n33
input/output, 115
INS. *See* International Necronautical Society
Interface Effect, The (Galloway), 113
interaction, primacy of, 49
Interaction Ritual (Goffman), 49
interiority, 8, 21, 100, 135, 254n29, 255n33
Internal Revenue Service (IRS), 30–33
International Necronautical Society (INS),
    29, 29–30, 156
Introduction to Cybernetics (Ashby), 115
IRS. *See* Internal Revenue Service
Ishiguro, Kazuo, 90, 109, 116–24
isotopias, 17–20, 87, 137, 141, 195, 206n40

Jakobson, Roman, 150
James, Henry, 18, 19, 88, 99, 141, 164, 169,
    206n47, 254n32
Jaspers, Karl, 94–95
Jennings, Peter, 131
Jünger, Ernst, 195, 259n34
juristical persons, 57–59, 155, 218n40

Kahn, Herman, 22–23, 238n85
Kant, Immanuel, 180–81

office as uncanny space, 83–89

official world: as board game, 174–75; boundaries, 9, 142; as denoting, 7; elements of, 3–4; extroversions in, 84–85; hyperactivity of, 16; observation in, 28; outside of, 183–86; premises of, 6–10; real/fictional in, 166; redoubling of reality, 148; reenactment zones, 42–43, 142; social systems of, 143, 170; suspended states, 178; use of term, 3, 6; words and things in, 144; as work of art, 7, 20

On Deep History and the Brain (Smail), 41–42

Oshii, Mamoru, 92

Pale View of Hills, A (Ishiguro), 117, 124

panopticon, 115–16

Parker, Dorothy, 150

Pentagon Papers, The, 22–23

personation, 49–50

personhood, 119, 155, 219n40, 241n14

photographic, 101, 222n22

Pink Panther, The (film), 142

place-value systems, 32, 85, 141

play, 88, 231n33, 251n8; playing dead, 170–74, 178–79, 184–85; playing society, 115, 168–70. *See also* games

Poe, Edgar Allen, 113, 148

Poincaré, Henri, 151

postal systems, 50–51, 64, 97–99

posthuman pyramid, 26

practical jokes, 127–28; fall of Berlin wall as, 128–33; in mystery novels, 148, 159; as socialized trance, 135, 137; in suspense novels, 30–35, 133–35, 137

practico-inert, use of term, 9

professionalism, 8, 13, 15–17, 29–31, 39, 41, 80, 121, 137, 151–53, 195–97

Protestant Ethic and the Spirit of Capitalism, The (Weber), 13

RAND Corporation, 112, 230–31n33, 239n89

reality, real/fictions, 92–93

Reality of the Mass Media, The (Luhmann), 41

reenactment, 16–17, 18, 21, 22; control and, 65; externalized, 78; in official world, 42–43, 142; reflexivity and, 73; registration and, 33; repeating and, 153–60; violence and, 214n4; without content, 28–29

reflexivity, 7–8; doubling and, 62–63, 222n22; modernity and, 21, 24, 36, 38, 54, 108, 112, 166; ouroboric, 35; reenactment, 73; self-reflection and, 238n85; self-reflexivity, 53–54, 165, 222n22, 254n29; social, 7, 51–55, 112, 166–67, 182; turns and, 107, 164–65, 167, 182, 186–87; violence and, 38, 176–77; zones, 10–11, 22. *See also* self-reference

reincarnation stories, 5, 13, 15, 75, 105, 155, 192, 205n37

reliable mindlessness, 70–71, 77, 137, 157

Remainder (T. McCarthy), 13, 28, 59, 142, 143–44, 153–60

repeating repeating, 153–60

reprogramming techniques, 15

reserved space, 85–86

Riefenstahl, Leni, 197

Riesman, Daniel, 105

Ripley's Game (Highsmith), 88–90, 95–98, 101–2, 105, 133–34

Rise of Silas Lapham, The (Howells), 83–85, 243n27

Road, The (C. McCarthy), 27, 38, 189–90, 209n4

rules of irrelevance, 96, 111, 229n30

Running Wild (Ballard), 65

Sartre, Jean-Paul, 9, 152

Savigny, Friedrich Carl von, 57–59

Scarry, Elaine, 245n16

Schabowski, Günter, 129, *130*

Schivelbusch, Wolfgang, 133, 151

science and pornography, 208–9n2

Scientology, 8, 15, 75, 113, 192, 205n37

Sebald, W. G., 25, 158

secrets, 99–100, 179

self-boosterism, 8–9, 15–17, 113

self-conditioning, 6, 41, 51–52, 93, 95, 104, 149, 168, 175